THE OFFICIAL® PRICE GUIDE TO

CLOCKS

Frederick W. Korz

HOUSE OF COLLECTIBLES

Random House Reference

New York

Important Notice: All the information, including valuations, in this book has been compiled from the most reliable sources, and every effort has been made to eliminate errors and questionable data. Nevertheless, the possibility of error, in a work of such immense scope, always exists. The publisher will not be held responsible for losses that may occur in the purchase, sale, or other transaction of items because of information contained herein. Readers who feel they have discovered errors are invited to *write* and inform us, so they may be corrected in subsequent editions. Those seeking further information on the topics covered in this book are advised to refer to the complete line of *Official® Price Guides* published by the House of Collectibles.

© 2003 Frederick W. Korz

Published by House of Collectibles, 1745 Broadway, New York, NY 10019. Distributed by the Random House Reference, a division of Random House Inc., New York, and simultaneously in Canada by Random House of Canada Limited, Toronto.

House of Collectibles is a registered trademark and the colophon is a trademark of Random House, Inc.

 www.houseofcollectibles.com

Printed in the United States of America

Photographs of clocks not individually credited are from the author's collection.

ISBN 0-609-80973-3

10 9 8 7 6 5 4 3 2 1

First Edition

CONTENTS

Acknowledgments

The author extends his sincere appreciation to the following for their contributions and support throughout this endeavor: My wife, Virginia, who has patiently and lovingly put up with all of my nonsense and clocks; my friend Saul Richman who shared a lifetime of professional experience; Sandra Andacht who makes it all seem easy; Bob Schmitt and Kent Andersen without whose advice and support this work would not have been possible; my editors, Dorothy Harris and Roger Generazzo, who took good care of this fledgling author; all the members of the National Association of Watch and Clock Collectors who graciously answered my questions and allowed me to photograph their clocks; Tuan Anh Tran who has supplied me with so much of my reference library; Chapter 2 and Chapter 88 of the NAWCC whose guest speakers and marts supplied raw material for this book; my students at C. W. Post, Long Island University whose questions helped me shape this work; and the following family and friends who graciously allowed me to include photos of their clocks in this book: Charles H. Korz, Jeanne and Richard Wagner, Madeline and Paul Alessi, Janet and David Marcus, Zahna and Alex Zilberberg, Mary and William Sterling, Barbara and Victor DiPaola, Robert Schneider, and the Timex Museum.

Introduction

I have tried to write and produce the sort of book that would have been helpful when I started collecting clocks forty years ago.

When I purchased my first clock I didn't have a clue as to what I had bought. I didn't know anything about the clock or even if I had paid too much. I just knew that I liked the way the clock looked and I was curious about how it worked.

My local library was of little help, having next to nothing on the subject of clocks. I learned how my clock worked by taking it apart and putting it back together enough times until I understood its operation.

The clock turned out to be a small 30-hour spring-driven OG shelf clock made by E. N. Welch, and the price was $5.

Now I was hooked, and I started to pick up clocks at garage and house sales, antiques shops, even at occasional country auctions. I bought many clocks that today I would not even glance at. It was during this time that I met a gentleman who was a retired clockmaker. He introduced me to the National Association of Watch and Clock Collectors, and I joined.

Since then, I've spent years acquiring the clocks I really wanted, learning how to repair and restore clocks, and evaluating and appraising clocks for others.

This book has been distilled from my own experiences. I hope it will be of use to the novice collector as well as to those who have already acquired a few clocks. I hope my many antiques dealer friends will find it handy to identify and help price clocks that they buy for resale. Most of all, I hope this is a book that you will take into the field.

Remember that this is only your starting point to enter a world of time and its measurement. Somewhere in these pages you will discover that part of the story that will capture your imagination and lead you into further exploration beyond this work. If that happens, then this book will have been successful.

Happy hunting!

CHAPTER 1

Beginnings:
A Survey of Clocks

The Ancient World

The start of our measurement of time is lost in prehistory. By the advent of written history, all the world's major civilizations had methods of measuring time. Most used light and shadow or the constant flow of water or sand to record time's passage.

Variations of the sundial were a common feature in the ancient civilizations of the Mediterranean. The clepsydra was a primitive water clock in which water dripped through a small hole. It registered time by the level collected in the receiving container or by the level of the water remaining in the starting vessel. By the second century B.C., the Greeks had adapted the dial and added a pointer to the clepsydra. It was said to have been used to time speakers in Athenian courts. Greek trade spread eastward into the Middle East, southward into Egypt, and westward into the Roman Empire, and Greek technology went with it. As the Roman Empire disintegrated and was replaced by the "Barbarian Kingdoms," which in turn would give rise to medieval and modern-day Europe, water clocks, sundials, hourglasses, and "candle clocks" remained as the empire's legacy. Of all of these devices, the sundial was most accurate. It was found in every public place.

Mechanical Clocks

The origin and first use of the mechanical weight-driven clock are lost to us. Research into the invention of the mechanical weight-driven clock is made more difficult by the fact that the Latin term *horologium* is used to indicate the sundial, water clock, and mechanical clock. It is impossible in manuscripts from the ninth to the thirteenth century A.D. to tell which of these devices is being mentioned. However, by the late thirteenth century, evidence exists that the mechanical weight-driven clock was in use. Through the study of the heavens and the evolution of astronomy, civilizations around the world built a framework for measuring time. We are most familiar with the Western framework of a year divided into months, a month divided into days, and a day divided into hours.

To trace the history of the clock we must go back to Roman society, which ordered daily life with signals at three-hour intervals. With the end of the Roman Empire, the Catholic Church maintained these intervals as the basis for its canonical hours. In the seventh century the papacy decreed that monastery bells should be rung at seven intervals during the day and night at the canonical hours of matins, lauds, prime, terce, sext, none, and vespers. This simple decree created an urgent need for an instrument for measuring time that would function both day and night and allow the monastery bells to be struck at the right hour. This led to the development of the mechanical weight-driven clock.

The fourteenth century saw the day divided into twenty-four equal hours, which replaced the canonical system. The newly developed mechanical clock was now redesigned to register these equal hours. As time came to play a greater role in people's lives, the clock moved out of the monastery and into newly constructed bell towers appearing in towns and cities throughout Europe. Human life was changed forever.

Public Clocks

In the fifteenth century, hours were divided into sixty minutes and minutes into sixty seconds. The earliest public clocks had neither dials nor striking mechanisms, as they only gave indication to the human striker to sound the hour on the bell in the bell tower. It is interesting to note that the word *clock* derives from the word for *bell*. By 1410, clocks had been developed to include a hammer that automatically struck the bell, eliminating the need for a human striker. The addition of a dial with a pointer followed shortly after. Now town dwellers could tell the hours at night by listening to the bells and during the day by looking at the dial as well as listening to the bells. These early clocks incorporated many small improvements developed over several centuries, the products of many different minds. However, these clocks were so inaccurate that for the next couple of centuries they were adjusted periodically by comparing their time with the sundial that was found in every public square.

Early Problems

The development of the mechanical clock was hindered by the lack of control over the motive power of the clock, which was driven by a falling weight. Weights as motive power to drive geared wheels had been known since ancient times. A weight attached to a rope wound around a drum would cause the drum to revolve as the weight fell. The problem in utilizing this form of motive power in a clock is that unless the speed of the drum is regulated, the weight falls faster and faster, making it useless.

The problem was solved with the development of a wheel with triangular teeth, which came to be called the "crown wheel" because it resembled a crown. The crown wheel was the last and fastest geared wheel driven by the weight. The revolution of this wheel was stopped by two pallets fixed to a vertical shaft called a "verge." These pallets alternately caught and released the crown wheel. This alternation regulated the motion of the geared wheels in the same way that a governor regulates the speed of a modern engine.

The action of the crown wheel's teeth pushed the pallets first one way and then the other. This caused the verge to move back and forth, releasing the gear train in a constant (or "tick-tock") motion. To further control the power of the weight, a crossbar with adjustable weights hanging from it was attached to the upper end of the verge. Now the crown wheel oscil-

Folliot Escapement

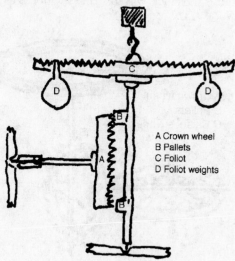

A Crown wheel
B Pallets
C Foliot
D Foliot weights

lated between the verge and the heavy crossbar, which had the effect of further regulating the gear train. The clock was slowed when the weights were moved to ends of the bar and sped up when they were moved toward the center. The crossbar with its two weights came to be called a "foliot." The last or crown wheel came to be known as the "escape wheel," a name it retains to this day. The pallets plus the escape wheel received the name "escapement."

During the fourteenth century, a domestic or chamber clock evolved, although we do not know in which part of Western Europe they were first made. They were well known by the fifteenth century, and numbers of French, German, and Italian examples exist in the world's museums.

Chamber Clocks

Obviously, a tower clock could not fit inside a house. The existing mechanism had to be made smaller and a new form of regulator devised to replace the heavy and cumbersome foliot. The new form of regulator took the shape of a wheel. The shaft of the wheel was attached to the top of the verge, which caused it to function in the same way as the weighted crossbar of the foliot escapement. Called a "balance wheel," it was regulated differently than the foliot. To make a balance wheel go faster, one increased the clock weight, and to slow it, one decreased the weight.

The gear trains of these early chamber clocks were fitted into open frames with four corner posts. If the clock only told the time, there was just one gear train, but if the clock was to strike the hours as well, there had to

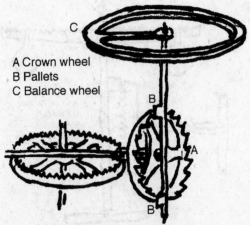

A Crown wheel
B Pallets
C Balance wheel

Balance Wheel Escapement

be two gear trains and two weights. Some clocks were fitted with an alarm, so there could be as many as three gear trains with three weights suspended below the open-frame case. As these clocks were weight-driven, they had to be hung on the wall to allow the weights to descend.

With the appearance of the domestic clock came the first attempts to decorate the clock. Besides dial decoration, the frame corner posts and the bell surmounting the movement now began to be embellished as well, often in the form of Gothic architecture.

Spring-driven Clock

The need to produce a portable clock that could be moved from room to room and place to place encouraged the development of the spring-driven clock movement. This mechanism appeared during the later fifteenth century. In the 1540s, the famous Nuremberg locksmith Peter Heinlein produced a spring-driven clock that was small enough to be carried.

However, these first spring-driven clocks had a serious problem. The coiled spring when fully wound exerted greater force than when it was

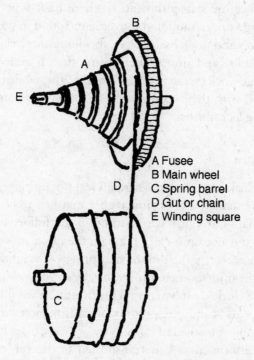

A Fusee
B Main wheel
C Spring barrel
D Gut or chain
E Winding square

Fusee System

running down. As this affected the accuracy of the clock, some method had to be developed to make the spring exert a constant force from start to finish. Two mechanisms were devised: the first, called the stackfeed, was discarded with the development of the second, called the fusee. The principle of both was similar, making the spring work harder when fully wound and gradually easing up as the power of the coiled spring diminished. The fusee was a conical drum mounted above the spring's barrel, or drum. Gut or chain connected the two drums. When the spring was wound, the gut or chain was correspondingly drawn down onto the spring barrel. When the spring was fully wound, the fusee was hardest to turn, but it got easier as the spring wound down. This arrangement produced a constant consistent release of the spring's motive power. The fusee was used in spring-driven clocks as early as 1525 and is still found in fine spring clocks today.

Although the invention of the fusee would eventually allow the miniaturization of the spring-driven clock into the pocket watch, development was still hindered by the cost and the skill necessary to produce reliable spring steel. For these reasons, weight-driven clocks dominated clock technology for centuries.

By the end of the sixteenth century, three basic types of clocks had evolved: the large tower-mounted movements found in public areas such as church belfries and town hall towers, the domestic or chamber weight-driven wall clocks, and the smaller spring-driven table and traveling clocks. The large clocks were made by blacksmiths, while the domestic or chamber clocks, with their requirements for smaller components, fell to the realm of the locksmiths.

The Pendulum

Although the clock had advanced a great deal since its inception centuries before, it still remained a poor timekeeper that had to be reset each day from the sundial. The cause was focused in the foliots and the balance wheels, which did not uniformly regulate the clock movements as they were both influenced by the pull of the spring or weight. This problem was solved in the mid-seventeenth century by the adoption of the pendulum to regulate clock escapements . This invention would transform the world of clocks and cause the production of timepieces to explode. The pendulum is subject to the law of gravity, which causes it to swing uniformly. The uniform motion is transmitted to the verge and from the verge to the rest of the gear train. The pendulum thus becomes the mas-

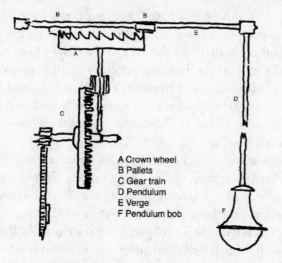

A Crown wheel
B Pallets
C Gear train
D Pendulum
E Verge
F Pendulum bob

Verge escapement showing a bob pendulum

ter of the clock as it determines the speed by which energy will be released in the form of hours, minutes, and seconds. If the speed is too fast, the pendulum bob is lowered and the clock runs slower, and if it is too slow, the bob is raised.

The properties of the pendulum that made it ideal as a clock regulator were discovered by the famous Italian astronomer Galileo Galilei. The application of the pendulum to a clock was made by the great Dutch astronomer and mathematician Christiaan Huygens in the late 1650s. In 1657, Huygens assigned his invention to Salomon Coster, a clockmaker at The Hague who produced the first practical pendulum clocks.

In less than a decade, pendulum clocks had replaced foliot and balance wheel clocks throughout Europe. The only exceptions were traveling clocks and watches.

Clockmaking Centers

By the end of the seventeenth century, very definite centers of clockmaking had developed and were rapidly expanding into national industries with distinct clock forms.

SOUTHERN GERMANY

Before the advent of the pendulum, the largest center of clockmaking was in southern Germany, in such cities as Augsburg and Nuremberg. Here clockmaking was closely associated with workers in gold and silver. South German prosperity in the sixteenth century was focused on mining, agriculture, and trade that tied the area to the cities of the northern Renaissance and the southern Renaissance cities of Italy and the Mediterranean. The goldsmiths and silversmiths of Augsburg and Nuremberg were famous for their elaborate clocks and clockwork creations fit for kings and emperors. This was a clockmaking center whose clientele was the "rich and famous."

As religious wars and dynastic struggles destroyed the economic fortunes of southern Germany, clockmaking centers shifted westward into Holland, France, and England. Following the Thirty Years War, Germany was assigned to the political backwaters of Europe, and its clockmaking leadership fell into an eclipse. German clocks of the eighteenth century followed French styles and tastes. Only the curious folk clock tradition of the Germanic Alps, with its reliance upon wooden movements, would remain. Not until the nineteenth century, after unification and industrialization, would German clockmakers and their industry once again become world famous.

HOLLAND

The expansion of Dutch commerce in Europe and overseas during the sixteenth and seventeenth centuries made wealthy Holland a natural site and market for clockmaking. Huygens's adaptation of the pendulum led to clocks of new design. Most noticeable were the wooden case, the mounting of the gear trains between two brass plates, and the addition of a minute hand. The iron-framed chamber clock now became an obsolete antique.

In Holland the new form of table clock was quickly dubbed the *Haagse Klokje*, or the Hague Clock. This design, which would play such a major role in the evolution of case design, soon appeared in England and spread across Belgium to France, where this design was known as *Religieuses*, because their decorations were often religious.

With the decline of Dutch economic fortunes and power in the eighteenth and nineteenth centuries, the clockmakers of Holland increasingly followed the English lead, and the tall-case, or grandfather, clock came to dominate their production.

Outside the cities, older and more provincial forms of Dutch wall clocks continued to be made. These older forms showed the Dutch reluctance to give up the weight-driven movement as the French had. They took the form of wall clocks and have names such as *Zaanse* (from the

Zaan River district north of Amsterdam), *Stoelklok* (meaning "chair clock," as it had the appearance of sitting on a small chair) and *Staartklok* (meaning "tail clock," as it had a long lower backboard in front of which a long pendulum swung, looking like a tail).

ENGLAND

The pendulum clock appears to have come to London with John Fromanteel, an English clockmaker of Dutch descent who worked with Salomon Coster learning how to make the new clocks. By 1658, London newspapers were advertising pendulum clocks. As England would usurp the commercial and colonial prominence of Holland by the end of the seventeenth century, so the English would also take the lead in clock movement design and innovation; they would not be relinquish it until the nineteenth century, when America took the lead. In quick succession, the English invented major improvements that converted the mechanical clock into a very accurate and reliable timekeeper. The London clockmaker Robert Hooke, a member of the Royal Society, demonstrated the advantages of a long pendulum with a new form of escapement called an "anchor escapement" in 1669. It rapidly replaced the verge and crown wheel escapement. By 1800, the anchor escapement had become the custom in virtually every English clock. From this escapement would come the development of tall-case clocks of great accuracy, as well as complex and accurate table clocks which the English would call bracket clocks.

Anchor escapement

FRANCE

Pendulum-regulated movement quickly crossed the border from the Lowlands into France. France in the seventeenth century continued to develop both a centralized monarchy and economy, so it was not strange that the heart of French clockmaking was located in the tightly controlled guilds of Paris. It was there that master French craftsmen produced the magnificent clocks so closely associated with French style and

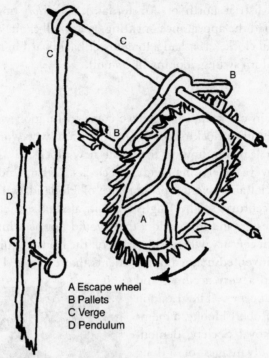

A Escape wheel
B Pallets
C Verge
D Pendulum

Anchor escapement—note that the escape wheel is now
parallel with the drive train and replaces the crown wheel.

taste that would come to dominate European fashion during the eighteenth century.

French clockmakers early in their history virtually standardized a
few variations of the pendulum movement which remained basically un-
changed until the twentieth century. These well-made movements were
fitted into increasingly innovative casework reflecting the times, art, design, and politics of France. With the exception of the country clocks,
today called Morbiers, French clocks were designed either to sit on a table
or a mantel, or to hang on the wall. Even those few freestanding floor
clocks that vaguely resemble tall-case clocks can be seen upon examination to more closely resemble table clocks that have been mounted on
pedestals, or plinths.

By the beginning of the eighteenth century, European clockmakers
were producing a great variety of accurate timepieces in three basic forms:
the wall clocks evolving from the weight-driven chamber clock mounted
on a wall so the clock weights could descend; the tall case, also developed
from the weight-driven wall clock but now fitted with a long pendulum

anchor escapement and cased to protect the pendulum and weights; and the table clock, which grew from the early balance wheel, spring-driven clocks.

This brief history omits the watch, which traces its origin back to the earliest table clocks. Watch history is usually considered a separate tale, and this work is devoted to clocks.

AMERICA

Although there are no examples of American clocks made earlier than the eighteenth century, English-trained clockmakers resided and worked in seventeenth-century New England and New York. By the early and mid-eighteenth century, it is not surprising to find that American clockmaking closely followed British styles and patterns, and many examples and records of the work of this time exist. In the second half of the century, American clockmakers began to show traits that distinguished their clocks from the British and others.

The great difference between American and European clocks occurred first in production, and this appeared toward the end of the eighteenth century. To understand what happened requires recrossing the Atlantic to Europe. In France until the French Revolution, clockmaking was tightly controlled by the royal government and the guilds. There were comparatively few clockmakers, and they were concentrated in Paris and a few other places. This system trained few apprentices, further restricting the expansion of the industry. In the British Isles, it was quite different. The guild system had far less of a stranglehold. Clockmakers and their apprentices were found throughout the United Kingdom, and the training of many apprentices further expanded the industry.

British-trained clockmakers were found in the American colonies by the beginning of the eighteenth century. At first, these clockmakers followed the British tradition, producing similar handcrafted products. In fact, handcrafted clocks flourished in American urban areas until about 1825 and in rural areas until 1850. The vast majority of the production was the impressive tall-case clock. After 1800, less expensive wooden-movement tall-case clocks were made in quantity to meet an expanded market. By about 1815, American wooden-movement shelf clocks began their appearance and the production expanded further. By 1825, shelf clocks were being mass produced, reducing their price, and the market expanded yet again.

At the end of the 1830s, the inexpensive brass shelf clock movement appeared and quickly replaced the wooden-works clocks. From 1840 to

1870, the American clock industry consolidated into seven giant clock-making companies located in Connecticut and New York.

Why did this development occur in the United States and not in Britain or France? Fortunately for America, the guild system never crossed the Atlantic. From the outset, most American clockmakers focused upon production as the way to profit. Unhampered by guild restrictions, America was open to new ideas and new methods and would adapt facets of the English Industrial Revolution developing in the eighteenth century to clock production before their British counterparts. England would "lay the egg that America would hatch."

The Birth of an Industry

Early American clocks were almost all tall case, although some table or bracket clocks were made in Boston and Philadelphia. By the last quarter of the eighteenth century, the Willard family of Grafton, Massachusetts, was introducing wall and shelf clocks in the form of the now famous banjo clock and the Massachusetts shelf clock. Both were far smaller than tall-case clocks, quicker and less expensive to produce, and satisfied an increasing public demand. At the same time that American makers were producing these smaller clocks, some were also cutting production costs by increasing the number of their apprentices and having them "specialize" by producing many similar parts which were then fitted into other parts produced by other apprentices until a complete movement was assembled. Still other makers bought precast parts, dials, and hands from British manufacturers and did the final finishing and assembling in their shops, marketing a product that bore their name. All three techniques reduced costs.

A maker in 1760 could produce 12 to 20 tall-case clocks a year, but by utilizing any or all of the techniques noted above, production doubled by 1800.

One Connecticut example illustrates how these sequences increased production, lowered costs, and increased profits. Thomas Harland, born in England in 1735 and trained as a clockmaker, crossed the Atlantic in 1773, settling in Norwich, Connecticut, where he opened a shop producing clocks and America's first watches. An examination of his clocks shows that he was utilizing his apprentices and journeymen in an effort to standardize parts and increase his production.

Among Harland's workers was Daniel Burnap. He completed his apprenticeship in 1780 and set up in business in East Windsor, Connecticut, and improved on his master's methods by importing large numbers of precast clock components from England. His apprentices and journeymen finished these components and assembled them into complete movements, rather than producing clocks from scratch. Profits increased along with production. Apprenticed to Burnap was Eli Terry, who learned the techniques of standardizing and accelerating the process of clockmaking. Terry then took the next step forward by introducing water-powered machinery, making use of abundant and inexpensive timber resources to achieve mass production and revolutionize nineteenth-century clockmaking.

Eli Terry left Daniel Burnap in 1792 and began producing both brass- and wooden-works tall-case clocks using the methods of batch production that he had learned as an apprentice. In 1806, the brothers Edward and Levi Porter of Waterbury, Connecticut, placed an order with Terry for 4,000 30-hour tall-case wooden clock movements to be completed in three years. Terry would supply the movement, the dial, the hands, the weights, and the pendulum, but not the cases. In the first year of the contract, Terry set up his factory and production line. In the second year, he manufactured 1,000 clocks, finishing the final 3,000 and meeting his contract in 1809.

During these three years, Terry had hired two joiners, Seth Thomas and Silas Hoadley, to help in the production. With the contract completed in 1809 and having proved the commercial success of mass production, Terry sold his operation in 1810 to Thomas and Hoadley. They continued the operation until 1813, when Thomas sold his share to Hoadley and set up in business for himself.

The great American clock industry had its roots in the Terry revolution. It grew and flourished as both clockmakers and businessmen throughout New England adopted Terry's method of production, bought wooden movements from makers such as Thomas and Hoadley, or began to design and manufacture their own wooden movements. Terry's successors would increase production to hundreds of thousands of components per year in less than 150 years. Mass production of components in one factory would reduce the price of a clock to a tiny fraction of the cost of a handcrafted one and put clocks into virtually every home.

These were heady times for the Connecticut River Valley as its tall-case wooden-movement clocks were peddled up and down the East Coast of the United States. By the 1820s, sales of Connecticut tall-case wooden-movement clocks were peaking and market demand was appearing for a new and different style of clock: the shelf clock. Again, the name of Eli Terry dominated events.

After selling his factory and operation to Thomas and Hoadley in 1810, Terry acquired a gristmill, sawmill, and carding shop on the Naugatuck River (a tributary of the Connecticut River) and here, between 1810 and 1814, he developed a wooden-works movement of different design and reduced size for use in a shelf clock. He applied for a patent for this movement, and it was granted in 1816. The movement was housed in a handsome Federal-style case with a reverse glass painted (see Glossary) panel in the lower section of the door. The wooden dial was hand painted, the hands stamped from soft steel, and the whole topped with three brass finials. This was his famous pillar and scroll mantel clock, which many believe is the most handsome of all American clocks.

The public liked the clock because it was attractive, suiting the style and fashion of the period. In addition, it was self-contained: unlike the tall-case clocks, the buyer did not have to purchase a separate case, and it could be easily moved from room to room. Peddlers and merchants liked it because it was easy to transport and easy to sell. The mantel clock signaled the end for wooden-works tall-case clocks, although they would continue to be made until the 1830s. The future of the American clockmaking industry would be based upon these smaller clocks.

Again, the success of Terry's shelf clock caused an expansion of the industry. More makers, such as Boardman, Wells, Jerome, and others, joined Thomas, Hoadley, and the Terry family in producing shelf clocks. Many of these men, Seth Thomas among them, bought the right to make these clocks from Terry, while others such as Jerome developed wooden movements that would circumvent the Terry patent. Most important was that all these movements were being cased as shelf clocks. This was the peak of wooden-works movement production. Thirty-hour wooden-works clocks retailed for less than $10. By the late 1830s, their popularity was waning, although they would still be manufactured in some numbers until the early 1840s.

The Panic of 1837

In 1837, America went into a massive economic depression bad enough to be called the Panic of 1837. The effect on the clockmaking industry was devastating. The wholesale price for a wooden-works shelf clock in 1837 was forced down from $9 to $4. Many firms collapsed and declared bankruptcy; hard hit were companies with little in the way of financial reserves to tide them over the bank failures and little hope of new capital.

One of the companies that almost failed was Jerome and Company, a firm founded by Chauncey Jerome that included his brother Noble Jerome. Chauncey Jerome, like Thomas and Hoadley, did not start off as a trained clockmaker. He was a carpenter by trade who had gotten his introduction to the industry making clock cases for Hotchkiss and Pierpont in New Jersey in 1812 and by doing the same work for Eli Terry in 1816. Throughout his career, Chauncey Jerome's strength was in clock case design. His brother Noble would design and build the clock movements that Chauncey envisioned. By the early 1820s, the Jeromes, along with Elijah Darrow, were successfully marketing wooden-works shelf clocks driven by a movement that circumvented Terry's patent. It was called a "groaner" after the noise made by the intermeshing gears.

This movement, and later Terry movements, were housed in a Chauncey Jerome–designed case that he called a "bronze looking-glass clock" (more commonly known today as a "pillar and splat clock.") The half columns of this case were stenciled with bronze and brass powder in the fashion of much of the furniture of the late 1820s and early 1830s. The lower panel in the door was a mirror, although later cases replaced the mirror with a reverse glass painted scene. These cases were a commercial success and superseded the popularity of Terry's pillar and scroll clock.

By the 1837 depression the Jerome Clock Co. had expanded as far as the Southern states, where Jerome had established plants that assembled clocks from parts fabricated in Connecticut, avoiding Southern state taxes on finished movements produced outside the region.

In his autobiographical notes and letters, Chauncey Jerome relates that he was in Richmond, Virginia, contemplating possible bankruptcy and looking at one of his wooden works clocks "when it popped" into his head that he could make a one-day brass clock movement more cheaply than a wooden works movement. He reasoned that the case would cost no more, as the dials, glasses, and weights would be the same, but the movement would be smaller and cost less to make. There has long been a dispute as to whether the Jeromes can claim the title of being the actual inventors of the cheap one-day brass movement. Far more important, however, are Chauncey's skills as a promoter and businessman.

Noble Jerome designed the movement, which was granted a patent in 1839, and Chauncey obtained the financing. The movement was housed in a simple box framed with ogee molding and outfitted with a brass dial. The public turned this clock into the most popular American clock ever produced, and Jerome and Company was saved. The clock was manufactured by various companies in incredible numbers between 1840 and 1890. These clocks could be wholesaled at $1.50 apiece. Other manufacturers scrambled to catch up with the Jeromes.

Clock Springs

Growing industrialization in America caused further changes in clock production. Among the most important of these was the development of cheap, reliable coil springs. Weights were generally used to drive clocks until the 1840s, when affordable and reliable springs began to become available. Before the 1840s, coiled springs had been imported from Europe, but they were too expensive to be used profitably in inexpensive mass-produced clocks. Silas B. Terry (son of Eli Terry) was the first to develop a way of tempering and producing a coil spring cheaply, for which he obtained a patent in 1830. By mid-century, spring-driven clocks were fast replacing weight-driven clocks. This advance allowed manufacturers to produce smaller clocks, as the space necessary for the weights to travel downward was no longer required. Spring-driven mechanical clocks would be the mainstay of the clockmaking industry until about 1930, when the rapid expansion of rural electrification in the United States enabled most manufacturers to concentrate on producing electric clocks.

Consolidation and Domination

By the middle of the nineteenth century, the American clockmaking industry had coalesced into the major manufacturers that many of us remember today. The companies that dominated the industry throughout the second half of the nineteenth century and into the twentieth century were:

The Ansonia Clock Company, founded in 1850 in Derby, Connecticut. From 1854 to 1878, the company made clocks in Ansonia, Connecticut. In 1878, after reorganization, the company moved to Brooklyn, New York. This company was among the most prolific of manufacturers and may well have had the most extensive line of clocks. By World War I, Ansonia had sales agents and offices around the world. The company's failure to keep abreast of changes after the war caused a decline in quality and production. By 1929, the company was in bankruptcy and a creditors' committee sold all its clockmaking machinery to the Soviet Union, where it became the core of the state-run clockmaking industry.

The E. Ingraham Company was founded by Elias Ingraham, a cabinetmaker who had come to Bristol, Connecticut, to make clock cases for various wooden-works manufacturers. In 1844, after coming out of a bankruptcy caused by the Panic of 1837, Ingraham entered into partnership with Elisha C. Brewster to manufacture clocks. One of their early successes was the production of the Jerome one-day brass movement to meet the demand for this new clock. In 1845, Ingraham designed the steeple case, which became one of the most popular cases developed in the 19th century. In 1885, the company introduced the black-painted mantel clock in imitation of the French Black Marble mantel clocks. This model was so popular that more than 220 variations of it were produced before production ended in the 20th century. Watches and wristwatches were added to the catalog in 1914 and 1930. Ingraham electric clocks appeared by 1932, and production of spring-driven clocks ceased during World War II, in 1942. Twenty-five years later, the company ceased to exist when it was sold to McGraw-Edison and Company and all clockmaking operations ceased.

The E. N. Welch Manufacturing Company was founded by Elisha Niles Welch, who had begun his career by making clock weights and clock bells. In 1856, when he purchased the bankrupt clockmaking business of Jonathan C. Brown, Welch became the largest clock manufacturer in Bristol, Connecticut. Welch died in 1887 and his son James drove the company deeply into debt. Production ceased in 1893 as the company paid off its debt, but production resumed in 1897.

In 1902, James Welch died and the company came into the hands of the major shareholders, William Sessions and his nephew Albert Sessions. They changed the company name in 1903 to the Sessions Clock Company. Sessions continued Welch's line of clocks, particularly black mantel and oak-cased kitchen clocks. The Great Depression of the 1930s brought new financial problems, and after 1935 Sessions made only electric clocks. The company was sold in 1958 to Consolidated Electronics Industries Corporation of New York, which then sold its clockmaking division to United Metal Goods Company of Brooklyn, New York, a maker of electric clocks.

The New Haven Clock Company was founded in 1853 to produce cheap brass movements for the Jerome Clock Company. When Jerome went bankrupt in 1855, the New Haven Clock Company bought it. In a year, the expanded company began to manufacture entire clocks. By 1880, it had offices in Europe and Asia. New Haven sold not only its own clocks, but also those of F. Kroeber of New York City, Ingraham of Bristol, and E. Howard of Boston. By 1890, New Haven had grown so large that it marketed only its own clocks. Added to the line in 1880 and 1917 were inexpensive pocket watches and wristwatches. The company had major financial problems in the 1940s and 1950s, and finally closed in 1959. All properties were auctioned off in 1960.

The Seth Thomas Clock Company was founded in 1810 by Seth Thomas. Always a good businessman, he had diversified his financial interests from the beginning and was able to weather the Panic of 1837. Under Seth Thomas, the company was very conservative and reluctant to introduce new ideas or modes of production. The company made money by letting others be the pioneers. By 1850, the company had switched fully to the production of brass clocks and was producing more than 24,000 clocks a year. Thomas organized the Seth Thomas Clock Company as a joint stock company in 1853 with himself as president and major shareholder. After his death in 1859, the company was run by his sons Aaron, Edward, and Seth, Junior. Business was expanded with an emphasis on spring-driven and calendar clocks, and starting in 1882, watches were added to the line, with production continuing until 1915. The company became well known for its regulators and tower clocks.

During the 1930s depression, the Seth Thomas Clock Company became a division of General Time Corporation. After World War II, the company ceased making movements and purchased them from outside domestic sources and from overseas. In 1970, the company lost a stockholders' fight, and the business, which included Westclox, became a division of Talley Industries of Seattle, Washington.

The Waterbury Clock Company was a major producer of clocks from 1857 to 1944 and watches from 1880 to the 1970s. The company was founded and located in Waterbury, Connecticut. Until the 1870s, it made a small number of its own clocks. Most of the company's profits after 1875 came from selling its own movements housed in cast iron, pot metal, and bronze cases purchased from other sources. In the late 1880s, Waterbury added calendar clocks to its line, and in 1880 it began to produce inexpensive nonjeweled watches. By 1917, when the United States entered World War I, its production of clocks and watches had surpassed 23,000 per year. The Great Depression put Waterbury into receivership in 1933 and all clock production ceased. Watches continued in production until 1944, when that operation was sold to United States Time Corporation. Watch production continues today as part of Timex.

The William Gilbert Clock Company began in 1828 when William Gilbert went into partnership with George Marsh. In 1841, Gilbert, along with Lucius Clarke, purchased the Riley Whiting clock factory from Whiting's widow. Clarke sold out to Gilbert four years later. The Gilbert Clock Company would survive until 1964 when the clockmaking division was sold to the Spartus Corporation of Chicago, Illinois. The company's most prosperous years were between 1880 and 1907, when it produced a good variety of both mantel and wall clocks. The company was severely hurt by the recession of 1907, but it finally came out of debt by 1925. The Great Depression found the company in receivership in 1932, but once again it emerged from debt in 1934. Gilbert continued manufacturing clocks during World War II by using nonmetal cases.

By the beginning of the twentieth century, clocks, once only the possession of the affluent, had now become available to everyone. As society, increasingly powered by commerce and manufacturing, became more time-driven, the demand for clocks continued to increase sharply. In greatest demand were inexpensive, smaller clocks. The American clockmaking industry from the end of the 18th century on would follow this trend. The Industrial Revolution beginning in the nineteenth century made this possible at the same time that it created an ever-increasing demand. The necessity of a public clock on the church steeple or in the town hall was replaced by the inexpensive, mass-produced mantel or wall clock.

This trend was true not only in America but also around the world. Inexpensive, mass-produced clocks arrived along with the industrialization. Local clockmaking industries either adapted or disappeared under the onslaught of American clocks. By the last quarter of the nineteenth century, the American clockmaking industry was filling this need around the globe. Various countries reacted to the American invasion in various ways. In the British Isles, American clocks, ironically, almost destroyed the industry from which they had evolved. After 1870, most of the clocks marketed in the British Isles were imported from America, Germany, and France. The greatly diminished native British industry survived by producing clocks more generally aimed at the affluent market and rarely challenged the mass-produced import.

France's clockmaking industry survived and flourished thanks to a combination of tactics. French tariffs in the 19th century tended to protect domestic industries and markets, and this kept most American clocks from the French market. French tradition and dominance of style and fashion throughout the 19th century caused an expansion of the market for French clocks outside France. Thousands of French clocks and movements crossed the sea to Britain and America to meet the demands of the middle class and the wealthy for high style and fashion.

After unification in 1871, Germany's clockmaking industry adapted by adopting American manufacturing and business techniques. Clocks from the Black Forest factories of companies such as Gustav Becker, Lenzkirche, and the Hamburg-American Clock Company began to challenge American dominance with cheaper prices by the turn of the twentieth century.

In Japan, after the opening of trade with the West in the 1850s and 1860s, the entire clockmaking industry was revamped. The indigenous earlier system of recording and observing time was discarded and Western concepts of time and clocks adopted. In the 1870s, the Japanese, like the Germans, adopted the framework and structure of the American industry. The Japanese produced faithful copies of many American clocks. These knockoffs, produced by such companies as Seiko, dominated the Japanese domestic market as Japan westernized.

Between the World Wars

The period between World War I and World War II saw a decrease of clock manufacturing throughout most of the world. Those mechanical clocks still being produced were often inferior in all ways to their prewar counterparts. With certain notable exceptions, the designs were cheaper and coarser. The world was turning to the electric clock, and depressed economic conditions did not seem to demand the variety of styles of an earlier, more prosperous day. Fewer fine clocks were being produced, and those were not for the mass market.

World War II virtually destroyed the industry, and of the companies that limped along after the war, one by one succumbed to bankruptcy or merger. The market that had made the clock a desired, and in many cases, a prized, possession was severely shrunken.

Time still governs much of our lives, but now it does so with the battery-operated electronic movement which is so inexpensive that we often discard our timepieces rather than change the battery.

Some mechanical clocks are still produced for niche markets. India made copies of some nineteenth-century American movements that were housed in reproduction American cases. Korea did a bit better by reproducing clocks with 31-day movements that more closely resemble their American originals. China produces battery-operated clocks in case forms that have "traditional" names, such as "Colonial Style," but whose shapes are new creations. In today's markets, case materials are plastics more often than not, and we are supposed to admire a "genuine simulated wood finish." Mass-produced German mechanical movements are housed in clock cases of various sizes and shapes around the world. The retailer often touts the vaunted craftsmanship and quality of the "German movement," but here, too, the quality has diminished.

Although this may seem a very negative way to end an introduction to the history of clocks that continues to this day, it really functions to direct you back to the reason that you are reading this book—back to a wonderful world of collecting and exploring time and timepieces. You will find irresistible the lure of a type or period of clock, or a country's or maker's clocks. Soon you will have to possess your own bit of the past and share the author's passion for Time.

CHAPTER 2

How Much and What Kind?

Clock Values

This book will help you identify the clocks that you will most frequently find and acquaint collectors with the range of values that they might expect to pay in the marketplace.

As the identification of a clock is determined by a number of factors so, too, is its value.

Although there are exceptions to what follows, these generalizations usually hold true.

1. Rarer handcrafted clocks will command higher prices than mass-produced ones.
2. All things being equal, older clocks generally command higher prices than newer clocks.
3. Striking clocks cost more than time-only clocks.
4. The more mechanical features, such as second hands, calendar, quarter strike, Westminster chimes, and the like, that a clock has, the higher the price it will command.
5. Mint original-condition clocks will always be worth more than clocks that have had parts restored or replaced.
6. Clocks that can clearly be identified by signed movements or dials or have their original labels or manufacturer's logo will cost you more than those missing these features.
7. Clock cases that have been refinished bring lower prices than those that retain their original finish in good condition.
8. Clock cases with missing or replaced parts also bring lower prices.
9. Clocks or clock cases that have been altered as well as those clocks reconstructed from the parts of other clocks ("marriages") will always bring lower prices.

10. Popularity of a particular type or model of clock will increase its market value. The opposite is equally true in decreasing values.
11. Your own particular desire to own certain clocks can have the effect of driving up the value when you compete with others for those clocks. This is particularly true at auctions.

The prices listed in this book were determined by many of the factors above. Instead of establishing a single fixed value for a type of clock, which is impossible, impractical, and foolish, a price range has been determined and printed at the end of each section's listings. These price ranges represent the average auction range for the clocks listed in this book.

The individual prices listed in this book derive from actual auction results. The reader must realize that retail prices will be higher to account for costs and profit margin. There is no value listed that is older than 1999 unless indicated. The latest values date from auctions held during fall 2002.

However, this is merely a guide, as any clock is worth only what the buyer is willing to pay for it.

Clock Types

All mechanical timepieces can be divided into six basic types. Three of these types are covered in this guide.

1. *Tower Clocks*—Very large clocks designed to operate in towers and steeples and be seen from a distance. These clocks span the centuries from the thirteenth to the twentieth and can be considered public clocks. As these clocks are collected by small numbers of people and as they rarely come up for sale, I have not included them in this guide.
2. *Tall-Case Clocks*—Large clocks designed to stand upon the floor. In England, where this style evolved during the seventeenth century, they are called long-case clocks. In America they are called tall-case or grandfather clocks, the latter name coming from a popular song of the 1870s (see Glossary).
3. *Wall Clocks*—designed to hang upon the wall to save space or originally to provide room for the clock weights to descend. Appearing as early as the fourteenth century as miniaturized tower clocks, they developed into major elements of commercial and domestic decor by the twentieth century.

4. *Shelf Clocks*—Smaller clocks designed to sit upon a surface such as a table, shelf, or bracket. They grew from the medieval chamber or domestic clock, which sat upon a table and was considered to be portable. They have been made in many different case styles. In England, shelf clocks are called *bracket clocks.* The term *mantel clock,* synonymous with *shelf clock,* became popular during the second half of the nineteenth century, when Victorian "tastemakers" used the term because they believed it conveyed a greater sense of gentility and status. *Shelf clock, bracket clock, table clock,* and *mantel clock* all refer to similar smaller clocks that stand on a surface other than the floor.

5. *Pocket Watches*—Small portable clocks meant to be carried in a pouch or pocket. They appear around the end of the sixteenth century, and their production continued into the twentieth century. They are traditionally treated separately from larger clocks as a unique division of timepieces and are therefore not covered in this work.

6. *Wristwatches*—Very small portable clocks meant to be worn on the wrist. They evolved in World War I from the military need for a small watch that could be easily consulted without fumbling in a pocket or pouch during combat. As unique a division as pocket watches, they are not included in this guide.

In each of our clock divisions (tall-case, wall, and shelf) I have further sorted the listed clocks by country of origin (American, British, Dutch, French, Austrian, German, and Swiss). Within each national division I have listed the most common styles in chronological or alphabetical order.

Names and Labels

By the first quarter of the nineteenth century, American clockmakers were identifying their products by adding paper labels to the inside of the backboard. They were placed in the bottom section of the case behind the pendulum and bell or gong. These labels, besides showing the maker's name, also contained operating instructions. Today these labels give us clues to help date the clock.

With the passing of wooden-works movements, which were rarely marked, brass movements were usually stamped with the maker's name.

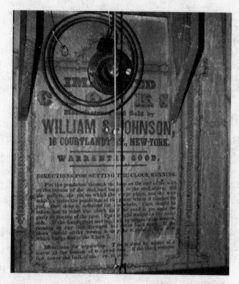

30-hour wooden-works time and strike, ca. 1841–48. W. Johnson was at 16 Courtlandt Street, New York City, during those years.

30-hour wooden-works time and strike, ca. 1831–34. E. Hotchkiss moved to Burlington, Vermont, in 1831 and went bankrupt in 1834.

30-hour wooden-works time, strike, and alarm movement, ca. 1820–42. Seth Thomas made wooden works clocks at Plymouth Hollow between 1820 and 1842, when the company switched to brass movements.

Because company names and locations changed over time, they can be useful in helping to date your clock. To aid your hunt, I have included here some brief information about the major companies, with names used and dates. Check the bibliography for more detailed sources.

SETH THOMAS CLOCK TREE

After selling out to Silas Hoadley in 1813 (see above), **Seth Thomas** opened his own business and made clocks under his own label (Seth Thomas) from 1813 to 1853. Reorganized in 1853 as the **Seth Thomas Clock Co.**, the company manufactured clocks until 1930, when it became a division of General Time Instrument Co. In 1949, it became a division of General Time Corporation. In 1970, General Time was sold, and the Seth Thomas division became a part of Talley Industries.

CHAUNCEY JEROME CLOCK TREE

Chauncey Jerome was employed by Eli Terry from 1816 to 1822. He formed **Jeromes and Darrow,** which made clocks from 1828 to 1833. Chauncey and his brother Noble produced clocks from 1835–1837 as **Chauncey and Noble Jerome. Jerome and Co.** was formed in 1840 and produced clocks until 1855, when it failed. The name and assets were purchased by the **New Haven Clock Company,** which made clocks under that label until 1956 when it was reorganized as the **New Haven**

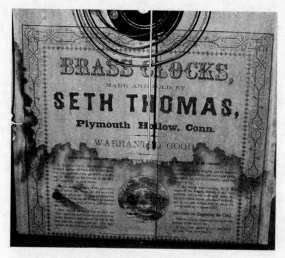

30-hour brass weight-driven time and strike movement, ca. 1842–53. Seth Thomas made brass movement clocks under this name until 1853, when the name changed to Seth Thomas Clock Co.

Clock and Watch Company, which in turn went out of business in 1960.

THE WATERBURY CLOCK TREE

The Waterbury Clock Company was formed in 1857 and made clocks under that label until 1944 when they were purchased and became a part of U.S. Time Corporation. The name no longer exists, having been incorporated along with the Ingersol watch label into today's Timex Corporation.

THE GILBERT CLOCK TREE

William L. Gilbert made clocks as **Marsh, Gilbert and Co.** from 1828 to 1835 and as **Birge, Gilbert and Co.** in 1835. The company was reorganized as **Birge and Gilbert** in 1835. Birge and Gilbert failed in 1837 and Gilbert joined Chauncey and Noble Jerome plus Zelotes Grant to form **Jeromes, Gilbert, Grant and Co.** from 1836 to 1840. By 1841, he had formed **Clark, Gilbert and Co.,** which was reorganized as **W. L. Gilbert and Co.** in 1845. This became **Gilbert and Clark** from 1848 to 1851 and then **W. L. Gilbert and Company** from 1851 to 1866. It was reformed again as the **Gilbert**

30-hour brass weight-driven time and strike,
ca. 1857–80. Jerome and Co. was owned by the New
Haven Clock Co. by this time but continued to use
this label for its exports to England until the 1880s.

Steeple clock, 30-hour brass time and strike movement,
ca. 1875–90. New Haven Clock Co. bought Jerome and Co.
in 1855 and made clocks under this name until 1956. The
lower glass tablet suggests the date.

Mfg. Co. until 1877, when the name became the **William L. Gilbert Clock Co.** This name stood until 1934. Reorganized once again in 1934, the company became **The William L. Gilbert Clock Corp.** until 1957. That year, it was sold and became part of the General Gilbert Corp. In 1964, the company's assets were bought by the Spartus Corp.

THE INGRAHAM CLOCK TREE

Elias Ingraham made clocks as **Ingraham and Bartholomew** from 1831 to 1832. **Ingraham and Goodrich** made clocks from 1832 to 1833, when Ingraham began making clocks under his own label, **Elias Ingraham.** He used this label from 1835 to 1840. Various partners changed the label to **Ray and Ingraham** (1841–44), **Brewster and Ingraham** (1844–52), and **E. and A. Ingraham** (1852–56). The label was **Elias Ingraham and Co.** from 1857 to 1860, **E. Ingraham and Co.** from 1861 to 1880, **The E. Ingraham Co.** from 1880 to 1884, **The E. Ingraham Co.** from 1884 to 1958, and finally the **Ingraham Co.** from 1958 to 1967. After 1967, it became a division of McGraw-Edison and Company.

THE BROWN/WELCH/SESSIONS CLOCK TREE

J. C. Brown started making clocks in the 1830s, and his name appears as part of **Bartholomew, Brown and Co.** from 1832 to 1835. This becomes

Double-decker 8-day weight-driven time and strike movement, ca. 1835–39. J. C. Brown used this label between 1835 and 1839.

the **Forrestville Manufacturing. Co.** between 1835 and 1839, then **Hills, Brown and Co.** from 1840 to 1842. Brown used two labels between 1842 and 1849: **J. C. Brown and Co.** and **The Forrestville Mfg. Co.** By 1850, the label read **Forrestville Clock Manufactory, J. C. Brown.** By 1864, it had become the **E. N. Welch Manufacturing Co.** In 1903, the name was changed to the **Sessions Clock Co.** In 1956, the name became **The Sessions Clock Co.** The company closed in 1968.

CHAPTER 3

Tall-Case Clocks

Commonly called grandfather clocks in America today, they are more properly known as tall-case or long-case clocks. They came into existence shortly after the invention of the anchor escapement (1670s) in England, which encouraged the enclosing of pendulum and weights within a case. The term *grandfather clock* is American and derives from a popular song of the 1870s called "My Grandfather's Clock."

Tall-case clocks were the most common clocks in America until the 1830s and in the British Isles until the 1860s. This style of clock was also found in Holland, Scandinavia, and Germany. Cased examples of Morbier wall clocks represent France's tall-case clocks, although there are those who would argue that these examples did not really start out as floor clocks as the movements were designed and manufactured to hang on the wall without a case.

Within these six clock areas pictured the collector will still be able to find affordable examples.

Although rare month- and yearlong clocks do exist, most tall-case clocks are generally found in just two forms; 30-hour clocks that must be wound every day and 8-day versions that are wound once a week.

With rare exceptions, 8-day tall-case clocks command a higher value in the market than do 30-hour clocks. Signed tall-case clocks are more valuable than unsigned clocks.

Almost all these clocks include both time and strike movements. They commonly strike a bell. Later tall-case clocks (late nineteenth and twentieth century) often strike coils, rods, or tubular chimes.

Seventeenth-, eighteenth-, and early-nineteenth-century clocks had solid wood case doors, with or without a lenticle (more common in Continental tall-case clocks). After the middle of the nineteenth century it became usual to find fully glazed trunk doors.

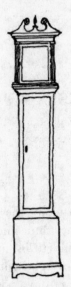

English and American tall-case clocks,
late eighteenth century

Tall-case clock, ca. 1940

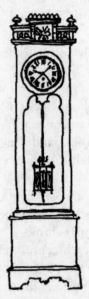

Regulator floor clock, ca. 1880

French, Morbier clock

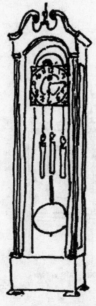

Hall clock, ca. 1890

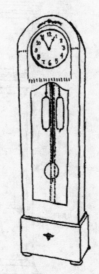

German clock, ca. 1900

To this day, most tall-case clocks are weight-driven, although spring-driven movements were fitted into some mass-produced clocks around the turn of the twentieth century.

Tall-Case Tops

The tops or hoods of tall-case clocks come in a variety of shapes that can be helpful in clock identification.

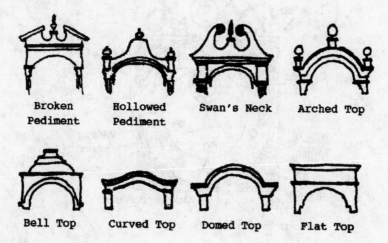

Broken Pediment

Hollowed Pediment

Swan's Neck

Arched Top

Bell Top

Curved Top

Domed Top

Flat Top

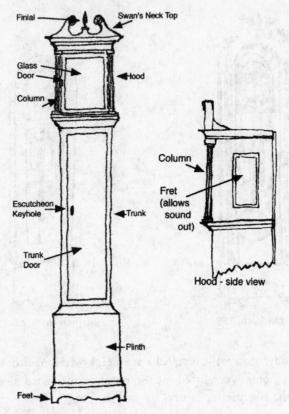

Basic tall-case nomenclature

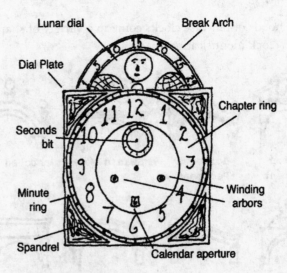

Basic dial nomenclature

Tall-Case Clock Value Range

The following value ranges represent auction prices. The range of prices is designed to allow the buyer to determine a fair retail value for various types, categories, and periods of American, English, Dutch, French, and German tall-case clocks. It presupposes that clocks of great rarity, uniqueness, and importance have been removed from consideration, as the purpose of this work is to acquaint the reader with the market prices of the most frequently encountered, and therefore most available, clocks.

American Tall-Case Clocks

I have divided American tall-case clocks into the following periods and types.

I. Tall-case clocks produced between ca. 1750 and ca. 1840, including 30-hour tall-case clocks and 8-day tall-case clocks.

II. Tall-case clocks produced between ca. 1840 and ca. 1870.

III. Regulator floor clocks and hall clocks produced between ca. 1870 and ca. 1910.

IV. All types of tall-case clocks produced between ca. 1900 and ca. 1950.

V. All types of tall-case clocks including custom and kit-built clocks produced from ca. 1950 to the present day.

Some things to remember: The highest prices are realized for signed clocks in their original cases in excellent original condition. The lowest prices are realized for clocks with faults such as damaged cases, dials, movements, marriages, poor restorations, and missing parts. Recased tall-case movements will always sell for less than movements in their original cases. Signed tall-case clocks will always sell for more than comparable unsigned clocks. Thirty-hour wooden-works tall-case clocks retail for less than the rarer 8-day wooden-works tall-case clocks. Eight-day brass-movement tall-case clocks sell for more than 30-hour brass-works tall-case clocks.

CATEGORY I

TALL-CASE CLOCKS PRODUCED BETWEEN CA. 1750
AND CA. 1840
American 30-hour Wooden-Works Tall-Case Clocks

American, New England, ca. 1825, 30-hour wooden-works tall-case clock, painted dial, unsigned, refinished pine case, flat top, $747

American, Maine, ca. 1820,
30-hour wooden-works time and
strike tall-case clock, unsigned,
walnut case, $900.

American, New England, ca. 1820, 30-hour wooden-works tall-case clock,
    painted dial, unsigned, cherry case, flat top, $1,350

	LOW	MID	HIGH
30-hour Wooden-Works Time and Strike Tall-Case Clocks, Unsigned (ca. 1775–1840)	$800–$1,000	$2,500	$3,500

American, Connecticut, ca. 1820,
30-hour wooden-works time,
seconds, calendar, and strike tall-
case clock, Thomas and Hoadley
movement, cherry case, $3,000.

American, New York, ca. 1830, 30-hour wooden-works time seconds and strike tall-case clock, M. Leavenworth, painted pine case, $4,500. Credit: NAWCC Eastern States Regional.

American, Maine, ca. 1820–25, 30-hour wooden-works time and strike tall-case clock, signed Edwards, grain painted pine case, $3,750. Credit: R. O. Schmitt Fine Arts.

American, Connecticut, ca. 1816–30, 30-hour wooden-works time, seconds, calendar, and strike tall-case clock, signed Seth Thomas, pine case, dial needs restoration, $2,000. Credit: R. O. Schmitt Fine Arts.

American, Connecticut, ca. 1801–30, 30-hour wooden-works tall-case clock, painted dial, signed Riley Whiting, Winchester, mahogany case, arched top, $2,645

American, Connecticut, ca. 1820, 30-hour wooden-works tall-case clock, painted dial, signed (Silas) Hoadley, Plymouth, pine case, arched top, $1,380

American, Ohio, ca. 1815–25, 30-hour wooden-works tall-case clock, painted dial, signed Luman Watson, Cincinnati, cherry and mahogany case, swan's neck top, $4,704

American, Ohio, ca. 1820–30, 30-hour wooden-works tall-case clock, painted dial, signed Luman Watson, Cincinnati, cherry case, swan's neck top, $4,802

American, Connecticut, ca. 1825, 30-hour wooden-works tall-case clock, painted dial, signed Seth Thomas, Plymouth, painted pine and poplar case, swan's neck rail top, $2,530

American, Connecticut, ca. 1830, 30-hour wooden-works tall-case clock, painted dial, signed Riley Whiting, Winchester, birch case, arched top, $3,520

American, Connecticut, ca. 1770–80, 30-hour wooden-works tall-case clock, brass dial, signed Ashel Cheney, birch and cherry case, arched top, $6,037

American, Connecticut, ca. 1760–80, 30-hour wooden-works tall-case clock, painted dial, signed Benjamin Cheney, cherry case, swan's neck top, $3,162

American, Connecticut, ca. 1825, 30-hour wooden-works tall-case clock, painted dial, signed (Silas) Hoadley, Plymouth, painted pine case, arched top, $4,025

	LOW	MID	HIGH
30-hour Wooden-Works Time and Strike Tall-Case Clocks, Signed (ca. 1775–1840)	$1,500	$4,500	$6,500

TYPICAL FORMS OF THE AMERICAN 30-HOUR WOODEN MOVEMENT

American, Connecticut, ca. 1816,
30-hour wooden-works tall-case clock,
Seth Thomas, pine case, $2,000. Credit:
R. O. Schmitt Fine Arts.

American, Connecticut, ca. 1816,
30-hour wooden-works tall-case clock,
Hoadley, painted pine case, $4,750.
Credit: NAWCC Eastern States Regional.

American, New York, ca. 1830, 30-hour
wooden works, Mark Leavenworth,
Albany, New York. Credit: NAWCC
Eastern States Regional.

American, Connecticut, ca. 1830, 30-hour
wooden works, strikes a cast iron bell on
the top of the plates, indicates the hours,
minutes, seconds, and day of the month.

American, New York, ca. 1830, 30-hour wooden-works tall-case clock, signed Curtis, painted pine case, $3,500. Credit: NAWCC Eastern States Regional.

American, Maine, ca. 1820, 30-hour wooden-works tall-case clock, signed S. Edwards, pine case, $3,750. Credit: R. O. Schmitt Fine Arts.

American Brass Works Tall Case Clocks

American, New England, ca. 1810, 8-day brass-movement tall-case clock, painted dial, unsigned, cherry case, domed top, $1,265

American, New England, ca. 1800, 8-day brass-movement tall-case clock painted moon dial, unsigned, mahogany case, swan's neck top, $8,625

American, Maryland, ca. 1801–25, 8-day brass-movement tall-case clock, painted dial, unsigned, Baltimore, faux grained cherry case, arched top, $2,587

American, unknown, ca. 1830, 8-day brass-movement tall-case clock, painted dial, unsigned, mahogany case, swan's neck top, $1,680

American, Pennsylvania, ca. 1810, 8-day brass-movement tall-case clock painted moon dial, unsigned, walnut case swan's neck top, $6,160

American, Pennsylvania, ca. 1780–1800, 8-day brass-movement tall-case clock, painted dial, unsigned, cherry case, swan's neck top, $6,612

American, New Hampshire, ca. 1820, 8-day time, seconds, calendar, and strike brass movement, unsigned, mahogany case, $7,500. Credit: R. O. Schmitt Fine Arts.

American, New Hampshire, ca. 1820, 8-day time, seconds, calendar, and strike brass movement, unsigned, cherry case, $5,500. Credit: R. O. Schmitt Fine Arts.

American, New York, ca. 1775–1800, 8-day brass-movement tall-case clock, painted dial (damaged), unsigned, mahogany case, swan's neck top, $4,950.

American, New Hampshire, ca. 1805–15, 8-day wood plate movement with brass and steel gears, tall-case clock, painted dial, unsigned, cherry case, arched top, $2,072

American, New England, ca. 1820, 8-day time, seconds, calendar, and strike brass movement, unsigned, mahogany case, $3,500.

American, Massachusetts, ca. 1760–70, 8-day brass-movement tall-case clock, painted dial, unsigned, wood case, stained to resemble mahogany, arched top, $13,800

American, New England, ca. 1800, 8-day brass-movement tall-case clock, painted dial, unsigned, cherry case, arched top, $7,187

American, New England, ca. 1760–80, 8-day brass-movement tall-case clock, painted dial, unsigned, cherry and maple case, arched top, $3,162

American, New England, ca. 1790–1800, 8-day brass-movement tall-case clock, painted dial, unsigned, mahogany case, swan's neck top, $1,035

	LOW	MID	HIGH
8-day Brass Time and Strike Tall-Case Clocks, Unsigned (ca. 1750–1820)	$2,000	$8,500	$12,500+

American, Pennsylvania, ca. 1805–15, 8-day brass-movement tall-case clock with painted moon dial, Daniel Oyster, Reading, mahogany case, hollowed pediment, $8,050

American, Pennsylvania, ca. 1775–85, 30-hour brass-movement tall-case clock, painted dial, Benjamin Morris, Hilltown, carved pine case (damaged), swan's neck top (broken arch), $2,200

American, New Hampshire, ca. 1825, 8-day time, seconds, calendar, moon, and strike brass movement, signed Benjamin Morrell, cherry and maple case, $9,100. Credit: R. O. Schmitt Fine Arts.

American, New Hampshire, ca. 1825, 8-day time, seconds, calendar, and strike brass movement, signed James Cross, tiger maple case, $7,200. Credit: R. O. Schmitt Fine Arts.

American, New York, ca. 1798, 8-day time-only brass movement, signed Nathaniel Dominy, pine case, $5,000. Credit: R. O. Schmitt Fine Arts.

American, Pennsylvania, ca. 1800, 30-hour brass-movement tall-case clock, brass dial, George Hoff Sr., walnut case, flat top, $1,300

American, Pennsylvania, ca. 1795–1805, 8-day brass-movement tall-case clock, painted dial, Samuel Hill, Harrisburg, walnut case, swan's neck top (broken arch), $6,325

American, Pennsylvania?, ca. 1770, 8-day brass-movement tall-case clock, brass dial, John Fisher, mahogany case, flat top, $9,744

American, Massachusetts, ca. 1765–75, 8-day brass-movement tall-case clock, brass dial, Nath. Mulliken, Lexington, mahogany and cherry case, arched top (broken), $7,638

American, Massachusetts, ca. 1800–15, 8-day brass-movement tall-case clock, painted dial, David Wood, Newburyport, cherry and maple case, arched top, $8,813

American, Pennsylvania, ca. 1815–25, 8-day brass-movement tall-case clock, painted dial, Henry Wismer, Bucks County, cherry case, swan's neck top, $5,875

American, Massachusetts, ca. 1800–10, 8-day brass-movement tall-case clock, painted dial, Joseph Mulliken, Concord, cherry case, arched top, $4,700

American, Massachusetts, ca. 1755–65, 8-day brass-movement tall-case clock, silvered brass dial, Nathaniel Mulliken, Lexington, cherry case, bell top, $12,925

American, Massachusetts, ca. 1805–15, 8-day brass-movement tall-case clock, painted dial, Nathaniel Munroe, Concord, mahogany case, arched top, $5,288

American, Massachusetts, ca. 1755–65, 8-day brass-movement tall-case clock, brass dial, Nathaniel Mulliken, Lexington, walnut case, bell top, $7,638

American, Pennsylvania, ca. 1800, 8-day brass-movement tall-case clock, brass dial, William Campbell, Shippensburg, cherry case, swan's neck top, $9,687

American, New Jersey, ca. 1800–10, 8-day brass-movement tall-case clock, painted dial, Isaac Brokaw, Bridge Town, mahogany case, hollowed pediment top, $10,575

American, Pennsylvania, ca. 1785–95, 30-hour brass-movement tall-case clock, painted dial, Michael Striepy, Bucks County, poplar and oak case, flat top, $4,312

American, Pennsylvania, ca. 1780–90, 30-hour brass-movement tall-case clock, painted dial, Jacob Solliday, Bucks County, walnut case, swan's neck top, $4,312

American, Massachusetts, ca. 1780, 8-day brass-movement tall-case clock, painted dial, Ezekiel Reed, Bridgewater, stained pine case, swan's neck top, $2,875

American, Massachusetts, ca. 1780–90, 8-day brass-movement tall-case clock, painted dial, Nathaniel Munroe, cherry and sycamore case, arched top, $8,337

American, New Hampshire, ca. 1760–80, 8-day brass-movement tall-case clock, brass dial, Timothy Chandler, Concord, cherry case, swan's neck top, $7,762

American, Connecticut, ca. 1784–1800, 8-day brass-movement tall-case clock, brass dial, Daniel Burnap, East Windsor, cherry case, hollowed pediment top, $11,500

American, Connecticut, ca. 1784–1800, 8-day brass-movement tall-case clock, brass dial, Daniel Burnap, East Windsor, cherry case, hollowed pediment top, $8,912

American, Massachusetts, ca. 1790–1800, 8-day brass-movement tall-case clock, painted dial, Simon Willard, Roxbury, cherry case, arched top, $10,925

American, Massachusetts, ca. 1750–80, 8-day brass-movement tall-case clock, brass dial, Nathaniel Mulliken, Lexington, chestnut case, flat top, $9,200

	LOW	MID	HIGH
8-day Brass Time and Strike Tall-Case Clocks, Signed (ca. 1750–1820)	$4,500	$8,500	$12,500+

CATEGORY II

TALL-CASE CLOCKS PRODUCED BETWEEN CA. 1840 AND CA. 1870

This category is virtually nonexistent in the marketplace, so it is impossible to establish a reliable price range.

American, New York, ca. 1850, time-only 8-day three-register movement, enameled dial, William F. Ladd, New York, mahogany case, Gothic arch top, $13,800

American, New York, ca. 1850, time-only, 8-day three-register movement, enameled dial, Blunt & Co., New York, mahogany case, Gothic arch top, $12,650

American, Ohio, ca. 1860, 8-day brass time and strike movement, painted dial, unsigned, heavily carved mahogany case, swan's neck top, $2,310

American, South Carolina, ca. 1850, 8-day brass time and strike movement, painted dial, unsigned, cherry case, swan's neck top, $4,600

American, New York, ca. 1850, 8-day time-only three-register movement, William F. Ladd, mahogany Gothic revival case, $13,800. Credit: Prices4Antiques.com.

American, Ohio, ca. 1860, 8-day time and strike movement, painted dial, unsigned, heavily carved mahogany case, $2,310. Credit: Prices4Antiques.com.

CATEGORY III

REGULATOR FLOOR CLOCKS AND HALL CLOCKS PRODUCED BETWEEN CA. 1870 AND CA. 1910

American, New Hampshire, ca. 1845, 8-day time only, regulator movement, silvered brass dial, Belden D. Bingham, Nashua, mahogany case, round top, $47,040

American, Connecticut, ca. 1850–70, 8-day, Regulator No. 8 movement, enameled dial, William L. Gilbert Clock Co., walnut Egyptian Revival case, $14,375

American, Connecticut, ca. 1895–05, 8-day Regulator No. 9 movement, enameled dial, William L. Gilbert Clock Co., walnut Renaissance Revival case, $5,720

American, Connecticut, ca. 1876–86, 8-day Regulator No. 7 movement, enameled dial, William L. Gilbert Clock Co., walnut Renaissance Revival case, $13,440

American, Connecticut, ca. 1886–96, 8-day Regulator No. 8 movement, enameled dial, Waterbury Clock Co., cherry architectural case, $10,080

American, New Hampshire, ca. 1840–50, jeweler's regulator, signed Belden D. Bingham, $47,040. Credit: R. O. Schmitt Fine Arts.

American, Connecticut, ca. 1876–86, Regulator No. 7, signed William L. Gilbert Clock Co., $13,440. Credit: R. O. Schmitt Fine Arts.

American, Connecticut, ca. 1900–10, 8-day Regulator No. 71 movement, enameled dial, Waterbury Clock Co., quarter sawn oak, architectural-style case, $11,760

American, Connecticut, ca. 1875–85, 8-day Regulator No. 15 movement, brass dial, Seth Thomas Clock Co., walnut Renaissance Revival case, $23,520

	LOW	MID	HIGH
Regulator Floor Clocks, Top-of-the-Line Factory-Produced Clocks (ca. 1870–1910)	$7,000	$12,000	$30,000+

HALL CLOCKS

American, Connecticut, ca. 1900, 8-day time and strike hall tall-case clock (base of clock contains a Regina disc player), Seth Thomas Clock Co., mahogany architectural-style case, $10,637

American, Massachusetts, ca. 1890, 8-day time and strike hall tall-case clock with silvered brass dial and elaborate chimes, Shreve, Crump & Low, Boston, carved oak case, flat top, $5,280

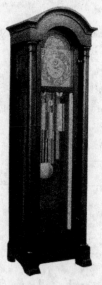 

American, ca. 1895, hall clock with English movement striking five tubular chimes, unsigned, $4,000. Credit: Prices4Antiques.com.

American, ca. 1916, hall clock, 8-day Herschede movement striking nine tubular chimes, signed Colonial Mfg. Co., $5,432. Credit: R. O. Schmitt Fine Arts.

American, New York, ca. 1900, 8-day time and strike hall tall-case clock (three train English movement striking bells, J. J. Eliott), Tiffany & Co., New York, heavily carved oak case, swan's neck top, $28,600

American, unknown, ca. 1910, 8-day time and strike hall tall-case clock (strikes on nine tubular chimes), G. R. Clock and Mantel Company, mahogany architectural-style case, $4,887

American, Massachusetts, ca. 1888, 8-day time and strike hall tall-case clock, E. Howard & Co., Boston, mahogany architectural-style case, large urn finial top, $23,100

American, New York?, ca. 1905, 8-day time and strike hall tall-case clock (three train English movement striking tubes, J. J. Eliott), unsigned, mahogany architectural-style case, $28,600

American, Michigan, ca. 1916, 8-day time and strike hall tall-case clock (Herschede movement striking nine tubes), Colonial Mfg. Co., Zeeland, mahogany architectural-style case, $5,432

American, New York, ca. 1885–95, 8-day time and strike hall tall-case clock (strikes on nine tubes), Tiffany & Co., New York, heavily carved mahogany Gothic-style case, $15,680

American, New York, ca. 1890, 8-day time and strike hall tall-case clock (strikes on nine tubes), Tiffany & Co., New York, heavily carved walnut case, $22,400

American, New York?, ca. 1900, 8-day time and strike hall tall-case clock (strikes on five tubes), unsigned, mahogany Gothic-style case, $2,800

American, Massachusetts, ca. 1895, 8-day time and strike hall tall-case clock (strikes on four tubes), John B. Varick Co., Manchester, mahogany architectural-style case, $2,645

	LOW	MID	HIGH
Hall Floor Clocks (ca. 1880–1910)	$2,500	$8,500	$30,000+

CATEGORY IV

ALL TYPES OF TALL-CASE CLOCKS PRODUCED
BETWEEN CA. 1900 AND CA. 1950

American, Pennsylvania, ca. 1905, 8-day time and strike tall-case clock, brass and steel moon dial, J. E. Caldwell & Co., Philadelphia, heavily carved mahogany case, swan's neck top, glazed door, $11,000

American, New York, ca. 1915, 8-day time and strike Arts and Crafts tall-case clock, signed J. G. Stickley, $50,000. Credit: Prices4Antiques.com.

American, ca. 1905, 8-day time and strike Arts and Crafts tall-case clock, signed Charles Rolhfs, $63,750. Credit: Prices4Antiques.com.

American, ca. 1890–1900, late Victorian tall-case clock with bronze and porcelain mounts, unsigned, $1,792. Credit: Prices4antiques.com.

American, Connecticut, ca. 1910, 8-day time and strike tall-case clock, brass and steel moon dial, Waterbury Clock Co., Hall Clock No. 58, mahogany Federal style case, swan's neck top, glazed door, $1,980

American, Pennsylvania?, ca. 1885, 8-day time and strike tall-case clock, painted dial, unsigned, mahogany case, rounded top, glazed door, $2,090

American, unknown, ca. 1915, 8-day spring-driven tall-case clock, painted dial, unsigned, oak Mission-style case, fret-decorated top, glazed door, $316

American, Illinois, ca. 1910, 8-day spring-driven tall-case clock, brass and steel moon dial, Toby Clock Co., Chicago, inlaid mahogany case, swan's neck top, glazed door, $11,200

American, New York, ca. 1924, 8-day spring-driven tall-case clock, striking tuned rods, silvered metal dial, Ansonia Clock Co., New York, Standing No. 9, mahogany Art Deco–style case, glazed door, $770

American, Massachusetts, ca. 1925, electric time-only tall-case clock, silvered metal dial, Standard Electric Time Co., Springfield, oak case, glazed door, $412

American, unknown, ca. 1925, 8-day time and strike tall-case clock, brass numerals on wood dial, unsigned, oak Arts and·Crafts–style case, glazed door, $1,100

American, unknown, ca. 1925, 8-day time and strike tall-case clock, brass dial, unsigned, oak Arts and Crafts–style case, glazed door, $1,705

American, unknown, ca. 1925–30, 8-day spring-driven tall-case clock, brass dial, unsigned, oak Arts and Crafts–style case, $550

American, unknown, ca. 1925–30, 8-day spring-driven tall-case clock, brass numerals on wood dial, unsigned, oak Arts and Crafts–style case, slag glass glazed door, $275

American, unknown, ca. 1925–30, 8-day time and strike tall-case clock, brass numerals on wood dial, unsigned, oak Arts and Crafts–style open case, $522

American, unknown, ca. 1925–35, electric tall-case clock, brass numerals on wood dial, unsigned, oak Arts and Crafts–style open case, $345

American, unknown, ca. 1925, 8-day spring-driven tall-case clock, brass numerals on wood dial, unsigned, oak Arts and Crafts–style case, glazed door, $672

American, unknown, ca. 1920, 8-day time and strike tall-case clock, brass and painted dial, unsigned, oak Arts and Crafts–style case, glazed door, $1,120

	LOW	MID	HIGH
Late-Nineteenth and Early-Twentieth-Century Tall-Case Clocks (ca. 1910–1950)	$200–$700	$2,500	$5,500+

CATEGORY V

MID- AND LATE-TWENTIETH-CENTURY TALL-CASE CLOCKS

American, Ohio, ca. 1940–50, electric clock and radio tall-case clock, painted dial, Crosley Radio Co., Cincinnati, Playtime Model 1-M, walnut case with birch bird's-eye inlay, double finial crest top, $460

American, Ohio, ca. 1940–50, electric clock and radio tall-case clock, painted dial, Crosley Radio Co., Cincinnati, Model 59 Tower Radio, walnut Art Deco case, Sangamo electric clock, $517

American, unknown, ca. 1950–60, 8-day time and strike tall-case clock, brass moon dial, unsigned, mahogany Chippendale-style case, swan's neck top, $977

American, unknown, ca. 1950–60, 8-day time and strike tall-case clock, brass dial, unsigned, mahogany Chippendale-style case, swan's neck top, glazed door, $935

American, ca. 1960–1970, 8-day time and strike tall-case clock, unsigned, $977. Credit: Prices4antiques.com.

American, New York, ca. 1940–50, electric clock tall-case clock, painted metal dial, General Electric Co., Telechron, mahogany case, pediment top (broken), $28

American, Pennsylvania, ca. 1930–50, 8-day time and strike tall-case clock, (eight tubular chimes), brass and steel moon dial, J. E. Caldwell, Philadelphia, mahogany case, scrolled top, glazed door, $6,600

American, Massachusetts, ca. 1950–60, 8-day time and strike tall-case clock, (five tubular chimes), brass and steel moon dial, Howard Miller Clock Co., Model 610166, burl walnut case, bombe base, shaped top, $800

American, California, ca. 1990–2000 8-day time and strike tall-case clock, enameled numerals on brass dial, Gazo Family Clock Co., San Diego, mahogany Austrian Baroque–style case, open trunk, $1,725

	LOW	MID	HIGH
Mid- and Late-Twentieth-Century Tall-Case Clocks (ca. 1950–present)	$500	$1,000	$2,500+

British Tall-Case Clocks

British tall-case clocks sell for less than comparable American tall-case clocks in U.S. markets. They sell for higher prices in their home market. This is generally true of any nation's clocks.

Most English tall-case clocks, particularly those which have reached our shores, are marriages of dials, movements, and cases that began life as parts of different clocks. Today this is usually acceptable to the collector.

English 30-hour tall-case clocks sell for considerably less than English 8-day tall-case clocks. This provides an attractive collecting opportunity.

Later large English hall clocks striking tubular chimes retail in America for less than comparable American hall clocks and provide another collecting opportunity.

BRITISH EIGHTEENTH- AND NINETEENTH-CENTURY TALL-CASE CLOCKS

30-hour Tall-Case Clocks

English, Provincial, ca. 1760–80, 30-hour time, strike, calendar, brass weight-driven movement tall-case clock, brass dial with applied cast spandrels, Red Lynch, elmwood case with lenticle in door, flat top, $1,380

English, Birmingham, ca. 1720–55, 30-hour time, seconds, calendar, and strike brass movement, silvered brass dial, signed Edward Gratrex, oak case, flat top, $1,600.

English, Birmingham, ca. 1720–55, 30-hour time, seconds, calendar, and strike brass movement, signed Edward Gratrex, $1,600.

English, Marketharbour, ca. 1820–30, 30-hour time, calendar, and strike brass movement, painted white dial, signed Thomas Bates, oak case, flat top, $1,500.

English, Darlington, ca. 1820–25, 30-hour time, calendar, and strike brass movement, painted white dial, signed Samuel Thompson, $1,600.

English, Birmingham, ca. 1720–55, 30-hour time, strike, seconds, calendar, brass weight-driven movement tall-case clock, silvered brass dial with applied cast spandrels, Edward Gratrex, oak case, solid door, flat top, $1,600

English, Provincial, ca. 1810–30, 30-hour time, strike, calendar, brass weight-driven movement tall-case clock, painted dial with painted spandrels, T. Leeming, mahogany and oak case, swan's neck top, $1,610

English, Pontefract, ca. 1800, 30-hour time, calendar, and strike, brass weight-driven movement tall-case clock, brass moon dial with applied cast spandrels and painted moon disk, Benjamin Booth, oak and mahogany case, swan's neck top, $1,485

English, Macclesfield, ca. 1780, 30-hour time and strike, brass weight-driven movement tall-case clock, brass dial with applied cast spandrels, Ashton, oak case, flat top, $920

	LOW	MID	HIGH
30-hour Time and Strike Clocks with Brass and Painted White Dials (ca. 1730–1850)	$800	$2,000	$3,500

8-day Tall-Case Clocks

English, Provincial, ca. 1800–20, 8-day brass time and strike, weight-driven movement tall-case clock, painted arched dial with painted spandrels, unsigned, walnut case, Gothic style door, swan's neck top, $1,410

English, Provincial, ca. 1790–1820, 8-day brass time and strike, weight-driven movement tall-case clock, painted arched dial with painted spandrels, unsigned, mahogany and walnut case, arched door, domed top, $2,540

English, Provincial, ca. 1820–40, 8-day brass time and strike, weight-driven movement tall-case clock, painted arched dial with painted spandrels, unsigned, mahogany and pine case, swan's neck top, $1,540

English, Provincial, ca. 1790–1820, 8-day brass time, seconds, calendar, and strike, weight-driven movement tall-case clock, painted arched moon dial with painted spandrels, unsigned mahogany case, domed top with open fretwork and finials, $7,920

English, ca. 1760, 8-day brass time and strike weight-driven movement. With minor variations, this was the movement used in most British tall-case clocks throughout the eighteenth century and well into the nineteenth century. Credit: Wagner Collection.

English, ca. 1770, brass square dial with later addition of top arch with a rocking ship. This square brass dial was found on most British tall-case clocks from the seventeenth century until the last quarter of the eighteenth century. Credit: Wagner Collection.

English, ca. 1790, painted or white dial. The painted dial was found on most English tall-case clocks from the last quarter of the eighteenth century to the final days of the nineteenth century. Credit: Alessi Collection.

English, Provincial, ca. 1820–40, 8-day brass time and strike, weight-driven movement tall-case clock, painted arched dial with painted spandrels, unsigned, mahogany case, shortened base, flat top with a pierced foliate crest, $1,150

English, Provincial, ca. 1780–1810, 8-day brass time, seconds, calendar, and strike, weight-driven movement tall-case clock, painted arched moon dial with painted spandrels, unsigned, mahogany and pine case, Gothic style door, swan's neck top, $2,530

English, Provincial, ca. 1835–45, 8-day brass time, seconds, calendar, and strike, weight-driven movement tall-case clock, painted arched moon dial with painted spandrels, unsigned, mahogany case, shortened base, swan's neck top, $1,980

English, Chester, ca. 1762–81, 8-day brass time, seconds, calendar, and strike, weight-driven movement tall-case clock, brass arched dial with applied spandrels, Robert Cawley, mahogany case, arched door, domed top with three finials, $7,593

English, Lydiat, ca. 1735–45, 8-day brass time, seconds, strike, weight-driven movement tall-case clock, brass arched dial with applied spandrels, Taylor, walnut case, arched door, domed top with three finials, $3,920

English, Rochdale, ca. 1755–65, 8-day brass time, seconds, calendar, and strike, weight-driven movement tall-case clock, brass square dial with applied spandrels, Samuel Buttonworth, heavily carved ebonized oak case, bell top, $1,792

English, Dumfries, ca. 1740–80, 8-day brass time and strike, weight-driven movement tall-case clock, brass arched dial with applied spandrels, Grindal Black, japanned case, arched door, hollowed top with three finials, $4,830

English, London, ca. 1740–50, 8-day brass time, seconds, calendar, and strike, weight-driven movement tall-case clock, brass arched dial with applied spandrels, Gershom Butcher, black japanned case with chinoiserie decoration, arched door, bell top with two finials, $3,910

English, Maidstone, ca. 1760–80, 8-day brass time, seconds, calendar, and strike, weight-driven movement tall-case clock, brass arched dial with applied spandrels, Jonathan Cutbush, mahogany inlaid case, arched door, domed top with three finials, $5,750

English, London, ca. 1670–80, 8-day brass time, seconds, calendar, and strike, weight-driven movement tall-case clock, brass square dial with applied spandrels, signed William Cattell, marquetry floral design inlaid case, lenticle door, flat top, $13,200

English, Falkirk, ca. 1750–60, 8-day brass time, seconds, calendar, and strike weight-driven movement tall-case clock, brass arched dial with applied spandrels, John Galbraith, walnut case, arched door, swan's neck top with one finial, $10,080

	LOW	MID	HIGH
English 8-day Clocks with Brass and Painted White Dials (ca. 1730–1870)	$1,500–$2,000	$5,500	$10,000–$12,000

BRITISH TALL-CASE CLOCKS PRODUCED BETWEEN CA. 1880 AND CA. 1910

English, Provincial, ca. 1860–70, 8-day brass time-only weight-driven floor regulator, painted dial, unsigned, walnut Gothic-style case, Gothic arch glazed door, Gothic top with three wooden finials, $9,200

English, Bristol, ca. 1751–93, 8-day time and strike tall-case clock, signed William Priest, $7,000–$9,000. Credit: Wagner Collection.

English, Manchester, ca. 1790, 8-day time and strike tall-case clock, signed Joseph Scholfield, $9,000–$10,000. Credit: Alessi Collection.

English, ca. 1815–25, 8-day time and strike tall-case clock, painted dial, unsigned, $1,410. Credit: Prices4Antiques.com.

English, ca. 1835–50, 8-day time and strike tall-case clock, painted dial, unsigned, $1,980. Credit: R. O. Schmitt Fine Arts.

English, ca. 1860–70, 8-day time-only regulator floor clock, unsigned, $9,200. Credit: Prices4Antiques.com.

English, ca. 1895–1905, 8-day time and strike weight-driven tall-case clock, unsigned, $1,500. Credit: Prices4Antiques.com.

English, Exeter & Eastbourne, ca. 1885–95, 8-day fusee (three train) time and strike (choice of bells or gongs) weight-driven bracket clock mounted on a seventy-inch-high base, W. Bruford & Son, ebonized carved oak case and base, $3,300

English, unknown, ca. 1895–1905, 8-day brass time and strike weight-driven tall-case clock, brass dial, unsigned, walnut case with a glazed trunk door, domed top, $1,500

	LOW	MID	HIGH
British Tall-Case Clocks (ca. 1880–1910)	$1,500	$5,500	$9,000

TWENTIETH-CENTURY BRITISH TALL-CASE CLOCKS PRODUCED CA. 1920–PRESENT

English, London, ca. 1925–35, 8-day brass time and strike spring-driven tall-case clock (55" high), metal and wood square dial, Enfield Clock Co., oak Art Deco–style case, $504

English, Leicester, ca. 1943–53, electric time-only master clock, painted dial, Gent & Co., Ltd., oak case, glazed door, flat top, $715

English, ca. 1930, 8-day time and strike tall-case clock, Art Deco style, signed Enfield Clock Co., $504. Credit: R. O. Schmitt Fine Arts.

English, ca. 1948, electric master time-only clock, signed Gent and Co., $715. Credit: R. O. Schmitt Fine Arts.

	LOW	MID	HIGH
Twentieth-Century Tall-Case Clocks (ca. 1920–present)	$500	$900	$1,500

French Tall-Case Clocks

Virtually all French tall-case clocks are Morbier/Comtoise wall clocks that have been cased to produce floor clocks. These well-built clocks can still be obtained at reasonable prices, although prices are steadily rising.

French, Provincial, ca. 1820–50, 8-day time and strike (with repeat) weight-driven Morbier clock, porcelain dial with stamped brass trim, unsigned, oak Normandy-style case, domed top, lenticle door, $2,185

French, Provincial, ca. 1825–35, 8-day brass time and strike weight-driven tall-case clock showing English influence, porcelain and brass dial with cast brass trim, Tho. Mayer, faux grain painted case, domed top, glazed door, $1,375

French, Provincial, ca. 1880–90, 8-day time and strike Morbier clock mounted on a wall bracket. Most Morbier clocks were never cased. Names found on dials are not makers, but rather the owner's or retailer's. The movements are housed in iron boxes. $600.

French, Morbier, closeup showing the porcelain dial with the name Guerin. The dial is surrounded by a stamped brass trim with painted highlights.

French, Morbier, side view showing the closed door of the sheet iron case that encloses the movement, the wall bracket, and the tops of the heavy cast-iron weights.

French, ca. 1830, 8-day time and strike tall-case clock, $1,375. Credit: R. O. Schmitt Fine Arts.

French, ca. 1880–90, 8-day time and strike Morbier clock, $1,375. Credit: Prices4Antiques.com.

French, ca. 1830, 8-day time and strike Morbier clock, cased, $1,700. Credit: Marcus Collection.

French, Provincial, ca. 1885–95, 8-day time-only (with center seconds hand) weight-driven Morbier clock, porcelain dial, unsigned, mahogany case, flat top, full glazed door, $3,080

French, Provincial, ca. 1750–1820, 8-day time and strike (on 5 gongs with repeat) weight-driven Morbier clock, porcelain dial with stamped brass surround, unsigned, walnut Normandy-style case, domed top, lenticle door, $2,300

French, Provincial, ca. 1820–50, 8-day time and strike (with repeat) weight-driven Morbier clock, porcelain dial with stamped brass surround, unsigned, oak Normandy-style case, domed top, lenticle door, $1,500

French, Provincial, dated 1881, 8-day time and strike (with repeat) weight-driven Morbier clock, porcelain dial with stamped brass surround and matching pendulum, Saunier, swelled-waist case, flat top, glazed door, $1,540

	LOW	MID	HIGH
Morbier Time and Strike Clocks with Repeat (ca. 1790–1930)	$850–$900	$1,500–$2,500	$3,000–$4,000

German, Austrian, and Dutch Tall-Case Clocks

German tall-case clocks of the late nineteenth and the twentieth century have traditionally realized the lowest retail prices in the American tall-case clock market. This is changing, but opportunities still exist to purchase some fine clocks at reasonable prices.

Austrian tall-case clocks have always commanded higher prices than their German counterparts, not only because of their scarcity, but also because of their reputation for higher quality (which is not always true).

Dutch tall-case clocks combine aspects of the English school (seen in the dials) and the German school (seen in the cases). Dutch tall-case clocks consistently bring higher prices than their German and Austrian counterparts.

German, Furtwangen, ca. 1850–60, 8-day weight-driven movement and spring-driven organ clock (not in working order), painted and enameled dial, Joseph Schmacher, hardwood case, solid door, architectural top, $4,400

German, Black Forest, ca. 1880–90, 8-day time and strike tall-case clock with a Berman music box and 13 discs, enamel and brass dial, clock un-

German, ca. 1850–60, 8-day time-only tall-case clock with spring-driven organ, unsigned, $4,400. Credit: R. O. Schmitt Fine Arts.

German, ca. 1897, 8-day time and strike open-well tall-case clock, unsigned, $3,999. Credit: NAWCC Eastern States Regional.

German, ca. 1920, 8-day time and strike hall clock, unsigned, $990. Credit: R. O. Schmitt Fine Arts.

German, ca. 1880–90, 8-day time and strike tall-case clock with music box, unsigned, $12,320. Credit: Prices4Antiques.com.

signed, music box signed Berman, walnut ornate Renaissance Revival–style case, $12,320

German, Black Forest, ca. 1892–1902, 8-day brass time and strike weight-driven tall-case clock, enameled dial, Gustav Becker, walnut Old German–style case, full glazed door, $2,016

German, Black Forest, a. 1895–1905, 8-day brass time and strike weight-driven tall-case clock, brass and silver dial, Lenzkirch, oak brass-ornamented Old German–style case, open well, $5,500

German, unknown, ca. 1905–15, 8-day brass time and strike weight-driven tall-case clock, painted metal moon dial, Peerless, mahogany Chippendale-style case, glazed trunk door, swan's neck top, $1,650

German, Black Forest, ca. 1915–25, 8-day brass time and strike (eight tuned rods) weight-driven hall clock, embossed brass dial, unsigned, oak Gothic–style case, glazed trunk door, round top, $990

German, Black Forest, ca. 1915–1925, 8-day brass time and strike weight-driven tall-case clock, metal dial, Lenzkirch, walnut case, glazed trunk door, flat top, $440

German, Black Forest, ca. 1915–25, 8-day brass time and strike (eight tuned rods) weight-driven tall-case clock, metal dial, Lenzkirch, oak fumed case, glazed trunk door, flat top, $1,650

Austrian, ca. 1920, 8-day time and strike tall-case clock, unsigned, $1,680. Credit: R. O. Schmitt Fine Art.

	LOW	MID	HIGH
German Tall-Case Clocks (ca. 1880–1920)	$800–$900	$1,500–$42,000	$5,000+

Austrian, Vienna, ca. 1915–25, 8-day brass time and strike (Grand Sonnerie) weight-driven tall-case clock, metal dial, unsigned, veneered Jugenstil (Austrian and German Art Deco)-style case, fully glazed door, $1,680

	LOW	MID	HIGH
Austrian Tall-Case Clocks (ca. 1875–1910)	$1,500–$2,000	$5,000	$8,000–$9,000+

Dutch, Amsterdam, ca. 1760–90, 8-day brass time, seconds, calendar, and strike tall-case clock, brass arched moon dial with applied spandrels, T. Bern Klingenberg, heavily inlaid case, bombe base, trunk door with lenticle, $12,100

Dutch, Amsterdam, ca. 1760–90, 8-day brass time, seconds, calendar, and strike tall-case clock, brass arched moon painted dial with applied spandrels, H. Huysl, burlwood case, bombe base, trunk door with lenticle, $8,050

Dutch, ca. 1750–80, 8-day time and strike tall-case clock, unsigned $12,100. Credit: Prices4Antiques.com.

Dutch, ca. 1790–1820, 8-day time and strike tall-case clock, unsigned $2,703. Credit: Prices4Antiques.com.

Dutch, maker unknown, ca. 1790–1820, 8-day brass time and strike tall-case clock, painted arched wooden dial, unsigned, japanned case with Chinese motifs, shaped trunk door with lenticle, domed top, $2,703

	LOW	MID	HIGH
Dutch Tall-Case Clocks (ca. 1720–1840)	$2,500–$3,000	$6,000–$8,000	$9,000–$15,000+

CHAPTER 4

Wall Clocks

Wall clocks are clocks whose cases are designed to hang on a wall, as opposed to mantel clocks, which sit on a table or mantel, or tall-case clocks, which sit on the floor. Wall clocks first appeared in the late medieval period.

In the days of weight-driven movements, placing the clock on the wall allowed the weight to travel a longer distance and the clock to run longer before it had to be rewound. With the advent of the spring-driven movement, wall clocks freed up surface space and became part of a wall's decor.

Wall clocks are divided by function, style, and case design. I have further divided them by country.

Among American clocks the following common types can be identified:

Advertising clocks
Anglo-American clocks
Arts and Crafts clocks
Banjo clocks
Calendar clocks
Gallery and octagon clocks
Ionic or figure eight clocks
Lyre clocks
Marble dial clocks
Mirror clocks
Regulator clocks
Round and octagon drop clocks
Ship or marine clocks

Two regulator wall clocks, last quarter of the nineteenth century. Credit: NAWCC TIMEXPO 2002.

English wall clock forms include:

> Anglo-American clocks
> Gallery clocks
> Post office clocks

Among Dutch clocks we can identify:

> Staartklok
> Stoelklok

French wall clocks include:

> Cartel clocks (bronze and wood)
> Gallery clocks
> Morbier clocks
> Picture frame clocks
> Regulator clocks
> Time and barometer clocks

Austrian, German, and Swiss wall clocks can be found as:

> Alt Deutsch (Old German) clocks
> Balcony clocks

Black Forest clocks
Box clocks
Cuckoo clocks
Dial clocks
Open ell clocks
Regulator clocks

American Wall Clocks

American wall clocks appeared toward the last part of the eighteenth century with the Willard banjo clock. They were produced in greatest numbers during the nineteenth century. For collectors this category includes some of the rarest and some of the most common American clocks.

ADVERTISING CLOCKS in their simplest form are clocks that have had advertising added to their case or glass and in their most complex form are clocks whose mechanism controls the display of advertising copy (see Sidney advertising clock on p. 70). They were most common during the fifty years between 1875 and 1925.

American, ca. 1870, Atkins Clock Co., *J. P. Steinmann Jeweler,* 25", 8-day
time-only movement, very good condition, $800

American, ca. 1897, 8-day time-only movement, good condition, signed Baird Clock Co., $2,000. Credit: NAWCC Eastern States Regional.

American, ca. 1913, *J. W. Owsley Jeweler,* 37", 8-day time-only movement, good condition, signed Gilbert Clock Co., $455. Credit: R. O. Schmitt Fine Arts.

American, ca. 1888, signed Sidney Advertising Clock Co., 64", 8-day time-only movement, clock in restored condition, $5,000. Credit: NAWCC Eastern States Regional.

American, ca. 1890, Baird Clock Co., *Vanner & Prest's Molliscorium,* 30.5", 8-day time-only movement, very good condition, $1,350

American, ca. 1890, Baird Clock Co., *Clapperton's Six Cord Spool,* 30.5", 8-day time-only movement, very good condition, $1,050

American, ca. 1893, Baird Clock Co., *Mayo's Tobacco,* 30.5", 8-day time-only movement, very good condition, $2,450

American, ca. 1895, Baird Clock Co., *Coca Cola,* 30.5", 8-day time-only movement, good condition, scarce early Coca-Cola advertising, $4,750

American, ca. 1897, Baird Clock Co., *Use Sapolio—It Saves Time.* 29.75", 8-day time-only movement, good condition (illustrated), $2,100

American, ca. 1910, Baird Clock Co., *Vanner & Prest's Molliscorium,* 30.5", 8-day time-only movement, good condition, $1,100

American, ca. 1913, Gilbert Clock Co., *J. W. Owsley Jeweler,* 37", 8-day time-only movement, good condition (illustrated), $455

American, ca. 1913, Gilbert Clock Co., "Washington" model case, *Calumet Baking Powder,* 38", 8-day time-only movement, very good condition, $250

American, ca. 1920, Gilbert Clock Co., *Old Mr. Boston,* 22", 8-day time-only movement, good condition, $175

American, ca. 1911, Ingraham Clock Co., "Western Union" model case, *Freihofer's Quality Cakes,* 38", 8-day time-only movement, good condition and scarce advertiser, $1,000

American, ca. 1925, Ingraham Clock Co., "Landau" model case, *Arnold & Co., Jewelers, Anne Arbor,* 38", 8-day time-only movement, very good condition, $400

American, ca. 1940, International Time Recording Co., *Anaconda—From Mine to Consumer,* 34", 8-day time-only movement, good condition, $230

American, ca. 1910, Sessions Clock Co., "Regulator E" model case, *D. M. Stultz, Jeweler, Culpeper, VA,* 38.5", 8-day time-only movement, very good condition, $500

American, ca. 1910, Sessions Clock Co., "Regulator H" model case, *Good-Year Wing Foot Heels,* 36", 8-day time-only movement, very good condition, $500

American, ca. 1915, Sessions Clock Co., "Regulator #4" model case, *Meyers Jeweler, Watches,* 38.5", 8-day time-only movement, good condition, $400

American, ca. 1890, Seth Thomas Clock Co., "Regulator #17" model case, *The New York, New Haven RR,* 68", 8-day time and seconds regulator movement, very good condition, excellent clock with very scarce original porcelain railroad plaque, $5,000

American, ca. 1888, Sidney Advertising Clock Co., 64", 8-day time-only movement, good clock in restored condition (illustrated), $5,000

American, ca. 1895, Sydney Advertising Clock Co., *Omaha Jewelers,* 70", 8-day time-only movement, very good condition, $4,100

American, ca. 1920, unknown maker, *None Such Mincemeat,* 9.5", 8-day time-only movement, good condition, $525

American, ca. 1920, unknown maker, *Gold Prize Coffee,* 32", 8-day time-only movement, good condition, $500

American, ca. 1875, Welch Clock Co., "Regulator #2" model case, *Wayne State Bank,* 53", 8-day time and seconds regulator movement, good condition, $2,200

American, ca. 1900, Welch Clock Co., *Colby Wringer Company,* 22", 8-day time and strike movement, good condition, $400

American, ca. 1880, Yale Clock Co., *Reed's Gilt Edge Tonic Cures,* 17.5", 8-day time-only movement, good condition with "medical" advertiser, $820

	LOW	MID	HIGH
Advertising Wall Clocks, 8-Day Clocks (ca. 1870–1920)	$200–$500	$1,000–$2,500	$3,000–$6,000

ANGLO-AMERICAN CLOCKS were American movements shipped to England and cased in English-made cases. This was often done to increase profits, as Connecticut mass-produced movements were less expensive than domestic English movements.

American/English, ca. 1870, Connecticut movement cased in an English inlaid mahogany school clock, 28", 8-day time and strike movement, $500

American/English, ca. 1870, Connecticut movement cased in an English round top drop school clock, 27", 8-day time and strike movement, $180

American/English, ca. 1870, Connecticut movement cased in an English round top drop school clock, 29", 8-day time and strike movement, $160

American/English, ca. 1870, Connecticut movement cased in an English mahogany rolling pin clock, 37", 8-day time and strike movement, $350

American/English, ca. 1875, Connecticut movement cased in an English inlaid rosewood school clock, 28", 8-day time and strike movement, $300

American/English, ca. 1875, Connecticut movement cased in an English inlaid walnut school clock, 29", 8-day time and strike movement, $275

American/English, ca. 1880, Connecticut movement cased in an English papier-mâché clock with mother-of-pearl inlay, 28", 8-day time and strike movement, $410

American/English, ca. 1870, 8-day time and strike movement cased in an English walnut wall regulator clock, signed Welch Manufacturing Co., $500. Credit: R. O. Schmitt Fine Arts.

American/English, ca. 1870, 8-day time and strike movement cased in a mirrored English mahogany wall clock, 33", signed Jerome and Co., $360. Credit: R. O. Schmitt Fine Arts.

American/English, ca. 1880, 8-day time and strike Connecticut movement cased in an English inlaid mahogany octagon drop clock, 28.5", signed Jerome and Co., $525. Credit: R. O. Schmitt Fine Arts.

American/English, ca. 1880, Connecticut movement cased in an English inlaid mahogany octagon drop clock, 28.5", 8-day time and strike movement (illustrated), $525

American/English, ca. 1880, Ingraham Clock Co., movement in an English mahogany case, 32", 8-day time and strike movement, $425

American/English, ca. 1860, Jerome and Co., movement cased in an English walnut round top drop school clock, 22.5", 8-day time and strike movement, $350

American/English, ca. 1870, Jerome and Co., movement cased in a mirrored English mahogany wall clock, 33", 8-day time and strike movement (illustrated), $360

American/English, ca. 1880, Seth Thomas Clock Co., movement cased in an English round top drop school clock, 24", 8-day time and strike movement, $200

American/English, ca. 1870, Welch Manufacturing Co., movement cased in an English walnut wall regulator, 31", 8-day time and strike movement (illustrated), $500

American/English, ca. 1870, Welch Manufacturing Co., movement cased in an English burl walnut wall clock, 31", 8-day time and strike movement, $900

	LOW	MID	HIGH
Anglo-American Wall Clocks, 8-Day Clocks (ca. 1870–1890)	$150–$400	$500–$700	$800–$1,000

ARTS AND CRAFTS CLOCKS (also called Mission style) appeared in America before World War I and disappeared by the mid-1930s. This design followed the parallel development of the Mission or Arts and Crafts style of furniture design in America. Many of these clocks are very reasonably priced for their quality. However, the growing popularity of Arts and Crafts furniture will sooner than later move the price of these clocks higher and higher.

American, ca. 1920, Sessions Clock Co., "San Jose" model, 25", 8-day time and strike, good original condition (illustrated), $120

American, ca. 1920, Sessions Clock Co., cut-out motif with brass numerals, 15", 8-day time and strike, good original condition (illustrated), $259

American, ca. 1920, Sessions Clock Co., "San Jose" model, 25", 8-day time and strike, good original condition, $69

American, ca. 1925, Sessions Clock Co., "San Jose" model, 25", 8-day time and strike, good original condition, $94

American, ca. 1915, unknown, circular dial with pewter numerals, pendulum wrong, 19", 8-day time only, good original condition, $633

American, ca. 1930, unknown, square oak with brass chapter ring, 12", 8-day time only, excellent condition, $392

American, ca. 1920, 8-day time and strike movement, San Jose model, 25", signed Sessions Clock Co., $120. Credit: R. O. Schmitt Fine Arts.

American, ca. 1910, 8-day time-only movement, pendulum is incorrect, 19", unsigned, $120. Credit: Prices4Antiques.com.

American, ca. 1920, cut-out motif with brass numerals, good original condition, 8-day time and strike, 15", signed Sessions Clock Co., $259.

	LOW	MID	HIGH
Arts and Crafts–Style Clocks (ca. 1910–30)	$50–$150	$200–$350	$400–$600

BANJO CLOCKS were the first truly American-designed clocks. Simon Willard of Massachusetts created this clock sometime between 1800 and 1802. The original versions were time-only weight-driven clocks. Later versions would be spring-driven and include a strike. The name comes from their obvious resemblance to a banjo. Collectors should be aware that original Willard banjo clocks command high prices and that forgeries abound. It has become common to encounter banjo clocks of lesser makers which have had their dials altered with counterfeit Willard signatures/names.

American, ca. 1924, Ansonia Clock Co., 18.5", 8-day time-only weight-driven movement, $2,300

American, ca. 1840, Bingham, B. D., 49", 8-day time-only weight-driven movement, $1,850

American, ca. 1907, Chelsea Clock Co., 33", 8-day time-only weight-driven movement, $1,500

American, ca. 1930, Chelsea Clock Co., "Willard" model case, 32", 8-day time-only weight-driven movement, $1,025

American, ca. 1938, Chelsea Clock Co., 41", 8-day time-only weight-driven movement, $700

American, ca. 1938, Chelsea Clock Co., "Willard" model case, 34", 8-day time and strike movement, $850

American, Massachusetts, ca. 1840, 8-day time-only weight-driven movement, 33", unsigned, $700. Credit: R. O. Schmitt Fine Arts.

Typical 8-day weight-driven banjo movement. Credit: R. O. Schmitt Fine Arts.

American, ca. 1940, Chelsea Clock Co., "Willard" model case, 42", 8-day time and strike movement, $2,600

American, ca. 1970, Chelsea Clock Co., 40", 8-day time and strike movement, $800

American, ca. 1995, Cline, Wayne, diamond head case, 20.5", 8-day time and strike movement, $1,000

American, ca. 1840, Curtis, Lemuel, 29.5", 8-day time-only weight-driven movement, $5,000

American, ca. 1929, Gilbert Clock Co., 29.5", 8-day time and strike spring-driven movement, $275

American, ca. 1840, Hatch, George, 29", 8-day time-only weight-driven movement, $1,050

American, ca. 1920, Herschede Clock Co., 42", 8-day time-only weight-driven movement, $2,250

American, ca. 1840, Howard Clock Co., 49", 8-day time-only weight-driven movement, $1,850

American, ca. 1850, Howard Clock Co., #2 Banjo (size and model), 44", 8-day time-only weight-driven movement (illustrated), $7,250

American, ca. 1857, Howard Clock Co., #3 Banjo (size and model), 38", 8-day time-only weight-driven movement, $6,200

American, ca. 1850, 8-day time-only weight-driven movement, #2 Banjo, 44", signed Howard Clock Co., $7,250. Credit: R. O. Schmitt Fine Arts.

American, ca. 1929, 8-day time and strike (Westminster chimes) spring-driven movement, "Willard" model case, 42", signed New Haven Clock Co., $300. Credit: R. O. Schmitt Fine Arts.

American, ca. 1857, Howard Clock Co., #5 Banjo (size and model), 29", 8-day time-only weight-driven movement, $1,250

American, ca. 1880, Howard Clock Co., #5 Banjo (size and model), 29", 8-day time-only weight-driven movement, $2,100

American, ca. 1890, Howard Clock Co., #2 Banjo (size and model), 44", 8-day time-only weight-driven movement, $2,300

American, ca. 1900, Howard Clock Co., #5 Banjo (size and model), 29", 8-day time-only weight-driven movement, $2,800

American, ca. 1984, Howard Clock Co., 38", 8-day time-only weight-driven movement, $1,600

American, ca. 1850, Howard and Davis, #4 Banjo (size and model), 32", 8-day time-only weight-driven movement, $2,400

American, ca. 1850, Howard and Davis, #1 Banjo (size and model), 50", 8-day time-only weight-driven movement, $4,000

American, ca. 1850, Howard and Davis, #4 Banjo (size and model), 38", 8-day time-only weight-driven movement, $1,300

American, ca. 1850, Howard and Davis (a marriage of case and movement), 52", 8-day time-only weight-driven movement, $600

American, ca. 1855, Howard and Davis, #4 Banjo (size and model), 32", 8-day time-only weight-driven movement, $1,500

American, ca. 1855, Howard and Davis, 38", 8-day time-only weight-driven movement, $3,000

American, ca. 1915, Ingraham Clock Co., 18.5", 8-day time and strike spring-driven movement, $140

American, ca. 1915, Ingraham Clock Co., "Nyzanza" model, 39", 8-day time-only spring-driven movement, $225

American, ca. 1925, Ingraham Clock Co., "Nyzanza" model, 39", 8-day time-only spring-driven movement, $70

American, ca. 1978, Kilbourn, William A., 34", 8-day time-only weight-driven movement, $1,200

American, ca. 1907, Little and Eastman, 33", 8-day time-only weight-driven movement, $1,000

American, ca. 1827, Merrill, Jacob, 30.75", 8-day time-only weight-driven movement, $12,500

American, ca. 1923, New Haven Clock Co., 40", 8-day time and strike spring-driven movement, $110

American, ca. 1925, New Haven Clock Co., "Wilson" model, 40.5", 31-day time and strike spring-driven movement, $1,300

American, ca. 1925, New Haven Clock Co., "Whitney" model, 30", 8-day time and strike spring-driven movement, $250

American, ca. 1927, New Haven Clock Co., 39", 8-day time and strike spring-driven movement, $275

American, ca. 1928, New Haven Clock Co., 25.25", 8-day time-only spring-driven movement, $110

American, ca. 1928, New Haven Clock Co., "Winetka" model, 18", 8-day time and strike spring-driven movement, $410

American, ca. 1929, New Haven Clock Co., "Willard" model, 42", 8-day time and strike (Westminster chimes), spring-driven movement (illustrated), $300

American, ca. 1930, New Haven Clock Co., "Whitney" model, 30", 8-day time and strike spring-driven movement, $150

American, ca. 1830, Sawin, John, 30", 8-day time and alarm weight-driven movement, $3,400

American, ca. 1925, Sessions Clock Co., "Washington" model, 27", 8-day time and strike spring-driven movement, $100

American, ca. 1929, Sessions Clock Co., "Halifax" model, 27.5", 8-day time and strike spring-driven movement, $140

American, ca. 1929, Seth Thomas Clock Co., #2 model, 28", 8-day time and strike spring-driven movement, $90

American, ca. 1920, Seth Thomas Clock Co., "Dover" model, 19.75", 8-day time-only spring-driven movement, $170

American, ca. 1929, Seth Thomas Clock Co., "Ramsgate" model, 21", 8-day time and strike spring-driven movement, $225

American, ca. 1930, Seth Thomas Clock Co., "Delaware" model, 23", quartz movement installed, price is for the case alone, $75

American, ca. 1930, Seth Thomas Clock Co., 30", 8-day time-only spring-driven movement, $120

American, ca. 1966, Stennes, Elmer, 33.5", 8-day time-only weight-driven movement, $2,250

American, ca. 1972, Stennes, Elmer, 40", 8-day time-only weight-driven movement, $2,850

American, ca. 1840, Tifft, H., 29", 8-day time-only weight-driven movement, $900

American, Massachusetts, ca. 1825, maker unknown, 34", 8-day time-only weight-driven movement, $750

American, Massachusetts, ca. 1830, maker unknown, 49", 8-day time and seconds weight-driven movement, $6,000

American, Massachusetts, ca. 1830, maker unknown, 33", 8-day time-only weight-driven movement (illustrated), $700

American, Massachusetts, ca. 1835, maker unknown, a marriage of a movement and a case, 32.75", 8-day time-only weight-driven movement, $450

American, Massachusetts, ca. 1835, maker unknown, 40", 8-day time-only weight-driven movement, $1,500

American, Massachusetts, ca. 1840, maker unknown, 32", 8-day time-only weight-driven movement, $575

American, Massachusetts, ca. 1840, maker unknown, 37", 8-day time-only weight-driven movement, $500

American, Massachusetts, ca. 1850, maker unknown, 33", 8-day time-only weight-driven movement, $700

American, Massachusetts, ca. 1850, maker unknown, 34", 8-day time-only weight-driven movement, $1,025

American, Massachusetts, ca. 1850, maker unknown, 28", 8-day time-only weight-driven movement, $950

American, Massachusetts, ca. 1850, maker unknown, 29", 8-day time-only weight-driven movement, $525

American, Massachusetts, ca. 1855, maker unknown, a marriage of a movement and a case, 34", 8-day time-only weight-driven movement, $450.

American, Massachusetts, ca. 1855, maker unknown, a marriage of a movement and a case, 34", 8-day time-only weight-driven movement, $525.

American, Massachusetts, ca. 1855, maker unknown, 28.5", 8-day time-only weight-driven movement, $500

American, Massachusetts, ca. 1860, maker unknown, a marriage of a movement and a case, 42", 8-day time-only weight-driven movement, $475

American, Massachusetts, ca. 1870, maker unknown, a marriage of a movement and a case, 41", 8-day time-only weight-driven movement, $400

American, Massachusetts, ca. 1900, maker unknown, a marriage of a movement and a case, 35", 8-day time-only weight-driven movement, $450

American, 1920, Waltham Clock Co., 30", 8-day time-only weight-driven movement, $500

American, ca. 1925, Waltham Clock Co., "Willard" model, 40", 8-day time-only weight-driven movement, $1,325

American, ca. 1925, Waltham Clock Co., 41", 8-day time-only weight-driven movement, $2,200

American, ca. 1925, Waltham Clock Co., 21", 8-day time-only movement, $100

American, ca. 1930, Waltham Clock Co., 42", 8-day time-only weight-driven movement, $2,300

American, ca. 1930, Waltham Clock Co., 42", 8-day time-only weight-driven movement, $1,000

American, ca. 1930, Waltham Clock Co., 42", 8-day time-only weight-driven movement, $1,900

American, ca. 1910, Waterbury Clock Co., "Willard #3" model, 42.25", 8-day time-only weight-driven movement, $1,300

American, ca. 1912, Waterbury Clock Co., "Willard #5" model, 34", 8-day time-only weight-driven movement, $1,400

American, ca. 1950, Zeeland (Colonial) Clock Co., "Willard" model, 40", 8-day time and strike spring-driven movement, $350

	LOW	MID	HIGH
American Banjo Clocks, 8-Day Clocks (ca. 1800–1995)	$200–$800	$1,000–$3,000	$5,000–$8,000

CALENDAR CLOCKS are clocks that show the date and often the month and day of the week. The concept and mechanism can be found on clocks that date from as early as the sixteenth century. By the middle of the nineteenth century, clocks with sophisticated and inventive calendar mechanisms had become extremely popular in America, and virtually every major maker produced them. Some of the most interesting were produced by the Ithaca Calendar Clock Co. Both wall and mantel calendar clocks were produced. Wall calendar clocks are shown here. Shelf versions are listed under Mantel Clocks.

American, ca. 1900, Ansonia Clock Co., "Drop octagon Extra Cal.," 24", 8-day time, strike, and date, fair condition, refinished oak case (illustrated), $308

American, ca. 1900, E. Ingraham and Co., "Dew Drop" model, 24", 8-day time and date, good condition with new dial and no label, oak case (illustrated), $429

American, ca. 1907, E. Ingraham and Co., Western Union, 36", 8-day time and date, very good original condition, $550

American, ca. 1920, E. Ingraham and Co., "Northwestern" model, 39", 8-day time and date, very good condition, oak case (illustrated), $412

American, ca. 1866, Ithaca Calendar Clock Co., figure eight model, 21", 8-day time and date, very good original finish, iron case (illustrated), $3,110

American, ca. 1920, 8-day time and date, 39", signed Ingraham Clock Co., $412. Credit: R. O. Schmitt Fine Arts.

American, ca. 1910, 8-day time and date, 39", signed Sessions Clock Co., $242. Credit: Prices4Antiques.com.

American, ca. 1910, 8-day time and date, 38.5", signed Sessions Clock Co., $504. Credit: R. O. Schmitt Fine Arts.

American, ca. 1900, 8-day time and date, 38", signed Gilbert Clock Co., $632. Credit: R. O. Schmitt Fine Arts.

American, ca. 1875, Ithaca Calendar Clock Co., No. 6 Hanging Library, 28", 8-day time, strike, and date, very good condition, refinished walnut case, $750

American, ca. 1875, Ithaca Calendar Clock Co., No. 1 Regulator, 49", 8-day time and date, very good refinished walnut case, $5,000

American, ca. 1880, Ithaca Calendar Clock Co., double dial, 28", 8-day time and date, fair condition, refinished rosewood case, replaced dials (illustrated), $357

American, ca. 1878, Ithaca Clock Co., No. 2 Bank, 61", 8-day time and date, fair condition, restored walnut case, $3,750

American, ca. 1880, Ithaca Clock Co., No. 7 double dial, 26", 8-day time and date, good condition, refinished walnut case (illustrated), $1,155

American, ca. 1870, L. F. and W.W. Carter, round drop double dial wall calendar clock, 57", 8-day time and date, good original condition (illustrated), $3,360

American, ca. 1881, New Haven Clock Co., American Regulator, 8-day T. P. Calendar, 48", 8-day time and date, good condition, refinished oak case, $750

American, ca. 1890, New Haven Clock Co., octagon case, 11", 8-day time, strike, and date, fair condition with some veneer damage (illustrated), $235

American, ca. 1880, Gale
astronomical calendar clock, 30",
signed Welch Clock Co., $5,830.
Credit: R. O. Schmitt Fine Arts.

American, ca. 1900, 8-day time and date,
"Dew Drop" model, 23.5", signed Ingraham
Clock Co., $429. Credit: R. O. Schmitt Fine
Arts.

American, ca. 1890, lever movement, 11",
signed New Haven Clock Co., $235. Credit:
R. O. Schmitt Fine Arts.

American, ca. 1900, 8-day time,
strike, and date, 24", signed Ansonia
Clock Co., $308. Credit: R. O.
Schmitt Fine Arts.

American, ca. 1900, 8-day time and date, 27.5", signed Gilbert Clock Co., $252. Credit: R. O. Schmitt Fine Arts.

American, ca. 1910, 8-day time and date, 33", signed Sessions Clock Co., $420. Credit: Prices4Antiques.com.

American, ca. 1900, 8-day time, strike, and date, 22.5", signed Waterbury Clock Co., $178. Credit: Prices4Antiques.com.

American, ca. 1890, 8-day time, strike, and date, 24", signed Welch Clock Co., $247. Credit: Prices4Antiques.com.

American, ca. 1910, Sessions Clock Co., Regulator No. 2, 38.5", 8-day time and date, very good condition, oak case, $400

American, ca. 1910, Sessions Clock Co., Regulator, 39", 8-day time and date, good condition, old finish oak case (illustrated), $242

American, ca. 1910, Sessions Clock Co., "Regulator E," 39", 8-day time and date, very good original finish, oak case (illustrated), $504

American, ca. 1915, Sessions Clock Co., Regulator, 38", 8-day time and date, good condition, oak case with replaced glass, $275

American, ca. 1910, Sessions Clock Co., octagon long-drop clock, 33", 8-day time and date, good condition, pressed oak case (illustrated), $420

American, ca. 1868, Seth Thomas Clock Co., Office Calendar No. 3, 24", 8-day time, strike, and date, excellent condition, rosewood veneered case, $4,000

American, ca. 1870, Seth Thomas Clock Co., Office Calendar No. 1, 40", 8-day time and date, excellent condition, rosewood veneered case, $2,750

American, ca. 1890, Waterbury Clock Co., "Calendar No. 36," 28", 8-day time and date, very good original finish, oak case (illustrated), $2,352

American, ca. 1910, Waterbury Clock Co., octagon drop clock, 23", 8-day time, strike, date, good condition, rosewood veneered case (illustrated), $178.

American, ca. 1880, double dial, 25", signed Ithaca Calendar Clock Co., $1,155. Credit: Prices4Antiques.com.

American, ca. 1890, double dial, 28", signed Waterbury Clock Co., $2,352. Credit: R. O. Schmitt Fine Arts.

American, ca. 1865, double dial, 57",
signed Carter Clock Co., $3,360. Credit:
R. O. Schmitt Fine Arts.

American, ca. 1880, double dial, 28",
signed Ithaca Calendar Clock Co., $357.
Credit: Prices4Antiques.com.

American, ca. 1880, Welch, E. N. and Co., "Gale Drop No. 1," 30", 8-day
time, strike, and astronomical calendar, excellent original condition
(illustrated), $5,830

American, ca. 1890, Welch, E. N. and Co., No. 1 drop calendar clock, 24",
8-day time, strike, and date, good condition, octagonal rosewood veneered case (illustrated), $247

American, ca. 1866, double dial,
21", signed Ithaca Calendar Clock
Co., $3,110. Credit: R. O. Schmitt
Fine Arts.

American, ca. 1885, Welch, Spring and Co., Damrosch, 41", 8-day time and date, fair condition, walnut case, $1,000

American, ca. 1900, William L. Gilbert Clock Co., Washington model time and date store regulator, 38", 8-day time and calendar, good original condition, oak case (illustrated), $632.

American, ca. 1900, William L. Gilbert Clock Co., "Admiral" model, 28", 8-day time and date, good condition, refinished oak case (illustrated), $252

American, ca. 1913, William L. Gilbert Clock Co., "Observatory," 368-day time and date, fair condition, oak case stripped and stained, $350

	LOW	MID	HIGH
American Calendar Clocks (ca. 1860–1925)	$200–$500	$1,500–$2,500	$3,000–$6,000

GALLERY AND OCTAGON CLOCKS are spring-driven wall clocks that appeared in considerable numbers around the middle of the nineteenth century. Most often they are time-only clocks; they may or may not have pendulum movements. They were usually found in institutional and commercial settings. Among the rarer and more valuable specimens are those with double wind and fusee movements.

American, ca. 1914, 8-day time only, 10⅞", signed Waterbury Clock Co., $105. Credit: R. O. Schmitt Fine Arts.

American, ca. 1870, 30-hour time and seconds, 6", signed L. Hubbell, $225. Credit: R. O. Schmitt Fine Arts.

American, ca. 1850, 8-day fusee time only, 15", signed Chauncey Jerome, $2,100. Credit: R. O. Schmitt Fine Arts.

American, ca. 1880, 8-day time only, 11", signed Waterbury Clock Co., $150. Credit: Timex Collection.

American, ca. 1852, Brewster and Ingraham, round gallery clock, 16.5", 8-day time only, fair condition, cracked glass and case repainted gold, $400

American, ca. 1920, Howard and Co., round gallery clock, 24", electric (DC) slave clock, very good refinished oak case, $1,800

American, ca. 1870, Hubbell, L., octagon gallery clock, 6", 30-hour lever time and seconds, excellent original condition (illustrated), $225

American, ca. 1875, Ingraham, E. and Co., round gallery clock, "Gallery 10 Inch" model, 14", 8-day time only, very good original condition, $825

American, ca. 1850, Jerome, Chauncey, octagon gallery clock, 10.25", 30-hour lever time, seconds, and strike, fair condition, $130

American, ca. 1850, Jerome, Chauncey, round gallery clock, 15", 8-day fusee time only, very good original condition, cherry and rosewood case (illustrated), $2,100

American, ca. 1880, Kroeber, F., round gallery clock, "Maltese" model, 27.5", 8-day time and strike, very good restored walnut case, $600

American, ca. 1857, Marine Mfg. Co., octagon gallery clock, 9", 8-day time-only marine movement, fair condition, rosewood case, $1,200

American, ca. 1860, New Haven Clock Co., octagon gallery clock, 8.75", 30-hour lever time and seconds, poor condition, $70

American, ca. 1880, Seth Thomas Clock Co., ten-sided gallery clock, 13",
30-hour lever time, seconds, and strike, very good condition, small veneer damage, $275

American, ca. 1886, Seth Thomas Clock Co., round metal gallery clock, "8
Inch Banner Lever" model, 10.75", 30-hour lever time and seconds,
good condition, $175

American, ca. 1868, Smith, A. D., round gallery clock, 13", 8-day time and
seconds marine movement, very good original condition, $650

American, ca. 1915, Standard Electric Time Co., round gallery clock, 30.5",
electric clock, good condition, $500

American, ca. 1880, Waterbury Clock Co., octagon gallery clock, "Six Inch
Lever Time" model, 8.75", 8-day lever time and seconds, good condition mahogany case with some veneer damage, $160

American, ca. 1891, Waterbury Clock Co., octagon gallery clock, 10.5",
30-hour time, seconds, and strike, fair condition, repainted dial and
time side not working, $150

American, ca. 1914, Waterbury Clock Co., octagon gallery clock, "Oak
Lever" model, 10⅞", 8-day lever time only, very good condition (illustrated), $105

American, ca. 1915, Waterbury Clock Co., round gallery clock, 30", 30-day
double-wind time only, good condition oak case, $1,500

American, ca. 1880, Welch, Spring and Co., round gallery clock, 19.5",
8-day double-wind time and seconds, excellent original condition, walnut case (illustrated), $2,200

American, ca. 1880, round gallery
clock, 8-day double-wind time
and seconds, excellent condition,
walnut case, 19.5", signed Welch,
Spring and Co., $2,200. Credit:
R. O. Schmitt Fine Arts.

	LOW	MID	HIGH
Gallery and Octagon Clocks (ca. 1850–1930)	$100–$400	$500–$800	$1,000–$3,000

IONIC OR FIGURE EIGHT CLOCKS are products of mid-nineteenth-century America. They are basically 8-day brass movements housed in cases that have two round segments. The top, and larger part, houses the movement and dial, and the smaller bottom houses the pendulum bob. "Ionic" refers to the name of the case model that was produced by E. Ingraham and Co. The name "Ionic" has stuck, although the generic term "figure eight" comes closer to defining the shape of these clocks. Not all major American clock makers produced these clocks. Those models produced by makers such as Ansonia and Ingraham bring far lower prices in the marketplace than the fine E. Howard clocks. Collectors should be aware that the Japanese produced copies of the Ionic clock in the late nineteenth and early twentieth centuries. Sometimes the unscrupulous remove the Japanese logos and labels and attempt to sell these clocks as American.

American, ca. 1885, Ansonia Clock Co., Ionic wall clock, "KOBE" model, 21.5", 8-day time, strike, and alarm, as-found condition, alarm mechanism missing (illustrated), $280

American, ca. 1885, 8-day time, strike, and alarm, 21.5", signed Ansonia Clock Co., $280. Credit: R. O. Schmitt Fine Arts.

American, ca. 1885, 8-day time only, 22", signed E. Ingraham and Co., $385. Credit: R. O. Schmitt Fine Arts.

American, ca. 1860, 8-day time-only,
33", signed George D. Hatch, $2,600.
Credit: R. O. Schmitt Fine Arts.

American, ca. 1890, 8-day time-only,
33", signed E. Howard and Co., $6,300.
Credit: R. O. Schmitt Fine Arts.

American, ca. 1885, Ansonia Clock Co., Ionic wall clock, "KOBE" model, 21.5", 8-day time and strike, good restored condition, paper dial replaced and wrong hands, $300

American, ca. 2000, Cline, Wayne R., figure eight miniature clock, 19", 8-day lever time-only, excellent condition, $1,000

American, ca. 1860, Hatch, George D., figure eight round bottom clock, 33", 8-day time-only, excellent original condition (illustrated), $2,600

American, ca. 1870, Howard, E. and Co., figure eight clock, "No. 9 Regulator" model, 37.5", 8-day time-only, good condition with some restoration, $900

American, ca. 1890, Howard, E. and Co., figure eight clock, "No. 10 Regulator" model, 33", 8-day time-only, good original condition (illustrated), $6,300

American, ca. 1870, Ingraham, E. and Co., Ionic wall clock, 24", 8-day time and strike, good condition, $300

American, ca. 1880, Ingraham, E. and Co., Ionic wall clock, 22", 8-day time-only, fair condition, rosewood case, $532

American, ca. 1885, Ingraham, E. and Co., Ionic wall clock, 22", 8-day time-only, good restored condition (illustrated), $385

	LOW	MID	HIGH
Ionic and Figure Eight Clocks (ca. 1860–1900)	$200–$500	$1,000–$5,000	$2,000–$8,000

LYRE CLOCKS were introduced around 1810. They have design features similar to those of the banjo clock but more closely resemble the musical instrument known as the lyre. These clocks are rare and command steep prices in the market. They are beyond the means of the average beginning collector.

American, ca. 1830, Boston area maker, lyre clock, 41.5", 8-day time only, good condition with some restoration, $2,000

American, ca. 1979, Campos, Foster, dated lyre clock, 39", 8-day time only, excellent condition (illustrated), $3,900

American, ca. 1979, Campos, Foster, dated lyre clock, 42", 8-day time only, excellent condition, $2,850

American, ca. 1830, Chandler, Abiel, lyre clock, 43", 8-day time only, good condition, refinished case, $17,250

American, ca. 1850, Forestville Mfg. Co., Connecticut lyre, 28", 8-day time only, good condition, tablet is cracked (illustrated), $3,410

American, ca. 1979, 8-day time only, 39", signed Foster Campos, $3,900. Credit: R. O. Schmitt Fine Arts.

American, ca. 1850, 8-day time only, 28", signed Forestville Manufacturing Co., $3,410. Credit: R. O. Schmitt Fine Arts.

American, ca. 1950, 8-day Chelsea time only, banjo movement, 39", unsigned, $1,850. Credit: R. O. Schmitt Fine Arts.

American, ca. 1825, Sawin and Dyer, lyre clock, 40", 8-day time only, good condition, $13,800

American, ca. 1830, maker unknown, lyre clock, 32", 8-day time only, good condition with some replacements, $1,485

American, ca. 1840, maker unknown, lyre clock made for Skinner of Boston, 40", 8-day time only, good condition, $9,900

American, ca. 1950, maker unknown, 1950s case with a Chelsea banjo movement, 39", 8-day time only, very good condition (illustrated), $1,850

	LOW	MID	HIGH
Lyre Clocks (ca. 1810–60)	$1,500–$3,000	$5,000–$8,000	$12,000–$25,000

MARBLE DIAL CLOCKS occur occasionally in the mid nineteenth century but become far more common between ca. 1875 and 1920. These wall clocks were generally found in institutions and commercial establishments, but rarely in homes. The nature of their dials made them quite heavy and, in a sense, fragile. Numerous surviving examples show dial damage. The steep market price of these clocks makes them difficult for the novice collector to collect. They have investment potential.

American, ca. 1920, Self Winding Clock Co., marble dial with bronze numerals, 24", electric movement, battery, very good condition, $1,064

American, ca. 1875, Howard, E. and Co., marble dial and case, 43", 8-day time only, very good condition (illustrated), $2,520

American, ca. 1875, 8-day time only, 43", signed E. Howard and Co., $2,520. Credit: Prices4Antiques.com.

American, ca. 1923, 8-day time only, 28", signed E. Howard and Co., $2,296. Credit: R. O. Schmitt Fine Arts.

American, ca. 1923, Howard, E. and Co., marble dial with bronze numerals, 28", 8-day time only, good condition (illustrated), $2,296

American, ca. 1875, Howard, E. and Co., marble dial with painted numerals, 29", 8-day time only, fair condition, lower part of marble missing and replaced by wood, $952

American, ca. 1905, Seth Thomas Clock Co., marble dial with bronze numerals, 20", 15-day double-wind movement, good original condition (illustrated), $1,176

American, ca. 1857, Howard, E. and Co., marble dial with painted numerals, custom made, 51", 8-day time only, very good condition, $9,350

American, ca. 1915, Howard, E. and Co., marble dial with bronze numerals, 35", 8-day time only, fair condition, incorrect pendulum, $990

American, ca. 1900, Howard, E. and Co., marble dial with silvered bronze numerals, 80", 8-day time only, good condition, one of the pendulum jars leaking, $5,264

American, ca. 1901, Howard, E. and Co., marble dial with original bronze hands and trim, 50", 8-day time only, good original condition, replaced pendulum, $1,210

	LOW	MID	HIGH
Marble Dial Clocks (ca. 1850–1920)	$1,000	$2,000–$4,000	$5,000–$8,000

American, 15-day double-wind, time only, 20", signed Seth Thomas Clock Co., $1,176. Credit: R. O. Schmitt Fine Arts.

MIRROR CLOCKS of the first half of the nineteenth century were simply Federal- and Empire-style mirrors with a clock in a wooden case added to the back. The earliest examples were made in New Hampshire and Vermont. The movements were 8-day brass time-only or time and strike weight-driven works. The mirror clock is usually very handsome and colorful. They are very popular with collectors of American clocks, and their prices have risen steadily in the marketplace. Always check for major restoration work on these clocks, especially on the painted tablets.

American, ca. 1825, Chadwick, Joseph, Federal split column mirror clock, 31.5", 8-day time and strike weight-driven, good condition, case refinished and some regilding (illustrated), $3,335

American, ca. 1830, Collins, A., Federal split column mirror clock, 30", 8-day time only weight-driven, good condition, painted glass around dial replaced, $1,904

American, ca. 1830, Freeman and Hoyt, Federal-style mirror clock with scroll top and corner rosettes, 32.5", 8-day time and strike weight-driven, good condition (illustrated), $1,400

American, ca. 1818, Ives, Joseph, pilaster and scroll mirror clock, 51", 8-day time and strike Ives movement, fair condition, dial tablet is flaking, $3,960

American, ca. 1850, Ives, Joseph, Federal quarter column mirror clock, 54", 8-day time and strike weight-driven, fair condition, movement and dial replaced with another Ives movement, $1,344

American, ca. 1825, 8-day time-only New Hampshire mirror clock, 33", signed Benjamin Morrill, $3,740. Credit: R. O. Schmitt Fine Arts.

American, ca. 1825, 8-day time and strike New Hampshire mirror clock, 31.5", signed Joseph Chadwick, $3,335. Credit: Prices4Antiques.com.

American, ca. 1825, Morrill, Benjamin, Federal split column mirror clock, 30", 8-day time and strike weight-driven, very good original condition, $10,350

American, ca. 1825, Morrill, Benjamin, Federal split column mirror clock, 31.25", 8-day time and strike weight-driven, good condition, some restoration, $3,737.50

American, ca. 1825, Morrill, Benjamin, Federal split column mirror clock, 30", 8-day time only weight-driven, very good condition, replaced tablet (illustrated), $3,740

American, ca. 1830, Morrill, Benjamin, Federal split column mirror clock, 30", 8-day time only weight-driven, good condition, mirror replaced, $1,210

American, ca. 1831, Munger and Benedict, Empire-style split column mirror clock, 31", 8-day time only weight-driven, good condition, small cracks in tablet, $3,575

American, ca. 1880, New Haven Clock Co., Federal split column mirror clock, 30", 8-day spring-driven time only, very good condition (illustrated), $145

American, ca. 1829, Randall, Isaac, Federal split column mirror clock, 31", 8-day time only weight-driven, very good condition, some restoration, $3,025

American, ca. 1880, 8-day time only spring-driven, 30", signed New Haven Clock Co., $145. Credit: Prices4Antiques.com.

American, ca. 1830, 8-day time and strike, 32.5", signed Freeman and Hoyt, $1,400. Credit: Prices4Antiques.com.

American, ca. 1890, Waltham Clock and Watch Co., Federal-style mirror clock, 37", 8-day watch movement, poor condition, case damage, $151

American, ca. 1890, Waltham Clock and Watch Co., Federal split column mirror clock, 36", 8-day watch movement, very good condition, $336

American, ca. 1820, Wingate, Frederick, Federal split column mirror clock, 32", 8-day time and strike weight-driven, good condition, restored, $5,500

American, ca. 1830, Wingate, Frederick, Empire-style split column mirror clock, 33", 8-day time and strike weight-driven, good condition, glass dial surround is new, $1,650

	LOW	MID	HIGH
Mirror Clocks (ca. 1820–90)	$150–$800	$1,500–$3,000	$5,000–$10,000

REGULATOR CLOCKS have precise and accurate movements, long compensated pendulums, and deadbeat escapements. They were frequently found in workshops and institutions where exact time was required. In their earliest days, these clocks were handcrafted by individual clockmakers and were considered to be the pinnacle of their maker's expertise. These clocks command exceedingly high prices in the market.

By the second half of the nineteenth century, true regulator clocks were being produced by the major clock manufacturers. They occupied the top of their lines and commanded their highest prices. By this time, the buying public was used to equating the name "Regulator" with "accurate, high-priced clock." Realizing that they could use this to their marketing advantage, manufacturers began to add the word "Regulator" to the model name, label, and glass of mass-produced, inexpensive clocks. By the twentieth century, thousands of these inexpensive clocks had been sold. There is a huge difference in between these moderately accurate clocks called regulators and actual regulators.

To help the reader identify the differences between wall regulators, I have divided this category into:

Box regulators
Large regulators
Octagon and round drop regulators
Square drop regulators
Vienna- or German-style regulators

The reader will quickly note the disparity in market price between categories and within categories and be able to discern the actual regulators from the others.

BOX REGULATORS were inexpensive movements mounted in inexpensive rectangular cases that only distantly resembled their expensive cousins. They were very common in the late nineteenth and early twentieth centuries. They were often found in stores and sometimes carry advertising.

American, ca. 1915, Gilbert, William L. Clock Co., box regulator, 34.5", 8-day time and date, good condition, $198

American, ca. 1925, Gilbert, William L. Clock Co., box regulator, Model No. 3022, 34.5", 8-day time only, very good original condition, $302

American, ca. 1913, Gilbert, William L. Clock Co., box regulator, Model "University," 34", 8-day time only, good condition with restoration, $330

American, ca. 1910, Ingraham Clock Co., box regulator, 39", 8-day time and date, good condition, $402

American, ca. 1907, Ingraham Clock Co., box regulator, Model "Western Union," 36", 8-day time only, good original condition (illustrated), $330

American, ca. 1900, 8-day time and date, box regulator, 39", signed Sessions Clock Co., $242. Credit: Prices4Antiques.com.

American, ca. 1890, 8-day time only, 39", signed Seth Thomas Clock Co., $145. Credit: Prices4Antiques.com.

American, ca. 1935, International Time Recorder, box regulator, 26", 8-day time only double-wind, very good condition, $275

American, ca. 1910, New Haven Clock Co., box regulator, 36", 8-day time only, good condition, $115

American, ca. 1915, New Haven Clock Co., box regulator, Model "Referee," 36", 8-day time and date, good condition with replacements, $250–$350

American, ca. 1910, Sessions Clock Co., box regulator, 39", 8-day time and date, good condition (illustrated), $242

American, ca. 1920, Sessions Clock Co., box regulator, mini store regulator, 19", 8-day time and strike, good original condition, $330–$360

American, ca. 1915, Sessions Clock Co., box regulator, Model "Regulator E," 38.5", 8-day time only, fair original condition, $302

American, ca. 1910, Sessions Clock Co., box regulator, Model "Regulator No. 2," 39", 8-day time only, good condition, $172

American, ca. 1905, Seth Thomas Clock Co., box regulator, 34", 8-day time and seconds, fair condition, flaking paint on dial, $504

American, ca. 1920, Seth Thomas Clock Co., box regulator, 35", 8-day time only, fair condition, $280

American, ca. 1915, Seth Thomas Clock Co., box regulator, 39", 8-day time only, fair condition (illustrated), $145

American, ca. 1910, 8-day time only, 37",
signed Waterbury Clock Co., $364.
Credit: Prices4Antiques.com.

American, ca. 1907, 8-day time only, 36",
signed E. Ingraham Clock Co., $330.
Credit: R. O. Schmitt Fine Arts.

American, ca. 1910, Waterbury Clock Co., box regulator, 37", 8-day time
only, good condition, $172

American, ca. 1910, Waterbury Clock Co., box regulator, Model "Crane,"
36.5", 8-day time only, good refinished condition (illustrated), $364

	LOW	MID	HIGH
Box Regulator Clocks (ca. 1880–1925)	$100–$150	$250–$350	$450–$600

LARGE REGULATORS were the industry's flagships, appearing in the catalogs mainly between ca. 1875 and ca. 1910.

American, ca. 1886, New Haven Clock Co., large wall regulator, Model No.
25, 34", 8-day time only, fair condition, $364

American, ca. 1885, Ansonia Clock Co., large wall regulator, Model No. 16,
84", 8-day time only, excellent original condition, oak case, $5,600

American, ca. 1890, Ansonia Clock Co., large wall regulator, Model No. 16,
84", 8-day time and seconds, very good condition, $3,920

American, ca. 1890, Ansonia Clock Co., large wall regulator, Model No. 4,
84", 8-day time and seconds, excellent condition, walnut case, $5,880

American, ca. 1895, Ansonia Clock Co., large wall regulator, Model No. 4,
84", 8-day time only, excellent original condition, $7,280

American, ca. 1891, 8-day time and seconds, Regulator No. 9, 76", signed Waterbury Clock Co., $15,680. Credit: R. O. Schmitt Fine Arts.

American, ca. 1885, 8-day time and seconds, 80", signed Waterbury Clock Co., $7,000. Credit: NAWCC Eastern States Regional.

American, ca. 1885, Ansonia Clock Co., large wall regulator, Model No. 14, 71", 8-day time and seconds, good condition, $9,075

American, ca. 1910, Chelsea Clock Co., large wall regulator, 36", 8-day time only, very good condition, $2,800

American, ca. 1900, Chelsea Clock Co., large wall regulator, Model No. 5, 48", 8-day time only, very good condition, $8,120

American, ca. 1895, Gilbert, William L. Clock Co., large wall regulator, Model No. 10, 52.5", 8-day time and seconds, excellent restored condition, $5,880

American, ca. 1891, Gilbert, William L. Clock Co., large wall regulator, Model No. 11, 50", 8-day time and seconds, very good condition, $3,584

American, ca. 1900, Gilbert, William L. Clock Co., large wall regulator, Model No. 16, 8-day time and seconds, very good condition, $12,320

American, ca. 1900, Howard, E. and Co., large wall regulator, Model No. 58, 51", 8-day time only, good original condition, $6,608

American, ca. 1890, Howard, E. and Co., large wall regulator, Model No. 58-8, 40", 8-day time only, good restored condition, $5,040

American, ca. 1885, Howard, E. and Co., large wall regulator, Model No. 59-6, 38", 8-day time only, very good condition, oak case, $3,960

American, ca. 1874, 8-day Swiss pinwheel movement, Regulator No. 27, 89", signed F. Kroeber, $12,880. Credit: R. O. Schmitt Fine Arts.

American, ca. 1903, 8-day time and seconds, Regulator No. 65, 82", signed Waterbury Clock Co., $12,040. Credit: R. O. Schmitt Fine Arts.

American, ca. 1977, Howard, E. and Co., large wall regulator, Model No. 59-8, 46", 8-day time only, excellent original condition, $2,090

American, ca. 1889, Howard, E. and Co., large wall regulator, Model No. 89, 65", 8-day time and seconds, very good condition, oak case, $4,480

American, ca. 1875, Howard, E. and Co., large wall regulator, No. 12, 60", 8-day time and seconds, very good condition, $5,824

American, ca. 1880, Jones, George A., large wall regulator, 55", 8-day time and seconds, good condition, refinished case, $4,200

American, ca. 1874, Kroeber, F., large wall regulator, Model No. 27, 89", 8-day time and seconds, excellent restored condition (illustrated), $12,880

American, ca. 1880, Kroeber, F., large wall regulator, Model No. 33, 45.5", 8-day time only, excellent original condition, $4,200

American, ca. 1875, Kroeber, F., large wall regulator, Model No. 43, 39.5", 8-day time and strike, fair condition, missing top trim, $1,008

American, ca. 1880, New Haven Clock Co., large wall regulator, Jeweler's No. 3, 86", 8-day time and seconds, good condition, $4,950

American, ca. 1905, New Haven Clock Co., large wall regulator, Model "Grecian," 51", 8-day time and seconds, good condition, $2,158

American, ca. 1887, Self Winding Clock Co., large wall regulator, Model No. 6, 45", time and seconds, electric battery, poor condition, missing bottom decorative trim, $726

American, ca. 1887, Self Winding Clock Co., large wall regulator, Model No. 8, 42", time and seconds, electric battery, fair condition, $880

American, ca. 1884, Seth Thomas Clock Co., large wall regulator, Model No. 17, 68", 8-day time and seconds, excellent original condition, $6,325

American, ca. 1890, Seth Thomas Clock Co., large wall regulator, Model No. 19, 75", 8-day time only, very good condition, $29,120

American, ca. 1909, Seth Thomas Clock Co., large wall regulator, Model No. 32, 68", 8-day time only, good restored condition, $5,376

American, ca. 1922, Seth Thomas Clock Co., large wall regulator, Model No. 4, 42", 8-day time and seconds, good condition, $2,145

American, ca. 1884, Seth Thomas Clock Co., large wall regulator, Model No. 6, 49", 8-day time and seconds, excellent restored condition, $4,816

American, ca. 1909, Seth Thomas Clock Co., large wall regulator, Model No. 63, 76", 8-day time only, excellent condition, $20,160

American, ca. 1885, maker unknown, large wall jeweler's regulator, 88.5", 8-day time only, very good condition, $3,960

American, ca. 1885, maker unknown, large wall jeweler's regulator, 84", 8-day time and seconds, very good condition, mahogany case, $3,450

American, ca. 1890, maker unknown, large wall regulator, 63", Swiss pinwheel movement, poor condition, case is missing top and bottom trim, $2,860

American, ca. 1880, maker unknown, large wall regulator, "Hartford No. 9," 97", 8-day time only, very good condition, $7,475

American, ca. 1896, Waterbury Clock Co., large wall regulator, Model "Kendall," 52", 8-day time and seconds, very good original condition, $3,472

American, ca. 1891, Waterbury Clock Co., large wall regulator, Model No. 11, 52.5", 8-day time only, good condition, repapered dial, $4,032

American, ca. 1893, Waterbury Clock Co., large wall regulator, Model No. 17, 56.5", 8-day time and seconds, good restored condition, $2,128

American, ca. 1893, Waterbury Clock Co., large wall regulator, Model No. 21, 55.5", 8-day time and seconds, good restored condition, $1,008

American, ca. 1903, Waterbury Clock Co., large wall regulator, Model No. 65, 81.5", 8-day time only, excellent condition (illustrated), $12,040

American, ca. 1880, Waterbury Clock Co., large wall regulator, Model No. 9, 88", 8-day time only, excellent restored condition, $15,680

American, ca. 1891, Waterbury Clock Co., large wall regulator, Model No. 9, 76", 8-day time and seconds, excellent original condition (illustrated), $15,680

American, ca. 1880, Welch, Spring and Co., large wall regulator, Model No. 1, 68", 8-day time and seconds only, double weights, very good condition, $7,840

American, ca. 1889, Welch, Spring and Co., large wall regulator, Model No. 11, 60", 8-day time and seconds, good condition, $3,360

American, ca. 1885, Welch, Spring and Co., large wall regulator, Model No. 12, 65", 30-day double spring time only, good condition, $3,584

American, ca. 1880, Welch, Spring and Co., large wall regulator, Model No. 4 B.W., 39.5", 8-day time only, excellent condition, $5,320

American, ca. 1885, Welch, Spring and Co., large wall regulator, Model No. 5 B.W., 52", 8-day time only, good restored condition, $5,040

American, ca. 1880, Welch, Spring and Co., large wall regulator, Model No. 6, 41", 8-day time only, good restored condition, $5,600

American, ca. 1881, Welch, Spring and Co., large wall regulator, Model No. 6, 52", 8-day time and seconds, good restored condition, $3,360

American, ca. 1883, Welch, Spring and Co., large wall regulator, Model No. 7, 47", 8-day time only, good restored condition, $6,160

American, ca. 1885, Welch, Spring and Co., large wall regulator, Model No. 8, 66", 8-day time only, good condition, $10,080

American, ca. 1889, Welch, Spring and Co., large wall regulator, Model No. 9, 39", 30-day time only, excellent condition, $5,254

	LOW	MID	HIGH
Large Regulators (ca. 1875–1920)	$1,500–$2,000	$3,000–$8,000	$10,000–$20,000

OCTAGON AND ROUND DROP "BOTTOM LINE" REGULATORS appeared before the mid-nineteenth century. The smaller and less expensive "Regulator" models appeared and were widely marketed between 1875 and 1925. The Regulator was made and marketed throughout this period, finally succumbing to the electric office clock. Many smaller and less expensive models are the same movements and cases that without the "Regulator" name are the clocks that we know as the "schoolhouse" clock (see Round and Octagon Drop Wall Clocks).

American, ca. 1901, Ansonia Clock Co., octagon drop regulator, Model "Office Regulator," 32", 8-day time, seconds, and strike, good condition (illustrated), $588

American, ca. 1890, Ansonia Clock Co., octagon drop regulator, Model "Office Regulator," 31", 8-day time only, excellent condition, $140

American, ca. 1915, Ansonia Clock Co., octagon drop regulator, Model "Regulator A," 32", 8-day time only, good condition, refinished oak case, $330

American, ca. 1901, Ansonia Clock Co., octagon drop regulator, Model "Regulator A," 32", 8-day time and date, fair condition, new bezel and repainted case, $522

American, ca. 1906, Ansonia Clock Co., octagon drop regulator, Model "Regulator A," 32", 8-day time and strike, good condition, $532

American, ca. 1900, Ansonia Clock Co., octagon drop regulator, Model "Regulator B," 32", 8-day time and strike, good condition, repapered dial, $495

American, ca. 1910, Gilbert, William L. Clock Co., octagon drop regulator, Model B, 29", 8-day time only, very good condition, oak case , $336

American, ca. 1911, Ingraham Clock Co., octagon drop regulator, Model "Hartford," 32", 8-day time only, good condition (illustrated), $364

American, ca. 1920, maker unknown, round drop regulator, 32", 8-day time only, very good condition, $275

American, ca. 1900, Welch, E. N. Mfg Co., octagon drop regulator, Model "Gentry," 26", 8-day time only, fair condition (illustrated), $140

American, ca. 1911, 8-day time only, 32", signed Ingraham Clock Co., $364. Credit: R. O. Schmitt Fine Arts.

American, ca. 1901, 8-day time, seconds, and strike, 32", signed Ansonia Clock Co., $588. Credit: R. O. Schmitt Fine Arts.

American, ca. 1900, 8-day time and strike, 24", signed E. N. Welch Manufacturing Co., $448. Credit: R. O. Schmitt Fine Arts.

American, ca. 1878, 8-day time only, 26", signed E. N. Welch Manufacturing Co., $140. Credit: R. O. Schmitt Fine Arts.

American, ca. 1878, Welch, Spring and Co., round drop regulator, 24", 8-day time and strike, fair condition, case has been partially stripped (illustrated), $448

American, ca. 1880, Welch, Spring and Co., round drop regulator, Model 3, 35", 8-day time-only two-weight movement, fair condition, $660

	LOW	MID	HIGH
Octagon and Round Drop "Bottom Line" Regulators (ca. 1875–1925)	$100–$200	$300–$400	$500–$600

OCTAGON AND ROUND DROP REGULATORS, TOP-OF-THE-LINE MODELS

American, ca. 1900, Ansonia Clock Co., round drop regulator, Model "General," 68", 8-day time-only two-weight movement, very good restored condition, $3,920

American, ca. 1920, Ansonia Clock Co., round drop regulator, Model "Standard Regulator," 37", 8-day time and seconds, very good refinished condition, $1,155

American, ca. 1860, Atkins Clock Co., round drop regulator, 44", 8-day time only, excellent original condition, $4,872

American, ca. 1925, 8-day time only, Regulator No. 34, 32.5", signed Waltham Clock Co., $1,210. Credit: R. O. Schmitt Fine Arts.

American, ca. 1900, 8-day time only, Regulator No. 70, 31", signed E. Howard and Co., $2,200–$3,000. Credit: R. O. Schmitt Fine Arts.

American, ca. 1865, Atkins Clock Co., round drop regulator, 24.5", 8-day time and strike, good condition, dial repainted, $672

American, ca. 1885, Boston Clock Co., round drop regulator, 34", 8-day time only, good condition, $2,310

American, ca. 1920, Chelsea Clock Co., round drop regulator, Model No. 1, 34", 8-day time only, good restored condition, $1,568

American, ca. 1832, Curtis and Dunning, round drop regulator, 36", 8-day time only, very good condition, $8,800

American, ca. 1895, Eastman Clock Co., round drop regulator, Model Pendulum No. 1, 33", 8-day time only, fair condition, case has been stripped, $1,792

American, ca. 1890, Howard, E. and Co., round drop regulator, made for Western Union, 43", 8-day time only, good condition, $9,800

American, ca. 1890, Howard, E. and Co., round drop regulator, Model No. 4, 32", 8-day time only, very good condition, $3,584

American, ca. 1900–20, Howard, E. and Co., round drop regulator, Model No. 70, 31", 8-day time only, excellent condition (illustrated), $2,200–$3,000

American, ca. 1890, New Haven Clock Co., octagon drop regulator, Model Admiral, 62", 30-day time and seconds only, excellent original condition, $2,970

American, ca. 1920, 8-day time and seconds, Regulator No. 2, 36", signed Seth Thomas Clock Co., $1,870. Credit: R. O. Schmitt Fine Arts.

American, ca. 1880, 8-day time and seconds, Office Regulator No. 2, 41", signed New Haven Clock Co., $1,400. Credit: R. O. Schmitt Fine Arts.

American, ca. 1880, New Haven Clock Co., octagon drop regulator, Model "Office No. 2," 41", 8-day time and seconds, good original condition (illustrated), $1,400

American, ca. 1910, New Haven Clock Co., round drop regulator, Model "Glenor," 36.5", 8-day time and seconds, good refinished condition, $3,808

American, ca. 1890, Seth Thomas Clock Co., octagon drop regulator, Model No. 3, 41", 8-day time and seconds, very good original condition, walnut case, $3,025

American, ca. 1875, Seth Thomas Clock Co., round drop regulator, Model No. 1, 37", 8-day time and seconds, very good condition, $1,100

American, ca. 1920, Seth Thomas Clock Co., round drop regulator, Model No. 2, 36", 8-day time and seconds, very good condition (illustrated), $1,870

American, ca. 1920, Seth Thomas Clock Co., twelve-sided drop regulator, Model No. 3, 44", 8-day time and seconds, good condition, $2,464

American, ca. 1830, Stowell, Abel, round drop regulator, 31", 8-day time only, good condition, $1,610

American, ca. 1870, Taylor, George and Co., round drop regulator, 30", 8-day time only, very good condition, refinished case, $2,016

American, ca. 1855, Terry, Silas B., round drop regulator, 33", 8-day time only, very good original condition, $2,310

American, ca. 1900–25, Waltham Clock Co., round drop regulator, Model No. 34, 32.5", 8-day time only, good condition (illustrated), $1,210

American, ca. 1910, Waterbury Clock Co., round drop regulator, Model No. 66, 58", 8-day time and seconds, very good oak case, $4,480

American, ca. 1905, Waterbury Clock Co., round drop regulator, Model No. 20, 38", 8-day time, seconds, and strike, good original condition, $1,456

American, ca. 1915, Waterbury Clock Co., round drop regulator, Model No. 80, 41", 8-day time and seconds, excellent restored condition, $1,904

American, ca. 1880, Welch, Spring and Co., round drop regulator, Model No. 3, 35", 8-day time and strike, excellent original condition, $5,264

American, ca. 1878, Welch, Spring and Co., round drop regulator, Model No. 4, 30", 8-day time, strike, and date, excellent original condition, $2,576

	LOW	MID	HIGH
Octagon and Round Drop Regulators, Top-of-the-Line Models (ca. 1860–1925)	$1,500–$2,000	$3,000–$5,000	$6,000–$8,000

SQUARE DROP REGULATORS are high-quality regulators produced at the end of the nineteenth and beginning of the twentieth century.

American, ca. 1890, Howard, E. and Co., square drop regulator, Model No. 75, 34", 8-day time only, fair condition (illustrated), $3,850

American, ca. 1905, Seth Thomas Clock Co., square drop regulator, Model No. 7, 45", 8-day time and seconds, very good condition (illustrated), $10,920

American, ca. 1905, Seth Thomas Clock Co., square drop regulator, Model No. 7, 45", 8-day time and seconds, very good condition, $12,320

American, ca. 1905, Seth Thomas Clock Co., square drop regulator, Model No. 8, 52", 8-day time and seconds, very good condition, $9,800

American, ca. 1909, Seth Thomas Clock Co., square drop regulator, Model No. 25, 32", 8-day time and seconds, as-found, $1,375

	LOW	MID	HIGH
Square Drop Regulators (ca. 1875–1915)	$1,500–$3,000	$4,000–$6,000	$10,000–$12,000

American, ca. 1905, 8-day time and seconds, Regulator No. 7, 45", signed Seth Thomas Clock Co., $10,920. Credit: R. O. Schmitt Fine Arts.

American, ca. 1890, 8-day time only, Boston Regulator No. 75, 34", signed E. Howard and Co., $3,850. Credit: R. O. Schmitt Fine Arts.

VIENNA- OR GERMAN-STYLE REGULATORS were produced at the end of the nineteenth century in imitation of the many European imports coming into America, mainly from Germany.

American, ca. 1880, Howard, E. and Co., Vienna/German-style regulator, No. 60, 80", 8-day time and seconds, good condition, walnut case, $3,808

American, ca. 1890, Kroeber, F., Vienna/German-style regulator, 47", 8-day time and seconds, fair condition (illustrated), $743

American, ca. 1890, New Haven Clock Co., Vienna/German-style regulator, 51", 8-day time only, fair condition, flaking dial (illustrated), $495

American, ca. 1890, Waterbury Clock Co., Vienna/German-style regulator, 37.5", 8-day time and strike, excellent original condition, $935

	LOW	MID	HIGH
Vienna/German-Style Regulators (ca. 1885–1900)	$500–$999	$1,000–$2,999	$3,000–$4,000

ROUND AND OCTAGON DROP SCHOOLHOUSE CLOCKS, at the peak of their production, were the most numerous of American wall clocks. Their

American, ca. 1890, 8-day time and seconds, Genuine Vienna Regulator, 47", signed F. Kroeber, $743. Credit: R. O. Schmitt Fine Arts.

American, ca. 1890, 8-day time only, 51", signed New Haven Clock Co., $495. Credit: R. O. Schmitt Fine Arts.

cases contained each manufacturers' mainline (mostly 8-day) movements. The least expensive versions were time only. Midrange clocks contained time and strike movements, and calendar movements were added to the most expensive of these clocks. "Short-drop" clocks have a shorter pendulum than their "long-drop" counterparts. These movements can also be found in box regulators, Arts and Crafts, and some round and octagon regulators. They still exist in very large numbers and appear in numerous shops and auctions. Beware of the unscrupulous seller who disguises Japanese versions of these clocks as American.

American, ca. 1870, Ansonia Clock Co., octagon short-drop schoolhouse clock, sold by Kroeber, 24", 8-day time and strike, very good condition, $550

American, ca. 1900, Ansonia Clock Co., octagon short-drop schoolhouse clock, 25", 8-day time and strike, excellent original condition, $336

American, ca. 1900, Ansonia Clock Co., octagon short-drop schoolhouse clock, 19", 8-day time only, very good condition, $357

American, ca. 1890, Atkins, octagon short-drop schoolhouse clock, 25", 8-day time and strike, very good condition, $1,064

American, ca. 1915, Gilbert, William L. Clock Co., octagon short-drop school-house clock, "Admiral" model, 28", 8-day time only, good condition, $275

Two American schoolhouse wall clocks offered for sale at
TIMEXPO in Waterbury, Connecticut, May 2002.

American, ca. 1850, Jerome, Chauncey, octagon short-drop schoolhouse
clock, 22.5", 8-day time and strike fusee movement, good condition,
$1,980

American, ca. 1880, New Haven Clock Co., octagon long-drop schoolhouse
clock, 32", 8-day time and strike, good condition (illustrated), $470

American, ca. 1910, Sessions Clock Co., octagon short-drop schoolhouse
clock, 26", 8-day time only, good condition, $176

American, ca. 1885, Seth Thomas Clock Co., octagon short-drop schoolhouse clock, 24", 8-day time only, very good condition, $330

American, ca. 1898, Seth Thomas Clock Co., octagon long-drop schoolhouse clock, "Globe" model, 32", 8-day time only, very good condition,
$605

American, ca. 1915, Seth Thomas Clock Co., octagon long-drop schoolhouse clock, 33.5", 8-day time only, very good condition, $225

American, ca. 1918, Seth Thomas Clock Co., octagon short-drop schoolhouse clock, 23.5", 8-day time only, fair condition, $275

American, ca. 1920, Seth Thomas Clock Co., mini round short-drop schoolhouse clock, 18", 8-day time only, very good condition, $150

American, ca. 1910, Waterbury Clock Co., round short-drop schoolhouse
clock, 24.5", 8-day time only, very good condition (illustrated), $275

American, ca. 1912, Waterbury Clock Co., octagon short-drop schoolhouse
clock, "Arion" model, 25", 8-day time only, fair condition, $220

American, ca. 1880, octagon short-drop schoolhouse clock, 8-day time only, 25", signed Waterbury Clock Co., $250. Credit: Timex Museum Collection.

American, ca. 1880, octagon long-drop schoolhouse clock, 8-day time and strike, 32", signed New Haven Clock Co., $470. Credit: R. O. Schmitt Fine Arts.

American, ca. 1910, round short-drop schoolhouse clock, 8-day time only, 25", signed Waterbury Clock Co., $275. Credit: R. O. Schmitt Fine Arts.

American, ca. 1910, octagon short-drop schoolhouse clock, "barber's clock," 8-day time only, 25", signed Waterbury Clock Co., $500. Credit: Timex Museum Collection.

American, ca. 1920, Waterbury Clock Co., octagon short-drop schoolhouse
clock, 25", 8-day time and strike, fair condition, $77

	LOW	MID	HIGH
Round and Octagon Drop Schoolhouse Clocks (ca. 1850–1930)	$100–$250	$300–$500	$700–$900

SHIP OR MARINE CLOCKS have been popular with collectors since the
beginning of the twentieth century. Among America's major makers, the
Seth Thomas Clock Company dominated the market. There are many of
these clocks on the market today. An interesting area of ships' clocks is the
group produced during World War II with nonmetallic cases.

American, ca. 1927, Chelsea Clock Co., ship's bell clock in carved oak case,
9.5", 8-day time and strike, good condition, broken hammer, $280

American, ca. 1880, Seth Thomas Clock Co., ship's bell clock in oak case, 9",
8-day time, seconds, and strike, very good condition (illustrated), $616

American, ca. 1890, Seth Thomas Clock Co., ship's bell clock in nickel-
plated brass case with outside bell, 10.5", 8-day time, seconds, and
strike, good original condition, $440

American, ca. 1940, ship's bell clock,
8-day time and strike, 7", signed Seth
Thomas Clock Co., $350.

American, ca. 1912, ship's bell clock and
stand, "No. 5," 8-day time only, 7",
signed Waterbury Clock Co., $450.
Credit: Timex Museum Collection.

American, ca. 1880, 8-day time, seconds, and strike, oak case, 9", signed Seth Thomas Clock Co., $616. Credit: Prices4antiques.com.

American, ca. 1935, 30-hour time, seconds, and strike, brass case, 7", signed Seth Thomas Clock Co., $364. Credit: R. O. Schmitt Fine Arts.

American, ca. 1900, Seth Thomas Clock Co., ship's bell clock in brass case with outside bell, 11", 30-hour time, seconds, and strike, good condition, missing label, $412

American, ca. 1925, Seth Thomas Clock Co., ship's bell clock in brass case with outside bell, 10.5", 8-day time, seconds, and strike, good condition, missing back plate, $302

American, ca. 1935, Seth Thomas Clock Co., ship's bell clock in brass case, 7", 30-hour time, seconds, and strike, very good condition (illustrated), $364

American, ca. 1936, Seth Thomas Clock Co., ship's bell clock in brass case with outside bell, "Monitor" model, 10.5", 30-hour time, seconds, and strike, good condition, $495

American, ca. 1943, Seth Thomas Clock Co., ship's clock in a Bakelite case, 7.75", 8-day time and seconds, good condition with repair to the case, $264

American, ca. 1943, Seth Thomas Clock Co., ship's clock in a phenolic resin case, 11", 8-day time and seconds, very good condition, $242

	LOW	MID	HIGH
Ship or Marine Clocks (ca. 1885–1945)	$200	$300–$450	$500–$800

English Wall Clocks

For most American collectors, foreign clocks are not the normal collecting base. However, fascinating and wonderful areas of collecting exist beyond our shores. There are, of course, fewer foreign clocks available in the United States for purchase than domestic ones. The great expansion of the American clock industry by the middle of the nineteenth century was responsible for this situation. The mass import of American clocks started by Chauncey Jerome greatly changed and diminished the English industry—ironically, the same industry that provided the foundation for America's.

This section is confined to those types of clocks that have made their way to American shores in some numbers. Under **Tall-Case Clocks** there is a large section on British clocks, and in this section, listed among **American Wall Clocks,** are the very interesting **Anglo-American Clocks**, which could easily be included here.

Beyond these, some rarer types of wall clocks will be mentioned, but most of the valuations are confined to **gallery** and **drop dial** clocks. Until World War I, most of these clocks were powered by the well-made, very reliable and notable English fusee movements. British workmanship between the 1700s and the 1930s was of high caliber and used the best materials.

Interest in British clocks has been steadily growing, and prices are rising.

LANTERN CLOCKS were among the earliest of British timepieces. In its beginnings, this style of clock was considered a wall clock, as it sat on a bracket on the wall which allowed the weights a longer distance to fall and fewer rewindings. Although appearing in the seventeenth century, it was made well into the eighteenth, and reproductions were made in the nineteenth and twentieth centuries. Although lantern clocks were made in considerable numbers, those available in the market bring prices that discourage most novice collectors.

	LOW	MID	HIGH
Lantern Clocks (ca. 1620–1750)	$2,000–$3,000	$5,000–$7,000	$8,000–$10,000

TAVERN OR "ACT OF PARLIAMENT" CLOCKS are weight-driven, time-only wall clocks with a large dial and narrow trunk. For a full explanation, see "Act of Parliament" in the Glossary.

English, ca. 1700, lantern clock mounted on bracket, maker unknown, $2,500. Credit: NAWCC TIMEXPO 2002.

Side view.

English, ca. 1800, maker unknown, Act of Parliament, case marked Justin Vulliamy (not the maker), 49.5", 8-day time only, good condition with some restoration (illustrated), $8,580

English, ca. 1810, maker unknown, Act of Parliament, chinoiserie case, 45", 8-day time only, good condition with restoration, $2,070

English, ca. 1810, maker unknown, Act of Parliament, chinoiserie case, 62.5", 8-day time only, good condition with restoration, $3,220

English, ca. 1625, 30-hour time and strike, extensive restoration, 16", maker unknown, $2,200. Credit: R. O. Schmitt Fine Arts.

English, ca. 1800, 8-day time only, maker unknown. Case is marked "Justin Vulliamy, London" who was not the maker of this clock. It was a common practice in the provinces to add the name of a prominent maker. $8,580. Credit: R. O. Schmitt Fine Arts.

	LOW	MID	HIGH
Act of Parliament or Tavern Clocks (ca. 1795–1840)	$2,500	$7,000	$12,000+

HOODED CLOCKS are essentially 8-day time and strike fusee movements installed in mahogany or oak hoodlike cases and mounted on wall brackets.

	LOW	MID	HIGH
Hooded Clocks (ca. 1820–1900)	$1,500	$2,000	$2,500

GALLERY CLOCKS are round wall clocks usually having 8-day time-only fusee movements. They can be rather large; they were often made to hang on the walls of public institutions such as post offices, railway stations, libraries, and the like. Gallery clocks are called dial clocks in England or sometimes railway or post office clocks. Prices for these clocks have been rising steadily in recent years.

English, ca. 1866, Cattaneo and Co., Leeds, gallery clock, 15", 8-day time only fusee, good condition with worn dial (illustrated), $600

English, ca. 1830, Cochran, Samuel, gallery clock, 15", 8-day time only fusee, very good condition, $2,912

English, ca. 1845, Dent, Edward James, gallery clock, 15", 8-day time only fusee, excellent condition (illustrated), $1,500

English, ca. 1930, Empire Clock Co., gallery clock, 16", 8-day time only, good condition, stripped case, $123

English, ca. 1830, 8-day time and strike
fusee movement, hooded wall clock,
19.5", signed T. H. Watkins,
Birmingham, $1,595. Credit: R. O.
Schmitt Fine Arts.

Side view.

English, ca. 1866, 8-day time-only fusee
movement, 15", signed Cattaneo and Co.,
$600.

English, ca. 1930, 8-day time and
strike movement, 16", signed
Enfield Clock Co., $200. Credit:
DePaola Collection.

English, ca. 1845, 8-day time and strike fusee movement, gallery clock, 15", signed Edward James Dent, $1,500. Credit: Marcus Collection.

English, ca. 1930, Enfield Clock Co., gallery clock, 16", 8-day time and strike, good condition, repainted dial (illustrated), $200

English, ca. 1940, Garrard, gallery clock, 13.5", 8-day time only, fair condition, badly flaking dial, $145

English, ca. 1890, Hall, G., gallery clock, 18.5", 8-day time-only fusee, good condition, mahogany-stained oak case, $504

English, ca. 1905, Ingram Bros., gallery clock, 16", 8-day time-only fusee, very good condition, $728

English, ca. 1925, Olsen, Chris, gallery clock with rope molding, imported movement, 9", 8-day time and seconds Swiss lever movement, fair condition, $77

English, ca. 1930, Potts and Sons, gallery postal clock, 15", 8-day time-only fusee, very good condition, $660

English, ca. 1848, Schwer gallery clock, 12", 30-hour German weight movement, good condition, $72

English, ca. 1890, maker unknown, gallery clock, 16", 8-day time-only fusee, very good condition, $190

English, ca. 1890, maker unknown, gallery clock, 15", 8-day time-only fusee, fair condition, worn dial, $400

English, ca. 1900, maker unknown, gallery clock, 15", 8-day time-only fusee, fair condition, missing pendulum, $302

English, ca. 1910, maker unknown, gallery clock made for and labeled General Post Office, 23", 8-day time-only fusee, fair condition, homemade pendulum, $825

English, ca. 1910, maker unknown, gallery clock, 15", 8-day time-only German fusee, poor condition, $190

English, ca. 1930, maker unknown, gallery postal clock with royal insignia, 14.75", 8-day time-only fusee, restored with repainted dial, $605

English, ca. 1890, Webster, gallery clock, 11", 8-day time-only fusee, fair condition, badly flaking dial, $1,344

	LOW	MID	HIGH
Gallery Clocks (ca. 1820–40)	$75–$150	$250–$650	$850–$1,500

Dutch Wall Clocks

The Dutch wall clocks that we know today evolved from provincial forms that first appeared in the province of Friesland. There are two major forms: the *Stoelklok* (chair clock), which appeared early in the eighteenth century, and the *Staartklok* (tail clock) that appeared at the beginning of the nineteenth century. Both clocks shared similar 8-day and 30-hour weight-driven time, strike, and often alarm movements. They were made until the end of the nineteenth century. Twentieth-century reproductions abound, and new Dutch clocks with very different German movements are even more abundant.

Dutch, ca. 1850, maker unknown, Staartklok, 60", 30-hour time and strike weight-driven movement, very good condition, $1,792

Dutch, ca. 1870, maker unknown, Staartklok, 44", 30-hour time and strike weight-driven movement, fair condition, some finial damage, $1,568

Dutch, ca. 1820, maker unknown, Stoelklok, 27", 30-hour time and strike weight-driven movement, fair condition, $840

Dutch, ca. 1890, maker unknown, Stoelklok, silver case and enameled dial, 5.5", 30-hour time and strike weight-driven movement, excellent condition, $935

Dutch, ca. 1840, maker unknown, Staartklok, 58", 8-day time, date, alarm, and strike, very good condition (illustrated), $2,090

Dutch, ca. 1795, Hindriks, M.A., Staartklok, 55", 30-hour time and strike weight-driven movement, fair condition, replaced finials, $805

Dutch, ca. 1800, maker unknown, Stoelklok, 29", 30-hour time and strike weight-driven movement, very good original condition (illustrated), $1,705

Dutch, ca. 1800, 30-hour time and strike, Stoelklok, 29", maker unknown, $1,705. Credit: R. O. Schmitt Fine Arts.

Dutch, ca. 1780, 30-hour time and strike, Stoelklok, 29", maker unknown, $2,500. Credit: NAWCC museum Collection.

Dutch, ca. 1860, 30-hour time and strike, Staartklok, 59", maker unknown, $1,800. Credit: NAWCC TIMEXPO 2002.

Dutch, ca. 1840, 8-day time, date, alarm, and strike, Staartklok, 58", maker unknown, $2,090. Credit: R. O. Schmitt Fine Arts.

Dutch, ca. 1840, maker unknown, Staartklok, 51", 30-hour time and strike weight-driven movement, good condition, $880

Dutch, ca. 1840, maker unknown, Staartklok, 49", 30-hour time and strike weight-driven movement, good condition, alarm is missing, $715

	LOW	MID	HIGH
Dutch Clocks, Stoelkloks and Staartkloks (ca. 1720–1890)	$500–$1,000	$1,500–$2,000	$2,500–$3,000

French Wall Clocks

French wall clocks appeared in America during the early decades of the nineteenth century. They arrived as part of America's fascination with the new styles of furniture, art, and clothing that accompanied the French Revolution and Napoleonic periods. As the century progressed, more and more French clocks were imported, and they often became status symbols among the growing middle class.

The later twentieth century saw the importation of many French provincial clocks known as Morbier or Comtoise clocks.

Most French clocks house very reliable and well-made brass movements whose designs had been standardized and used since the late eighteenth century. The provincial clocks house sturdy iron-framed movements that continued to use the crown verge escapement well into the nineteenth century.

I believe that most French clocks offer the collector excellent value for their price. A recent upward spiraling of their prices indicates the continuing popularity of these clocks.

CARTEL CLOCKS were produced in France starting about 1750. The term "cartel" at first meant "dial clock," although in modern usage it refers to a specific style of elongated wall clock. The cases of these clocks were usually made from bronze and "fire-gilded." Later nineteenth-century versions were cased in brass, brass-plated spelter, and wood. For convenience, I have separated the metal-cased from the wooden-cased clocks. Eighteenth-century cartel clocks bring very high prices and are beyond the reach of most beginning collectors. The clocks illustrated and listed below are mainly from the latter part of the nineteenth century, when this style of clock underwent a renaissance of popularity.

French, ca. 1880, Louis XIV–style gilded bronze cartel clock, 8-day time and strike, 31", unmarked, $1,200. Credit: NAWCC Mid-Eastern States Regional 2002.

French, ca. 1890, Louis XVI–style gilded brass cartel clock, 8-day time and strike, 34", unmarked, $1,400. Credit: NAWCC Mid-Eastern States Regional 2002.

French, ca. 1750, Caffieri, Jacques, Louis XV–style gilt bronze cartel clock, 33", 8-day time and strike, excellent condition, $27,600

French, ca. 1870, Japy Frères, Baroque-style gilt bronze cartel clock, 21", 8-day time and strike, very good condition (illustrated), $605

French, ca. 1870, Japy Frères, Rococo-style gilt bronze cartel clock, 18.5", 8-day time and strike, excellent original condition, $440

French, ca. 1870, Lepool, E. P., Rococo-style gilt bronze cartel clock, 30", 8-day time and strike, excellent condition, $2,750

French, ca. 1885, Marti, Louis XIV–style gilt bronze cartel clock, 24.5", 8-day time and strike, very good condition, $1,265

French, ca. 1880, Planchon, Louis XIV–style gilt bronze cartel clock, 20.5", 8-day time and strike, excellent condition, $2,090

French, ca. 1860, maker unknown, figural-style gilt bronze cartel clock, 20", 8-day time only, very good condition, $672

French, ca. 1885, maker unknown, Louis XIV–style gilt bronze cartel clock, 14", 8-day time and strike, good condition, $880

French, ca. 1885, maker unknown, Louis XIV–style gilt bronze cartel clock, 34", 8-day time and strike, very good condition, $880

French, ca. 1870, maker unknown, Louis XV–style gilt bronze cartel clock, 21", 8-day time and strike, excellent original condition, $1,150

French, ca. 1870, Baroque-style gilt bronze cartel clock, 8-day time and strike, 21", Japy Frères, $605. Credit: R. O. Schmitt Fine Arts.

French, ca. 1900, Rococo-style pressed brass cartel clock, 8-day time and strike, 22", unmarked, $476. Credit: R. O. Schmitt Fine Arts.

French, ca. 1850, maker unknown, Rococo-style gilt bronze cartel clock, 20", 8-day time and strike, very good condition, $2,070

French, ca. 1880, maker unknown, Rococo-style gilt bronze cartel clock, 24", 8-day time and strike, very good condition, $1,035

French, ca. 1900, maker unknown, Rococo-style gilt bronze cartel clock, 22", 8-day time and strike, very good condition, $448

French, ca. 1900, maker unknown, Rococo-style pressed brass cartel clock, 22", 8-day time and strike, excellent condition (illustrated), $476

	LOW	MID	HIGH
French Metal-Cased Cartel Clocks (ca. 1750–1910)	$350–$700	$800–$1,500	$2,500–$3,500

FRENCH WOOD-CASED CARTEL CLOCKS were extremely popular in the last quarter of the nineteenth century and are rather rustic in style compared to their metal-cased brethren.

French, ca. 1885, maker unknown, carved oak cartel clock, 26", 8-day time and strike, good original condition, $990

French, ca. 1885, maker unknown, carved oak cartel clock, 24", 8-day time and strike, fair condition, $797

French, ca. 1890, walnut-cased cartel clock, 8-day time and strike, 29", unknown maker, $250.

French, ca. 1880, carved oak-cased cartel clock, 8-day time and strike, 33", unknown maker, $550. Credit: R. Schneider Collection.

French , ca. 1890, maker unknown, carved oak cartel clock, 25", 8-day time and strike, good original condition, $308

French, ca. 1890, maker unknown, carved oak cartel clock, 28", 8-day time and strike, very good original condition, $532

French, ca. 1890, maker unknown, carved oak cartel clock, 28", 8-day time and strike, very good original condition, $506

French, ca. 1890, maker unknown, carved oak cartel clock, 28", 8-day time and strike, excellent condition, $715

French, ca. 1900, maker unknown, carved oak cartel clock, 33", 8-day time and strike, very good original condition, $385

French, ca. 1850, maker unknown, carved walnut cartel clock, 31.5", 8-day time and strike, excellent condition, $1,870

French, ca. 1880, maker unknown, carved walnut cartel clock, 23", 8-day time and strike, good original condition, $247

French, ca. 1880, maker unknown, carved walnut cartel clock, 29", 8-day time and strike, very good original condition, $874

French, ca. 1890, maker unknown, carved walnut cartel clock, 27", 8-day time and strike, very good condition, movement replaced, $896

French, ca. 1890, maker unknown, carved walnut cartel clock, 29", 8-day time and strike, very good original condition, $616

French, ca. 1890, maker unknown, carved walnut cartel clock, 25", 8-day time and strike, very good original condition, $440

French, ca. 1890, maker unknown, carved walnut cartel clock, 26", 8-day time and strike, good original condition, $742

French, ca. 1890, maker unknown, carved walnut cartel clock, 24.5", 8-day time and strike, very good original condition, $1,100

French, ca. 1890, maker unknown, carved walnut cartel clock, 23.5", 8-day time and strike, good original condition, $385

French, ca. 1900, maker unknown, carved walnut cartel clock, 28", 8-day time and strike, good original condition, $467

	LOW	MID	HIGH
French Wood-Cased Cartel Clocks (ca. 1850–1900)	$200–$400	$500–$800	$1,000–$2,000

FRENCH GALLERY CLOCKS were never produced in great numbers. They appear in France during the last half of the nineteenth century. This style was far more abundantly produced in Germany, the United States, and England. For the most part, they were domestic, utilitarian timepieces. They can still be found in fair numbers, and their prices make them attractive to the collector.

French, ca. 1870, wood-cased gallery clock, 8-day time and strike, 15", unmarked, $192. Credit: R. O. Schmitt Fine Arts.

French, ca. 1900, brass-cased gallery clock, 8-day time only, 20", unmarked, $196. Credit: R. O. Schmitt Fine Arts.

French, ca. 1870, unmarked, round wood-cased gallery clock, 15", 8-day
time and strike, very good original condition (illustrated), $192

French, ca. 1880, unmarked, round porcelain-cased gallery clock, 16", 8-day
time and strike, very good condition, wrong hands, $550

French, ca. 1880, unmarked, round wood-cased gallery clock, 19", 8-day
time and strike, good condition, minor veneer chips, $137

French, ca. 1890, unmarked, round brass-cased gallery clock, 21", 8-day
time and strike, very good original condition, $165

French, ca. 1900, unmarked, round brass-cased gallery clock, 20", 8-day
time only, very good condition, replaced paper dial (illustrated),
$196

French, ca. 1900, unmarked, round wood-cased gallery clock, 14.5", 8-day
time and strike, fair condition, stripped case and wrong hands, $77

	LOW	MID	HIGH
French Gallery Clocks (ca. 1860–1910)	$75–$100	$150–$200	$250–$500

FRENCH MORBIER CLOCKS are sturdy iron-framed clocks that were produced in the northeastern area of France near Switzerland. In this region
of France, the Domestic or Gothic clocks of the sixteenth and seventeenth centuries had evolved into rugged clocks with a distinctive
upright rack in the striking mechanism. The strike repeats approximately two minutes after the hour. These movements have long pendulums with either verge (earlier pre-1850 movements) or anchor
escapements. They first appear as a distinct type of clock around 1750.
The vast majority of these clocks were treated as wall clocks and usually
sat on brackets. However, significant numbers were cased as tall-case
clocks (see Tall-Case Clocks).

The dials of Morbier wall clocks are most often porcelain and contain
the name of the owner or retailer. They are crested by or surrounded with
a decorative cast or pressed brass trim. It is these trims, along with their
equally decorative pendulums, that have made these clocks so popular
with decorators.

The name stems from the village of Morbier, where many of these
movements were made. They are also known as Morez or Comtoise
clocks. Since World War II, many of these clocks have been imported to
the United States. Their prices still place them in the realm of affordable
and collectible clocks. Beware of reproductions made in the 1970s and
1980s in eastern Europe.

French, ca. 1880, Morbier wall clock, 8-day time and strike, 21", unmarked, $500.

French, ca. 1880, with pendulum, 55", $500.

French, ca. 1830, maker unknown, Morbier or Comtoise clock, wall mounted, 60", 8-day time and strike with repeat, weight-driven, very good condition, $770

French, ca. 1840, maker unknown, Morbier or Comtoise clock, wall mounted, 55", 8-day time and strike with repeat and alarm, weight-driven, fair condition, $528

French, ca. 1840, maker unknown, Morbier or Comtoise clock, wall mounted, 58", 8-day time and strike with repeat, weight-driven, fair condition, lead-filled soup cans as weights, $440

French, ca. 1855, maker unknown, Morbier or Comtoise clock, wall mounted, 58", 8-day time and strike with repeat, weight-driven, good condition, $884

French, ca. 1860, maker unknown, Morbier or Comtoise clock, wall mounted, 57", 8-day time and strike with repeat, weight-driven, restored condition, $1,210

French, ca. 1860, maker unknown, Morbier or Comtoise clock, wall mounted, 53", 8-day time and strike with repeat, weight-driven, very good condition, $840

French, ca. 1860, maker unknown, Morbier or Comtoise clock, wall mounted, 57", 8-day time and strike with repeat, weight-driven, very good condition, $495

French, ca. 1860, maker unknown, Morbier or Comtoise clock, wall mounted, 52", 8-day time and strike with repeat, weight-driven, good condition, missing alarm mechanism, $600

French, ca. 1870, maker unknown, Morbier or Comtoise clock, wall mounted, 54", 8-day time and strike with repeat, weight-driven, fair condition, German weights, $467

French, ca. 1870, maker unknown, Morbier or Comtoise clock, wall mounted, 54", 8-day time and strike with repeat, weight-driven, fair condition, missing weights, $392

French, ca. 1875, maker unknown, Morbier or Comtoise clock, wall mounted, 54", 8-day time and strike with repeat, weight-driven, good condition, $784

French, ca. 1875, maker unknown, Morbier or Comtoise clock, wall mounted, 52", 8-day time and strike with repeat, weight-driven, as-found condition, $770

French, ca. 1875, maker unknown, Morbier or Comtoise clock, wall mounted, 53", 8-day time and strike with repeat, weight-driven, good condition, replaced dial and wall bracket, $440

French, ca. 1880, maker unknown, Morbier or Comtoise clock, wall mounted, 54", 8-day time and strike with repeat, weight-driven, very good condition, $770

French, ca. 1880, maker unknown, Morbier or Comtoise clock, wall mounted, 56", 8-day time and strike with repeat, weight-driven, very good condition, $412

French, ca. 1890, maker unknown, Morbier or Comtoise clock, wall mounted, 54", 8-day time and strike with repeat and date, weight-driven, excellent original condition, $672

French, ca. 1890, maker unknown, Morbier or Comtoise clock, wall mounted, 53", 8-day time and strike with repeat, weight-driven, very good condition, $476

French, ca. 1840, maker unknown, Morbier or Comtoise clock, wall mounted, original folding pendulum, 15", 8-day time and strike with repeat, weight-driven, good condition, reproduction weights, $728

	LOW	MID	HIGH
French Morbier Clocks (ca. 1750–1920)	$300–$450	$500–$700	$800–$1,200

FRENCH "PICTURE FRAME" CLOCK is the name given to domestic wall clocks whose frames were reminiscent of picture frames, many decorated with mother-of-pearl, which were common during the second half of the nineteenth century. These clocks were not considered sophisticated as their alternate name, "baker's clock," indicates. However, the movements are generally good, solid 8-day time and strike products of the nineteenth-century French clockmaking industry. Like the Morbier clocks, these unpretentious clocks have been imported in large numbers since World War II. Abundant and affordable, these clocks offer an opportunity to the beginning collector.

French, ca. 1890, Japy Frères, picture frame or baker's clock, brass inlay, 24", 8-day time and strike, good condition, $385

French, ca. 1870, maker unknown, picture frame or baker's clock, 19", 8-day time and strike, very good condition, walnut case, $467

French, ca. 1880, maker unknown, picture frame or baker's clock, 25", 8-day time and strike, very good condition, $224

French, ca. 1870, maker unknown, picture frame or baker's clock, mother-of-pearl inlay, 24", 8-day time and strike, fair condition, $336

French, ca. 1870, maker unknown, picture frame or baker's clock, mother-of-pearl inlay, 24", 8-day time and strike Morbier movement, good original condition, iron framed, $385

French, ca. 1880, picture frame clock, 8-day time and strike, 18", unmarked, $300.

French, ca. 1880, picture frame clock, 8-day time and strike, 19", unmarked, $588. Credit: R. O. Schmitt Fine Arts.

French, ca. 1870, maker unknown, picture frame or baker's clock, mother-of-pearl inlay, 25", 8-day time and strike, iron framed, Morbier movement, very good condition, $543

French, ca. 1875, maker unknown, picture frame or baker's clock, mother-of-pearl inlay, 24", 8-day time and strike, good condition, dial slightly warped, $504

French, ca. 1880, maker unknown, picture frame or baker's clock, mother-of-pearl inlay, 24", 8-day time and strike, good condition, clear glass missing from door, $302

French, ca. 1880, maker unknown, picture frame or baker's clock, mother-of-pearl inlay, 19", 8-day time and strike, iron framed, Morbier movement, very good condition (illustrated), $588

French, ca. 1885, maker unknown, picture frame or baker's clock, mother-of-pearl inlay, 25", 8-day time and strike, iron framed, Morbier movement, very good condition, $577

French, ca. 1890, maker unknown, picture frame or baker's clock, mother-of-pearl inlay, 26", 8-day time and strike, excellent condition, walnut case, $513

French, ca. 1875, maker unknown, picture frame or baker's clock, reverse painted glass dial, 28", 8-day time and strike, iron framed, Morez movement, excellent condition, $495

French, ca. 1890, maker unknown, picture frame or baker's clock, reverse painted glass dial, 24", 8-day time and strike, poor condition, water damage, $156

	LOW	MID	HIGH
French Picture Frame Clocks (ca. 1860–1900)	$150–$250	$300–$450	$500–$650

FRENCH REGULATOR CLOCKS are rare forms within the scope of French clocks. There are basically two types; the true "Regulator" (see Glossary) and those clocks that were produced to take advantage of the popularity of the mass-produced German pseudo-Viennese "Regulators." Notice the similarity between the Japy Frères "Regulator" below and the German "Regulators" found later in this section.

French, ca. 1880, Japy Frères, wall regulator, 37", 8-day time and strike, good condition, walnut case with missing trim (illustrated), $448

French, ca. 1880, wall regulator, 8-day time and strike, 37", Japy Frères, $448. Credit: R. O. Schmitt Fine Arts.

French, ca. 1900, astronomical wall regulator, 15-day time only, skeleton dial, 65", unmarked, $6,060. Credit: R. O. Schmitt Fine Arts.

French, ca. 1870, maker unknown, wall regulator, 61", 8-day pinwheel movement, excellent condition, mahogany case, $2,128

French, ca. 1880, Japy Frères, wall regulator, 37", 8-day time and strike, excellent condition, walnut case, $715

French, ca. 1900, maker unknown, astronomical wall regulator, 65", 15-day time only, skeleton dial, very good restored condition (illustrated), $6,050

	LOW	MID	HIGH
French Regulator Clocks	$500–$600	$700–$900	$1,500–$2,500

FRENCH TIME AND BAROMETER CLOCKS are an interesting group of clocks that appeared in the closing decades of the nineteenth century. They were typically carved wood cartel cases (see French wood-cased cartel clocks) that housed 8-day time and strike movements plus an aneroid barometer and a thermometer.

French, ca. 1890, maker unknown, carved wood cartel case containing a clock, barometer, and thermometer, 44", 8-day time and strike, very good condition, walnut case, $1,540

French, ca. 1900, time, barometer, and thermometer clock, 8-day time and strike, 46", unmarked, $616. Credit: R. O. Schmitt Fine Arts.

French, ca. 1890, time, barometer, and thermometer clock, 8-day time and strike, 36", unmarked, $471. Credit: R. O. Schmitt Fine Arts.

French, ca. 1890, maker unknown, carved wood cartel case containing a clock, barometer, and thermometer, 36", 8-day time and strike, good condition, walnut case, piece of backboard replaced (illustrated), $471

French, ca. 1890, maker unknown, carved wood cartel case containing a clock, barometer, and thermometer, 38", 8-day time and strike, good condition, walnut case, $880

French, ca. 1890, maker unknown, carved wood cartel case containing a clock, barometer, and thermometer, 39.5", 8-day time and strike, excellent condition, walnut case, $1,092

French, ca. 1890, maker unknown, carved wood cartel case containing a clock, barometer, and thermometer, 36", 8-day time and strike, good condition, split in the door, $247

French, ca. 1890, maker unknown, carved wood cartel case containing a clock, barometer, and thermometer, 34", 8-day time and strike, fair condition, some damage to the barometer, $220

French, ca. 1890, maker unknown, carved wood cartel case containing a clock, barometer, and thermometer, 38", 8-day time and strike, fair condition, replaced movement and altered dial, $412

French, ca. 1900, maker unknown, carved wood cartel case containing a clock, barometer, and thermometer, 46", 8-day time and strike, good condition, massive walnut case (illustrated), $616

French, ca. 1890, maker unknown, cast-iron cartel case containing a clock, barometer, and thermometer, 25", 8-day time and strike, very good condition, $440

	LOW	MID	HIGH
French Time and Barometer Clocks (ca. 1885–1905)	$200–$400	$500–$700	$800–$1,500

FRENCH WESTMINSTER CHIME CLOCKS were produced from 1900 into the 1930s. They were marketed to compete with German box clocks, which were entering France in large numbers after World War I. French Westminster chime clocks were produced for only a short time, yet they are unique, very affordable, and just beginning to be collected.

French, ca. 1905, Becker, Gustav, Louis XVI–style Westminster, chime clock, 33", 8-day time, chime, and strike German movement, very good condition, walnut case, $495

French, ca. 1925, maker unknown, Art Deco Westminster chime clock, 25", 8-day time, chime, and strike, good condition, oak case with replaced dial (illustrated), $110

French, ca. 1930, Westminster chime wall clock, 8-day time, chime, and strike, 23", unmarked, $220. Credit: R. O. Schmitt Fine Arts.

French, ca. 1925, Westminster chime wall clock, 8-day time, chime, and strike, 25", unmarked, $110. Credit: R. O. Schmitt Fine Arts.

French, ca. 1925, maker unknown, Art Deco Westminster chime clock, 27",
8-day time, chime, and strike, good original condition, oak case, $192

French, ca. 1930, maker unknown, Art Deco Westminster chime clock,
23", 8-day time, chime, and strike, good condition, walnut case (illustrated), $220

French, ca. 1935, maker unknown, Art Deco Westminster chime clock, 23",
8-day time, chime, and strike, excellent condition, walnut case, $159

French, ca. 1935, maker unknown, Art Deco Westminster chime clock, 23",
8-day time, chime, and strike, fair condition, walnut case with beveled
leaded glass in door, $201

French, ca. 1900, maker unknown, box clock–style Westminster chime
clock, 32", 8-day time, chime, and strike, Morbier movement, good condition, walnut case, $605

French, ca. 1935, Vedette, Art Deco Westminster chime clock, 24", 8-day
time, chime, and strike, good condition, walnut case, $121

	LOW	MID	HIGH
French Westminster Chime Clocks (ca. 1905–39)	$100–$200	$300–$400	$500–$600

Austrian Wall Clocks

Until the end of World War I in 1918, Austria was the core of a widespread and multicultural empire. Austria straddles much of the Alps and
has historic ties to the north, west, east, and south, so there is little wonder
that these influences are reflected in much of Austrian life. Such was the
case in Austrian clockmaking. The German alpine clockmaking methods
and forms can be found in Austrian Picture Frame clocks, while French
style and movement design can be discerned in Austrian Portico clocks,
and the world-famous Vienna Regulators benefited from both the French
and German traditions. However, these clocks did not slavishly follow
French and German models, but developed a uniqueness as demonstrated by their distinctly Austrian 2-day movements.

Austrian clocks have always demonstrated the highest level of craftsmanship and use of materials. They usually fetch higher prices at auction
then similar clocks from neighboring France and Germany.

AUSTRIAN PICTURE FRAME CLOCKS are not unique to Austria as they were
also produced in France and Germany, but they are considered the most

desirable to the collector. Part of the long tradition of Austrian clockmaking, these clocks have often been overshadowed by the more famous Vienna Regulators. Two types exist, the 30-hour weight-driven clocks that followed the manufacturing traditions of the Black Forest region of Germany, and the 2-day spring-driven clocks that followed the traditions of the Viennese makers. Austria was one of the few areas in Europe that regularly produced 2-day movements well into the nineteenth century when others had standardized their production for 30-hour and 8-day movements.

Austrian, ca. 1820, Bauer, J. G., grand sonnerie square picture frame clock, 19", 2-day time and strike, very good original condition (illustrated), $1,400

Austria, ca. 1820, maker unknown, animated (woodcutter) square picture frame clock, 20", 2-day time and strike, very good original condition, $2,240

Austria, ca. 1810, maker unknown, grand sonnerie square picture frame clock, 21.5", 2-day time and strike, as-found fair condition, missing outer door, $448

Austria, ca. 1860, maker unknown, oval picture frame clock, 11", 30-hour time and strike, weight-driven, excellent condition (illustrated), $504

Austrian, ca. 1860, picture frame clock, 30-hour time and strike, 11", unmarked, $504. Credit: Price4antiques.com.

Austrian, ca. 1820, grand sonnerie picture frame clock, 2-day time and strike, 19", signed J. G. Bauer, $1,400. Credit: R. O. Schmitt Fine Arts.

Austria, ca. 1795, maker unknown, square picture frame clock, 16", 2-day time and strike, fair condition, front glass cracked, $550

	LOW	MID	HIGH
Austrian Picture Frame Clocks (ca. 1790–1880)	$400–$500	$700–$900	$1,000–$3,000

AUSTRIAN REGULATOR CLOCKS are the basis upon which the fame of Austria's clockmaking industry rests. At their best, there were no finer movements produced in Europe, and at their worst, they were well-made, reliable timepieces. This type of clock would be imitated in Germany, France, Switzerland, and the United States. Never mass-produced in Austria, as they were in Germany and the United States, the name "Vienna Regulator" would be usurped and used to sell inferior foreign clocks.

Below is a series of Austrian regulators illustrating the major case styles.

Austrian, ca. 1880, maker unknown, Alt Deutsch–(old German–) style wall regulator, 52", 8-day grand sonnerie, weight-driven, very good condition with replaced top, $1,120

Austrian, ca. 1900, Berrmayr, Carl, Baroque-style wall regulator, 50", 8-day grand sonnerie, weight-driven, very good original condition, walnut case, $2,970

Austrian, ca. 1890, maker unknown, Baroque-style wall regulator, 48", 8-day grand sonnerie, weight-driven, very good restored condition, $3,300

Austrian, ca. 1905, maker unknown, Baroque-style wall regulator, 51", 8-day grand sonnerie, weight-driven, very good original condition case, $4,125

Austrian, ca. 1850, Brutman, F. and Sohn, Biedermeier mini–style wall regulator, 29", 8-day time only, weight-driven, excellent restored condition (illustrated), $1,045

Austrian, ca. 1835, maker unknown, Biedermeier-style wall regulator, 39", 8-day time only, weight-driven, very good condition case, $6,600

Austrian, ca. 1840, maker unknown, Biedermeier-style wall regulator, 34.5", 8-day time only, weight-driven, very good restored condition, $3,080

Austrian, ca. 1845, maker unknown, Biedermeier-style wall regulator, 39", 2-day grand sonnerie, weight-driven, fair condition, cresting missing (illustrated), $1,960

Laterndluhr regulator, ca. 1830, 46.5".
Credit: R. O. Schmitt Fine Arts.

Biedermeier regulator, ca. 1845, 39".
Credit: R. O. Schmitt Fine Arts.

Mini regulator, ca. 1850, 29". Credit:
R. O. Schmitt Fine Arts.

Serpentine regulator, ca. 1860, 33.5".
Credit: R. O. Schmitt Fine Arts.

Mini regulator, ca. 1880, 34". Credit: R. O. Schmitt Fine Arts.

Extra large shingle-style top, ca. 1880, 61". Credit: R. O. Schmitt Fine Arts.

Arch top regulator, ca. 1900, 42". Credit: R. O. Schmitt Fine Arts.

Art Deco regulator, ca. 1920, 40". Credit: R. O. Schmitt Fine Arts.

Austrian, ca. 1850, maker unknown, Biedermeier-style wall regulator, 33.5", 8-day time only, weight-driven, very good restored condition, $1,650

Austrian, ca. 1910, Bauer, W., box clock–style wall regulator, 26", 8-day time only, weight-driven, poor condition, oak case, replacement movement, $128

Austrian, ca. 1920, Herz, M., box clock–style wall regulator, 41", 8-day grand sonnerie, weight-driven, as-found fair condition, missing gong and hammers, $504

Austrian, ca. 1860, Lechner, dwarf serpentine-style wall regulator, 37", 8-day time only, weight-driven, excellent restored condition, $1,155

Austrian, ca. 1860, maker unknown, dwarf serpentine-style wall regulator, 31", 8-day time only, weight-driven, very good condition, walnut case, missing cresting, $840

Austrian, ca. 1860, maker unknown, dwarf-serpentine style wall regulator, 39", 8-day grand sonnerie, weight-driven, very good condition, restored case, $3,190

Austrian, ca. 1920, Baumann, F. and Cie, Jugendstil-style wall regulator, 29", 8-day time only, weight-driven, excellent condition, mahogany case, $660

Austrian, ca. 1920, Gebrüder Resch, Jugendstil-style wall regulator, 34.5", 8-day time and strike, weight-driven, excellent condition, walnut case, $357

Austrian, ca. 1915, Meindl, Mathias, Jugendstil-style wall regulator, 40", 8-day time and strike, weight-driven, good condition, rosewood case with beveled glass, $2,205

Austrian, ca. 1830, maker unknown, Laterndluhr (lantern clock) wall regulator, 46.5", 3-month time and seconds, weight-driven, good refinished condition (illustrated), $13,865

Austrian, ca. 1880, maker unknown, plain architectural-style mini wall regulator, 32", 8-day time only, weight-driven, poor condition, many replacements (illustrated), $470

Austrian, ca. 1865, maker unknown, plain architectural-style wall regulator, 39", 8-day time and strike, weight-driven, good original condition, some damage to the hands, $588

Austrian, ca. 1900, maker unknown, plain architectural-style wall regulator, 42", 8-day time and strike, weight-driven, fair condition, oak case, mismatched weights (illustrated), $560

Austrian, ca. 1900, maker unknown, plain architectural-style wall regulator, 43.5", 8-day time only, weight-driven, very good original condition, replaced finials, $840

Austrian, ca. 1860, Höfler, Hermann, serpentine-style wall regulator, 40", 8-day time only, weight-driven, very good restored condition, $1,430

Austrian, ca. 1860, Kirch, Josef, serpentine-style wall regulator, 31.5", 3-month time and seconds, weight-driven, good original condition, $6,160

Austrian, ca. 1860, maker unknown, serpentine-style wall regulator, 33.5", 8-day time only, weight-driven, very good restored condition (illustrated), $1,210

Austrian, ca. 1860, maker unknown, serpentine-style wall regulator, 48.5", 8-day grand sonnerie, weight-driven, very good restored condition, $2,640

Austrian, ca. 1855, Blaschko, W., Vienna-style wall regulator, 58", 30-day time and seconds, weight-driven, excellent restored condition, $1,760

Austrian, ca. 1875, Gebrüder Resch, Vienna-style wall regulator, 55", 8-day grand sonnerie, weight-driven, good condition, walnut case, replaced cresting, $1,120

Austrian, ca. 1885, Gebrüder Resch, Vienna-style wall regulator, 39", 8-day time and strike, weight-driven, excellent original condition, $1,375

Austrian, ca. 1880, Suchy, Carl and Söhne, Vienna-style wall regulator, 38", 8-day time only, weight-driven, excellent restored condition, $1,650

Austrian, ca. 1865, maker unknown, Vienna-style wall regulator, 54", 8-day grand sonnerie, weight-driven, fair condition, walnut case, $1,210

Austrian, ca. 1870, maker unknown, Vienna-style wall regulator, 38", 8-day time only, weight-driven, good condition case, $1,456

Austrian, ca. 1880, maker unknown, Vienna-style wall regulator, 45", 8-day time and strike, weight-driven, fair condition, damage to the cresting, missing bottom finial, $672

Austrian, ca. 1880, maker unknown, Vienna-style wall regulator, 45", 8-day time and strike, weight-driven, fair condition, mahogany case, $690

Austrian, ca. 1880, maker unknown, Vienna-style wall regulator, 48", 8-day time and strike, weight-driven, good original condition, walnut case, $504

Austrian, ca. 1880, maker unknown, Vienna-style wall regulator, 53", 8-day time and strike, weight-driven, very good restored condition, $952

Austrian, ca. 1885, maker unknown, Vienna-style wall regulator, 37", 8-day time and strike, weight-driven, very good condition, restored case, $2,200

Austrian, ca. 1890, maker unknown, Vienna-style wall regulator, 50.5", 8-day time and strike, weight-driven, poor condition, walnut case, weights missing, $212

Austrian, ca. 1880, maker unknown, Vienna-style wall regulator, 61", 8-day time and strike, weight-driven, very good original condition (illustrated), $2,240

Austrian, ca. 1895, maker unknown, Vienna-style wall regulator, 69", 8-day grand sonnerie, weight-driven, excellent original condition, $5,600

	LOW	MID	HIGH
Austrian Regulator Clocks (ca. 1820–1930)	$500–$1,000	$2,000–$4,000	$6,000–$8,000+

German Wall Clocks

German wall clocks are the products and descendants of the clockmaking industry of southwestern Germany, the region we know as the Black Forest. Here clockmaking started as a folk industry with wood-cased, wood plate, and metal-geared wall clocks produced at home and sold to clock peddlers. By the first half of the nineteenth century, this home industry was producing parts for clocks that were now being assembled by others and sold throughout Europe.

As America's mass-produced clocks began to displace these inexpensive German products, the Black Forest clockmakers began to combine, cooperate, and merge. The new industry was increasingly organized like the American model, demonstrated by the number of clocks that were American in style and form as well as the number of companies that used "American" in their titles.

By the late 1870s, aided by German political unification in 1871, the clockmaking industry was coalescing into four or five major companies. Besides producing French- and American-style clocks, these companies were now producing uniquely German clocks.

By the 1890s, German clocks were beginning to displace American clocks in some European markets. They had penetrated the highly protected French market and were being exported in large numbers to America. This expansion and prosperity would continue until World War I.

The clock styles included here represent those that collectors most commonly encounter. These clocks are well-constructed and reliable.

Their reputation has continued to this day, although contemporary German clocks don't always deserve it.

GERMAN BALCONY CLOCKS appeared at the end of the nineteenth century and reflect the industrial prosperity and, some say, excesses of, German society under Kaiser Wilhelm II. These clocks may not appeal to every collector, as they appear massive hanging on the wall. At the bottom of each of these clocks is the balcony from which these clocks take their name.

Germany, 1890, Lenzkirch, balcony-style oak wall clock, 32", 8-day time and strike on wire gong, excellent condition, oak case with extensive bronze trim (illustrated), $2,860

Germany, 1890, Lenzkirch, balcony-style oak wall clock, 37", 8-day time and strike on wire gong, good condition, oak case with one piece of bronze trim missing (illustrated), $3,850

Germany, 1890, maker unknown, balcony-style oak wall clock, 38", 8-day time and strike on wire gong, excellent condition, oak case with bronze trim, $1,848

German, ca. 1890, balcony wall clock, 8-day time and strike on wire gong, 32", Lenzkirch, $2,860. Credit: R. O. Schmitt Fine Arts.

German, ca. 1890, balcony wall clock, 8-day time and strike on wire gong, 37", Lenzkirch, $3,850. Credit: R. O. Schmitt Fine Arts.

	LOW	MID	HIGH
German Balcony Clocks (ca. 1885–1910)	$1,000	$2,000–$3,000	$4,000+

GERMAN BLACK FOREST CARVED (CUCKOO) CLOCKS appeared in the late eighteenth and early nineteenth centuries. Animation and music were soon added to the time and strike capabilities of these clocks, and most collectors today refer to them as "cuckoo clocks."

The movements in these clocks are not the highest examples of German clockmaking, but are always fascinating. Their major attraction has been the beauty of the case carvings. They reached their peak in the last quarter of the nineteenth century. Twentieth-century production of these clocks has concentrated on increasing production, lowering costs, and developing a garish souvenir. These comments notwithstanding, cuckoo clocks remain highly collectible, and prices are rising steadily.

Germany, ca. 1920, maker unknown, Black Forest cuckoo clock, cuckoo and quail carvings, 25", 30-hour time, cuckoo, and strike, fair condition, one mismatched weight (illustrated), $412

German, ca. 1920, Black Forest cuckoo clock, 30-hour time, cuckoo, and strike, 25", maker unknown, $412. Credit: R. O. Schmitt Fine Arts.

German, ca. 1890, Black Forest cuckoo clock, 30-hour time, cuckoo, and strike, 27", maker unknown, $600–$800. Credit: NAWCC Museum.

German, ca. 1885, Black Forest
cuckoo clock, 30-hour time,
cuckoo, and strike, 47",
unknown maker, $3,584.
Credit: Prices4antiques.com.

Germany, ca. 1885, maker unknown, Black Forest cuckoo clock, deer and
game carvings, 47", 30-hour time, cuckoo, and strike, excellent condition, $4,760

Germany, ca. 1910, maker unknown, Black Forest cuckoo clock, deer and
game carvings, 25", 30-hour time, cuckoo, and strike, very good condition, $616

Germany, ca. 1885, maker unknown, Black Forest cuckoo clock depicting
eagle attacking antelope, 47", 8-day time, cuckoo, and strike, excellent
condition (illustrated), $3,584

Germany, ca. 1890, maker unknown, Black Forest cuckoo clock depicting
eagle attacking antelope, 47", 8-day time, cuckoo, and strike, very good
condition, $3,584

Germany, ca. 1910, maker unknown, Black Forest cuckoo clock, eagle crest
and stag with dog, 37", 8-day time, cuckoo, and strike, excellent condition, $1,176

	LOW	MID	HIGH
German Black Forest Carved Clocks (ca. 1800–present)	$100–$200	$400–$600	$1,000+

GERMAN BOX CLOCKS were the clocks for the middle class in the catalogs
of the first quarter of the twentieth century. This was the moneymaking
clock of the German industry. Modernistic, handsome, and inexpensive to
produce, they were manufactured by the thousands. All the major companies made them, including Junghans, Gustav Becker, and Lenzkirch.

Today they can be found in such far-flung locations as France, Germany, England, Canada, Japan, and America. They are good, solid, reliable clocks striking on steel rods. Abundant and affordable, these clocks often start the novice's collection.

Germany, ca. 1910, Hensinger, Karl, box clock with beveled glass in door, 30", 8-day time and strike on rods, very good condition, $225

Germany, ca. 1910, maker unknown, box clock with beveled glass in door, 32", 8-day time and strike, wire gong, excellent condition, mahogany case, $350

Germany, ca. 1920, maker unknown, box clock with beveled glass in door, 30", 8-day time and strike on rods, good condition, refinished walnut case, $110

Germany, ca. 1925, Becker, Gustav, box clock with ebonized oak case and beveled glass in door, 31", 8-day time and strike, bim-bam on rods, very good condition, one pane of glass cracked (illustrated), $300

Germany, ca. 1920, Japy Frères, Westminster chime box clock with inlay and beveled glass in door, 32", 8-day time, chime, and strike on rods, excellent condition, mahogany case (illustrated), $650

Germany, ca. 1920, maker unknown, Westminster chime box clock with inlay and beveled glass in door, 31", 8-day time, chime, and strike on rods, very good original condition, oak case, $644

German, ca. 1925, box clock, 8-day time and strike on rods, 31", signed Gustav Becker, $300.

German, ca. 1920, box clock, 8-day time, chimes, and strike on rods, 32", signed Japy Freres, $650.

German, ca. 1925, box clock,
8-day time and strike, 32",
unsigned, $350.

Germany, ca. 1920, maker unknown, Westminster chime box clock with
    inlay and beveled glass in door, 29.5", 8-day time, chime, and strike on
    rods, very good original condition, oak case, $532

	LOW	MID	HIGH
German Box Clocks (ca. 1910–39)	$100–$200	$300–$400	$500–$600

GERMAN OPEN-WELL CLOCKS evolved from the provincial Dutch clocks of
the early nineteenth century. These clocks have pendulums that hang in
the open, below the boxed movement and dial. This style of clock can be
found in France, England, and America. It became quite popular in Germany and remained in catalogs until the 1930s.

Germany, ca. 1906, Junghans, Berlin-style open-well clock with Alt
    Deutsch aspects, 41", 8-day time and strike on gong, very good condi-
    tion, walnut case, $687

Germany, ca. 1910, Junghans, Berlin-style open-well clock with Alt
    Deutsch aspects, 33", 8-day time and strike on gong, good condition,
    oak case, replaced eagle on crest, $412

Germany, ca. 1880, maker unknown, Berlin-style open-well clock with Alt
    Deutsch aspects, 44", 8-day time and strike on gong, excellent condi-
    tion, walnut case, $1,017

German, ca. 1906, open-well clock, 8-day time and strike on wire gong, 41", signed Junghans, $687. Credit: R. O. Schmitt Fine Arts.

German, ca. 1930, open-well clock, 8-day time, chime, and strike on wire gong, 38.5", maker unknown, $504. Credit: R. O. Schmitt Fine Arts.

Germany, ca. 1925, maker unknown, Berlin-style open-well clock with Art Nouveau aspects, 32.5", 8-day time and strike on gong, very good condition, case with retouched dial numerals, $330

Germany, ca. 1880, Lenzkirch, miniature open-well clock in Baroque style, 16", 8-day time only, excellent original condition, walnut case, extensive bronze trim, $1,485

Germany, ca. 1930, maker unknown, Westminster chime open-well clock in Art Deco style, 34.5", 8-day time, chime, and strike on rods, good condition, oak case (illustrated), $504

	LOW	MID	HIGH
German Open Well Clocks (ca. 1880–1930)	$300–$400	$500–$600	$800–$1,000+

GERMAN REGULATOR CLOCKS patterned after the famous Vienna Regulators appear as early as the 1870s, although they become even more popular during the 1880s and 1890s. As in America, there were "Regulators" and "regulators." Germany produced top-of-the-line true regulators as well as bottom-of-the-line clocks called regulators that lacked true regulator movements. The tremendous success of these clocks virtually

German, ca. 1880, regulator wall clock, 8-day time only, 44", maker unknown, $840. Credit: R. O. Schmitt Fine Arts.

German, ca. 1900, regulator wall clock, 8-day time and strike, 34", maker unknown, $464. Credit: R. O. Schmitt Fine Arts.

destroyed the Austrian clock industry and forced American makers to introduce their own line of "Vienna Regulators."

Germany, ca. 1878, Becker, Gustav, Vienna-style regulator wall clock in figure eight case, 36", 8-day time and seconds, weight-driven, excellent original condition, $1,650

Germany, ca. 1890, Becker, Gustav, grand sonnerie regulator wall clock, 49", 8-day time and strike on steel rods, weight-driven, excellent original condition, $3,360

Germany, ca. 1890, Becker, Gustav, regulator wall clock in the Alt Deutsch style, 35", 8-day time and strike on gong, good condition, walnut case, $145

Germany, ca. 1890, Becker, Gustav, Vienna-style regulator wall clock, 52", 8-day time and strike, weight-driven, good condition, $716

Germany, ca. 1895, Becker, Gustav, regulator wall clock in the Alt Deutsch style, 50", 8-day time and strike on gong, weight-driven, very good condition, walnut case, $825

Germany, ca. 1910, Becker, Gustav, regulator wall clock in the Jugendstil style, 35.5", 8-day time and strike on steel rods, weight-driven, good condition, walnut case, one piece of molding missing, $504

German, ca. 1920, 8-day time and strike, 51", signed Freiburg Clock Co., $687. Credit: R. O. Schmitt Fine Arts.

German, ca. 1925, 8-day time and strike, 27", Junghans, $157.

Germany, ca. 1880, Bob, Lorenz, Black Forest regulator wall clock, 28", 8-day time and strike on gong, good condition case, some missing trim, $440

Germany, ca. 1900, E-P Leipzig, Vienna-style regulator wall clock, 46", 8-day time and strike on gong, very good original condition, $1,008

Germany, ca. 1920, Freiburg United Clock Factories, regulator wall clock in the Alt Deutsch style, 51", 8-day time, seconds, and strike, weight-driven, good condition, original finish (illustrated), $687

Germany, ca. 1890, Junghans, regulator wall clock in the serpentine style, 34", 8-day time and strike, good condition, walnut case, $385

Germany, ca. 1910, Junghans, regulator wall clock in the Jugendstil style, 32.5", 8-day time and strike on steel rod, very good original condition, cut glass in the door, $784

Germany, ca. 1925, Junghans, regulator wall clock in the Alt Deutsch style, 27", 8-day time and strike, very good original condition (illustrated), $157

Germany, ca. 1900, Kienzle, simple architectural style regulator wall clock, 32", 8-day time and strike on gong, very good condition, oak case, $448

Germany, ca. 1880, Lenzkirch, Vienna-style regulator wall clock, 32", 8-day time and strike on gong, good condition, case with replaced top and bottom trim, $308

Germany, ca. 1890, Mayer, miniature brass facade regulator wall clock, 16.5", 8-day time only, very good original condition, $2,016

Germany, ca. 1880, maker unknown, Vienna-style regulator wall clock, 44", 8-day time only, weight-driven, good condition, walnut case (illustrated), $840

Germany, ca. 1890, maker unknown, regulator wall clock in the Alt Deutsch style, 34", 8-day time and strike on bell, good condition, walnut case with one missing finial (illustrated), $464

Germany, ca. 1900, maker unknown, regulator wall clock in the Alt Deutsch style, 44", 8-day time and strike on gong, good condition, walnut case, $448

Germany, ca. 1900, maker unknown, regulator wall clock in the Alt Deutsch style, 36", 8-day time only, very good condition, walnut case, two finials replaced, $504

	LOW	MID	HIGH
German Regulator Clocks (ca. 1875–1930)	$150–$300	$500–$800	$1,000–$2,000+

GERMAN ROUND DIAL CLOCKS appeared around the middle of the nineteenth century and developed from the Black Forest clockmaking tradition. The great majority have 30-hour time and strike weight-driven movements. These clocks were exported far and wide. They are interesting clocks that remain affordable to the novice collector.

Germany, ca. 1890, maker unknown, Black Forest octagon dial wall clock, 12", 30-hour time and strike, wood plate/brass gears, weight-driven, good condition, missing weights, $247

Germany, ca. 1880, Ganter, A., Black Forest round dial wall clock, 12", 30-hour time and strike, wood plate/brass gears, weight-driven, fair condition, homemade replacement pendulum (illustrated), $247

Germany, ca. 1890, maker unknown, Black Forest round dial wall clock, 12", 30-hour time and strike, wood plate/brass gears, weight-driven, good condition, missing weights (illustrated), $250

Germany, ca. 1910, Hamburg American Clock Co., gallery clock, 16.5", 8-day time and strike, good condition, oak case, $341

Germany, ca. 1870, Lenzkirch, gallery clock, made for the French market, 12", 8-day time and strike, good condition, $420

German, ca. 1880, round dial wall clock, 30-hour time and strike, 12", signed A. Ganter, $247. Credit: R. O. Schmitt Fine Arts.

German, ca. 1890, round dial wall clock, 30-hour time and strike, 12", unknown maker, $250.

	LOW	MID	HIGH
German Round Dial Clocks (ca. 1850–1920)	$150–$200	$300	$400

Swiss Wall Clocks

Swiss clocks followed the patterns and forms of Switzerland's neighbors France, Germany, and Austria. Swiss wall clock prices mirror that of their neighbors.

Switzerland, ca. 1910, Blanc, Henri, Swiss Graham escapement, quarter strike wall regulator clock, 42", 8-day time and strike on gongs, fair condition, walnut case, both gongs broken (illustrated), $495

Switzerland, ca. 1905, Japy Frères, Swiss wall regulator in Alt Deutsch–style case, 47", 8-day time and strike, good condition, walnut case, finial damage, $330

Switzerland, ca. 1905, Japy Frères, Swiss wall regulator in Alt Deutsch–style case, 39", 8-day time and strike on gong, good condition, walnut case, replaced cresting, $752

Swiss, ca. 1910, wall regulator, 8-day time and strike (on the quarters), 42", signed Henri Blanc, $495. Credit: R. O. Schmitt Fine Arts.

Switzerland, ca. 1870, maker unknown, Swiss picture clock with music box, 28" by 23", 8-day time and strike, starts music box after striking, very good condition, $3,920

Switzerland, ca. 1850, maker unknown, Swiss pinwheel wall regulator clock , 58", 8-day time and second, weight-driven, good condition, mahogany case, beveled glass door, $1,760

CHAPTER 5

Shelf Clocks

Shelf clocks are designed to sit upon a surface other than the floor. They first appeared in the form of the domestic chamber or Gothic clock during the fourteenth and fifteenth centuries. With the development of the pendulum, anchor escapement, and reliable spring steel, the shelf clock's movement became even more compact. Compact accurate movements allowed shelf clocks to evolve into the most numerous and varied forms ever produced.

To aid in identification, these clocks are divided by country of origin and style. The collector will easily find most of these clocks, and it is hard to imagine a collection beginning with any other type of clock.

American Shelf Clocks

American shelf clocks have existed since the eighteenth century, when bracket clocks in the English style were first produced in the colonies. Not long after the American Revolution, New England clockmakers such as the Willards began to produce new styles known today as Massachusetts shelf clocks (1780–1830).

The real explosion in shelf clocks began when Eli Terry successfully introduced mass production in the first quarter of the nineteenth century. Price reductions from factory production made the shelf clock affordable to all. Development of cheap, reliable spring steel and rolled brass by midcentury created an industry that would dominate the world's markets by 1900.

Thousands of these shelf clocks are running today and provide collection opportunities for both novice and advanced collectors. I have tried to include all those examples that the collector can expect to find offered for sale.

Arts and Crafts– or Mission-style clocks, ca. 1900–29
Beehive clocks, ca. 1840–80

German, nineteenth-century mantel clock. Credit: NAWCC TIMEXPO 2002.

Black mantel clocks, ca. 1875–1910
Calendar clocks, ca. 1850–90
China and porcelain clocks, 1895–1915
Column and cornice clocks, ca. 1838–80
Column and splat clocks, ca. 1826–38
Cottage clocks, ca. 1840–1914

NAWCC TIMEXPO 2002.

NAWCC TIMEXPO 2002.

Crystal regulator clocks, ca. 1885–1920
Double- and triple-decker clocks, ca. 1830–50
Figural clocks, ca. 1890–1914
Hollow-column clocks, ca. 1840–49
Iron-front clocks, ca. 1845–70
Late mahogany clocks, ca. 1900–1920
Massachusetts shelf clocks, ca. 1780–1830
Novelty clocks, ca. 1840–present

American nineteenth- and twentieth-century mantel clocks

English, ca. 1860 skeleton clock. Credit: A. Zilberberg Collection.

French, ca. 1880 table clock. Credit: A. Zilberberg Collection.

Ogee or OG clocks, ca. 1838–1914
Pillar and scroll clocks, ca. 1818–35
Roundside clocks, ca. 1838–40 and 1860s
Steeple clocks, ca. 1840–1940
Tambour clocks, ca. 1915–50
Terry patent box clock, ca. 1816
Transition clocks, ca. 1830–40

French, ca. 1880 mantel clock. Credit: A. Zilberberg Collection.

Walnut and oak gingerbread clocks, ca. 1875–1910
Walnut clocks, ca. 1865–95

ARTS AND CRAFTS- OR MISSION-STYLE MANTEL CLOCKS grew from the popularity of the late-nineteenth-century English Arts and Crafts movement, whose craftsmen favored the use of oak and handmade hardware in their furniture. This English style crossed the Atlantic and established itself in America, where it was known both as Arts and Crafts and Mission style. America's clock industry produced clocks and cases that complemented this new furniture.

Although it is still available at reasonable prices, the rising value of Mission furniture is forcing Mission clock prices ever higher. Most desirable among these mantel clocks are those which strike upon a series of nested bells.

American, ca. 1915, Gilbert, William L., oak Arts and Crafts (Mission) mantel clock, 18.5", 8-day time and strike, fair condition, $140

American, ca. 1917, Gilbert, William L., oak Arts and Crafts (Mission) mantel clock, "SANTA ROSA" model, 19", 8-day time and strike, very good condition, $165

American, ca. 1910, 19", New Haven Clock Co., $470.
Credit: Prices4Antiques.com.

American, ca. 1905, 21.75", New Haven Clock Co., $373.
Credit: Prices4Antiques.com.

American, ca. 1915, New Haven Clock Co., oak Arts and Crafts (Mission) mantel clock, 19", 8-day time and strike, good refinished condition (illustrated), $470

American, ca. 1920, New Haven Clock Co., oak Japanese-style Arts and Crafts (Mission) mantel clock, 21.75", 8-day time and strike, good original condition (illustrated), $373

American, ca. 1920, Oscar Onken Co., oak Arts and Crafts (Mission) mantel clock, 20", 8-day time and strike, good condition, $275

	LOW	MID	HIGH
Arts and Crafts (Mission) Mantel Clocks (ca. 1900–29)	$100–$200	$300–$500	$600–$1,000

BEEHIVE SHELF CLOCKS derive their name from the similarity between their cases and the straw beehives that dotted the mid-nineteenth-century rustic landscape. They can also be called Gothic arch or lancet case clocks. Beehive clocks appeared in 1841 and remained in production until the early 1900s.

These were America's first mass-produced clocks powered by coil springs. Coil springs allowed production of smaller shelf clocks and lessened demand for weight-driven clocks.

The beehive case was introduced by Brewster and Ingraham in 1841 and, being unprotected by patent, was quickly copied by other makers. Many of these clocks remain on the market, and their reasonable prices make them very collectible. The earliest examples have brass coil springs and command high prices.

American, ca. 1860, Ansonia Brass Co., beehive shelf clock, 19", 30-hour brass time and strike spring-driven movement, very good condition, $134

American, ca. 1840, Brewster, E. C. and Co., beehive shelf clock, 19", 8-day brass time and strike spring-driven movement, good condition, $1,232

American, ca. 1840, Brewster, E. C. and Co., beehive shelf clock, 19", 8-day brass time and strike spring-driven movement, good condition, $2,800

American, ca. 1840, Brewster, E. C. and Co., beehive shelf clock, 19", 8-day brass time and strike spring-driven movement, very good condition, $1,210

American, ca. 1845, Brewster and Ingraham, beehive shelf clock, 19", 8-day brass time and strike spring-driven movement, good condition, replaced lower glass, $330

American, ca. 1870, beehive clock, 8-day time and strike, 18.5", signed Jerome and Co., $137. Credit: R. O. Schmitt Fine Arts.

American, ca. 1860, beehive clock, 30-hour time and strike, 19", signed Connecticut Clock Co., $123. Credit: Prices4Antiques.com.

American, ca. 1850, Brewster and Ingraham, beehive shelf clock, 19", 8-day brass time and strike spring-driven movement, good condition, $504

American, ca. 1844, Brewster and Ingraham, beehive shelf clock, 19", 8-day brass time and strike spring-driven movement, excellent condition, $1,008

American, ca. 1850, beehive clock, 8-day time and strike, 19", signed J. C. Brown, $1,760. Credit: Prices4Antiques.com.

American, ca. 1844, Brewster and Ingraham, beehive shelf clock, 19", 8-day brass time and strike spring-driven movement, fair condition, missing tablet, $112

American, ca. 1845, Brewster and Ingraham, beehive shelf clock, 19", 8-day brass time and strike spring-driven movement, good condition, $504

American, ca. 1845, Brewster and Ingraham, beehive shelf clock, 19", 8-day brass time and strike spring-driven movement, good condition, some replacements, $560

American, ca. 1845, Brewster and Ingraham, beehive shelf clock, 18.75", 8-day brass time and strike spring-driven movement, good condition, minor veneer damage, $235

American, ca. 1848, Brown, J. C., beehive shelf clock, 19", 8-day brass time and strike spring-driven movement, excellent original condition, $2,189

American, ca. 1848, Brown, J. C., beehive shelf clock with ripple trim, 18.75", 8-day brass time and strike fusee movement, good condition (illustrated), $1,760

American, ca. 1848, Brown, J. C., beehive shelf clock with ripple trim, 19", 8-day brass time and strike spring-driven movement, good condition, repapered dial and reproduction tablet, $1,375

American, ca. 1848, Brown, J. C., beehive shelf clock with ripple trim, 19", 8-day brass time and strike spring-driven movement, good condition, small flaking on dial, $2,016

American, ca. 1850, Brown, J. C., beehive shelf clock with ripple trim, 18.75", 8-day brass time and strike spring-driven movement, very good condition, faded tablet, $2,200

American, ca. 1855, Brown, J. C., beehive shelf clock with ripple trim, 15.25", 30-hour brass time and strike spring-driven movement, excellent condition, $4,125

American, ca. 1845, Brown, J. C., miniature beehive shelf clock, 15.25", 8-day brass time and strike spring-driven movement, fair condition, paint loss, cracked glass, and veneer damage, $4,730

American, ca. 1848, Brown, J. C., miniature beehive shelf clock, 15.5", 8-day brass time and strike spring-driven movement, fair condition, replaced movement and veneer loss, $616

American, ca. 1848, Brown, J. C., miniature beehive shelf clock with ripple trim, 15.5", 8-day brass time and strike spring-driven movement, good condition, $6,050

American, ca. 1850, Connecticut Clock Co., beehive shelf clock, 18.5",
30-hour brass time and strike spring-driven movement, fair condition,
veneer damage on lower part of door (illustrated), $123

American, ca. 1848, Forestville Mfg. Co., beehive shelf clock with ripple
trim, 19", 8-day brass time and strike spring-driven movement, good
condition, $2,640

American, ca. 1855, Ingraham, E. and A., beehive shelf clock, 18", 8-day
brass time and strike spring-driven movement, good original condition,
$230

American, ca. 1845, Jerome, Chauncey, beehive shelf clock, 19", 8-day brass
time and strike fusee movement, good condition, $522

American, ca. 1845, Jerome, Chauncey, beehive shelf clock, 18.5", 8-day
brass time and strike fusee movement, fair condition, $252

American, ca. 1845, Jerome, Chauncey, beehive shelf clock, 19", 8-day brass
time and strike spring-driven movement, fair condition, cracked glass
and veneer loss, $196

American, ca. 1855, Jerome, Chauncey, beehive shelf clock, 19", 8-day brass
time and strike spring-driven movement, fair condition, raised veneer
and damaged tablet (illustrated), $137

American, ca. 1870, Jerome and Co. (New Haven Clock Co.), beehive shelf
clock, 18.5", 8-day brass time and strike spring-driven movement, good
condition, refinished case, $137

American, ca. 1870, New Haven Clock Co., beehive shelf clock, 19", 30-hour
brass time and strike spring-driven movement, poor condition, $44

American, ca. 1870, New Haven Clock Co., beehive shelf clock, 18.5", 8-day
brass time and strike spring-driven movement, very good condition,
$336

American, ca. 1845, Terry and Andrews, beehive shelf clock, 19", 8-day
brass time and strike spring-driven movement, fair condition, $247

American, ca. 1850, Terry and Andrews, beehive shelf clock, 19", 30-hour
brass time and strike spring-driven movement, poor condition, all veneer removed and restained, $145

American, ca. 1850, Terry and Andrews, beehive shelf clock, 19", 8-day
brass time and strike spring-driven movement, poor dismantled condition, $134

American, ca. 1850, Terry and Andrews, beehive shelf clock, 19", 8-day
brass time and strike spring-driven movement, very good condition,
$574

American, ca. 1850, Terry and Andrews, beehive shelf clock, 19", 8-day brass time and strike spring-driven movement, very good condition, $336

American, ca. 1870, Waterbury Clock Co., beehive shelf clock, 18.75", 8-day brass time and strike spring-driven movement, good condition, replaced dial, $112

American, ca. 1850, Welch, E. N., beehive shelf clock, 18.75", 8-day brass time and strike spring-driven movement, very good condition, $145

American, ca. 1860, Welch, E. N., beehive shelf clock, 19", 8-day brass time and strike spring-driven movement, fair condition, pendulum missing, $275

American, ca. 1860, Welch, E. N., beehive shelf clock, 19", 8-day brass time and strike spring-driven movement, good restored condition, $275

American, ca. 1860, Welch, E. N., beehive shelf clock, 19", 8-day brass time and strike spring-driven movement, good condition, $201

American, ca. 1870, Welch, E. N., beehive shelf clock, 19", 8-day brass time and strike spring-driven movement, good condition, $441

American, ca. 1870, Welch, E. N., beehive shelf clock, 18", 8-day brass time and strike spring-driven movement, good restored condition, $137

American, ca. 1875, Welch, E. N., beehive shelf clock, 20", 8-day brass time and strike spring-driven movement, poor condition, $82

American, ca. 1860, Welch, E. N., miniature beehive shelf clock, 15.25", 30-hour brass time and strike spring-driven movement, very good condition, $4,400

	LOW	MID	HIGH
Beehive Shelf Clocks (ca. 1841–1915)	$100–$200	$300–$500	$1,000+

BLACK MANTEL CLOCKS were a reaction to the popularity of imported black marble (actually slate) mantel clocks from France. American makers introduced their own versions around 1875. They remained among the industry's top sellers until around 1910, and now abound in antiques shops.

Most makers produced these clocks, but no company produced more than the Ansonia Clock Company of New York. Mindful of both domestic and foreign markets, American makers sold three types of the black mantel clock: black marble (slate) cases for the high end of the market, black enameled iron cases for the mid-range market, and black enameled wood cases for the low end.

These cases house 8-day spring-driven pendulum movements, often with outside escapements. They strike the hour and the half-hour on coil gongs. "Blacks" are readily available at reasonable prices, so buy them only in excellent condition.

American, ca. 1880, Ansonia Clock Co., black polished-slate architectural mantel clock, 12.5", 8-day time and strike spring-driven movement, fair condition, $187

American, ca. 1880, Ansonia Clock Co., black enameled-iron architectural mantel clock, "LA FRANCE" model, 11", 8-day time and strike spring-driven movement, good condition, $253

American, ca. 1880, Ansonia Clock Co., black polished-marble architectural mantel clock, 17", 8-day time and strike spring-driven movement, poor condition, $230

American, ca. 1883, Ansonia Clock Co., black hard-rubber architectural mantel clock, "MARBELITE NO. 8" model, 15.5", 8-day time and strike spring-driven movement, very good condition, $550

American, ca. 1886, Ansonia Clock Co., black enameled-iron architectural mantel clock, "PARMA" model, 12", 8-day time and strike spring-driven movement, good condition, $308

American, ca. 1886, Ansonia Clock Co., black enameled-iron architectural mantel clock, "LA DUCHESSE" model, 10.5", 8-day time and strike spring-driven movement, fair condition, $159

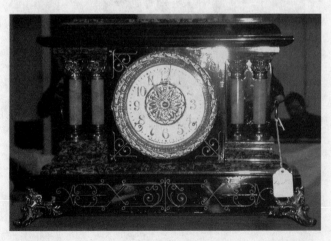

American, black mantel clock, enameled wood, restored, $400.
Credit: NAWCC Mid-Eastern States Regional 2002.

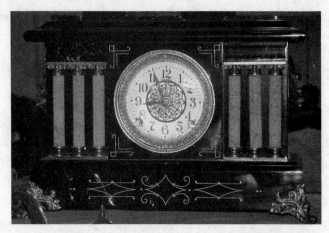

American, black mantel clock, enameled wood, restored, asking
price $400. Credit: NAWCC Mid-Eastern States Regional 2002.

American, ca. 1890, Ansonia Clock Co., black enameled-iron architectural
mantel clock, 11", 8-day time and strike spring-driven movement, very
good condition (illustrated), $121

American, ca. 1890, Ansonia Clock Co., black enameled-iron architectural
mantel clock, "ST CLAIR" model, 11", 8-day time and strike spring-
driven movement, very good condition, $275

Assorted American "blacks," enameled wood and iron
cases. Credit: NAWCC Mid-Eastern States Regional 2002.

Assorted American "blacks," enameled wood and iron cases.
Credit: NAWCC Mid-Eastern States Regional 2002.

American, ca. 1895, Ansonia Clock Co., black polished-marble architectural mantel clock, 10", 8-day time and strike spring-driven movement, very good condition, $220

American, ca. 1900, Ansonia Clock Co., black enameled-iron architectural mantel clock, "RICHELIEU" model, 9", 8-day time and strike spring-driven movement, very good condition, $286

American, ca. 1900, Ansonia Clock Co., black enameled-iron architectural mantel clock, "PALERMO" model, 10.25", 8-day time and strike spring-driven movement, good condition, $145

American, ca. 1904, Ansonia Clock Co., black polished-marble architectural mantel clock, "EL DARA" model, 14.5", 8-day time and strike spring-driven movement, good condition, $224

American, ca. 1904, Ansonia Clock Co., black polished-marble architectural mantel clock, 10.25", 8-day time and strike spring-driven movement, good condition, $253

American, ca. 1915, Gilbert, William L., black enameled-wood architectural mantel clock, 11", 8-day time and strike spring-driven movement, poor condition, $123

American, ca. 1920, Gilbert, William L., black enameled-wood architectural mantel clock, "CURFEW" model, 18", 8-day time and strike spring-driven movement, fair condition, $187

American, ca. 1885, black marble mantel clock,
10", signed Westbury Clock Co. $175. Credit:
Timex Museum.

American, ca. 1920, Gilbert, William L., black enameled-wood architectural mantel clock, "MODEL 220–A," 8.5", 30-hour time and alarm
spring-driven movement, very good condition, $88

American, ca. 1900, Ingraham and Co., black enameled-wood architectural
mantel clock, 10", 8-day time and strike spring-driven movement, fair
condition, repainted case, $62

American, ca. 1900, Ingraham and Co., black enameled-wood architectural
mantel clock, 10", 8-day time and strike spring-driven movement, poor
condition, stripped case, $56

American, ca. 1890, black slate case with marble
columns, 8-day time and strike, 9.5", signed Seth Thomas
Clock Co., $330. Credit: Prices4Antiques.com.

American, ca. 1885, black enameled-iron case, 8-day time and strike escapement, 11", signed Ansonia Clock Co., $121. Credit: Prices4Antiques.com.

American, ca. 1907, Ingraham and Co., black enameled-wood architectural mantel clock, 12", 8-day time and strike spring-driven movement, poor condition, $77

American, ca. 1910, Ingraham and Co., black enameled-wood architectural mantel clock, 11", 8-day time and strike spring-driven movement, fair condition, $88

American, ca. 1910, Ingraham and Co., black enameled-wood architectural mantel clock, 10", 8-day time and strike spring-driven movement, fair condition, $112

American, ca. 1920, Ingraham and Co., black enameled-wood architectural mantel clock, 11", 8-day time and strike spring-driven movement, good condition, $121

American, ca. 1890, New Haven Clock Co., black enameled-iron architectural mantel clock, "FORTUNA" model, 10", 8-day time and strike spring-driven movement, very good condition, $165

American, ca. 1900, New Haven Clock Co., black enameled-wood architectural mantel clock, 10", 8-day time and strike spring-driven movement, good condition, $110

American, ca. 1900, New Haven Clock Co., black enameled-iron architectural mantel clock, "FAIRFIELD" model, 10.5", 8-day time and strike spring-driven movement, very good original condition, $198

American, ca. 1900, New Haven Clock Co., black enameled-iron architectural mantel clock, 11", 8-day time and strike spring-driven movement, good condition, $112

American, ca. 1890, Sessions Clock Co., black enameled-wood architectural mantel clock, 10", 8-day time and strike spring-driven movement, good condition, $84

American, ca. 1910, Sessions Clock Co., black enameled-wood architectural mantel clock, 10", 8-day time and strike spring-driven movement, fair condition, $99

American, ca. 1880, Seth Thomas, black polished-marble architectural mantel clock, 9.5", 8-day time and strike spring-driven movement, very good condition (illustrated), $330

American, ca. 1895, Seth Thomas, black polished-marble architectural mantel clock, "NO. 1490," 10.5", 8-day time and strike spring-driven movement, very good condition, $212

American, ca. 1898, Seth Thomas, black adamantine-enameled-wood architectural mantel clock, 11", 8-day time and strike spring-driven movement, good original condition, $247

American, ca. 1899, Seth Thomas, black adamantine-enameled-wood architectural mantel clock, 10.5", 8-day time and strike spring-driven movement, very good condition, $214

American, ca. 1900, Seth Thomas, black adamantine-enameled-wood architectural mantel clock, 10.5", 8-day time and strike spring-driven movement, poor condition, missing feet, $159

American, ca. 1900, Seth Thomas, black adamantine-enameled-wood architectural mantel clock, 10", 8-day time and strike spring-driven movement, very good condition, $324

American, ca. 1900, Seth Thomas, black adamantine-enameled-wood architectural mantel clock, 11", 8-day time and strike spring-driven movement, good condition, $192

American, ca. 1900, Seth Thomas, black adamantine-enameled-wood architectural mantel clock, 11", 8-day time and strike spring-driven movement, good condition, $247

American, ca. 1900, Seth Thomas, black adamantine-enameled-wood architectural mantel clock, 11", 8-day time and strike spring-driven movement, good condition, $192

American, ca. 1900, Seth Thomas, black adamantine-enameled-wood architectural mantel clock, 10", 8-day time and strike spring-driven movement, fair condition, $302

American, ca. 1900, Seth Thomas, black adamantine-enameled-wood architectural mantel clock, 12", 8-day time and strike spring-driven movement, good condition, $156

American, ca. 1880, Waterbury Clock Co., black enameled-iron architectural mantel clock, 7.75", 30-hour time-only spring-driven movement, very good condition, $22

American, ca. 1880, Waterbury Clock Co., black enameled-iron architectural mantel clock, 10", 8-day time and strike spring-driven movement, very good condition, $84

American, ca. 1895, Waterbury Clock Co., black polished-marble architectural mantel clock, "NO. 2013," 11.25", 8-day time and strike spring-driven movement, very good condition, $282

	LOW	MID	HIGH
Black Mantel Clocks (ca. 1875–1920)	$100–$200	$300–$500	$600–$800

CALENDAR SHELF CLOCKS with perpetual calendar mechanisms made a reappearance in the mid-1850s. These time- and date-keepers increased in popularity throughout the 1860s, 1870s, and 1880s. A number of clockmakers made nothing else, and the calendar clock remained in manufacturers' catalogs into the twentieth century.

There are two distinct types, the single dial and double dial. Single dial calendar clocks are fitted with an extra hand that points to the day of the month, marked outside the minute ring. Double dial models indicate time only on the upper dial and all other information, such as day, date, and month, on the lower dial.

Almost all the movements are brass 8-day time and strike spring-driven and most are housed in walnut cases.

Single dial models command lower prices than double dials, and prices are increasing faster for the latter than for the former.

American, ca. 1880, Ansonia Clock Co., single dial calendar clock, "PARISIAN" model, 23.5", 8-day time, strike, date, and day, good original condition (illustrated), $448

American, ca. 1863, Carter, L. F. and W. W., double dial calendar clock, 21", 8-day time, strike, date, and day, excellent condition, $990

American, ca. 1895, Feishtinger, Charles W., double dial calendar clock, 22", 8-day time, strike, date, and day, very good walnut case, refinished, $1,540

American, ca. 1910, Ingraham and Co., single dial calendar clock, "GILA" model, 23", 8-day time, strike, and date, good pressed oak case, refinished, $247

American, ca. 1890, "Calendar No. 44," single dial calendar clock, 23.5", signed Waterbury Clock Co., $448. Credit: Prices4Antiques.com.

American, ca. 1881,"No. 3½ Parlor," double dial calendar clock, 20.5", signed Ithaca Clock Co., $1,848. Credit: R. O. Schmitt Fine Arts.

American, ca. 1880, Ingraham, E. and Co., double dial calendar clock, 22", 8-day time, strike, date, and day, very good condition, $1,064

American, ca. 1881, Ingraham, E. and Co., double dial calendar clock, "INGRAHAM CALENDAR" model, 21.5", 8-day time, strike, date, and day, good condition, walnut case, $1,008

American, ca. 1890, Ingraham, E. and Co., double dial calendar clock, "INGRAHAM CALENDAR" model, 21.5", 8-day time, strike, date, and day, fair condition, replaced backboard (illustrated), $672

American, ca. 1870, Ithaca Calendar Clock Co., double dial calendar clock, "FAVORITE NO. 3½" model, 19.25", 8-day time, strike, date, and day, good condition, $3,987

American, ca. 1874, Ithaca Calendar Clock Co., double dial calendar clock, "COTTAGE NO. 7" model, 22", 8-day time, strike, date, and day, good restored and refinished case, $448

American, ca. 1874, Ithaca Calendar Clock Co., double dial calendar clock, "NO. 10 FARMER" model, 21", 8-day time, strike, date, and day, good original condition, $784

American, ca. 1875, Ithaca Calendar Clock Co., double dial calendar clock, "CALENDAR NO. 8" model, 25", 8-day time, strike, date, and day, as found, missing trim, $660

American, ca. 1890, Ingraham Parlor
double dial calendar clock, 21.5", signed
Ingraham Clock Co., $672. Credit: R. O.
Schmitt Fine Arts.

American, ca. 1890, double dial,
"Calendar No. 44," 24", signed
Waterbury Clock Co., $550. Credit: R. O.
Schmitt Fine Arts.

American, ca. 1875, Ithaca Calendar Clock Co., double dial calendar clock,
   "CHRONOMETER" model, 33", 8-day time, strike, and date, good restored walnut case, $1,925

American, ca. 1875, Ithaca Calendar Clock Co., double dial calendar clock,
   "COTTAGE NO. 5" model, 20.5", 8-day time, strike, date, and day,
   fair condition, $1,120

American, ca. 1886, double dial,
"Calendar No. 44," 25", signed
Seth Thomas Clock Co., $1,320.
Credit: R. O. Schmitt Fine Arts.

American, ca. 1875, Ithaca Calendar Clock Co., double dial calendar clock, "NO. 8 SHELF LIBRARY" model, 25", 8-day time, strike, date, and day, good refinished condition, $728

American, ca. 1879, Ithaca Calendar Clock Co., double dial calendar clock, "CALENDAR NO. 5" model, 22.5", 8-day time, strike, date, and day, good refinished condition, $868

American, ca. 1880, Ithaca Calendar Clock Co., double dial calendar clock, 25.5", 8-day time, strike, date, and day, very good condition, $575

American, ca. 1880, Ithaca Calendar Clock Co., double dial calendar clock, "BELGRADE NO. 6½" model, 32", 8-day time, strike, date, and day, good refinished condition, $2,688

American, ca. 1880, Ithaca Calendar Clock Co., double dial calendar clock, "CALENDAR NO. 11" model, 21", 8-day time, strike, date, and day, very good restored condition, $907

American, ca. 1880, Ithaca Calendar Clock Co., double dial calendar clock, "CALENDAR NO. 9" model, 23.5", 8-day time, strike, date, and day, very good condition, $1,650

American, ca. 1880, Ithaca Calendar Clock Co., double dial calendar clock, "FAVORITE NO. 3½" model, 20.25", 8-day time, strike, date, and day, very good condition, $3,654

American, ca. 1880, Ithaca Calendar Clock Co., double dial calendar clock, "FAVORITE NO. 4½" model, 32", 8-day time, strike, date, and day, fair condition, partial loss of cresting, $1,320

American, ca. 1880, Ithaca Calendar Clock Co., double dial calendar clock, "FAVORITE NO. 4½" model , 31", 8-day time, strike, date, and day, very good condition, $3,024

American, ca. 1880, Ithaca Calendar Clock Co., double dial calendar clock, "GRANGER NO. 14" model , 26", 8-day time, strike, date, and day, good condition, replaced dial, $896

American, ca. 1880, Ithaca Calendar Clock Co., double dial calendar clock, "INDEX" model, 33", 8-day time, strike, date, and day, good condition, $1,430

American, ca. 1880, Ithaca Calendar Clock Co., double dial calendar clock, "NO. 10 FARMER" model, 25", 8-day time, strike, date, and day, good condition, crest tip replaced, $1,456

American, ca. 1880, Ithaca Calendar Clock Co., double dial calendar clock, "NO. 10 FARMER" model, 24", 8-day time, strike, date, and day, good condition, refinished walnut case, $962

American, ca. 1880, Ithaca Calendar Clock Co., double dial calendar clock, "NO. 10 FARMER" model, 24", 8-day time, strike, date, and day, fair condition, replaced top, $644

American, ca. 1880, Ithaca Calendar Clock Co., double dial calendar clock, "NO. 10 FARMER" model, 26", 8-day time, strike, date, and day, very good condition, $672

American, ca. 1880, Ithaca Calendar Clock Co., double dial calendar clock, "NO. 5 EMERALD" model, 33", 8-day time, strike, date, and day, good restored condition, $1,650

American, ca. 1880, Ithaca Calendar Clock Co., double dial calendar clock, "NO. 5" model, 23", 8-day time, strike, date, and day, good condition, $560

American, ca. 1881, Ithaca Calendar Clock Co., double dial calendar clock, "FAVORITE NO. 3½" model, 20.5", 8-day time, strike, date, and day, good condition (illustrated), $1,848

American, ca. 1885, Ithaca Calendar Clock Co., double dial calendar clock, "INDEX" model, 32", 8-day time, strike, date, and day, good restored walnut case, $1,925

American, ca. 1884, National Calendar Clock Co., double dial calendar clock, "FASHION" model, 32", 8-day time, strike, date, and day, good condition, some tablet loss, $1,100

American, ca. 1875, Southern Calendar Co., double dial calendar clock, "FASHION NO. 1" model, 29", 8-day time, strike, date, and day, good condition, $770

American, ca. 1875, Southern Calendar Co., double dial calendar clock, "FASHION NO. 5" model, 32", 8-day time, strike, date, and day, very good condition, $2,352

American, ca. 1876, Southern Calendar Co., double dial calendar clock, "FASHION NO. 2" model, 31", 8-day time, strike, date, and day, fair condition, walnut case , $660

American, ca. 1878, Southern Calendar Co., double dial calendar clock, 31", 8-day time, strike, date, and day, very good condition, $1,322

American, ca. 1878, Southern Calendar Co., double dial calendar clock, "FASHION NO. 4" model, 32", 8-day time, strike, date, and day, good restored condition, $1,650

American, ca. 1880, Southern Calendar Co., double dial calendar clock, "FASHION NO. 4" model, 32", 8-day time, strike, date, and day, good condition, refinished walnut case, $2,915

American, ca. 1880, Southern Calendar Co., double dial calendar clock, "FASHION NO. 5" model, 32", 8-day time, strike, date, and day, good restored condition, $1,925

American, ca. 1884, Southern Calendar Co., double dial calendar clock, "FASHION NO. 9" model, 32", 8-day time, strike, date, and day, good condition, replaced glass and hands, $1,210

American, ca. 1863, Seth Thomas, double dial calendar clock, 30.5", 8-day time, strike, date, and day, good condition, stripped rosewood case, $1,650

American, ca. 1865, Seth Thomas, double dial calendar clock, 30.5", 8-day time, strike, date, and day, good original condition, $1,344

American, ca. 1866, Seth Thomas, double dial calendar clock, "PARLOR CALENDAR NO. 1" model, 33", 8-day time, strike, date, and day, good condition, $588

American, ca. 1875, Seth Thomas, double dial calendar clock, "PARLOR CALENDAR NO. 1" model, 33", 8-day time, strike, date, and day, good condition, rosewood case, $770

American, ca. 1875, Seth Thomas, double dial calendar clock, "PARLOR CALENDAR NO. 3" model, 26.75", 8-day time, strike, date, and day, good condition, $672

American, ca. 1880, Seth Thomas, double dial calendar clock, "PARLOR CALENDAR NO. 3" model, 27", 8-day time, strike, date, and day, fair condition, $476

American, ca. 1885, Seth Thomas, double dial calendar clock, "PARLOR CALENDAR NO. 3" model, 26.5", 8-day time, strike, date, and day, good condition, $742

American, ca. 1885, Seth Thomas, double dial calendar clock, "PARLOR CALENDAR NO. 3" model, 27", 8-day time, strike, date, and day, good restored condition, $440

American, ca. 1885, Seth Thomas, double dial calendar clock, "PARLOR NO. 9" model , 29.5", 8-day time, strike, date, and day, good restored walnut case, $3,740

American, ca. 1886, Seth Thomas, double dial calendar clock, "PARLOR CALENDAR NO. 5" model, 20", 8-day time, strike, date, and day, fair condition, $840

American, ca. 1886, Seth Thomas, double dial calendar clock, "PARLOR CALENDAR NO. 5" model, 20", 8-day time, strike, date, and day, excellent restored condition, $935

American, ca. 1886, Seth Thomas, double dial calendar clock, "PARLOR CALENDAR NO. 6" model, 27", 8-day time, strike, date, and day, good restored and refinished case, $952

American, ca. 1886, Seth Thomas, double dial calendar clock, "PARLOR CALENDAR NO. 8" model, 27.5", 8-day time, strike, date, and day, excellent condition, $5,040

American, ca. 1886, Seth Thomas, double dial calendar clock, "PARLOR CALENDAR NO. 9" model, 29.5", 8-day time, strike, date, and day, very good condition, $6,160

American, ca. 1886, Seth Thomas, double dial calendar clock, "PARLOR NO. 4" model, 25", 8-day time, strike, date, and day, very good condition, walnut case (illustrated), $1,320

American, ca. 1886, Seth Thomas, double dial calendar clock, "PARLOR NO. 8" model, 27.5", 8-day time, strike, date, and day, good condition, $5,600

American, ca. 1890, Seth Thomas, double dial calendar clock, "PARLOR CALENDAR NO. 10" model, 36", 8-day time, strike, date, and day, excellent condition, $9,350

American, ca. 1896, Seth Thomas, double dial calendar clock, "PARLOR CALENDAR NO. 6" model, 27", 8-day time, strike, date, and day, good condition, $2,912

American, ca. 1900, Seth Thomas, double dial calendar clock, 26.75", 8-day time, strike, date, and day, fair condition, $603

American, ca. 1880, Waterbury Clock Co., double dial calendar clock, "CALENDAR NO. 4" model, 24", 8-day time, strike, date, and day, fair condition, $412

American, ca. 1880, Waterbury Clock Co., double dial calendar clock, "CALENDAR NO. 44" model, 24", 8-day time, strike, date, and day, fair condition, $660

American, ca. 1890, Waterbury Clock Co., double dial calendar clock, "CALENDAR NO. 44" model, 24", 8-day time, strike, and day, good refinished condition (illustrated), $550

American, ca. 1891, Waterbury Clock Co., single dial calendar clock, "BUFFALO" model, 26.75", 8-day time, strike, and date, good condition, walnut case, $880

American, ca. 1912, Waterbury Clock Co., double dial calendar clock, "CALENDAR NO. 43" model, 28.25", 8-day time, strike, date, and day, excellent restored oak case, $1,100

American, ca. 1885, Welch, E. N., double dial calendar clock, "ARDITI" model, 27", 8-day time, strike, date, and day, good condition, $1,904

American, ca. 1885, Welch, E. N., double dial calendar clock, "ARDITI" model, 27", 8-day time, strike, date, and day, good original condition, $1,100

American, ca. 1885, Welch, E. N., double dial calendar clock, "ARDITI" model, 27", 8-day time, strike, date, and day, good original condition, $1,210

American, ca. 1868, Welch, Spring and Co., double dial calendar clock, "ITALIAN NO. 3" model, 20", 8-day time, strike, and date, good condition, $660

American, ca. 1875, Welch, Spring and Co., double dial calendar clock, "ITALIAN NO. 3" model, 18", 8-day time, strike, date, and day, very good condition, $990

American, ca. 1875, Welch, Spring and Co., double dial calendar clock, "ITALIAN NO. 3" model, 18", 8-day time, strike, date, and day, fair condition, $660

	LOW	MID	HIGH
Calendar Shelf Clocks (ca. 1855–1920)	$300–$800	$900–$2,500	$3,500–$10,000+

CHINA-CASED MANTEL CLOCKS decorated thousands of American parlors and bedrooms by the turn of the twentieth century. The same 8-day movements that were often found in the black mantel clocks graced these clocks as well.

These highly decorated clocks were immensely popular, largely due to the handpainted china cases that were imported from Europe. Most popular were those from the Royal Bonn porcelain works in Germany.

Although numerous companies marketed these clocks, the Ansonia Clock Company dominated the market. The outbreak of World War I in 1914 curtailed the importation of cases and ended the popularity of these clocks.

They are still readily available but they are getting pricey, so the collector must carefully inspect cases for the chips and cracks that seriously reduce the value of these clocks.

American, ca. 1895, Ansonia Clock Co., Royal Bonn china mantel clock, "NO. 501" model, 13.25", 8-day time and strike spring-driven movement, very good condition, $896

American, ca. 1904, "La Manche," 14",
signed Ansonia Clock Co., $495. Credit:
R. O. Schmitt Fine Arts.

American, ca. 1905, "La Clairmont," 11",
signed Ansonia Clock Co., $495. Credit:
R. O. Schmitt Fine Arts.

American, ca. 1900, Ansonia Clock Co., china mantel clock, 11.5", 8-day
time and strike spring-driven movement, good condition, $330

American, ca. 1900, Ansonia Clock Co., Royal Bonn china mantel clock,
"GRANITE" model, 6.5", 30-hour time-only spring-driven movement,
very good condition, $212

American, ca. 1902, "Arabia,"
10.5", signed Ansonia Clock Co.,
$385. Credit: R. O. Schmitt
Fine Arts.

American, ca. 1900, Ansonia Clock Co., Royal Bonn china mantel clock, "LA MANCHE" model, 14", 8-day time and strike spring-driven movement, good condition, old crack in back, $1,250

American, ca. 1900, Ansonia Clock Co., Royal Bonn china mantel clock, "PAWNEE" model, 11.25", 8-day time and strike spring-driven movement, good condition, $440

American, ca. 1900, Ansonia Clock Co., Royal Bonn china mantel clock, "LA CRUZ" model, 11.5", 8-day time and strike spring-driven movement, very good condition, $522

American, ca. 1900, Ansonia Clock Co., china mantel clock, 11", 8-day time and strike spring-driven movement, good condition, $550

American, ca. 1901, Ansonia Clock Co., Royal Bonn china mantel clock, "LA VERA" model, 12.25", 8-day time and strike spring-driven movement, excellent original condition, $2,016

American, ca. 1901, Ansonia Clock Co., Royal Bonn china mantel clock, "LA CHAPELLE" model, 12", 8-day time and strike spring-driven movement, excellent original condition, $1,960

American, ca. 1901, Ansonia Clock Co., Royal Bonn china mantel clock, "LA CANTAL" model, 12", 8-day time and strike spring-driven movement, excellent original condition, $1,320

American, ca. 1902, Ansonia Clock Co., Royal Bonn china mantel clock, "LA LAYON" model, 14.5", 8-day time and strike spring-driven movement, excellent original condition, $1,760

American, ca. 1902, Ansonia Clock Co., Royal Bonn china mantel clock, "LA VERDON" model, 14.5", 8-day time and strike spring-driven movement, excellent condition, $1,815

American, ca. 1902, Ansonia Clock Co., Royal Bonn china mantel clock, "ARABIA" model, 10.25", 8-day time and strike spring-driven movement, good condition (illustrated), $385

American, ca. 1902, Ansonia Clock Co., Royal Bonn china mantel clock, "AMARA" model, 10.25", 8-day time and strike spring-driven movement, very good condition, $330

American, ca. 1904, Ansonia Clock Co., china mantel clock, 14", 8-day time and strike spring-driven movement, good condition, old 2" crack in the back, $495

American, ca. 1904, Ansonia Clock Co., Royal Bonn china mantel clock, "LA LOMME" model, 11", 8-day time and strike spring-driven movement, very good condition, $644

American, ca. 1904, Ansonia Clock Co., Royal Bonn china mantel clock, "LA CHAPELLE" model, 12", 8-day time and strike spring-driven movement, excellent original condition, $990

American, ca. 1904, Ansonia Clock Co., Royal Bonn china mantel clock, "LA MANCHE" model, 14", 8-day time and strike spring-driven movement, very good condition (illustrated), $495

American, ca. 1905, Ansonia Clock Co., Royal Bonn china mantel clock, 11.5", 8-day time and strike spring-driven movement, good condition, $364

American, ca. 1905, Ansonia Clock Co., Royal Bonn china mantel clock, "LA CHARNY" model, 11.5", 8-day time and strike spring-driven movement, excellent original condition, $1,848

American, ca. 1905, Ansonia Clock Co., Royal Bonn china mantel clock, "LA MAYENNE" model, 13.25", 8-day time and strike spring-driven movement, good condition, $605

American, ca. 1905, Ansonia Clock Co., Royal Bonn china mantel clock, "LA LORNE" model, 11.5", 8-day time and strike spring-driven movement, excellent condition, $935

American, ca. 1905, Ansonia Clock Co., Royal Bonn china mantel clock, "LA NORD" model, 11.75", 8-day time and strike spring-driven movement, excellent original condition, $1,344

American, ca. 1905, Ansonia Clock Co., Royal Bonn china mantel clock, "LA LAYON" model, 14.5", 8-day time and strike spring-driven movement, good condition, $1,680

American, ca. 1905, Ansonia Clock Co., china mantel clock, "EUCLID" model, 5.5", 30-hour time-only spring-driven movement, good condition, $247

American, ca. 1905, Ansonia Clock Co., Royal Bonn china mantel clock, "LA VENDEE" model, 14.5", 8-day time and strike spring-driven movement, fair condition, hairline cracks, $1,540

American, ca. 1905, Ansonia Clock Co., Royal Bonn china mantel clock, "LA ORNE" model, 10.75", 8-day time and strike spring-driven movement, excellent condition, $660

American, ca. 1905, Ansonia Clock Co., Royal Bonn china mantel clock, "THE RUSTIC" model, 11", 8-day time and strike spring-driven movement, good condition, $560

American, ca. 1905, Ansonia Clock Co., Royal Bonn china mantel clock, "REFLEX" model, 11", 8-day time and strike spring-driven movement, excellent original condition, $577

American, ca. 1905, Ansonia Clock Co., Royal Bonn china mantel clock, "LA ROCHE" model, 13.5", 8-day time and strike spring-driven movement, very good original condition, $1,551

American, ca. 1905, Ansonia Clock Co., Royal Bonn china mantel clock, "LA BRETAGNE" model, 15", 8-day time and strike spring-driven movement, excellent condition, $1,320

American, ca. 1905, Ansonia Clock Co., Royal Bonn china mantel clock, "LA FARGE" model, 11.25", 8-day time and strike spring-driven movement, excellent original condition, $467

American, ca. 1905, Ansonia Clock Co., Royal Bonn china mantel clock, "LA LORNE" model, 11.5", 8-day time and strike spring-driven movement, excellent original condition, $726

American, ca. 1905, Ansonia Clock Co., Royal Bonn china mantel clock, "LA ORB" model, 12.5", 8-day time and strike spring-driven movement, fair condition with chipped dial, $770

American, ca. 1905, Ansonia Clock Co., Royal Bonn china mantel clock, "LA CLAIRMONT" model, 11", 8-day time and strike spring-driven movement, fair condition, chipped (illustrated) $495

American, ca. 1910, Ansonia Clock Co., Royal Bonn china mantel clock, "LA LAYON" model, 14.5", 8-day time and strike spring-driven movement, very good original condition, $1,792

American, ca. 1910, Ansonia Clock Co., Royal Bonn china mantel clock, "LA FONTAINE" model, 11.25", 8-day time and strike spring-driven movement, good condition, $392

American, ca. 1910, Ansonia Clock Co., Royal Bonn china mantel clock, "RAINBOW" model, 11.25", 8-day time and strike spring-driven movement, excellent original condition, $385

American, ca. 1910, Ansonia Clock Co., Royal Bonn china mantel clock, "REVIEW" model, 11.25", 8-day time and strike spring-driven movement, good original condition, $440

American, ca. 1910, Ansonia Clock Co., Royal Bonn china mantel clock, "LA RIVIERE" model, 12.5", 8-day time and strike spring-driven movement, good condition, $990

American, ca. 1910, Ansonia Clock Co., Royal Bonn china mantel clock, "LA SAVOIA" model, 11.75", 8-day time and strike spring-driven movement, very good condition, $560

American, ca. 1910, Ansonia Clock Co., Royal Bonn china mantel clock, "LA TOUR" model, 11", 8-day time and strike spring-driven movement, good condition, $460

American, ca. 1910, Ansonia Clock Co., Royal Bonn china mantel clock, "LA MOSELLE" model, 14.25", 8-day time and strike spring-driven movement, very good condition, $1,386

American, ca. 1914, Ansonia Clock Co., Royal Bonn china mantel clock, "LA RAMBLA" model, 12", 8-day time and strike spring-driven movement, very good condition, $467

American, ca. 1915, Ansonia Clock Co., Royal Bonn china mantel clock, "LA SAVOIE" model, 11.25", 8-day time and strike spring-driven movement, good condition, $990

American, ca. 1915, Ansonia Clock Co., Royal Bonn china mantel clock, "LA SIENE" model, 11.5", 8-day time and strike spring-driven movement, excellent, condition, $385

American, ca. 1909, Gilbert, William L., china mantel clock, 4", 30-hour time-only spring-driven movement, fair condition, some chips on case, $84

American, ca. 1910, Gilbert, William L., china mantel clock, "MODEL #423," 10", 8-day time and strike spring-driven movement, very good condition, $330

American, ca. 1900, New Haven Clock Co., china mantel clock, 5.5", 30-hour time-only spring-driven movement, good condition, $22

American, ca. 1900, New Haven Clock Co., majolica case mantel clock, 12", 8-day time and strike spring-driven movement, very good condition, $1,064

American, ca. 1900, New Haven Clock Co., china mantel clock, 8.75", 8-day time and strike spring-driven movement, very good condition, $224

American, ca. 1900, New Haven Clock Co., china mantel clock, "HYPER-ION," 11.5", 8-day time and strike spring-driven movement, very good condition, $357

American, ca. 1905, maker unknown, china mantel clock, "LAGRANDE," 20.5", 8-day time and strike spring-driven movement, very good condition, $1,210

American, ca. 1895, Waterbury Clock Co., china mantel clock, "PARLOR #10," 8-day time and strike spring-driven movement, good condition, missing pendulum, $302

American, ca. 1910, Waterbury Clock Co., blue delft china mantel clock, 12", 8-day time and strike spring-driven movement, good condition, $577

	LOW	MID	HIGH
China-Cased Mantel Clocks (ca. 1890–1920)	$200–$500	$600–$900	$1,000–$3,000

COLUMN AND CORNICE SHELF CLOCKS first appeared in the late 1830s and remained in production until the 1880s. These clocks were steady money-makers for most of the major manufacturers.

Simple in style and easy to construct, they most often housed brass time and strike weight-driven movements (both 8-day and 30-hour) sounding on a coiled wire gong. Column and cornice clocks can be de-scribed as architectural with cyma curved molding making up the cornice and half or full columns flanking the door. Large versions of this clock are often double-deckers in that they have two doors, one above the other. The smaller versions are almost always one-door single-deckers. They are still available and reasonably priced.

American, ca. 1870, Andrews, F. C., column and cornice Empire-style single-decker shelf clock, 26", 30-hour brass time and strike, good condition, replaced tablet, $112

American, ca. 1840, Birge and Fuller, column and cornice Empire-style double-decker shelf clock, 32.5", 8-day brass time and strike, original found condition, flaking middle tablet, $364

American, ca. 1840, Birge and Fuller, column and cornice Empire-style double-decker shelf clock, 33", 8-day brass time and strike, good condition, repainted tablets and cracked dial, $280

American, ca. 1870, column and cornice shelf clock, 30-hour time and strike weight-driven movement, 25", signed Seth Thomas Clock Co., $250.

American, ca. 1860, column and cornice shelf clock, 30-hour time and strike weight-driven movement, 25", signed Seth Thomas Clock Co., $308. Credit: R. O. Schmitt Fine Arts.

American, ca. 1885, mini column and cornice shelf clock, 8-day time and strike spring-driven movement, 16", signed Seth Thomas Clock Co., $145. Credit: Prices4Antiques.com.

American, ca. 1840, column and cornice double-decker shelf clock, 8-day time and strike weight-driven movement, 32.75", signed Birge, Peck and Co., $402. Credit: Prices4Antiques.com.

American, ca. 1840, Birge and Fuller, column and cornice Empire-style double-decker shelf clock, 32.5", 8-day brass time and strike, original found condition, flaking middle tablet, $308

American, ca. 1835, Birge, Peck and Co., column and cornice Empire-style double-decker shelf clock, 32.75", 8-day brass time and strike, good condition, replaced dial and tablets (illustrated), $402

American, ca. 1845, column and cornice double-decker shelf clock, 8-day time and strike weight-driven movement, 34", signed Forestville Manufacturing Co., $1,960. Credit: R. O. Schmitt Fine Arts.

American, ca. 1838, Birge, Peck and Co., column and cornice Empire-style double-decker shelf clock, 33", 8-day brass time and strike, fair condition, flaking tablets, $495

American, ca. 1855, Birge, Peck and Co., column and cornice Empire-style double-decker shelf clock, 32.5", 8-day brass time and strike, fair condition, flaking tablets and missing veneer, $440

American, ca. 1855, Boardman, C., mini column and cornice Empire-style single-decker shelf clock, 18.5", 8-day fusee time and strike, good condition, $420

American, ca. 1845, Brewster, E. C., cornice single-decker shelf clock, 23.5", 30-hour time and strike spring-driven movement, good original condition, $280

American, ca. 1855, Brown, J. C. (Forestville Mfg. Co.), column and cornice Empire-style double-decker shelf clock, 33.5", 8-day brass time and strike, fair condition, missing columns, $275

American, ca. 1855, Brown, J. C. (Forestville Mfg. Co.), column and cornice Empire-style single deck shelf clock, 19", 30-hour brass time and strike, fair condition, veneer loss, $467

American, ca. 1840, Forbes, Wells, cornice top single-decker shelf clock, 29", 30-hour wooden works with alarm, fair condition, $148

American, ca. 1840, Forestville Mfg. Co., column and cornice Classical-style double-decker shelf clock, 37", 8-day brass time and strike, good condition, $550

American, ca. 1840, Forestville Mfg. Co., column and cornice Empire-style double-decker shelf clock, 32", 8-day brass time and strike, excellent condition, original tablets, $560

American, ca. 1845, Forestville Mfg. Co., column and cornice Empire-style double-decker shelf clock, 34", 8-day brass time and strike, excellent original condition (illustrated), $1,960

American, ca. 1850, Forestville Mfg. Co., column and cornice Empire-style double-decker shelf clock, 34", 8-day brass time and strike, very good refinished condition, $1,456

American, ca. 1850, Forestville Mfg. Co., column and cornice Empire-style double-decker shelf clock, 28", 30-hour brass time and strike, good condition, $1,925

American, ca. 1850, Jerome, Chauncey, column and cornice Empire-style single-decker shelf clock, 25", 30-hour brass time and strike, good original condition, $330

American, ca. 1855, Jerome, Chauncey, mini column and cornice Empire-style single-decker shelf clock, 18", 8-day brass time and strike, good condition, $257

American, ca. 1857, New Haven Clock Co., column and cornice Empire-style double-decker shelf clock, 20.5", 8-day brass time and strike, very good condition, $812

American, ca. 1860, New Haven Clock Co., column and cornice Empire-style single-decker shelf clock, 16", 30-hour brass time and strike, fair condition, missing lower veneer, $93

American, ca. 1860, New Haven Clock Co., mini column and cornice Empire-style single-decker shelf clock, 18", 8-day brass time and strike, good condition, $137

American, ca. 1835, Packard, Isaac, column and cornice single-decker shelf clock, 37", 30-hour Torrington time and strike wooden movement, good condition, $1,210

American, ca. 1855, Pratt, Daniel and Sons, column and cornice Empire-style double-decker shelf clock, 20.25", 8-day brass time and strike, good condition, new middle and lower tablets, $660

American, ca. 1840, Seth Thomas, Column and cornice Empire-style double-decker shelf clock, 32.5", 8-day brass time and strike, very good condition, original tablets, $575

American, ca. 1860, Seth Thomas, column and cornice Empire-style double-decker shelf clock, 32.25", 8-day brass time and strike, very good condition (illustrated), $308

American, ca. 1860, Seth Thomas, column and cornice Empire-style double-decker shelf clock,31.75", 8-day brass time and strike, good condition, label and tablet damage, $495

American, ca. 1860, Seth Thomas, column and cornice Empire-style double-decker shelf clock, 32", 8-day brass time and strike, good condition, $632

American, ca. 1870, Seth Thomas, column and cornice Empire-style double-decker shelf clock, 32", 8-day brass time and strike, good condition, $275

American, ca. 1875, Seth Thomas, column and cornice Empire-style double-decker shelf clock, 32.5", 8-day brass time and strike, good condition, reveneered, lower tablet new, $330

American, ca. 1875, Seth Thomas, column and cornice Empire-style double-decker shelf clock, 31.75", 8-day brass time and strike, fair condition, replaced cornice and part of backboard, $275

American, ca. 1880, Seth Thomas, column and cornice Empire-style double-decker shelf clock, 32.5", 8-day brass time and strike, original found condition, $308

American, ca. 1840, Seth Thomas, column and cornice Empire-style double-decker shelf clock, 32.5", 8-day brass time and strike, original found condition, $280

American, ca. 1840, Seth Thomas, column and cornice Empire-style single-decker shelf clock, 25", 30-hour brass time and strike, fair condition, replaced dial, $110

American, ca. 1855, Seth Thomas, column and cornice Empire-style single-decker shelf clock, 25", 30-hour brass time and strike, good original condition, $687

American, ca. 1855, Seth Thomas, column and cornice Empire-style single-decker shelf clock, 25", 30-hour brass time and strike, good original condition, some tablet loss, $72

American, ca. 1860, Seth Thomas, column and cornice Empire-style single-decker shelf clock, 19", 8-day brass time and strike, good original condition, $880

American, ca. 1860, Seth Thomas, column and cornice Empire-style single-decker shelf clock, 25", 30-hour brass time and strike, very good condition, $280

American, ca. 1860, Seth Thomas, column and cornice Empire-style single-decker shelf clock, 25", 30-hour brass time and strike, very good condition, $308

American, ca. 1867, Seth Thomas, column and cornice Empire-style single-decker shelf clock, 32.5", 30-hour brass time and strike, restored condition, $522

American, ca. 1868, Seth Thomas, column and cornice Empire-style single-decker shelf clock, 25", 30-hour brass time and strike, good condition, missing alarm mechanism, $330

American, ca. 1870, Seth Thomas, column and cornice Empire-style single-decker shelf clock, 18", 8-day brass time and strike, fair condition, missing lower veneer, $88

American, ca. 1870, Seth Thomas, column and cornice Empire-style single-decker shelf clock, 25", 8-day brass time and strike, good condition, cracked tablet and repainted dial, $412

American, ca. 1860, Seth Thomas, mini column and cornice Empire-style single-decker shelf clock, 19", 8-day brass time and strike, excellent condition, $616

American, ca. 1860, Seth Thomas, mini column and cornice Empire-style single-decker shelf clock, 18", 8-day brass time and strike, fair condition, paint loss, $165

American, ca. 1860, Seth Thomas, mini column and cornice Empire-style single-decker shelf clock, 16", 8-day brass time and strike, good condition (illustrated), $145

American, ca. 1868, Seth Thomas, mini column and cornice Empire-style single-decker shelf clock, 15.75", 8-day brass time, alarm, and strike, fair condition, $165

American, ca. 1886, Seth Thomas, mini column and cornice Empire-style single-decker shelf clock, 16", 30-hour brass time, alarm, and strike, fair condition, $140

American, ca. 1860, Seth Thomas for S. J. Southworth, Leeds Co., Canada, column and cornice Empire-style single-decker shelf clock, 25.5", 30-hour brass time and strike, restored condition, $165

American, ca. 1840, Spencer, Wooster and Co., column and cornice single-decker shelf clock, 34", 8-day rack and snail brass time and strike movement, good condition, some paint loss on the tablet, $1,650

American, ca. 1865, Spring, S. C. and Co., column and cornice single-decker shelf clock, 30.25", 8-day brass time, alarm, and strike, good condition, alarm disk missing, $784

American, ca. 1857, Terry, Silas, column and cornice Empire-style double-decker shelf clock, 32", 8-day brass time and strike, good condition, flaking tablets, $660

American, ca. 1860, Welch, E. N., column and cornice Empire-style double-decker shelf clock, 32.5", 8-day brass time and strike, very good condition, $495

American, ca. 1860, Welch, E. N., column and cornice Empire-style single-decker shelf clock, 25", 30-hour brass time and strike, fair condition, missing lower tablet, $121

	LOW	MID	HIGH
Column and Cornice Shelf Clocks (ca. 1838–85)	$100–$300	$400–$800	$1,000–$2,000

COLUMN AND SPLAT SHELF CLOCKS were developed when various makers (Chauncey Jerome among them), looking for a case design that would successfully challenge Eli Terry's pillar and scroll, developed long-pendulum wooden works clocks that came to be called "column and splat."

A column and splat clock is a vertical rectangle whose single door is flanked by columns (half, full, or flat) and topped by a splat-like crest. In some versions, these columns and splats are carved. In other versions, the columns and splats are stenciled. These clocks can sit flat upon the shelf or have carved lion's-paw or ball feet in front and turned feet in the back.

The doors are divided into two panels, the upper glass clear and the lower glass decorated on the reverse by painting and stenciling or by a combination of these techniques. The artwork on the lower tablets can be exceptional and greatly enhance the value of the clock. The cases are constructed of pine, mahogany, and mahogany-veneered pine. The dials are wood and often beautifully decorated.

Most of these cases house 30-hour wooden works time and strike weight-driven movements with an alarm. A smaller number have 8-day wooden works movements. They were produced as early as the mid-1820s and faded away with the Panic of 1837 and the appearance of the cheap Jerome brass movement. These were among the last of the early mass-produced clocks that still show handcrafted details.

Long out of favor, these clocks are slowly beginning to rise in value. Nonetheless, many remain with reasonable prices. Buy with a view to fine original condition and excellent dial and tablet.

American, ca. 1828, Boardman, stenciled half column and splat shelf clock, 34", 30-hour "Groaner"-type wooden movement, good as-found condition, $179

American, ca. 1840, Boardman and Wells, stenciled half column and splat shelf clock, 31.5", 30-hour time and strike wooden weight-driven movement, good as-found condition, old replacement mirror, $168

American, ca. 1826, Brace, Rodney, carved half column and splat shelf clock, 36", 30-hour Torrington wooden movement, good restored condition (illustrated), $1,064

American, ca. 1835, Forestville Manufacturing Co., stenciled half column and splat shelf clock, 33.25", 30-hour time and strike wooden weight-driven movement, good as-found condition, $337

American, ca. 1832, Hall, Asaph, flat column and splat shelf clock, 34.5", 30-hour time and strike wooden weight-driven movement, good as-found condition, $672

American, ca. 1835, Hoadley, Silas, stenciled half column and splat shelf clock, 36", 30-hour Hoadley "upside down" movement, good condition, $1,210

Stenciled Column and Splat Shelf Clocks

American, ca. 1833, column and splat shelf clock, 30-hour time and strike wooden movement, 34.5", signed Elisha Hotchkiss, $300.

American, ca. 1828, column and splat shelf clock, 30-hour time and strike wooden movement, 35", signed Seth Thomas Clock Co., $550.

Elisha Hotchkiss paper label, ca. 1833.

Lower tablet with stenciled margins and reverse glass painted centers, Seth Thomas Clock Co.

Flat Column and Splat Shelf Clock

David Dutton wood dial.

David Dutton pendulum bob.

American, ca. 1830, column and splat shelf clock, 30-hour time and strike wooden movement, 32", signed David Dutton, $350.

Carved and Footed Column and Splat Shelf Clocks

American, ca. 1835, column and splat shelf clock, 30-hour wooden movement, 35.5", signed Riley Whiting, $364. Credit: R. O. Schmitt Fine Arts.

American, ca. 1826, column and splat shelf clock, 30-hour Torrington wooden works, 36", signed Rodney Brace, $1,064. Credit: R. O. Schmitt Fine Arts.

American, ca. 1835, Hoadley, Silas, carved half column and splat shelf clock, 39", 30-hour Hoadley "upside down" movement, very good condition, dial with extra holes, $1,680

American, ca. 1833, Hotchkiss, Elisha, stenciled half column and splat shelf clock, 34.5", 30-hour time and strike wooden weight-driven movement, good condition, replacement tablet in door (illustrated), $300

American, ca. 1837, Jerome, Chauncey, stenciled half column and splat shelf clock, 31.75", 8-day brass time and strike weight-driven movement, good condition, lower tablet now with a Currier print, $123

American, ca. 1829, Jeromes and Darrow, stenciled half column and splat shelf clock, 33.5", 30-hour time and strike wooden weight-driven movement, very good condition, some veneer repairs, $300

American, ca. 1830, Jeromes and Darrow, stenciled half column and splat shelf clock, 33.5", 30-hour time and strike wooden weight-driven movement, good original condition, $364

American, ca. 1830, Jeromes and Darrow, stenciled half column and splat shelf clock, 33.5", 30-hour time and strike wooden weight-driven movement, fair condition, missing veneer, $156

American, ca. 1830, Jeromes and Darrow, stenciled half column and splat shelf clock, 33.5", 30-hour time and strike wooden weight-driven movement, good as-found condition, $123

American, ca. 1830, Jeromes and Darrow, stenciled half column and splat shelf clock, 33", 30-hour time and strike wooden weight-driven movement, very good condition, $190

American, ca. 1830, Jeromes and Darrow, stenciled half column and splat shelf clock, 35", 30-hour time and strike wooden weight-driven movement, very good condition, $252

American, ca. 1830, Lane, Mark, carved half column and splat shelf clock, 34", 30-hour time and strike wooden weight-driven movement, very good condition, some paint loss in the lower tablet, $840

American, ca. 1831, Mitchell, George, stenciled half column and splat shelf clock, 35.5", 30-hour time and strike wooden weight-driven movement, good condition, replacement mirror in door, $280

American, ca. 1837, Pratt, Daniel, Jr., flat column and splat shelf clock, 35.5", 30-hour time and strike wooden weight-driven movement, good original condition, $302

American, ca. 1830, Pratt and Frost, stenciled half column and splat shelf clock, 35", 30-hour time and strike wooden weight-driven movement, good condition with cracked top glass, $230

American, ca. 1835, Rawson, Jason R., flat column and splat shelf clock, 31", 30-hour time and strike wooden weight-driven movement, good condition, $84

American, ca. 1836, Stratton, Charles, flat bevel column and splat shelf clock, 34.5", 30-hour time, strike, and alarm wooden weight-driven movement, very good condition, some veneer repairs, $336

American, ca. 1833, Terry, Eli, Jr., stenciled half column and splat shelf clock with a short drop movement, 31.5", 30-hour time and strike wooden weight-driven movement, good condition, blank lower table, $336

American, ca. 1835, Terry, Eli, Jr., stenciled half column and splat shelf clock, 31.5", 30-hour time and strike wooden weight-driven movement, good condition, $151

American, ca. 1832, Terry, Eli and Sons, stenciled half column and splat shelf clock, 34.5", 8-day time and strike wooden movement, fair condition, missing hands and weights, $420

American, ca. 1834, Terry, Henry, stenciled half column and splat shelf
   clock, 28.5", 30-hour time and strike wooden weight-driven movement,
   fair condition, tablet poorly retouched, $200

American, ca. 1830, Terry, Silas, stenciled half column and splat shelf clock,
   34.5", 30-hour time and strike wooden weight-driven movement, very
   good condition, $336

American, ca. 1828, Seth Thomas, stenciled half column and splat shelf
   clock, 34.5", 30-hour time, strike, and alarm wooden weight-driven
   movement, good original condition, excellent original tablet (illustrated) $550

American, ca. 1830, Seth Thomas, stenciled half column and splat shelf
   clock, 34.5", 30-hour time and strike wooden weight-driven movement,
   good condition, lower tablet now clear, $145

American, ca. 1830, Seth Thomas, carved and stenciled half column and
   splat shelf clock, 37", 8-day time and strike wooden movement, good
   condition, replaced tablet, $1,624

American, ca. 1835, Whiting, Riley, carved half column and splat shelf
   clock, 35.5", 30-hour time and strike wooden weight-driven movement,
   fair condition, partially stripped case (illustrated) $364

	LOW	MID	HIGH
Column and Splat Shelf Clocks (ca. 1825–40)	$150–$250	$350–$600	$800–$1,500

COTTAGE SHELF CLOCKS are among the most ubiquitous of American
shelf clocks, rivaled in numbers only by "OG" and steeple clocks. The
simple, utilitarian cottage shelf clock was found in virtually every home,
usually in kitchens and bedrooms. Appearing as early as the 1840s, this
clock remained in production until World War I. Worldwide demand
caused the German industry to copy and export large numbers of them,
many to America.

In their simplest version, they are 30-hour time-only spring-driven
clocks. Many had alarm mechanisms. Within a short time of their introduction, 8-day models were offered for sale. Cases were simple with flat
or sloped tops. Decorating the lower door tablet was a transfer or later a
decal. Dials are painted metal and the hands are stamped from steel.

While cottage clocks are reasonably priced now, the value of clean
decorative examples has been rising steeply.

American, ca. 1855, Atkins Clock Co., mini cottage clock, 10.25", 30-hour time-only spring-driven movement, good condition, $196

American, ca. 1865, Atkins Clock Co., mini cottage clock, 10.25", 30-hour time-only spring-driven movement, good original condition, $179

American, ca. 1865, Atkins Clock Co., mini cottage clock, 10.25", 30-hour time and alarm spring-driven movement, very good original condition (illustrated), $252

American, ca. 1870, Atkins Clock Co., mini cottage clock, 10", 30-hour time-only spring-driven movement, fair condition, glass tablet replaced with a wood panel, $148

American, ca. 1850, Brewster and Ingraham, cottage clock, 14", 8-day time and strike spring-driven movement, good condition, $407

American, ca. 1855, Brown, J. C., cottage clock, 15.25", 8-day time, alarm, and strike spring-driven movement, good condition, $560

American, ca. 1845, Brown, J. C., cottage clock with ripple trim, 15", 30-hour time and strike spring-driven movement, good condition, $1,064

American, ca. 1845, Brown, J. C. cottage clock with ripple trim, 14", 8-day time and strike spring-driven movement, good condition, some flaking on tablet (illustrated), $1,904

American, ca. 1911, flat-top cottage clock, 8-day time, strike, and alarm spring-driven movement, 14.5", signed Seth Thomas Clock Co., $550. Credit: R. O. Schmitt Fine Arts.

American, ca. 1845, ripple-front flat-top cottage clock, 8-day time and strike spring-driven movement, 14", signed J. C. Brown, $1,904. Credit: R. O. Schmitt Fine Arts.

American, ca. 1865, slope-top cottage clock, 30-hour time and alarm spring-driven movement, 10.25", signed Atkins Clock Co., $252. Credit: R. O. Schmitt Fine Arts.

American, ca. 1860, slope-top cottage clock, 30-hour time, strike, and alarm spring-driven movement, 16.25", signed Jerome and Co., $123. Credit: Prices4Antiques.com.

American, ca. 1849, Brown, J. C., cottage clock with ripple trim, 15", 30-hour time, alarm, and strike spring-driven movement, fair condition, $364

American, ca. 1850, Brown, J. C., cottage clock with ripple trim, 15", 30-hour time and strike spring-driven movement, good condition, $770

American, ca. 1851, Brown, J. C., cottage clock with ripple trim, 15", 2-day time and strike spring-driven movement, good condition, $1,100

American, ca. 1870, Gilbert, William L., cottage clock, 13", 30-hour time and strike spring-driven movement, very good condition, $165

American, ca. 1860, Goodrich, Chauncey, mini cottage clock, 12.5", 30-hour time and alarm spring-driven movement, poor condition, missing the springs, $504

American, ca. 1900, Ingraham and Co., cottage clock, 13", 8-day time and strike spring-driven movement, very good original condition, $275

American, ca. 1880, Ingraham, E., cottage clock, 13", 30-hour time and strike spring-driven movement, fair condition, $99

American, ca. 1850, Jerome, Chauncey, cottage clock, 13", 8-day time and strike spring-driven movement, good original condition, $275

American, ca. 1850, Jerome, Chauncey, cottage clock, 12", 30-hour time-only spring-driven movement, good condition, $280

American, ca. 1850, Jerome, Chauncey, cottage clock, 13", 8-day time and strike fusee movement, good original condition, $687

American, ca. 1850, Jerome, Chauncey, cottage clock, 13", 8-day time and strike fusee movement, very good original condition, $561

American, ca. 1850, Jerome and Co., cottage clock, 12.5", 30-hour time-only spring-driven movement, good condition, $168

American, ca. 1850, Jerome and Co., cottage clock, 16.25", 30-hour time, alarm, and strike spring-driven movement, good condition (illustrated), $123

American, ca. 1860, Jerome and Co., cottage clock, 13.5", 8-day time, alarm, and strike spring-driven movement, good original condition, $364

American, ca. 1857, Jerome, S. B., cottage clock, 13", 8-day time and strike spring-driven movement, very good condition, $374

American, ca. 1855, Pratt, Daniel, cottage clock, 11", 30-hour time and alarm spring-driven movement, very good condition, some label damage, $257

American, ca. 1850, Sperry, Henry, cottage clock, 12", 30-hour time-only spring-driven movement, very good condition, $129

American, ca. 1848, Terry and Andrews, cottage clock, 15.5", 8-day time and strike spring-driven movement, very good condition, replaced hands, $522

American, ca. 1870, Terry Clock Co., cottage clock, 11.5", 30-hour time-only spring-driven movement, good condition, $192

American, ca. 1855, Terry Clock Co., mini cottage clock, 10.5", 30-hour time and strike spring-driven movement, good condition, $224

American, ca. 1852, Terry, Silas, cottage clock, 11.75", 30-hour time and alarm spring-driven movement, good condition, $1,456

American, ca. 1852, Terry, Silas, cottage clock, 10.25", 30-hour time-only spring-driven movement, poor condition, veneer removed from case, $198

American, ca. 1853, Terry, Silas, cottage clock, 10.5", 30-hour time-only spring-driven movement, good original condition, $364

American, ca. 1853, Terry, Silas, cottage clock, 10", 30-hour time-only spring-driven movement, good condition, $2,860

American, ca. 1855, Terry, Silas, cottage clock, 12.25", 8-day time, seconds, and strike spring-driven movement, very good condition, $672

American, ca. 1855, Terry, Silas, mini cottage clock, 10.5", 30-hour time-only spring-driven movement, fair condition, $420

American, ca. 1860, Seth Thomas, cottage clock, 14.5", 30-hour time and strike spring-driven movement, good condition, $132

American, ca. 1875, Seth Thomas, cottage clock, 14", 8-day time and strike spring-driven movement, very good condition, $385

American, ca. 1875, Seth Thomas, cottage clock, 14.25", 30-hour time-only spring-driven movement, good condition, alarm missing, $196

American, ca. 1876, Seth Thomas, cottage clock, 14.25", 30-hour time, alarm, and strike spring-driven movement, very good condition, $253

American, ca. 1880, Seth Thomas, cottage clock, 14", 8-day time and strike spring-driven movement, good restored condition, $220

American, ca. 1880, Seth Thomas, cottage clock, 14.25", 8-day time, alarm, and strike spring-driven movement, very good condition, $165

American, ca. 1911, Seth Thomas, cottage clock, 14.5", 8-day time, alarm, and strike spring-driven movement, very good original condition (illustrated), $550

American, ca. 1870, Seth Thomas, cottage clock, Tudor No. 3, 9.5", 30-hour time-only spring-driven movement, good restored condition, $448

American, ca. 1863, Seth Thomas, mini cottage clock, 9.5", 30-hour time-only spring-driven movement, fair condition, reveneered case, $192

American, ca. 1863, Seth Thomas, mini cottage clock, 9", 30-hour time-only spring-driven movement, good restored condition, $459

American, ca. 1865, Seth Thomas, mini cottage clock, 9", 30-hour time-only spring-driven movement, good condition, $280

American, ca. 1868, Seth Thomas, mini cottage clock, 9.5", 30-hour time only spring-driven movement, good restored condition, $220

American, ca. 1870, Seth Thomas, mini cottage clock, 9.25", 30-hour time and alarm spring-driven movement, good condition, $181

American, ca. 1870, Seth Thomas, mini cottage clock, 9.25", 30-hour time and alarm spring-driven movement, fair condition, $170

American, ca. 1870, Seth Thomas, mini cottage clock, 9", 30-hour time-only spring-driven movement, very good condition, $200

American, ca. 1870, Seth Thomas, mini cottage clock, 9.5", 30-hour time and alarm spring-driven movement, very good condition, $110

American, ca. 1870, Seth Thomas, mini cottage clock, 9.5", 30-hour time and strike spring-driven movement, good condition, $112

American, ca. 1875, Seth Thomas, mini cottage clock, 9.5", 30-hour time and alarm spring-driven movement, fair condition, $247

American, ca. 1875, Seth Thomas, mini cottage clock, 9.25", 30-hour time and alarm spring-driven movement, good original condition, $330

American, ca. 1875, Seth Thomas, mini cottage clock, 9.5", 30-hour time-only spring-driven movement, good condition, $212

American, ca. 1875, Seth Thomas, mini cottage clock, 9.5", 30-hour time and alarm spring-driven movement, good condition, $123

American, ca. 1875, Seth Thomas, mini cottage clock, 9.5", 30-hour time-only spring-driven movement, good condition with touched-up dial, $190

American, ca. 1875, Seth Thomas, mini cottage clock, 9.5", 30-hour time and alarm spring-driven movement, good condition, $123

American, ca. 1875, Seth Thomas, mini cottage clock, 9.5", 30-hour time and alarm spring-driven movement, good condition, $168

American, ca. 1876, Seth Thomas, mini cottage clock, 9", 30-hour time-only spring-driven movement, good condition, $224

American, ca. 1878, Seth Thomas, mini cottage clock, 9", 30-hour time-only spring-driven movement, very good restored condition, $201

American, ca. 1880, Seth Thomas, mini cottage clock, 9", 30-hour time-only spring-driven movement, very good condition, $357

American, ca. 1880, Seth Thomas, mini cottage clock, 9", 30-hour time-only spring-driven movement, good condition, $252

American, ca. 1886, Seth Thomas, mini cottage clock, 9", 30-hour time and alarm spring-driven movement, very good condition, $168

American, ca. 1895, Seth Thomas, mini cottage clock, 9", 30-hour time-only spring-driven movement, good condition, $190

American, ca. 1860, unknown, cottage clock, 13", 30-hour time and strike spring-driven movement, good condition, $106

American, ca. 1880, Waterbury Clock Co., cottage clock, 10.5", 30-hour time-only spring-driven movement, good condition, repapered dial, $88

American, ca. 1881, Waterbury Clock Co., cottage clock, 12.75", 8-day time and strike spring-driven movement, good original condition, $121

American, ca. 1870, Waterbury Clock Co., mini cottage clock, 6", 30-hour time-only spring-driven movement, good condition, $123

American, ca. 1880, Welch, E. N., cottage clock, 12", 30-hour time-only spring-driven movement, poor condition, $67

	LOW	MID	HIGH
Cottage Clocks (ca. 1845–1920)	$100–$200	$300–$700	$1,000–$2,000+

CRYSTAL REGULATOR MANTEL CLOCKS were an attempt to develop a domestic market started by French imports. As a style, these glass-cased mantel clocks originated in France during the second half of the nineteenth century. American versions appeared in the 1880s, but achieved their greatest popularity between 1900 and 1920.

The movements are 8-day time and strike that sound on a heavy wire gong. The escapement was often placed in front of the dial. On the best of these clocks, pendulums are compensated, often with two small vials of mercury. Lower-priced versions have simulated compensated pendulums.

Two types of case are commonly found, a flat-top version that resembles a carriage clock minus the handle and a far more ornate Baroque version that terminates in a decorative finial. The four sides of the case have beveled glass through which you can view the operation of the clock. There are two doors, one in front and one in the rear. High-end cases are gilded brass, while low-end cases are gilded spelter.

American, ca. 1910, Ansonia Clock Co., crystal regulator shelf clock, 9.75",
    8-day time and strike spring-driven movement, very good condition,
    $550

American, ca. 1910, crystal regulator, 8-day time and strike movement, 10.25", signed Boston Clock Co., $560. Credit: Prices4Antiques.com.

American, ca. 1915, crystal regulator, 8-day time and strike movement, 16.5", signed Ansonia Clock Co., $840. Credit: Prices4Antiques.com.

American, ca. 1914, Ansonia Clock Co., crystal regulator shelf clock, "CRYSTAL" model, 9.75", 8-day time and strike spring-driven movement, excellent condition, $500

American, ca. 1914, Ansonia Clock Co., crystal regulator shelf clock, "CRYSTAL REG. NO. 2" model, 17", 8-day time and strike spring-driven movement, very good condition, $3,740

American, ca. 1914, Ansonia Clock Co., crystal regulator shelf clock, "CRYSTAL REG. NO. 3" model, 18.25", 8-day time and strike spring-driven movement, excellent original condition, $4,400

American, ca. 1915, Ansonia Clock Co., crystal regulator shelf clock, "CRYSTAL REG. NO. 3" model, 17.5", 8-day time and strike spring-driven movement, very good condition, $548

American, ca. 1905, Ansonia Clock Co., crystal regulator shelf clock, "DORVAL" model, 8.75", 8-day time and strike spring-driven movement, good condition, $209

American, ca. 1920, Ansonia Clock Co., crystal regulator shelf clock, "DORVAL" model, 8.75", 8-day time and strike spring-driven movement, fair condition, some chipped and cracked glass, $192

American, ca. 1914, Ansonia Clock Co., crystal regulator shelf clock, "ELYSIAN" model, 16.5", 8-day time and strike spring-driven movement, good condition, $672

American, ca. 1904, Ansonia Clock Co., crystal regulator shelf clock, "EXCELSIOR" model, 20.5", 8-day time and strike spring-driven movement, fair condition, metalwork of the case painted gold, $1,760

American, ca. 1901, Ansonia Clock Co., crystal regulator shelf clock, "MARQUISE" model, 13", 8-day time and strike spring-driven movement, good condition, urn finial missing from the top, $616

American, ca. 1905, Ansonia Clock Co., crystal regulator shelf clock, "NORMA" model, 14", 8-day time and strike spring-driven movement, fair condition, bronze surface oxidized, $852

American, ca. 1917, Ansonia Clock Co., crystal regulator shelf clock, "PEER" model, 12", 8-day time and strike spring-driven movement, fair condition, $599

American, ca. 1880, Ansonia Clock Co., crystal regulator shelf clock, "SYMBOL EXTRA" model, 16", 8-day time and strike spring-driven movement, good condition, $532

American, ca. 1910, Ansonia Clock Co., crystal regulator shelf clock, "VIS-COUNT" model, 16.5", 8-day time and strike spring-driven movement, excellent condition (illustrated), $840

American, ca. 1900, Boston Clock Co., crystal regulator shelf clock, 10.25", 8-day time and strike spring-driven movement, good condition (illustrated), $560

American, ca. 1890, Boston Clock Co., crystal regulator shelf clock, "DELPHUS" model, 10.5", 8-day time and strike spring-driven movement, good original condition, $952

American, ca. 1900, Gilbert, William L., crystal regulator shelf clock, 10.5", 8-day time and strike spring-driven movement, very good condition, $357

American, ca. 1900, Gilbert, William L., crystal regulator shelf clock, "VISTA" model, 10.5", 8-day time and strike spring-driven movement, good condition, $412

American, ca. 1911, New Haven Clock Co., crystal regulator shelf clock, "THOREAU" model, 15.5", 8-day time and strike spring-driven movement, fair condition, gilding worn down to the copper base, $550

American, ca. 1911, New Haven Clock Co., crystal regulator shelf clock, "THOREAU" model, 15.25", 8-day time and strike spring-driven movement, excellent condition, $577

American, ca. 1920, Poole Electric, crystal regulator shelf clock, "SALEM" model, 11", electric movement, excellent condition, $56

American, ca. 1910, Seth Thomas, crystal regulator shelf clock, "CRYSTAL REG. NO. 4" model, 10.5", 8-day time and strike spring-driven movement, excellent original condition, $588

American, ca. 1905, Seth Thomas, crystal regulator shelf clock, "EMPIRE #5" model, 14", 8-day time and strike spring-driven movement, very good condition, $605

American, ca. 1917, Seth Thomas, crystal regulator shelf clock, "EMPIRE NO. 200" model, 9.5", 8-day time and strike spring-driven movement, very good condition, $308

American, ca. 1917, Seth Thomas, crystal regulator shelf clock, "EMPIRE NO. 300" model, 9.25", 8-day time and strike spring-driven movement, very good condition, $280

American, ca. 1909, Seth Thomas, crystal regulator shelf clock, "EMPIRE

NO. 65" model, 11", 8-day time and strike spring-driven movement, fair condition, $504

American, ca. 1909, Seth Thomas, crystal regulator shelf clock, "ORCHID NO. 4" model, 10.75", 8-day time and strike spring-driven movement, good condition, $280

American, ca. 1903, Waterbury Clock Co., crystal regulator shelf clock, "AVIGNON" model, 17.5", 8-day time and strike spring-driven movement, good condition, $599

American, ca. 1906, Waterbury Clock Co., crystal regulator shelf clock, "NAVARRE" model, 8.75", 8-day time and strike spring-driven movement, good as-found condition, $448

American, ca. 1912, Waterbury Clock Co., crystal regulator shelf clock, "TOULON" model, 10.5", 8-day time and strike spring-driven movement, very good condition, $440

	LOW	MID	HIGH
Crystal Regulator Mantel Clocks (ca. 1880–1925)	$200–$350	$500–$850	$1,500+

DOUBLE- AND TRIPLE-DECKER SHELF CLOCKS are 8-day wooden works with brass time and strike weight-driven clocks that appeared among the Connecticut clockmakers as early as the 1830s and disappeared shortly after the Civil War (1861–65).

Double- and triple-decker shelf clocks are large, standing three feet high or more. The cases are mahogany-veneered pine boxes. The fronts are divided into two or three sections of which two are doors. Each section is flanked by columns that can be carved, stenciled, or gilded. The lower tablet or tablets are reverse decorated with the same motifs found on pillar and scroll and column and splat clocks. Dials are handpainted wood in early production and painted metal in later years. Splats can be carved, architectural, or gilded molded plaster.

This is not a plentiful style, but prices are more often determined by decoration than rarity.

American, ca. 1825, Atkins and Downs for George Mitchell, carved splat and column triple-decker, 37", 8-day brass time and strike, good condition, $690

American, ca. 1835, Barnes, Bartholomew, and Co., carved splat and column triple-decker, 36", 8-day brass time and strike, original as found, $660

American, ca. 1835, double-decker shelf clock, 8-day brass time and strike weight-driven movement, 38", signed Forestville Manufacturing Co., $600.

American, ca. 1839, double-decker shelf clock, 8-day brass time and strike weight-driven movement, wood dial, carved splat, 36", signed Forestville Manufacturing Co., $650. Credit: NAWCC TIMEXPO 2002.

American, ca. 1835, double-decker shelf clock, 8-day brass time and strike weight-driven movement, wood dial, carved splat, architectural top and paw feet, 36", signed Forestville Manufacturing Co., Credit: NAWCC Eastern States Regional 2002.

American, ca. 1838, double-decker shelf clock, 8-day brass time and strike weight-driven movement, wood dial, gilded plaster splat, 37", signed A. J. Birge, $3,584. Credit: Prices4Antiques.com.

American, ca. 1845, triple-decker shelf clock, 8-day brass time and strike weight-driven movement, wood dial, carved splat, 38", signed Birge and Gilbert, $420. Credit: Prices4Antiques.com.

American, ca. 1833, 8-day strap brass time and strike weight-driven movement used in many double- and triple-decker shelf clocks. Credit: NAWCC Eastern States Regional 2002.

American, ca. 1830, Birge, A. J., column and splat double-decker, 36.5", 8-day brass time and strike, good as-found condition, mahogany case (illustrated), $3,584

American, ca. 1835, Birge Case Co., carved splat and column triple-decker, 36", 8-day brass time and strike, good condition, $632

American, ca. 1855, Birge and Gilbert, carved splat and column triple-decker, 38", 8-day brass time and strike, fair condition, middle tablet replaced, flaking dial (illustrated), $420

American, ca. 1838, Birge and Ives, carved splat and column triple-decker, 36", 8-day brass time and strike, very good condition with repainted tablet, $812

American, ca. 1835, Birge, John for George Mitchell, carved splat and column triple-decker, 37", 8-day brass time and strike, good condition, some paint missing from tablet, $1,782

American, ca. 1840, Birge, Mallory and Co., carved splat and column double-decker, 34", 8-day brass time and strike, poor condition, missing cresting and with replaced tablets, poor dial, $179

American, ca. 1840, Birge, Mallory, and Co., carved splat and column triple-decker, 39", 8-day brass time and strike, fair condition, replaced tablets, $196

American, ca. 1840, Birge, Mallory, and Co., carved splat and column triple-decker, 38", 8-day brass time and strike, good condition, $646

American, ca. 1840, Birge, Mallory, and Co., carved splat and column triple-decker, 31.5", 8-day brass time and strike, poor condition, missing crest, flaking mid tablet, clear lower tablet, $252

American, ca. 1840, Birge, Mallory, and Co., carved splat and column triple-decker, 39", 8-day brass time and strike, good condition, replaced middle tablet (illustrated), $476

American, ca. 1840, Birge, Mallory, and Co., carved splat and column triple-decker, 36", 8-day brass time and strike, good condition, $632

American, ca. 1840, Birge, Mallory, and Co., carved splat and column triple-decker, 25.5", 8-day brass time and strike, very good original condition, $2,200

American, ca. 1840, Birge, Mallory, and Co., carved splat and column triple-decker, 28", 30-hour brass time and strike, fair condition with repainted dial, $1,210

American, ca. 1845, Birge, Mallory, and Co., carved splat and column triple-decker, 38", 8-day brass time and strike, original as found, $770

American, ca. 1845, Birge, Mallory, and Co., carved splat and column, triple-decker, 32", 8-day brass time and strike, original, as found, $500

American, ca. 1840, Birge and Marsh, carved splat and column triple-decker, 36", 8-day brass time and strike, good condition, $532

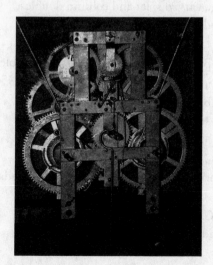

American, ca. 1850, triple-decker shelf clock, 8-day brass time and strike weight-driven movement, wood dial, molded and gilded plaster splat, 39", signed Birge and Mallory, $476. Credit: Prices4Antiques.com.

American, ca. 1855, Birge and Peck and Co., carved splat and column triple-decker, 33.25", 8-day brass time and strike, fair condition, missing feet, $550

American, ca. 1855, Birge and Peck and Co., carved splat and column triple-decker, 34", 8-day brass time and strike, good condition, missing feet, $336

American, ca. 1855, Birge and Peck and Co., carved splat and column triple-decker, 29.5", 8-day brass time and strike, poor condition, missing crest and feet, $179

American, ca. 1855, Birge and Peck and Co., carved splat and column triple-decker, 36.5", 8-day brass time and strike, very good original condition, $2,688

American, ca. 1835, Forestville Mfg., carved splat and column double-decker, 38", 8-day brass time and strike, original as found, some tablet flaking (illustrated), $600

American, ca. 1840, Forestville Mfg., cornice and column double-decker, 36.5", 8-day brass time and strike, very good condition, $308

American, ca. 1840, Forestville Mfg., cornice and column double-decker, 34.5", 8-day brass time and strike, fair condition, missing paint from tablets, $179

American, ca. 1840, Forestville Mfg., cornice and column double-decker, 37", 8-day brass time and strike, fair condition, missing glass, $550

American, ca. 1845, Forestville Mfg., carved splat and column double-decker, 39", 8-day brass time and strike, as-found condition, some restoration, $476

American, ca. 1845, Forestville Mfg., carved splat and column double-decker, 40", 8-day brass time and strike, very good condition, glass tablets retouched, $1,045

American, ca. 1835, Hotchkiss and Benedict, flat column and splat double-decker, 37.25", 8-day brass time and strike, very good condition, $1,456

American, ca. 1835, Hotchkiss and Benedict, flat splat and flat column double-decker, 38", 8-day brass time, seconds, and strike, very good condition, $1,650

American, ca. 1832, Ives, C. and L.C., carved splat and column triple-decker, 38", 8-day brass time and strike, good condition, wrong hands and replaced tablet, $1,512

American, ca. 1832, Ives, C. and L.C., carved splat and column triple-decker, 38", 8-day brass time and strike, good condition, lower tablets replaced, $880

American, ca. 1835, Jerome, Chauncey, carved splat and column, double-decker, 39", 8-day wood time and strike, good condition, $308

American, ca. 1840, Jerome, Chauncey and Noble, cornice and column double-decker, 35.25", 8-day brass time and strike, fair condition, missing paint from tablets, $420

American, ca. 1838, Jeromes and Darrow, cornice and column double-decker, 22", 30-hour wood time and strike, fair refinished condition, $392

American, ca. 1840, Marsh, G., column and splat double-decker, 35.5", 8-day brass time and strike, good as-found condition, mahogany case with damaged dial, $420

American, ca. 1833, Marsh, George and Co., carved splat and column double-decker, 41", 8-day wood time and strike, good condition, with replaced mirror, $660

American, ca. 1835, Mitchell and Atkins, cornice and column triple-decker, 35", 8-day wood time and strike, very good condition, $952

American, ca. 1831, Munger and Benedict, carved splat and column double-decker, 42", 8-day brass time, seconds, and strike, very good condition, $2,090

American, ca. 1835, Seymour, Williams and Porter, carved splat and column triple-decker, 32", 30-hour wood time and strike, good condition, missing feet, $224

American, ca. 1830, Spencer, Hotchkiss, and Co., carved splat and column triple-decker, 32", 8-day brass time, seconds, and strike, fair condition, $1,100

American, ca. 1828, Terry, Eli, and Sons, carved splat and column double-decker, 38.5", 8-day wood time and strike, very good condition, replaced tablet, $1,375

American, ca. 1830, Terry, Eli, and Sons, carved splat and column double-decker, 37", 8-day brass time, seconds, and strike, good condition, $1,155

American, ca. 1835, Terry, R. and J. B., carved splat and column triple-decker, 37", 8-day brass time and strike, original as-found condition, $504

American, ca. 1840, Terry, R. and J. B., cornice and column triple-decker, 37", 8-day brass time and strike, good condition, case stripped and refinished, $605

American, ca. 1838, Terry, Silas B., carved splat and column double-decker, 36", 8-day brass time and strike round-plate movement, very good condition, $2,750

American, ca. 1840, Terry, Silas B., carved splat and column double-decker, 36", 8-day brass time and strike, good condition, $1,008

American, ca. 1835, maker unknown, carved splat and column double-decker, 36", 8-day brass time and strike, good condition, $575

American, ca. 1838, Upson, Merrimans, and Co., carved splat and carved column triple-decker , 37", 8-day brass time and strike, good restored condition, $737

American, ca. 1835, Williams, Orton, Prestons, and Co., cornice and carved half-column double-decker, 35", 8-day wood time and strike, good as-found condition, mahogany case, $504

	LOW	MID	HIGH
Double- and Triple-Decker Shelf Clocks (ca. 1830–60)	$200–$400	$500–$900	$1,000–$3,000

FIGURAL MANTEL CLOCKS originated in France in the late eighteenth century. By the nineteenth century, they were being imported to America and appearing in the homes of the wealthy. The number of imports increased after the Civil War, but Connecticut manufacturers countered by introducing their own lines of figural clocks.

American figural clocks were cast and plated spelter cases fitted with many of the same 8-day brass spring-driven movements found in the black mantel clocks. The upper end of this line usually consisted of a rectangular footed base surmounted by a classical figure at one end and the clock at the other. The less expensive clocks combined clock and figure in one.

Never as popular as the blacks, they were produced from the 1870s until World War I. Price depends upon the casting details, movement, and demand.

American, ca. 1894, Ansonia Clock Co., figural mantel clock, "MERCURY" model, 15", 8-day time and strike spring-driven movement, good as-found condition (illustrated), $539

American, ca. 1894, Ansonia Clock Co., figural mantel clock, "MUSIC and POETRY" model, 20.5", 8-day time and strike spring-driven movement, fair condition, $1,456

American, ca. 1895, Ansonia Clock Co., figural mantel clock, maiden picking flowers figure, 24", 8-day time and strike spring-driven movement, good condition, $575

American, ca. 1870, figural mantel
clock, 30-hour time-only brass
spring-driven movement, 11.5",
signed Terry Clock Co., $412.
Credit: R. O. Schmitt Fine Arts.

American, ca. 1901, Ansonia Clock Co., figural mantel clock, "VASSAR"
   model, 11", 8-day time and strike spring-driven movement, fair condition, repainted with gold paint, $440

American, ca. 1910, Ansonia Clock Co., figural mantel clock, cavalier figure, 22", 8-day time and strike spring-driven movement, fair condition,
   repainted, $660

American, ca. 1894, figural mantel clock, "Mercury,"
8-day time and strike brass spring-driven movement,
15", signed Ansonia Clock Co., $539. Credit:
R. O. Schmitt Fine Arts.

American, ca. 1890, Boston Clock Co., figural mantel clock, Rip Van Winkle, 14.5", 30-hour time-only spring-driven movement, fair condition, $476

American, ca. 1915, Caldwell, E. F. and Co., figural mantel clock, 17.5", 8-day time-only spring-driven Chelsea movement, very good condition, $11,760

American, ca. 1878, Kroeber, Francis, figural mantel clock, "SAXONIA" model, 20.5", 8-day time and strike spring-driven movement, fair condition, most of the finish worn away, $896

American, ca. 1890, Kroeber, Francis, figural mantel clock, warrior, 22", 8-day time and strike spring-driven movement, very good condition, $450

American, ca. 1900, New Haven Clock Co., figural mantel clock, "CLOTHO" model, 16", 8-day time and strike spring-driven movement, very good original condition, $1,017

American, ca. 1930, Sterling Bronze Co., figural mantel clock, 11", 8-day time-only spring-driven Chelsea movement, good original condition, $1,344

American, ca. 1870, Terry Clock Co., figural mantel clock, 11.5", 30-hour time-only spring-driven movement, good condition (illustrated), $412

American, ca. 1877, Seth Thomas, figural mantel clock, "MUSIC and ART" model, 19", 8-day time and strike spring-driven movement, good condition, repainted in gold, $660

American, ca. 1890, Seth Thomas, figural mantel clock, "MUSIC and ART" model, 17", 8-day time and strike spring-driven movement, good condition with worn finish, $495

American, ca. 1875, Seth Thomas and Sons and Co., figural mantel clock, "MUSIC and ART" model, 17", 8-day time and strike spring-driven movement, excellent original condition, $880

American, ca. 1876, Seth Thomas and Sons and Co., figural mantel clock, 15", 8-day time and strike spring-driven movement, fair condition with repainting and dents, $467

American, ca. 1876, Seth Thomas and Sons and Co., figural mantel clock, Angel and Child, 17", 8-day time and strike spring-driven movement, good condition, $885

American, ca. 1880, maker unknown, figural mantel clock, 47", 8-day time and strike spring-driven movement, very good condition, $2,520

American, ca. 1895, maker unknown, figural mantel clock, 13", 8-day time and strike spring-driven movement, good condition, $495

American, ca. 1865, Waterbury Clock Co., figural mantel clock, "RO-
MANCE" model, 21", 8-day time and strike spring-driven movement,
good restored condition, $396

	LOW	MID	HIGH
Figural Mantel Clocks (ca. 1860–1920)	$350–$550	$650–$1,000	$1,500–$3,000+

HOLLOW COLUMN SHELF CLOCKS were made only in the 1840s by a few
Connecticut makers. These rather ungainly-looking clocks are all
weight-driven brass 30-hour and 8-day time and strike movements whose
weights descend within the hollow columns that flank the clock door.
Not too many exist, and their prices vary according to place and buyer.

American, ca. 1840, Clarke, Gilbert, and Co., hollow column shelf clock,
28.5", 30-hour brass time and strike movement, very good condition,
$812

American, ca. 1845, Clarke, Gilbert and Co., hollow column shelf clock,
28.5", 30-hour brass time and strike movement, good condition,
replaced lower tablet and missing upper glass, $1,430

American, ca. 1840, Hills, Goodrich, and Co., hollow column shelf clock,
28", "upside down" 30-hour brass time and strike movement, very good
condition, $616

American, ca. 1845, hollow
column shelf clock, 30-hour brass
time and strike weight-driven
movement, 33", signed Elisha
Manross, $275. Credit: R. O.
Schmitt Fine Arts.

American, ca. 1843, Hills, Goodrich, and Co., hollow column shelf clock, 31", "upside down" 30-hour brass time and strike movement, good condition, major restoration, $1,265

American, ca. 1845, Manross, Elisha, hollow column shelf clock, fake hollow columns, 33", 30-hour brass time and strike movement, good restored condition (illustrated), $275

American, ca. 1845, Manross, Elisha, hollow column shelf clock, fake hollow columns, 33.5", 8-day time and strike, very good condition, $660

American, ca. 1845, Manross, Elisha, hollow column shelf clock, 34", 8-day time and strike, good condition with top and middle tablets replaced, $687

	LOW	MID	HIGH
Hollow Column Shelf Clocks (ca. 1840–50)	$250–$500	$600–$900	$1,000–$2,000

IRON FRONT MANTEL CLOCKS are thoroughly American clocks produced from around 1845 to 1870. They are 30-hour and 8-day time and strike spring-driven clocks. Only the front is cast iron. The movement is housed in a wood box that is fastened to the rear of the iron front. Many of these clocks used the wonderful iron castings made in New York City by Müller and Sons. There are a few that have full iron cases, but I have chosen to list them among the black mantel clocks.

There are three distinct types. First are the unadorned cast-iron fronts usually painted black. Second are those clocks which have a painted scene applied to the iron front, and third are iron front clocks with mother-of-pearl decoration. Some cases have both a painted scene and mother-of-pearl decoration.

Long ignored by collectors, these clocks are slowly being sought out. Prices are still quite reasonable, and these clocks might well appeal to the novice collector.

American, ca. 1855, American Clock Co., cast-iron front clock, 12", 30-hour time-only spring-driven movement, good condition, $280

American, ca. 1865, American Clock Co., cast-iron front clock, 11.5", 30-hour time-only spring-driven movement, very good condition, $220

American, ca. 1850, American Clock Co., cast-iron front clock, 16", 30-hour time and strike spring-driven movement, poor condition, $50

American, ca. 1860, cast-iron front mantel clock with painted floral scene and mother-of-pearl decoration, 8-day time and strike movement, 21", signed Bristol Brass and Clock Co., $522. Credit: Prices4Antiques.com.

American, ca. 1865, cast-iron front clock, Müller and Sons, New York City casting, 8-day time and strike spring-driven movement, 23", signed F. Kroeber and Co., $522.

American, ca. 1855, American Clock Co., cast-iron front clock, 15", 30-hour time and strike spring-driven movement, good condition, $175

American, ca. 1850, Brewster and Ingraham, cast-iron front clock, 17", 8-day brass time and strike spring-driven movement, very good condition, $840

Rear of Kroeber clock showing wood case housing movement.

American, ca. 1852, Bristol Brass and Clock Co., cast-iron front clock, 21", 8-day brass time, alarm, and strike spring-driven movement, fair condition, missing alarm disk and lower crystal, $440

American, ca. 1855, Bristol Brass and Clock Co., cast-iron front clock, 17", 8-day brass time and strike spring-driven movement, good condition, $264

American, ca. 1860, Bristol Brass and Clock Co., cast-iron front clock, 21", 8-day brass time and strike spring-driven movement, very good condition (illustrated), $522

American, ca. 1845, Forestville Mfg. Co., cast-iron front clock, 14", 8-day brass time, alarm, and strike spring-driven movement, good condition, $224

American, ca. 1851, Goodwin, E. O., cast-iron front clock, 16", 8-day brass time and strike spring-driven movement, very good condition, $318

American, ca. 1855, Goodwin, E. O., cast-iron front clock, 18", 8-day brass time and strike spring-driven movement, very good condition, $181

American, ca. 1855, Jerome, Chauncey, cast-iron front clock, 23", 8-day brass time and strike spring-driven movement, excellent condition, $414

American, ca. 1865, Kroeber, Francis, cast-iron front clock, 23", 8-day brass time and strike spring-driven movement, very good condition (illustrated), $350

American, ca. 1860, Terhune and Edwards, cast-iron front clock, 20", 8-day brass time and strike spring-driven movement, excellent original condition, $440

American, ca. 1851, Terry, Downs, and Burwell, cast-iron front clock, 10.5", 30-hour time-only spring-driven movement, good condition, $448

American, ca. 1855, maker unknown, cast-iron front clock, 17.5", 30-hour time and strike spring-driven movement, very good condition , $140

American, ca. 1855, maker unknown, cast-iron front clock, 16", 30-hour time and strike spring-driven movement, very good condition, $220

American, ca. 1850, maker unknown, cast-iron front clock, 21", 8-day brass time and strike spring-driven movement, good condition, $660

American, ca. 1855, maker unknown, cast-iron front clock, 18", 8-day brass time and strike spring-driven movement, very good condition, $165

American, ca. 1850, Upson Bros., cast-iron front clock, 19", 8-day brass time and strike spring-driven movement, very good condition, $3,630

American Shelf Clock Tablets

One of the hallmarks of American shelf clocks during the nineteenth century was the use of decorated glass tablets in the lower portion of the door and sometimes on the glass surrounding the dial. They appear in the first mass-produced clocks. Here is an example showing subject and technique. The tablets were piecework painted by unknown local artists, usually women, who were paid about 50 cents a pane. Artist skill varied.

Pillar and scroll shelf clock, ca. 1830—Elisha Neal. Credit: R.O. Schmitt Fine Arts.

The early examples involved stenciling a border around the outside perimeter and an oval border in the center. These borders had gold leaf applied to them (see above). Another stenciled border could then be applied (see below) made of flowers, leaves, etc. with gilded highlights. The center of the panel was in reverse glass technique in which the final details were applied first and the background last. Finally a coat was applied to seal the painting. The clock now had a multi-layered painting with a clear oval window in the center showing the swinging pendulum.

Column and splat clock—door glass tablet—stencil and reverse glass technique—Seth Thomas.

Rear of glass tablet.

As competition and production among clockmakers increased, ways were sought to reduce production costs. The artwork on the glass tablets soon began to degrade as quicker and cheaper methods were adopted. The tablet near right shows one step taken by the late 1830s. Here an oval stencil was used to produce a gilded wreath on the glass pane and handpainting used only to apply the flowers with butterfly to the clear center. Finally an opaque coat of blue paint backed the wreath.

The tablet at far right was produced with a series of stencils. No freehand painting was necessary on this pane at all.

OG clock with wooden works, ca. 1839—William Johnson.

Flat OG clock with wooden works, ca. 1840—Boardman and Wells.

By the 1840s clockmakers began to use a technique that allowed them to transfer cheap prints to the reverse of the glass pane and then crudely apply colors. This technique produced a finished tablet that was even cheaper to make than stenciling and required less skill.

Cottage clock with colored transfer print, ca. 1845—J. C. Brown. Credit: R. O. Schmitt Fine Arts.

By the 1860s this technique was replaced by machine screened tablets as shown in the Atkins clock. Machine screening was replaced by even cheaper decals by the turn of the century. Well done original reverse glass tablets can considerably increase the value of a clock.

Cottage clock with machine screened tablet, ca. 1865—Atkins Clock Co. Credit: R. O. Schmitt Fine Arts.

Clock Dials

There are only a few dial shapes that have been used over the centuries: square, round, and arched. Other shapes exist but these are the most common.

Materials most used in dial construction include metal (brass, iron, zinc, and tin), wood, porcelain on metal, and occasionally stone and glass. The twentieth century added plastics to this list.

Brass was the preferred material for dials in England, Holland, and America from the seventeenth century until the last three decades of the eighteenth century, when iron dials began to replace the more expensive brass ones. To keep the iron dials from rusting, they were painted. A white base was the foundation on which the colorful decoration was applied. In America these dials are called "painted dials" and in the British Isles they are called "white dials."

English arched brass dial with cast spandrels, ca. 1760—Credit: J. & R. Wagner.

Because of the cost of brass in America, painted iron dials were being used on tall case clocks by the 1780s. Some of these dials were imported from England and others were produced here. However, even painted iron dials were too expensive for our first mass produced wooden works tall case clocks. American makers turned to wood for their dials and chose to decorate them in the English style (see the bottom of the following page). We would continue to use wooden dials until as late as the 1840s. After that period we turned to painted zinc or tin and shifted most of the decoration to the glass tablet in the door. Porcelain dials, in numbers, appear on American clocks in the last quarter of the nineteenth century in competition with European imports. Stone dials were rarely used by American makers and when they are, can be dated to the late nineteenth century.

English square brass dial, silvered with cast spandrels, ca. 1750–1760.

English round painted iron dial, ca. 1830. Credit: R. O. Schmitt Fine Arts.

English brass engraved arched dial with cast spandrels, ca. 1760–1770—W. Priest, Bristol. Credit: J. & R. Wagner.

English painted iron arched dial with painted center and spandrels, ca. 1790—J. Schofield, Manchester. Credit: M. & P. Alessi.

English painted iron arched dial with painted arch and spandrels, ca. 1820—S. Thompson, Darlington.

American painted wood dial with painted arch and spandrels, ca. 1830—J. Curtis, New York. Credit: NAWCC Eastern States Regional.

American Shelf Clock Wood and Metal Dials

American makers bought their dials from dial painters in the same way that they originally obtained their reverse glass decorated tablets. As time passed and competition increased, costs were reduced by installing less expensive dials—handpainted dials with less decoration. The early dials have raised spandrels and finely drawn patterns in the center done in gesso and gold/brass paint. The later wood dials first lose the center decoration and then the spandrels. After 1840 inexpensive rolled metal dials of zinc and tin became standard. They were rolled and cut by machine. At first painted and decorated by hand, they soon were made completely by machine.

ca. 1833

ca. 1830–1835

ca. 1835

ca. 1838–1839

Reverse of wooden dial—the vertical strips are mortised into the dial to keep the face from warping.

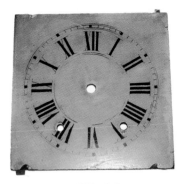

ca. 1840–1845

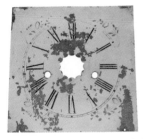

Handpainted tin dial with stenciled spandrels, ca. 1845.

Jerome brass dial, ca. 1850. The decoration around the dial is actually on the back of the glass.

Machine screened zinc dial, ca. 1860–1870.

French Figural Mantel Clocks

French clockmakers have always had the talent and the ability to wed style, craftsmanship and engineering to produce wonderful clocks. Among these was a type known as "figurals" as the cases incorporated human figures as part of the motif. Paralleling French art and décor, these clocks were produced for over a century. Today collectors and decorators eagerly seek these clocks and superlative examples command very high prices.

French figural mantel clock, ca 1820–1825—ormolu case depicting cupid capturing a classically clad maiden with a garland of flowers. Credit: R. O. Schmitt Fine Arts.

The earliest of these clocks (ca. 1780-1820) have allegorical or classical subjects and they have ormolu, bronze, and sometimes marble cases. They house silk suspension brass time-and-strike movements. The workmanship is of the highest quality. Notice that the design of these clocks is one of a smaller rectangle placed upon a larger and surmounted or flanked by figures (see bottom of previous page).

French figural mantel clock, ca. 1840—ormolu case depicting a young nobleman reading a book. Credit: NAWCC Eastern States Regional.

French figural mantel clock, ca. 1835—ormolu case depicting a seated lady in contemporary dress with a lute.

In the second period (ca. 1830-1850) these clocks began to take a more pyramidal form as they acquired splayed feet and the figures are part of a triangular design incorporating the dial (see above). The subjects begin to include contemporary historical and romantic themes. The cases remain mostly ormolu and the brass move ments are still usually silk thread suspension time and strike with metal or porcelain dials. Workmanship, while excellent, has declined.

There is a third period (ca. 1860-1870) when the pyramidal form is developed further (see right) and the cases are now gilded brass and bronze often with marble or alabaster components. Case design subjects are strongly allegorical and depict "Commerce," "Industry," etc. Movements are brass time and strike spring suspensions with porcelain dials. Workmanship is good but quality has declined compared to the earlier clocks.

French figural mantel clock, ca. 1865–1870—brass, bronze, and alabaster case—allegorical figure of "Commerce."

The years between 1880 and 1910 saw the final stage of these clocks. This was a period of mass production and design and quality suffered. Cases are poorly designed late Victorian romantic subjects and they are made of brass, plated spelter and white metal. Movements are reliable brass time and strike *pendules* with spring suspensions and porcelain dials.

French figural clock, ca. 1900—brass case, figures of young man playing a violin and a wine press above the clock. Credit: R. O. Schmitt Fine Arts.

French figural clock, ca. 1890—gilded spelter case, figure of a huntsman.

However, throughout the later nineteenth century French makers continued to make finer quality figural clocks as well although in far fewer numbers.

French figural clock, ca. 1880–1890—gilded brass and bronze case, figures of Mars and Cupid flank the dial which is topped with doves, excellent workmanship. Credit: Zylberberg Collection.

American, ca. 1860, Waterbury Clock Co., cast-iron front clock, 12.75",
    30-hour time-only spring-driven movement, fair condition, broken tip,
    $110

American, ca. 1860, Waterbury Clock Co., cast-iron front clock, 16",
    30-hour time and strike spring-driven movement, good condition, $148

	LOW	MID	HIGH
Iron-Front Mantel Clocks (ca. 1845–70)	$100–$350	$400–$700	$800–$1,000+

LATE MAHOGANY MANTEL CLOCKS saw a revival in the first decades of the twentieth century. These small mahogany-cased mantel clocks (plus a few in walnut and oak) were traditionally styled and are among the last domestic clocks produced by the American clockmaking industry. The flamboyant Victorian case styles were replaced by such classic ones as architectural, arched top, balloon, and Gothic arch.

    The 8-day time and strike spring-driven movements were the culmination of a century of clock design and manufacture. Most sound on deep-toned wire "cathedral" gongs. Others sound on series of nested bells, which produce wonderful tones.

    These clocks are still reasonably priced and are waiting to be discovered.

American, ca. 1929, Gothic-arch mantel clock, "Inglewood" model, 8-day time and strike (Westminster), 12.5", signed New Haven Clock Co., $165. Credit: R. O. Schmitt Fine Arts.

American, ca. 1909, arched-top, "Tory" model, 8-day time and strike, 13.5", signed Seth Thomas Co., $420. Credit: R. O. Schmitt Fine Arts.

American, ca. 1910, Gilbert, William L., mahogany architectural mantel clock, 9.75", 8-day time and strike spring-driven movement, very good condition, $50

American, ca. 1913, Gilbert, William L., mahogany arched-top mantel clock, 16.5", 8-day time and strike spring-driven movement, good restored condition, $275

American, ca. 1910, Ingraham, E., mahogany dome-top mantel clock, 12.25", 8-day time and strike spring-driven movement, good condition, $72

American, ca. 1920, New Haven Clock Co., mahogany balloon-top mantel clock, "TAUNTON" model, 11.5", 8-day time and strike spring-driven movement, very good condition, $467

American, ca. 1925, New Haven Clock Co., mahogany Gothic mantel clock, "ABBEY" model, 15.5", 8-day time and strike spring-driven movement, good condition, one missing finial, $357

American, ca. 1929, New Haven Clock Co., mahogany Gothic mantel clock, "INGLEWOOD" model, 12.5", 8-day time and strike Westminster movement, very good condition (illustrated), $165

American, ca. 1929, New Haven Clock Co., mahogany Gothic mantel clock, "INGLEWOOD" model, 12.5", 8-day time and strike Westminster movement, very good condition, $192

American, ca. 1910, Sessions Clock Co., mahogany arched-top mantel clock, 11", 8-day time and strike spring-driven movement, good condition, $88

American, ca. 1920, Sessions Clock Co., walnut dome-top mantel clock with Masonic emblems, 17.5", 8-day time and strike spring-driven movement, good condition, $577

American, ca. 1900, Seth Thomas Clock Co., walnut-cased mantel clock, "VALMA" model, 16.5", 8-day time and strike spring-driven movement, very good condition, $137

American, ca. 1902, Seth Thomas Clock Co., mahogany architectural mantel clock, "CORDOVA" model, 10.75", 8-day time and strike spring-driven movement, very good condition (illustrated), $770

American, ca. 1902, Seth Thomas Clock Co., oak broken-pediment mantel clock, "NAPLES" model, 12", 8-day time and strike spring-driven movement, very good condition, $784

American, ca. 1905, Seth Thomas Clock Co., mahogany architectural mantel clock, "WALES" model, 10.75", 8-day time and strike spring-driven movement, good original condition, $413

American, ca. 1909, Seth Thomas Clock Co., mahogany arched-top mantel clock, "TORY" model, 13.5", 8-day time and strike spring-driven movement, very good original condition (illustrated), $420

American, ca. 1909, Seth Thomas Clock Co., mahogany arched-top mantel clock, "ETON" model, 10", 8-day time and strike spring-driven movement, very good condition, $302

American, ca. 1909, Seth Thomas Clock Co., mahogany architectural mantel clock, "TURIN" model, 8.75", 8-day time and strike spring-driven movement, excellent original condition (illustrated), $392

American, ca. 1909, Seth Thomas Clock Co., mahogany balloon mantel clock, "FLORENCE" model, 12.25", 8-day time and strike spring-driven movement, good restored condition, $467

American, ca. 1909, Seth Thomas Clock Co., mahogany balloon mantel clock, "FLORENCE" model, 12.25", 8-day time and strike spring-driven movement, good restored condition, $341

American, ca. 1909, Seth Thomas Clock Co., mahogany balloon mantel clock, "PARMA" model, 12", 8-day time and strike spring-driven movement, poor condition (illustrated), $179

American, ca. 1915, round-top mantel clock, "Chime No. 11" model, 8-day time and strike (on five nested bells), 13.25", signed Seth Thomas Co., $756. Credit: R. O. Schmitt Fine Arts.

American, ca. 1909, balloon-case mantel clock, "Parma" model, 8-day time and strike, 12", signed Seth Thomas Co., $179. Credit: R. O. Schmitt Fine Arts.

American, ca. 1909, flat-top mantel clock, "Turin," 8-day time and strike, 8.75", signed Seth Thomas Co., $392. Credit: R. O. Schmitt Fine Arts.

American, ca. 1905, architectural mantel clock, 8-day time and strike (gong and bell), 9.5", signed Ansonia Clock Co., $200.

American, ca. 1909, Seth Thomas Clock Co., mahogany balloon mantel clock, "PARMA" model, 12", 8-day time and strike spring-driven movement, excellent restored condition, $715

American, ca. 1909, Seth Thomas Clock Co., mahogany balloon mantel clock, "SAVOY" model, 13.5", 8-day time and strike spring-driven movement, good restored condition, $231

American, ca. 1909, Seth Thomas Clock Co., mahogany Gothic mantel clock, "ESSEX" model, 9.5", 8-day time and strike spring-driven movement, good original condition, $176

American, ca. 1909, Seth Thomas Clock Co., mahogany Gothic mantel clock, "WHITBY" model, 12", 8-day time and strike spring-driven movement, very good condition, $275

American, ca. 1910, Seth Thomas Clock Co., mahogany architectural mantel clock, "CHIME CLOCK No. 1" model, 12.5", 8-day time and strike Westminster movement, good condition, $487

American, ca. 1910, Seth Thomas Clock Co., rosewood-adamantine-veneer architectural mantel clock, "DING DONG" model, 11.25", 8-day time and strike spring-driven movement, very good condition, $470

American, ca. 1910, Seth Thomas Clock Co., walnut dome-top mantel clock, 3.5", 8-day time and strike spring-driven movement, very good condition, $201

American, ca. 1913, Seth Thomas Clock Co., mahogany architectural mantel clock, "ANDES" model, 10", 8-day time and strike spring-driven movement, good condition, $192

American, ca. 1913, Seth Thomas Clock Co., mahogany dome-top mantel clock, "PROSPECT No. 2" model, 13", 8-day time and strike spring-driven movement, good condition, $143

American, ca. 1913, Seth Thomas Clock Co., oak architectural mantel clock, "CHIME CLOCK No. 51" model, 14", 8-day time and strike Westminster movement, good restored condition, $532

American, ca. 1914, Seth Thomas Clock Co., mahogany Gothic mantel clock, "CHIME No. 16" model, 18", 8-day time and strike spring-driven movement, excellent original condition, $979

American, ca. 1915, Seth Thomas Clock Co., mahogany arched-top mantel clock, "CHIME No. 255" model, 9.5", 8-day time and strike Westminster movement, fair condition, $1,320

American, ca. 1915, Seth Thomas Clock Co., mahogany architectural mantel clock, "CHIME CLOCK No. 00" model, 9.75", 8-day time and strike spring-driven movement, excellent original condition, $672

American, ca. 1915, Seth Thomas Clock Co., mahogany architectural mantel clock, "CHIME CLOCK No. 1" model, 13", 8-day time and strike Westminster movement, good original condition, $336

American, ca. 1910, architectural mantel clock,
8-day time and strike, 10.5", signed Seth Thomas Co.,
$250.

American, ca. 1915, Seth Thomas Clock Co., mahogany architectural mantel clock, "CHIME No. 1" model, 13.5", 8-day time and strike spring-driven movement, good condition, $330

American, ca. 1915, Seth Thomas Clock Co., mahogany architectural mantel clock, "CHIME No. 5" model, 14", 8-day time and strike spring-driven movement, very good condition (illustrated), $770

American, ca. 1915, Seth Thomas Clock Co., mahogany architectural mantel clock, "CHIME No. 5" model, 14", 8-day time and strike spring-driven movement, good condition, $495

American, ca. 1915, Seth Thomas Clock Co., mahogany dome-top mantel clock, "TUDOR" model, 8.75", 8-day time and strike spring-driven movement, good condition, $110

American, ca. 1915, Seth Thomas Clock Co., mahogany dome-top mantel clock, "CHIME CLOCK No. 11" model, 13.25", 8-day time and strike spring-driven movement, excellent original condition (illustrated), $756

American, ca. 1915, Seth Thomas Clock Co., mahogany Gothic mantel clock, "CHIME No. 14" model, 14", 8-day time and strike Westminster movement, excellent original condition, $1,148

American, ca. 1915, Seth Thomas Clock Co., mahogany Gothic mantel clock, "CHIME No. 14" model, 14", 8-day time and strike Westminster movement, very good original condition, $742

American, ca. 1915, Seth Thomas Clock Co., mahogany Gothic mantel clock, "CHIME No. 2002" model, 18", 8-day time and strike Westminster movement, excellent original condition, $2,860

American, ca. 1915, Seth Thomas Clock Co., mahogany Gothic mantel clock, "CHIME No. 214" model, 14", 8-day time and strike Westminster movement, very good condition, $2,090

American, ca. 1915, Seth Thomas Clock Co., mahogany Gothic mantel clock, "CHIME No. 264" model, 14", 8-day time and strike Westminster movement, good restored condition, $1,980

American, ca. 1915, Seth Thomas Clock Co., mahogany Gothic mantel clock, "CHIME No. 266" model, 18", 8-day time and strike Westminster movement, very good condition, $2,750

American, ca. 1915, Seth Thomas Clock Co., mahogany Gothic mantel clock, "CHIME No. 64" model, 14", 8-day time and strike spring-driven movement, good condition, $550

American, ca. 1915, architectural mantel clock, "CHIME No. 5" model, 8-day time and strike (four bells), 14", signed Seth Thomas Co., $770. Credit: R. O. Schmitt Fine Arts.

American, ca. 1902, architectural mantel clock, "Cordova" model, 8-day time and strike, 10.75", signed Seth Thomas Co., $770. Credit: R. O. Schmitt Fine Arts.

American, ca. 1917, Seth Thomas Clock Co., mahogany Gothic mantel clock, "PERTH" model, 11.5", 8-day time and strike spring-driven movement, good condition, 220

American, ca. 1920, Seth Thomas Clock Co., mahogany architectural mantel clock, "SONORA CHIME" model, 14", 8-day time and strike spring-driven movement, good condition, $616

American, ca. 1920, Seth Thomas Clock Co., mahogany dome-top mantel clock, "CHIME No. 11" model, 13.5", 8-day time and strike Westminster movement, good restored condition, $605

American, ca. 1920, Seth Thomas Clock Co., mahogany dome-top mantel clock, "CHIME No. 211" model, 13.2", 8-day time and strike Westminster movement, excellent original condition, $3,080

American, ca. 1920, Seth Thomas Clock Co., mahogany Gothic mantel clock, "CHIME No. 72" model, 14.75", 8-day time and strike Westminster movement, excellent original condition, $715

American, ca. 1922, Seth Thomas Clock Co., mahogany Gothic mantel clock, "CHIME No. 95" model, 11.25", 8-day time and strike spring-driven movement, good condition, $220

American, ca. 1925, Seth Thomas Clock Co., mahogany Gothic mantel clock, "CHIME No. 64-A" model, 14", 8-day time and strike spring-driven movement, good condition, $370

American, ca. 1930, Seth Thomas Clock Co., mahogany arched-top mantel clock, "SEVERN" model, 10", 8-day time and strike spring-driven movement, good condition, $357

American, ca. 1917, Waterbury Clock Co., mahogany arched-top mantel clock, "CHIME No. 501" model, 16.75", 8-day time and strike spring-driven movement, good restored condition, $577

American, ca. 1917, Waterbury Clock Co., mahogany arched-top mantel clock, "CHIME No. 501" model, 16.75", 8-day time and strike spring-driven movement, excellent original condition, $364

	LOW	MID	HIGH
Late Mahogany Mantel Clocks (ca. 1900–30)	$150–$300	$400–$700	$800–$1,000

MASSACHUSETTS SHELF CLOCKS appear during the last quarter of the eighteenth century, evolving from the work of the Willard family. They remained popular until about 1830.

Early Massachusetts shelf clocks vary in height from 25" to more than 40" and have brass anchor escapement weight-driven movements that run from two to eight days. The various case styles have many of the same features and details as tall-case clocks.

Massachusetts shelf clocks are priced out of the reach of most collectors, but numbers of more reasonably priced reproductions exist.

American, ca. 1813, Curtis, L., Massachusetts shelf clock, 35.5", 8-day time-only weight-driven movement, very good restored condition, $7,638

American, ca. 1825, Morrill, Benjamin, New Hampshire shelf clock in the Massachusetts style, 37", 8-day time-only weight-driven movement, very good condition with some replaced veneer and missing pendulum, $12,100

American, ca. 1810, Parker, Gardner, Massachusetts shelf clock, 35", 8-day time and alarm weight-driven movement, fair condition, $26,450

American, ca. 1820, Sawin, John, Massachusetts shelf clock, 38", 8-day time-only weight-driven movement, good condition with restored tablets (illustrated), $4,400

American, ca. 1820, Massachusetts shelf clock, 8-day time and alarm, weight-driven movement, 38", signed John Sawin, $4,400. Credit: R. O. Schmitt Fine Arts.

American, ca. 1815, Massachusetts shelf clock, 8-day time-only, weight-driven movement, 35", signed David Wood, $3,080. Credit: Prices4Antiques.com.

American, ca. 1808, Taber, Elnathan, Massachusetts shelf clock, 37", 8-day time-only weight-driven movement, very good restored condition, $14,950

American, ca. 1805, maker unknown, Massachusetts shelf clock, 38.5", 8-day time-only weight-driven movement, very good restored condition, $12,650

American, ca. 1970, maker unknown, Massachusetts shelf clock (reproduction), 34", 8-day time-only weight-driven movement, excellent condition, mahogany case, $336

American, ca. 1800, Willard, Aaron, Massachusetts shelf clock, 38", 8-day time-only weight-driven movement, very good restored condition, $20,700

American, ca. 1805, Willard, Aaron, Massachusetts shelf clock, 36", 8-day time-only weight-driven movement, very good restored condition, $21,850

American, ca. 1810, Willard, Aaron, Massachusetts shelf clock, 33.25", 8-day time-only weight-driven movement, good condition, restoration and restored tablet, $7,700

American, ca. 1810, Willard, Aaron, Massachusetts shelf clock, 32", 8-day time-only weight-driven movement, good condition with flaking lower tablet, $24,150

American, ca. 1817, Willard, Aaron, Jr., Massachusetts shelf clock, 35", 8-day time and strike weight-driven movement, very good restored condition, $7,475

American, ca. 1793, Wood, David, Massachusetts shelf clock, 29.5", 30-hour time and strike weight-driven movement, excellent condition, $387,500

American, ca. 1810, Wood, David, Massachusetts shelf clock, 38.375", 8-day time-only weight-driven movement, very good as-found condition, $6,875

American, ca. 1810, Wood, David, Massachusetts shelf clock, 35", 8-day time-only weight-driven movement, very good restored condition, $7,700

American, ca. 1815, Wood, David, Massachusetts shelf clock, 35", 8-day time-only weight-driven movement, fair condition with case replacements (illustrated), $3,080

	LOW	MID	HIGH
Massachusetts Shelf Clocks (ca. 1775–1830)	$3,000–$5,000	$8,000–$12,000	$20,000+

NOVELTY CLOCKS are clocks that for various reasons fall outside the mainstream. Every nation's clockmaking industry has produced these clocks. American novelty clocks appear as early as the 1840s.

There are hundreds of different novelty clocks, and their prices range across the scale. I have listed only a few of the most frequently encountered antique novelty clocks.

American, ca. 1893, Ansonia Clock Co., girl on swing novelty clock, "Jumper No. 1," 15", 30-hour time-only spring-driven movement, fair condition, replaced dial, $1,045

American, ca. 1894, Ansonia Clock Co., girl on swing novelty clock, "Jumper No. 1," 15", 30-hour time-only spring-driven movement, fair condition, replaced dial, $1,210

American, ca. 1894, Ansonia Clock Co., girl on swing novelty clock, "Jumper No. 1," 15", 30-hour time-only spring-driven movement, fair condition, $440

American, ca. 1894, Ansonia Clock Co., girl on swing novelty clock, "Swing No. 1," 11.5", 30-hour time-only spring-driven movement, good condition, $2,530

American, ca. 1900, novelty clock, good luck horseshoe, 30-hour time-only, 5", signed Ansonia Clock Co., $145. Credit: Prices4Antiques.com.

American, ca. 1840, novelty clock, tape measure, 30-hour time-only, 2.5", unknown maker, $134. Credit: Prices4Antiques.com.

American, ca. 1894, Ansonia Clock Co., girl on swing novelty clock, "Swing No. 1," 11.5", 30-hour time-only spring-driven movement, good condition, $577

American, ca. 1894, Ansonia Clock Co., girl on swing novelty clock, "Swing No. 2," 8", 30-hour time-only spring-driven movement, excellent original condition (illustrated), $2,530

American, ca. 1890, Ansonia Clock Co., horseshoe-shaped good luck novelty clock, 5", 30-hour time-only spring-driven movement, poor condition (illustrated), $145

American, ca. 1895, Ansonia Clock Co., stacked oars and anchor, "NAVY" novelty clock, 12.5", 30-hour time-only spring-driven movement, good condition, $715

American, ca. 1895, Ansonia Clock Co., stacked oars and anchor, "NAVY" novelty clock, 12.5", 30-hour time-only spring-driven movement, fair condition (illustrated), $336

American, ca. 1895, Ansonia Clock Co., stacked rifles and bugle, "ARMY" novelty clock, 12.5", 30-hour time-only spring-driven movement, good condition, $506

American, ca. 1850, Bradley and Hubbard, blinking eye novelty clock, "ADMIRAL" model, 16", 30-hour time-only spring-driven movement, good condition, $1,590

American, ca. 1936, novelty clock, Franklin D. Roosevelt electric clock, dial shows bartender shaking cocktails, 10.5", unknown maker, $165. Credit: Prices4Antiques.com.

American, ca. 1920, novelty clock, 30-hour time-only, 9", signed One Hand Clock Co., $224. Credit: Prices4Antiques.com.

American, ca. 1860, Bradley and Hubbard, blinking eye novelty clock, "ADMIRAL" model, 16.5", 30-hour time-only spring-driven movement, good condition, $880

American, ca. 1875, Bradley and Hubbard, blinking eye novelty clock, "ADMIRAL" model, 16", 30-hour time-only spring-driven movement, good restored condition, $616

American, ca. 1875, Bradley and Hubbard, blinking eye novelty clock, "ADMIRAL" model, 17", 30-hour time-only spring-driven movement, good condition, eyes restored, $1,035

American, ca. 1867, Bradley and Hubbard, blinking eye novelty clock, "SAMBO" model, 16", 30-hour time-only spring-driven movement, fair condition, $2,090

American, ca. 1870, Bradley and Hubbard, blinking eye novelty clock, "SAMBO" model, 15.5", 30-hour time-only spring-driven movement, fair condition, $2,750

American, ca. 1875, Bradley and Hubbard, blinking eye novelty clock, "SAMBO" model, 16", 30-hour time-only spring-driven movement, fair condition (illustrated), $2,184

American, ca. 1875, Bradley and Hubbard, blinking eye novelty clock, "SAMBO" model, 16", 30-hour time-only spring-driven movement, fair condition, repair to the back of the hat, $2,800

American, ca. 1867, Bradley and Hubbard, blinking eye novelty clock, "TOPSEY" model, 16.5", 30-hour time-only spring-driven movement, restored condition, $1,980

American, ca. 1872, Bradley and Hubbard, blinking eye novelty clock, "TOPSEY" model, 16.5", 30-hour time-only spring-driven movement, fair condition, repainted, $302

American, ca. 1860, Brown, George W., Briggs Rotary novelty clock, 7.75", 8-day time-only movement, fair condition with worn dial, $672

American, ca. 1865, Brown, George W., Briggs Rotary novelty clock, 8", 8-day time-only movement, excellent original condition, $1,457

American, ca. 1968, Horolovar Co., "Hickory, Dickory, Dock" mouse novelty clock (reproduction), 24.5", 8-day time and strike movement, excellent original condition, $840

American, ca. 1970, Horolovar Co., "Hickory, Dickory, Dock" mouse novelty clock (reproduction), 24.5", 8-day time and strike movement, very good condition (illustrated), $420

American, ca. 1970, Horolovar Co., "Hickory, Dickory, Dock" mouse novelty clock (reproduction), 24.5", 8-day time and strike movement, very good condition, $522

American, ca. 1878, novelty clock, "Briggs Rotary," 8-day, time only, 8.75", signed E. N. Welch Manufacturing Co., $896. Credit: R. O. Schmitt Fine Arts.

American, ca. 1870, novelty clock, "blinking eyes," 30-hour time-only, 16", signed Bradley and Hubbard, $2,184. Credit: Prices4Antiques.com.

American, ca. 1910, novelty clock, "spherical clock," 30-hour time-only, 2.25", signed New Haven Clock Co., $364. Credit: Prices4Antiques.com.

American, ca. 1970, novelty clock, reproduction "Hickory, Dickory, Dock" clock, 8-day time and strike, 25", signed Horolovar Co., $420. Credit: Prices4Antiques.com.

American, ca. 1970, Horolovar Co., "Hickory, Dickory, Dock" mouse novelty clock (reproduction), 24.5", 8-day time and strike movement, poor condition with missing numerals, $385

American, ca. 1948, Lux Clock Co., miniature tape measure novelty clock, 4.75", 30-hour time-only spring-driven movement, very good condition, $132

American, ca. 1950, Lux Clock Co., miniature tape measure novelty clock, 5", time-only electric movement, very good condition, $22

American, ca. 1950, Lux Clock Co., miniature tape measure novelty clock, 5", 30-hour time-only spring-driven movement, very good condition, $58

American, ca. 1910, New Haven Clock Co., spherical glass novelty clock with rhinestone bezel, 2.75", 30-hour time-only spring-driven movement, fair condition, dial has cracks, $224

American, ca. 1910, New Haven Clock Co., spherical glass novelty clock with rhinestone bezel, 2.75", 30-hour time-only spring-driven movement, very good condition, $112

American, ca. 1910, New Haven Clock Co., spherical glass novelty clock, 2.25", 30-hour time-only spring-driven movement, very good condition (illustrated), $364

American, ca. 1910, New Haven Clock Co. for Dungan and Klump, "Hickory, Dickory, Dock" mouse novelty clock, 43", 8-day time and strike movement, fair condition with repainting, $2,240

American, ca. 1910, New Haven Clock Co. for Dungan and Klump, "Hickory, Dickory, Dock" mouse novelty clock, 43", 8-day time and strike movement, fair condition, $1,430

American, ca. 1910, New Haven Clock Co. for Dungan and Klump, "Hickory, Dickory, Dock" mouse novelty clock, 43", 8-day time and strike movement, very good original condition, $2,860

American, ca. 1920, New Haven Clock Co. for Dungan and Klump, "Hickory, Dickory, Dock" mouse novelty clock, 43", 8-day time and strike movement, good condition, $690

American, ca. 1920, One Hand Clock Co., one-hand novelty clock, 9", 30-hour time-only spring-driven movement, very good condition (illustrated), $224

American, ca. 1920, One Hand Clock Co., one-hand novelty clock, 9", 30-hour time-only spring-driven movement, very good condition, $364

American, ca. 1925, One Hand Clock Co., one-hand novelty clock, 9", 30-hour time-only spring-driven movement, fair condition, $235

American, ca. 1894, novelty clock, "Swing No. 1," 30-hour time-only, 11.5", signed Ansonia Clock Co., $2,530. Credit: R. O. Schmitt Fine Arts.

American, ca. 1885, novelty clock, "Navy," 30-hour time-only, 12.5", signed Ansonia Clock Co., $336. Credit: R. O. Schmitt Fine Arts.

American, ca. 1880, maker unknown, blinking eye novelty clock, black man holding whiskey jug and guitar, 10", 30-hour time-only spring-driven movement, good condition, $1,540

American, ca. 1875, maker unknown, blinking eye novelty clock, standing dog, 7.75", 30-hour time-only spring-driven movement, poor condition, missing eyes, $140

American, ca. 1860, maker unknown, Briggs Rotary novelty clock, 8", 8-day time-only movement, very good condition, $448

American, ca. 1870, maker unknown, Briggs Rotary novelty clock, 8", 8-day time-only movement, very good condition, $420

American, ca. 1940, maker unknown, miniature tape measure novelty clock, 3", 30-hour time-only spring-driven movement, good condition (illustrated), $134

American, ca. 1936, maker unknown, Roosevelt political novelty clock, 10.5", time-only electric movement, poor condition, $220

American, ca. 1936, maker unknown, Roosevelt political novelty clock 10.5", time-only electric movement, very good original condition (illustrated), $165

American, ca. 1910, Waltham Watch Co., spherical glass novelty clock made for Tiffany and Co., 3.5", 30-hour time-only spring-driven movement, poor condition, missing stem, $336

American, ca. 1890, Waterbury Clock Co., horseshoe-shaped "DERBY" novelty clock, 5.75", 30-hour time-only spring-driven movement, very good original condition, $207

American, ca. 1878, Welch, E. N. Mfg. Co., Briggs Rotary novelty clock, 8.75", 8-day time-only movement, fair condition, $308

American, ca. 1878, Welch, E. N. Mfg. Co., Briggs Rotary novelty clock, 8.75", 8-day time-only movement, good condition (illustrated), $896

American, ca. 1878, Welch, E. N. Mfg. Co., Briggs Rotary novelty clock, 8", 8-day time-only movement, good condition with replaced dial, $605

American, ca. 1878, Welch, E. N. Mfg. Co., Briggs Rotary novelty clock, 9", 8-day time-only movement, good condition with replaced dome, $784

	LOW	MID	HIGH
Novelty Clocks (ca. 1840–present)	There are so many varieties in this category that it is impossible to create a meaningful range.		

OGEE (OG) SHELF CLOCKS are said to have originated as result of the Panic of 1837 and the economic depression that followed. Their popularity was such that they were produced from the late 1830s until World War I in 1914. Along with the cottage clock and the steeple clock, the ogee clock was found in huge numbers throughout the United States.

Legend holds that during the Panic of 1837, Chauncey Jerome (see Chapter One), faced with a looming bankruptcy, got the idea for an inexpensive brass clock movement that he thought might save his company. His brother Noble Jerome designed and produced a 30-hour rolled brass weight-driven movement which was housed in a simple pine case framed with easily obtained ogee molding. This inexpensive clock was an immediate success. The business was saved, and a new style of clock case was born. The other Connecticut makers were soon marketing their own "OG" clocks.

This clock style can be divided into the following types:

8-day brass movement spring-driven clocks, 18" high
8-day brass movement weight-driven clocks, 34" high
30-hour brass movement spring-driven clocks, 18" high
30-hour brass movement weight-driven clocks, 19" high
30-hour brass movement weight-driven clocks, 26" high
30-hour wooden movement weight-driven clocks, 26" high

The earliest Ogees have wooden dials.

These clocks are found everywhere, so buy only those in the finest condition!

American, ca. 1840, Andrews, L. and F., OG shelf clock, 27", 30-hour brass time and strike spring-driven movement, original as-found condition, wooden dial, $235

American, ca. 1870, Ansonia Clock Co., OG shelf clock, 26", 30-hour brass time and strike weight-driven movement, poor condition, flaking tablet, no weights, partial label, $67

American, ca. 1845, Atkins, Alden A., OG shelf clock, 26.5", 30-hour brass time and strike weight-driven movement, as-found condition, wooden dial, $288

American, ca. 1845, Atkins, Porter, OG shelf clock, 26", 30-hour brass time, alarm, and strike weight-driven movement, good condition, $127

American, ca. 1838, 30-hour time and strike
weight-driven wooden works movement used in
William Johnson OG shelf clock.

American, ca. 1845, Atkins and Porter, OG shelf clock, 26", 30-hour brass
time and strike weight-driven movement, good condition, wooden dial,
$251

American, ca. 1840, Birge and Mallory, OG shelf clock, 26", 30-hour brass
time and strike weight-driven movement, good condition, metal dial,
$224

American, ca. 1845, Blakeslee, R. J., OG shelf clock, 26", 30-hour brass time
and strike weight-driven movement, good condition, wooden dial, $196

American, ca. 1846, Blakeslee, R. J., OG shelf clock, 26", 30-hour brass time
and strike weight-driven lyre movement, good condition, wooden dial,
$271

American, ca. 1840, Boardman, C., OG shelf clock, 26", 30-hour brass time
and strike weight-driven movement, fair condition, replaced dial,
$110

American, ca. 1842, Brewster, E. C., OG shelf clock, 26", 30-hour brass
time and strike weight-driven movement, good restored condition,
$196

American, ca. 1850, Brewster, E. C., OG shelf clock, 26", 30-hour brass time
and strike weight-driven movement, poor condition, cracked glass,
veneer damage, metal dial, $190

American, ca. 1839, OG shelf clock, 30-hour time and strike, weight-driven wooden works movement, 30", signed Seth Thomas Co., $350.

American, ca. 1838, OG shelf clock, 30-hour time and strike, weight-driven wooden works movement, 26", signed William Johnson, $300.

American, ca. 1845, OG shelf clock, 30-hour brass time and strike weight-driven movement, 26", signed Jerome and Co., $150. Credit: NAWCC Eastern States Regional 2002.

American, ca. 1845, OG shelf clock, 30-hour Ives brass time and strike weight-driven movement, 24", signed F. C. Andrews, $450. Credit: NAWCC Eastern States Regional 2002.

American, ca. 1843, OG shelf clock, 30-hour Ives brass time and strike weight-driven movement, 27", signed Hills and Goodrich and Co., $1,000. Credit: NAWCC Eastern States Regional 2002.

American, ca. 1845, Brewster and Ingraham, mini OG shelf clock, 18", 30-hour brass time and strike spring-driven movement, good condition, replaced springs, $495

American, ca. 1850, Brewster and Ingraham, mini OG shelf clock, 17", 30-hour brass time and strike spring-driven movement, good condition, metal dial, $224

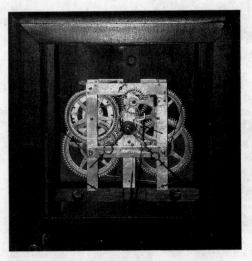

American, ca. 1838, 30-hour brass time and strike weight-driven movement used in OG clocks. Credit: NAWCC Eastern States Regional 2002.

American, ca. 1840, Brewster and Ingraham, mini OG shelf clock, 17.5", 30-hour brass time and strike spring-driven movement, excellent condition, $950

American, ca. 1845, Brewster and Ingraham, mini OG shelf clock, 17", 30-hour brass time and strike spring-driven movement, fair condition, stripped case, flaking metal dial, $196

American, ca. 1850, Brown, J. C., OG shelf clock, 29", 8-day brass time and strike weight-driven movement, poor condition, flaking tablet, veneer damage, no weights, $112

American, ca. 1855, Brown, J. C., OG shelf clock, 26", 30-hour brass time and strike weight-driven movement, fair condition with replaced lyre movement, metal dial, $145

American, ca. 1840, Byington, Lawyer, OG shelf clock, 27", 30-hour time and strike wooden works movement, good condition, wooden dial, replaced tablet, $141

American, ca. 1835, Downs, Ephraim, OG shelf clock, 26", 30-hour time and strike wooden works movement, good condition, wooden dial, $451

American, ca. 1855, Forestville Mfg. Co., OG case-on-case shelf clock, 31", 8-day brass time and strike weight-driven movement, excellent condition, wooden dial (illustrated), $1,120

American, ca. 1840; 8-day brass time and strike weight-driven movement used in OG clocks.
Credit: NAWCC Eastern States Regional 2002.

American, ca. 1842, OG shelf clock, 30-hour brass time and strike weight-driven movement, 26", signed Jerome, Gilbert and Grant. $250. Credit: NAWCC Eastern States Regional 2002.

American, ca. 1855, double door OG shelf clock, 8-day brass time and strike weight-driven movement, 31", signed Forestville Manufacturing Co., $1,120. Credit: Prices4Antiques.com.

American, ca. 1855, Forestville Mfg. Co., OG case-on-case shelf clock, 30.5", 8-day brass time and strike weight-driven movement, good condition, metal dial, $672

American, ca. 1850, Forestville Mfg. Co., OG shelf clock, 31", 8-day brass time and strike weight-driven movement, fair condition, replaced tablet, no hands or weights, wooden dial, $123

American, ca. 1860, Forestville Mfg. Co., OG shelf clock, 29", 8-day brass time and strike weight-driven movement, fair condition, veneer damage, flaking tablet, wooden dial, $179

American, ca. 1860, Gilbert, William L., OG shelf clock, 26", 30-hour brass time, alarm, and strike weight-driven movement, good condition, $201

American, ca. 1860, Gilbert, William L., OG shelf clock, 26", 30-hour brass time and strike weight-driven movement, good condition, $67

American, ca. 1845, Hills and Goodrich and Co., OG shelf clock, 31", 8-day brass time and strike weight-driven movement, excellent condition, fire-gilt columns, metal dial, $1,375

American, ca. 1850, Hills and Goodrich and Co., OG shelf clock, 30", 8-day brass time and strike weight-driven movement, good condition, fire-gilt columns, metal dial, $504

American, ca. 1839, Hoadley, Silas, OG shelf clock, 26", 30-hour brass time and strike weight-driven movement, original as-found condition, wooden dial, $308

American, ca. 1845, Hoadley, Silas, OG shelf clock, 26.75", 30-hour brass time and strike weight-driven movement, excellent condition, $550

American, ca. 1838, Ives, Joseph, OG shelf clock, 29.25", 8-day brass time and strike weight-driven movement, good condition, wooden dial, $448

American, ca. 1855, Jerome, C. and Co., OG shelf clock, 26", 30-hour brass time and strike weight-driven movement, fair condition, flaking tablet, metal dial, $112

American, ca. 1838, Jerome, Chauncey, OG shelf clock, 26", 30-hour brass time and strike weight-driven movement, good condition, wooden dial, $468

American, ca. 1840, Jerome, Chauncey, OG shelf clock, 25.5", 30-hour brass time and strike weight-driven movement, fair condition, veneer damage, wooden dial, no weights, $123

American, ca. 1844, Jerome, Chauncey, OG shelf clock, 26", 30-hour brass time and strike weight-driven movement, fair condition with veneer loss, flaking tablet, wooden dial, $77

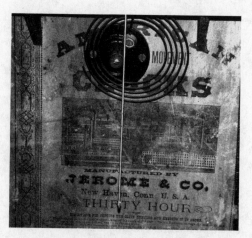

Label from preceding clock, which was made for export to England in the 1850s.

American, ca. 1850, OG shelf clock, 30-hour time and strike weight-driven movement, 26", signed Jerome and Co., $150. Credit: R. Wagner Collection.

American, ca. 1842, OG shelf clock, 30-hour time and strike weight-driven movement, 26", signed Chauncey Jerome, $150. Credit: NAWCC Eastern States Regional 2002.

American, ca. 1845, Jerome, Chauncey, OG shelf clock, 29", 8-day brass time and strike weight-driven movement, fair condition, $345

American, ca. 1850, Jerome, Chauncey, OG shelf clock, 26", 30-hour brass time and strike weight-driven movement, fair condition, zinc dial, $165

American, ca. 1855, Jerome, Chauncey, OG shelf clock, 26", 30-hour brass time and strike weight-driven movement, fair condition, metal dial, $165

American, ca. 1870, Jerome, Chauncey, OG shelf clock, 26", 30-hour brass time and strike weight-driven movement, fair as-found condition, metal dial, $110

American, ca. 1870, OG shelf clock, 30-hour time, alarm, and strike spring-driven movement, 18", signed Waterbury Clock Co., $125. Credit: Timex Museum.

American, ca. 1880, OG shelf clock, 30-hour time, alarm, and strike weight-driven movement, 27", signed Ansonia Clock Co., as found, $85. Credit: NAWCC Eastern States Regional 2002.

American, ca. 1845, Johnson, William S., mini OG shelf clock, 19", 30-hour brass time and strike weight-driven movement, excellent condition, wooden dial, $686

American, ca. 1838, Johnson, William S., OG shelf clock, 26", 30-hour time and strike wooden works movement, good condition, wooden dial (illustrated), $300

American, ca. 1839, Johnson, William S., OG shelf clock, 26", 30-hour time and strike wooden works movement, fair condition, wooden dial, $165

American, ca. 1855, Johnson, William S., OG shelf clock, 26", 30-hour brass time and strike weight-driven movement, fair condition, veneer damage, no weights, metal dial, $106

American, ca. 1840, Lane, Joel, OG shelf clock, 24", 30-hour brass time and strike weight-driven movement, fair original condition, cracked wooden dial, $134

American, ca. 1850, Manross, Elisha, OG shelf clock, 28.75", 8-day brass time and strike weight-driven movement, fair condition, replaced tablet, torn label, metal dial, $134

American, ca. 1870, New Haven Clock Co., mini OG shelf clock, 21.5", 30-hour brass time and strike weight-driven movement, very good original condition, $728

American, ca. 1870, New Haven Clock Co., mini OG shelf clock, 18", 30-hour brass time, alarm, and strike spring-driven movement, good condition with replaced dial, $95

American, ca. 1890, OG shelf clock,
30-hour brass time and strike spring-driven
movement, 26", signed E. N. Welch, $112.
Credit: Prices4Antiques.com.

American, ca. 1885, OG shelf clock,
30-hour brass time and strike spring-driven
movement, 16", signed Seth Thomas Co.,
$168. Credit: Prices4Antiques.com.

American, ca. 1880, New Haven Clock Co., mini OG shelf clock, 18.5",
8-day brass time and strike spring-driven movement, good condition,
metal dial, $61

American, ca. 1870, New Haven Clock Co., OG shelf clock, 25.75", 30-hour
brass time and strike weight-driven movement, fair condition, flaking
tablet, metal dial, $67

American, ca. 1880, New Haven Clock Co., OG shelf clock, 26", 30-hour
brass time, alarm, and strike spring-driven movement, fair condition
with veneer loss, metal dial, $175

American, ca. 1870, Seth Thomas, mini OG shelf clock, "Kitchen" model,
20", 30-hour brass time and strike spring-driven movement, fair original condition, metal dial, $121

American, ca. 1838, Seth Thomas, OG shelf clock, 24", 30-hour time and
strike wooden works movement, good condition, replaced tablet,
wooden dial, $350

American, ca. 1840, Smith, A. and Brother, OG shelf clock, 27", 30-hour
brass time and strike weight-driven movement, good condition,
wooden dial, $812

American, ca. 1840, Smith Clock Co., OG shelf clock, 31.50", 8-day brass
time and strike weight-driven movement, good condition, wooden dial,
$756

American, ca. 1845, Smith and Goodrich, mini OG shelf clock, 15.25",
30-hour time and strike fusee movement, very good condition, $336

American, ca. 1845, Smith and Goodrich, OG shelf clock, 26", 30-hour brass
time and strike weight-driven movement, fair condition, $110

American, ca. 1840, Smith, Henry C., OG shelf clock, 26", 30-hour brass
time and strike weight-driven movement, good condition, $100

American, ca. 1840, Smith, Henry C., OG shelf clock , 26.5", 30-hour brass
time and strike weight-driven movement, fair condition, repainting,
replacements, wooden dial, $140

American, ca. 1840, Sperry and Shaw, OG shelf clock, 27", 30-hour time
and strike wooden works movement, excellent original condition,
wooden dial, $625

American, ca. 1845, Terry and Andrews, OG shelf clock, 26", 30-hour brass
time, alarm, and strike weight-driven movement, very good condition,
metal dial, $247

American, ca. 1845, Terry and Andrews, OG shelf clock, 26", 30-hour brass
time and strike weight-driven movement, good original condition, $280

American, ca. 1870, Terry Clock Co., mini OG shelf clock, 10.25", 30-hour
brass time and strike spring-driven movement, poor condition, strike
mechanism missing, metal dial, $151

American, ca. 1840, Terry, Eli, mini OG shelf clock, 22.25", 30-hour brass
time and strike weight-driven movement, good condition, wooden dial,
$280

American, ca. 1890, OG shelf
clock, 30-hour brass time and
strike weight-driven movement,
26", signed Seth Thomas Co., $72.
Credit: Prices4Antiques.com.

American, ca. 1840, Terry, Henry, mini OG shelf clock, 19.75", 30-hour brass time and strike spring-driven movement, fair condition, refinished, cracked tablet, wooden dial, $756

American, ca. 1850, Terry, Silas, mini OG shelf clock, 14.5", 30-hour brass time and strike spring-driven movement, good condition, wooden dial with paint loss, $3,360

American, ca. 1840, Terry, Silas B., mini OG shelf clock, 20", 30-hour brass time and strike weight-driven movement, good condition, replaced tablet, wooden dial, $525

American, ca. 1860, Seth Thomas, mini OG shelf clock, 16", 30-hour brass time and strike spring-driven movement, very good original condition, $168

American, ca. 1870, Seth Thomas, mini OG shelf clock, 16", 30-hour brass time, alarm, and strike spring-driven movement, good condition, metal dial, $150

American, ca. 1855, Seth Thomas, OG shelf clock, 26", 30-hour brass time and strike weight-driven movement, poor condition, veneer damage, missing top glass, $95

American, ca. 1855, Seth Thomas, OG shelf clock, 25", 30-hour brass time and strike weight-driven movement, good condition, metal dial, $145

American, ca. 1865, Seth Thomas, OG shelf clock, 25.25", 8-day brass time and strike spring-driven movement, fair condition with veneer damage, $50

American, ca. 1870, Seth Thomas, OG shelf clock, 25", 8-day brass time and strike spring-driven movement, fair condition with repainted lower tablet, metal dial, $123

American, ca. 1870, Seth Thomas, OG shelf clock, 25.25", 30-hour brass time and strike weight-driven movement, fair condition, veneer damage, metal dial, no weights (illustrated), $72

American, ca. 1845, Union Mfg. Co., OG shelf clock, 26", 30-hour brass time and strike weight-driven movement, excellent original condition, wooden dial, $705

American, ca. 1850, maker unknown, OG shelf clock, 26", 30-hour brass time, alarm, and strike spring-driven movement, fair condition, metal dial, $137

American, ca. 1870, Waterbury Clock Co., mini OG shelf clock, 17.75", 8-day brass time and strike spring-driven movement, fair condition, replaced metal dial, missing bell, $134

American, ca. 1870, Waterbury Clock Co., mini OG shelf clock, 18.75", 30-hour brass time and strike spring-driven movement, good condition with replaced tablet, metal dial, $67

American, ca. 1875, Waterbury Clock Co., mini OG shelf clock, 19", 30-hour brass time and strike spring-driven movement, good condition, restoration, $165

American, ca. 1880, Waterbury Clock Co., mini OG shelf clock, 17.75", 8-day brass time and strike spring-driven movement, fair condition, replaced metal dial, $134

American, ca. 1880, Waterbury Clock Co., mini OG shelf clock, 19", 30-hour brass time and strike spring-driven movement, fair condition, flaking tablet, metal dial, $95

American, ca. 1880, Waterbury Clock Co., OG shelf clock, 25.75", 30-hour brass time and strike weight-driven movement, good condition, re-painted tablet, metal dial, no weights, $106

American, ca. 1864, Welch, E. N., mini OG shelf clock, 18", 30-hour brass time and strike spring-driven movement, good condition, $150

American, ca. 1880, Welch, E. N., mini OG shelf clock, 18.25", 30-hour brass time and strike spring-driven movement, fair condition, replaced metal dial and veneer damage, $123

American, ca. 1870, Welch, E. N., OG shelf clock, 27", 30-hour brass time and strike weight-driven movement, fair condition, replaced tablet, veneer damage, metal dial, $112

American, ca. 1839, Welton, H. and Co., OG shelf clock, 26", 30-hour brass time and strike weight-driven movement, very good condition, wooden dial, $227

American, ca. 1840, Welton, H. and Co., OG shelf clock, 26", 30-hour brass time and strike weight-driven lyre movement, fair as-found condition, $155

	LOW	MID	HIGH
Ogee (OG) Shelf Clocks (ca. 1837–1920)	$50–$100	$200–$400	$500–$900+

PILLAR AND SCROLL SHELF CLOCKS appeared in 1818, growing out of Eli Terry's attempt to develop a mass-produced wooden movement for a shelf clock. This late-Federal-style clock was an immediate success and remained in production until the 1830s.

American, ca. 1830, pillar and scroll shelf clock, 30-hour time and strike wooden works movement, 31", signed Elisha Neal, $2,016. Credit: R. O. Schmitt Fine Arts.

American, ca. 1830, pillar and scroll shelf clock, 30-hour time and strike wooden works movement, 30", unattributed, Credit: NAWCC TIMEXPO 2002.

Terry's patent protected this clock from imitators in the beginning, but it was soon licensed to others such as Seth Thomas. A number of innovative movement designs by other makers circumvented Terry's patent, and by the 1830s there were many makers producing this case design. Reproductions are still being made.

The pillar and scroll is considered by many to be America's most beautiful clock and desirable to most collectors. Expect to pay a good price for this clock even though a fair number still exist.

American, ca. 1990, Bruno, George, Connecticut pillar and scroll shelf clock (reproduction), 30", 30-hour wooden works movement, fine condition (this reproduction has the outside escapement), $1,568

American, ca. 1940, Chelsea Clock Co., Connecticut pillar and scroll shelf clock, 24", 8-day time and strike spring-driven movement, good as-found condition, $728

American, ca. 1929, Gilbert, William L., miniature Dresden model pillar and scroll shelf clock, 12.25", 8-day time and strike spring-driven movement, very good condition, $412

American, ca. 1828, Hoadley, Silas, Connecticut pillar and scroll shelf clock,

American, ca. 1827, pillar and scroll shelf clock, Terry 30-hour time and strike wooden works movement and wooden dial replacing original movement and dial, 28", signed Wadsworth, Lowensbury and Turner, $1,000.

29", 30-hour wooden weight-driven movement, fair condition, replaced parts , $797

American, ca. 1830, Holtzinger, Joseph, Pennsylvania pillar and scroll shelf clock, 31.5", 8-day time and strike, good condition, $2,750

American, ca. 1830, Neal, Elisha, New Hampshire pillar and scroll shelf clock, 31", 30-hour wooden weight-driven movement, very good restored condition (illustrated), $2,016

American, ca. 1825, North, Norris, Connecticut pillar and scroll shelf clock, 29", 30-hour wooden Torrington movement, very good condition, replaced tablet, $2,128

Tablet for clock above.

American, ca. 1820, Terry, Eli, Connecticut pillar and scroll shelf clock, 31", 30-hour wooden weight-driven movement, poor condition, missing crest parts, replaced tablet, $632

American, ca. 1830, Terry, Eli, Connecticut pillar and scroll shelf clock, 31", 30-hour wooden weight-driven movement, very good condition, mahogany case, $1,035

American, ca. 1830, Terry, Eli and Samuel, Connecticut pillar and scroll shelf clock, 31.5", 30-hour wooden weight-driven movement, good restored condition, $1,650

American, ca. 1830, Terry, Eli and Samuel, Connecticut pillar and scroll shelf clock, 32", 30-hour wooden weight-driven movement, good restored condition, $1,100

American, ca. 1830, Terry, Eli and Sons, Connecticut pillar and scroll shelf clock, 30.75", 30-hour wooden weight-driven movement, good condition, mahogany case, replaced tablet, $980

American, ca. 1818, Seth Thomas, Connecticut pillar and scroll shelf clock, 27.5", 30-hour wooden works with off-center pendulum, very good condition, minor restoration, $8,800

American, ca. 1830, Thomas, Seth, Connecticut pillar and scroll shelf clock, 29", 30-hour wooden works weight-driven movement, poor condition, case damage and missing finials, $952

American, ca. 1830, Seth Thomas, Connecticut pillar and scroll shelf clock, 31", 30-hour wooden weight-driven movement, very good condition, curly maple case, $2,420

American, ca. 1940, Seth Thomas, Connecticut pillar and scroll shelf clock, 20", 8-day time and strike spring-driven movement, very good condition, $632

American, ca. 1827, Wadsworth, Lownsbury, and Turner, Connecticut pillar and scroll shelf clock, 28", 30-hour wooden weight-driven movement, very good condition, mahogany case, $1,000

	LOW	MID	HIGH
Pillar and Scroll clocks (ca. 1818–35)	$500–$700	$900–$1,500	$2,500–$3,500+

ROUNDSIDE SHELF CLOCKS were produced by the Jeromes in the late 1830s and revived on a larger scale by the Seth Thomas Company in the 1860s. They were 30-hour brass time and strike weight-driven clocks when manufactured by the Jeromes, but became 8-day time and strike weight-driven clocks when made by Seth Thomas. The name refers to the rounded front corners of the case.

These clocks are not easy to find, but they are also not greatly in demand, so they are still reasonably priced.

American, ca. 1838, Jerome, Chauncey and Noble, roundside shelf clock, 22", 30-hour brass time and strike, good condition, extensive restoration, $308

American, ca. 1838, Jerome, Chauncey and Noble, roundside shelf clock, 22", 30-hour brass time and strike, good condition with replaced glass top and bottom (illustrated), $220

American, ca. 1839, Jerome, Chauncey and Noble, roundside shelf clock, 22", 30-hour brass time and strike, good condition, $357

American, ca. 1840, Jerome, Chauncey and Noble, roundside shelf clock, 22", 30-hour brass time and strike, good condition, $345

American, ca. 1863, Seth Thomas, roundside shelf clock, 30.5", 8-day brass time and strike, good condition, $700

	LOW	MID	HIGH
Roundside Shelf Clocks (ca. 1835–75)	$200–$299	$300–$400	$600–$800

American, ca. 1838, roundside shelf clock, 30-hour brass time and strike weight-driven movement, 22", signed C. and N. Jerome, $220. Credit: R. O. Schmitt Fine Arts.

STEEPLE SHELF CLOCKS were created by Elias Ingraham shortly after he introduced the beehive clock in 1840. This case style remained in production into the 1950s. Ingraham, who failed to take out a patent on this design, found that he had an immediate success that he could not protect. Many companies produced this design.

This clock has a sharp Gothic-arch case. It quickly came to be called a steeple clock for its resemblance to church with steeples. The clock has a gable top flanked by round columns surmounted with tapered spires. Most cases were veneered in mahogany, although numerous others were done in rosewood and walnut. Some models had applied ripple molding. Case variations range from no steeples to four steeples and from a single deck to a double deck.

Movements were spring-driven 30-hour or 8-day brass time and strike, often with an alarm.

Prices can range from $100 for a late 30-hour model to thousands of dollars for a double-decker (steeple-on-steeple) with a Joseph Ives wagon-spring movement.

American, ca. 1870, Ansonia Clock Co., miniature steeple clock with two
    steeples, 14.5", 30-hour time, alarm, and strike spring-driven move-
    ment, good condition, replaced dial, $134

An assortment of American steeple clocks for sale at NAWCC
Mid-Eastern States Regional 2002.

NAWCC TIMEXPO 2002.

American, ca. 1848, Atkins, M. W. and Co., steeple clock with two steeples, 19.75", 8-day time and strike spring-driven movement, very good condition, $515

American, ca. 1845, Atkins, Porter, and Co., steeple-on-steeple clock with two steeples, 28", 8-day time and strike spring-driven movement, good condition, cracked upper tablet, $2,912

American, ca. 1845, Atkins, Porter, and Co., steeple-on-steeple clock with two steeples, 28", 8-day time and strike spring-driven movement, very good condition, $2,912

NAWCC TIMEXPO 2002.

American, ca. 1880, steeple clock, 30-hour brass time and strike spring-driven movement, 21", signed New Haven Clock Co., $125.

American, ca. 1854, steeple clock without steeples, 30-hour time-only, 12.75", signed Forestville Hardware and Clock Co., $1,120. Credit: R. O. Schmitt Fine Arts.

American, ca. 1850, Beals, J. J., and Co., steeple clock with two steeples, 19.5", 30-hour time, alarm, and strike with a spring-driven movement, good condition, $156

American, ca. 1840, Birge and Fuller, steeple-on-steeple clock with four steeples, 26", 8-day time and strike with a wagon-spring movement, very good condition, $2,800

American, ca. 1845, Birge and Fuller, steeple-on-steeple clock with four steeples, 26", 8-day time and strike with a wagon-spring movement, very good condition, $1,344

American, ca. 1845, Birge and Fuller, steeple-on-steeple clock with four steeples, 26.5", 8-day time and strike spring-driven movement, very good condition (illustrated), $1,120

American, ca. 1848, Birge and Fuller, steeple-on-steeple clock with four steeples, 27.5", 8-day time and strike wagon-spring movement, good condition, $3,360

American, ca. 1848, Birge and Fuller, steeple-on-steeple clock with four steeples, 26.5", no movement, good condition, $308

American, ca. 1848, Birge and Fuller, steeple-on-steeple clock with four steeples, 24.25", 30-hour time and strike wagon-spring movement, very good condition, $2,128

American, ca. 1850, ripple-front steeple clock, 30-hour time, alarm, and strike, 20", signed J. C. Brown, $2,860. Credit: R. O. Schmitt Fine Arts.

American, ca. 1867, steeple clock, 30-hour time, alarm, and strike, 21", signed Waterbury Clock Co., $150. Credit: Timex Museum.

American, ca. 1848, Birge and Fuller, steeple-on-steeple clock with four steeples, 27.25", 8-day time and strike wagon-spring movement, very good condition, $3,920

American, ca. 1848, Birge and Fuller, steeple-on-steeple clock with four steeples, 26", 8-day time and strike spring-driven movement, very good condition (illustrated), $3,248

American, ca. 1848, Birge and Fuller, steeple-on-steeple clock with two steeples, 21.5", 30-hour time and strike wagon-spring movement, very good condition (illustrated), $20,900

American, ca. 1845, Boardman, Chauncey, steeple clock with two steeples, 19.75", 8-day time and strike brass fusee movement, fair condition, $280

American, ca. 1845, Boardman, Chauncey, steeple clock with two steeples, 20", 30-hour time and strike spring-driven movement, good condition, $336

American, ca. 1845, Boardman, Chauncey, steeple clock with two steeples, 20", 30-hour time and strike spring-driven movement, good condition with repainted dial, $302

American, ca. 1845, Boardman, Chauncey, steeple clock with two steeples, 19.75", 30-hour time and strike fusee movement, good condition, $308

American, ca. 1875, steeple clock, replaced lower tablet, 8-day time, alarm, and strike, 20", signed W. L. Gilbert, $200. Credit: Sterling Collection.

American, ca. 1880, steeple clock, 8-day time, alarm, and strike, 19", signed E. N. Welch, $235. Credit: Prices4Antiques.com.

American, ca. 1847, Boardman, Chauncey, steeple clock with two steeples, 19", 30-hour time, alarm, and strike spring-driven movement, very good condition, $176

American, ca. 1848, Boardman, Chauncey, steeple clock with two steeples, 20", 30-hour time and strike fusee movement, very good condition, $275

American, ca. 1850, Boardman and Wells, steeple clock with two steeples, 19.5", 30-hour time and strike fusee movement, fair condition, $252

American, ca. 1850, Brewster and Ingraham, steeple clock with an onion top and two steeples, 20", 8-day time and strike spring-driven movement, fair condition, $1,870

American, ca. 1845, Brewster and Ingraham, steeple clock with four steeples, 19.25", 8-day time and strike spring-driven movement, very good condition, $1,456

American, ca. 1845, Brewster and Ingraham, steeple clock with two steeples, 20", 8-day time and strike spring-driven movement, good condition, $235

American, ca. 1845, Brewster and Ingraham, steeple clock with two steeples, 21", 8-day time and strike spring-driven movement, very good condition, $2,128

American, ca. 1845, Brewster and Ingraham, steeple clock with two steeples, 20", 8-day time and strike spring-driven movement, poor condition with veneer damage, $123

American, ca. 1850, steeple clock, 8-day time, alarm, and strike brass spring, 20", signed Terry and Andrews, $644. Credit: Prices4Antiques.com.

American, ca. 1845, steeple-on-steeple clock, 8-day brass time and strike fusee movement, 26.5", signed Birge and Fuller, $1,120. Credit: Prices4Antiques.com.

American, ca. 1845, Brewster and Ingraham, steeple clock with two steeples, 20", 30-hour time and strike spring-driven movement, fair condition, $123

American, ca. 1845, Brewster and Ingraham, steeple clock with two steeples, 19.5", 8-day time and strike spring-driven movement, very good condition, $700

American, ca. 1845, Brewster and Ingraham, steeple clock with two steeples, 19.5", 30-hour time and strike spring-driven movement, good condition, $179

American, ca. 1845, Brewster and Ingraham, steeple clock with two steeples, 20", 8-day time and strike spring-driven movement, good condition with replaced dial, $364

American, ca. 1845, Brewster and Ingraham, steeple clock with two steeples, 20", 8-day time and strike spring-driven movement, fair condition with veneer damage and missing alarm, $392

American, ca. 1845, Brewster and Ingraham, steeple clock with two steeples, 18.75", 30-hour time and strike spring-driven movement, good condition, $308

American, ca. 1845, Brewster and Ingraham, steeple clock with two steeples, 20", 8-day time and strike spring-driven movement, fair condition with replaced dial, $89

American, ca. 1845, double steeple clock, 8-day time and strike, 26", signed Birge and Fuller, $3,248. Credit: Prices4Antiques.com.

American, ca. 1845, Brewster Mfg. Co., steeple clock with two steeples, 19.5", 30-hour time and strike spring-driven movement, fair condition with replaced tablet and repainted dial, $106

American, ca. 1855, Bristol Brass and Clock Co., steeple clock with two steeples, 20", 30-hour time and strike spring-driven movement, good condition, $550

American, ca. 1855, Brown, J. C., miniature steeple clock with two steeples, 16", 30-hour time and strike spring-driven movement, good condition, $1,064

American, ca. 1855, Brown, J. C., miniature steeple clock with two steeples

American, miniature single-steeple clock, 30-hour time and strike wagon-spring movement, 21.5", signed Birge and Fuller, $20,900. Credit: Prices4Antiques.com.

with ripple trim, 16", 30-hour time and strike spring-driven movement, very good condition, $6,875

American, ca. 1855, Brown, J. C., miniature steeple clock with two steeples with ripple trim, 16", 30-hour time and strike spring-driven movement, good condition, $1,430

American, ca. 1850, Brown, J. C., steeple clock with four steeples and ripple trim, 19.75", 8-day time and strike spring-driven movement, very good condition, $1,736

American, ca. 1855, Brown, J. C., steeple clock with two steeples, 19.75", 8-day time and strike spring-driven movement, good condition, $308

American, ca. 1850, Brown, J. C., steeple clock with two steeples and ripple trim, 20", 30-hour time, alarm, and strike spring-driven movement, excellent condition (illustrated), $2,860

American, ca. 1850, Connecticut Clock Co., steeple clock with two steeples and ripple trim, 19.5", 30-hour time and strike spring-driven movement, very good refinished condition, $2,920

American, ca. 1854, Forestville Hardware and Clock Co., miniature steeple clock with no steeples, 12.75", 30-hour time and strike spring-driven movement, good condition with retouched dial (illustrated), $1,120

American, ca. 1870, Gilbert, W. L., miniature steeple clock with two steeples, 14.75", 30-hour time-only ladder movement, fair condition, missing hands, $123

American, ca. 1880, Gilbert, W. L., steeple clock with two steeples, 19.75", 30-hour time, alarm, and strike spring-driven movement, good condition, $78

American, ca. 1848, Jerome, Chauncey, steeple clock with two steeples, 19.5", 30-hour time and strike spring-driven movement, good condition with a replaced movement, $196

American, ca. 1850, Jerome and Co., miniature steeple clock with two steeples, 15.5", 30-hour time, alarm, and strike spring-driven movement, fair condition with replaced dial and veneer loss, $106

American, ca. 1845, Johnson, W. S., steeple-on-steeple clock with four steeples, 23.5", 8-day time and strike spring-driven movement, very good condition, $1,008

American, ca. 1845, Johnson, W. S., steeple-on-steeple clock with four steeples, 23.25", 8-day time and strike spring-driven movement, good condition, $644

American, ca. 1850, Manross, Elisha, steeple clock with two steeples, 19.75", 30-hour time and strike spring-driven movement, good condition, $476

American, ca. 1850, Manross, Elisha, steeple clock with two steeples, 19.5", 30-hour time and strike spring-driven movement, good condition with minor veneer damage, $145

American, ca. 1850, Manross, Elisha, steeple clock with two steeples, 19.5", 30-hour time and strike spring-driven movement, fair condition with veneer damage, $134

American, ca. 1850, Manross, Elisha, steeple clock with two steeples, 19.75", 30-hour time and strike spring-driven movement, good condition with minor tablet loss, $280

American, ca. 1850, Manross, Elisha, steeple clock with two steeples, 20", 30-hour time and strike spring-driven movement, very good condition, $605

American, ca. 1845, Manross, Elisha, steeple-on-steeple clock with four steeples, 24", 8-day time and strike brass fusee movement, good condition, $1,344

American, ca. 1850, Manross, Elisha, steeple-on-steeple clock with four steeples, 23.5", 8-day time and strike fusee movement, fair condition, replaced tablet and veneer loss, $1,008

American, ca. 1850, Manross, Elisha, steeple-on-steeple clock with four steeples, 23.5", 8-day time and strike fusee movement, good condition, $2,464

American, ca. 1870, New Haven Clock Co., miniature steeple clock with two steeples, 14.5", 30-hour time and strike spring-driven movement, fair condition, $231

American, ca. 1870, New Haven Clock Co., miniature steeple clock with two steeples, 14.75", 30-hour time, alarm, and strike spring-driven movement, fair condition, $168

American, ca. 1875, New Haven Clock Co., steeple clock with two steeples, 20.5", 8-day time and strike spring-driven movement, fair condition with replaced dial and veneer loss, $95

American, ca. 1880, New Haven Clock Co., steeple clock with two steeples, 20", 30-hour time, alarm, and strike spring-driven movement, good condition, $112

American, ca. 1850, Pond and Barnes, steeple clock with two steeples, 19", 30-hour time and strike spring-driven movement, excellent condition, $385

American, ca. 1845, Pratt, Daniel, steeple-on-steeple clock with four steeples, 24", 30-hour time and strike wagon-spring movement, very good condition, $2,645

American, ca. 1870, Pratt, Daniel, and Sons, steeple clock with two steeples, 19", 30-hour time, alarm, and strike spring-driven movement, good condition, $302

American, ca. 1950, Seth Thomas, miniature steeple clock with two steeples, 14.5", electric time and strike movement, good condition, $11

American, ca. 1858, Seth Thomas, steeple clock with two steeples, 29", 30-hour time and strike spring-driven movement, very good condition, $781

American, ca. 1848, Sperry, C. S., steeple clock with four steeples, 21", 30-hour time and strike fusee movement, good condition with replaced dial, $588

American, ca. 1848, Sperry and Shaw, steeple clock with four steeples, 21", 30-hour time and strike fusee movement, good condition with alarm mechanism removed, $687

American, ca. 1850, Terry and Andrews, steeple clock with four steeples, 19", 8-day time, alarm, and strike spring-driven movement, good condition, $1,232

American, ca. 1850, Terry and Andrews, steeple clock with two steeples, 19", 8-day time and strike spring-driven movement, good restored condition, $297

American, ca. 1850, Terry and Andrews, steeple clock with two steeples, 20", 8-day time and strike spring-driven movement, good condition (illustrated), $644

American, ca. 1850, Terry and Andrews, steeple clock with two steeples, 20", 30-hour time strike spring-driven movement, good condition with replaced dial, $252

American, ca. 1850, Terry and Andrews, steeple clock with two steeples, 20", 30-hour time, alarm, and strike spring-driven movement, good condition, $308

American, ca. 1855, Terryville Mfg. Co., steeple clock with two steeples, 19.5", 30-hour time and strike spring-driven movement, good condition, $308

American, ca. 1865, Welch, E. N., steeple clock with two steeples, 19.5", 30-hour time, alarm, and strike spring-driven movement, good original condition, $190

American, ca. 1890, Welch, E. N., steeple clock with two steeples, 19", 8-day time, alarm, and strike spring-driven movement, fair condition, $235

American, ca. 1890, Welch, E. N., steeple-on-steeple clock with four steeples, 24.25", 8-day time and strike spring-driven movement, good condition, $1,008

	LOW	MID	HIGH
Steeple Shelf Clocks (ca. 1840–1940)	$100–$250	$450–$850	$1,000–$3,500+

TAMBOUR MANTEL CLOCKS are often called "camelback" or "Napoleon's hat" clocks. The case form originated in France during the nineteenth century. American clockmakers adopted the form as a mantel clock during the final flowering of American mechanical clocks in the 1920s. Many will remember this form as their grandparents' clock. It was produced from World War I (1914–18) into the 1950s, often with an electric movement.

Tambour clocks are found everywhere from yard sales to antiques shops. At present they are very reasonable in price, but as the supply dwindles and more and younger collectors enter the field, prices will rise. Buy only the best—Westminster chimes, wonderful cases, or Chelsea models in brass cases.

American, ca. 1914, Ansonia Clock Co., mahogany tambour mantel clock, "Cabinet No. 42" model, 6.5", 30-hour time-only spring-driven movement, poor condition, $44

American, ca. 1912, Chelsea Clock Co., brass-cased tambour mantel clock,

American, ca. 1917, tambour mantel clock, 8-day time and strike (Westminster chimes), 10", signed Waterbury Clock Co., $125. Credit: Timex Museum.

American, ca. 1925, tambour mantel clock, 8-day time and strike, 9.5", signed Seth Thomas, asking $100. Credit: NAWCC Eastern States Regional 2002.

"TAMBOUR No. 1," 9.5", 8-day time and strike spring-driven movement, very good original condition, $470

American, ca. 1916, Chelsea Clock Co., mahogany tambour mantel clock, "BABRO No. 32" model, 11", 8-day time and strike spring-driven movement, very good original condition, $1,092

American, ca. 1917, Chelsea Clock Co., brass-cased tambour mantel clock, made for Tiffany and Co., "TAMBOUR No. 3" model, 9", 8-day time and strike spring-driven movement, excellent original condition, $1,568

American, ca. 1917, Chelsea Clock Co., mahogany tambour mantel clock, "BABRO No. 30" model, 10", 8-day time and strike (ship's bell) spring-driven movement, good condition, $308

American, ca. 1920, tambour mantel clock, "TEMPO" model, 8-day time and strike, 9.5", signed Seth Thomas, $112. Credit: Prices4Antiques.com.

American, ca. 1925, tambour mantel clock, 8-day time and strike (Westminster chimes), 10", signed Seth Thomas, $72. Credit: Prices4Antiques.com.

American, ca. 1919, Chelsea Clock Co., terra cotta–cased tambour mantel clock, 11.5", 8-day time and strike spring-driven movement, fair condition, $280

American, ca. 1920, Chelsea Clock Co., brass-cased tambour mantel clock, "TAMBOUR No. 4" model, 12", 8-day time and strike (ship's bell) spring-driven movement, excellent condition, $784

American, ca. 1925, Chelsea Clock Co., mahogany tambour mantel clock made for Tiffany and Co., 8.5", 8-day time and strike spring-driven movement, good condition, $385

American, ca. 1920, Gilbert, William L., mahogany tambour mantel clock, 10", 8-day time and strike spring-driven movement, good restored condition, $27

American, ca. 1920, Herschede Clock Co., mini mahogany tambour mantel clock, 6", electric time and strike movement, very good condition, $44

American, ca. 1935, Ingraham Clock Co., mahogany tambour mantel clock, 10", 8-day time and strike "bim-bam" spring-driven movement, poor condition, $56

American, ca. 1915, Seth Thomas, mini mahogany novelty tambour mantel clock, 5.75", 30-hour time-only spring-driven movement, fair condition, $168

American, ca. 1916, Seth Thomas, mahogany tambour mantel clock, "PEER" model, 8", 8-day time and strike spring-driven movement, very good condition, $252

American, ca. 1920, Seth Thomas, mahogany tambour mantel clock, 9", 8-day time and strike spring-driven movement, good original condition, $143

American, ca. 1920, Seth Thomas, mahogany tambour mantel clock,

"TAMBOUR" model, 9.5", 8-day time and strike "ding-dong" spring-driven movement, very good restored condition, $140

American, ca. 1920, Seth Thomas, mini glass novelty tambour clock, 5.75", 30-hour time-only spring-driven movement, good condition, $84

American, ca. 1920, Seth Thomas, mahogany tambour mantel clock, "TEMPO" model, 9.5", 8-day time and strike spring-driven movement, very good condition (illustrated), $112

American, ca. 1920, Seth Thomas, mini mahogany tambour mantel clock, 4", 8-day time-only jeweled spring-driven movement, very good condition, $33

American, ca. 1925, Seth Thomas, mahogany tambour mantel clock, "PLY-MOUTH" model, 9", 8-day time and strike "ding-dong" spring-driven movement, poor condition, $60

American, ca. 1925, Seth Thomas, mahogany tambour mantel clock, "No. 124" model, 10", 8-day time and strike Westminster movement, good condition (illustrated), $72

American, ca. 1925, Seth Thomas, mahogany tambour mantel clock, 10", 8-day time and strike spring-driven movement, good condition, $44

American, ca. 1950, Seth Thomas, mahogany tambour mantel clock, "MEDBURY" model, 9.5", 8-day time and strike Westminster movement, excellent condition, $192

American, ca. 1955, Seth Thomas, mahogany tambour mantel clock, "PLY-MOUTH" model, 10", electric movement, poor condition, $77

American, ca. 1920, Waltham Clock Co., mahogany tambour mantel clock, 9.5", 8-day time and strike lever escapement spring-driven movement, fair condition, $352

	LOW	MID	HIGH
Tambour Mantel Clocks (ca. 1900–50)	$25–$50	$100–$300	$500–$1,000+

TERRY PATENT BOX SHELF CLOCKS are included only to illustrate Eli Terry's first marketed wooden works shelf clock from which the American shelf clock evolved.

TRANSITION SHELF CLOCKS appeared about 1830. These short-pendulum (short-drop) 30-hour wooden works clocks had some attributes of the pillar and scroll and the stenciled and carved column clocks. These clocks are referred to as transition clocks and were often produced to circumvent var-

American, ca. 1816, Eli Terry patent box clock, earliest model, 30-hour time and strike brass and wood movement, 20", signed Seth Thomas, sold at R. O. Schmitt auction on April 27, 2002, for $58,240. Credit: R. O. Schmitt Fine Arts.

American, ca. 1817, Eli Terry patent box clock, 30-hour time and strike brass and wood movement, 20", museum exhibit. Credit: NAWCC Museum.

ious patents and licenses. By 1840 they had disappeared. They are fairly scarce and underappreciated today.

In height and finials they resemble the pillar and scroll clocks while their columns and splats were carved or stenciled like their long-pendulum (long-drop) column and splat contemporaries.

American, ca. 1830, Blakeslee, M. and E., transition shelf clock with stenciled splat and half columns, 27.5", 30-hour wooden time and alarm movement, very good as-found condition (illustrated), $550

American, ca. 1830, Hoadley, Silas, transition shelf clock with stenciled half columns, 26", 30-hour wooden time and alarm movement, fair condition with tablet replaced (illustrated), $1,008

American, ca. 1830, Hodges, Erastus, transition shelf clock with stenciled splat and half columns, 27", 30-hour wooden time and strike movement, very good condition, missing hands, $560

American, ca. 1830, Jeromes and Darrow, transition shelf clock with stenciled splat and half columns, 28.5", 30-hour wooden time and strike movement, very good condition, $560

American, ca. 1830, Jeromes and Darrow, transition shelf clock with sten-

American, ca. 1830, transition shelf clock, 30-hour time and strike wooden works, 27.5", M. and E. Blakeslee, $550. Credit: Prices4Antiques.com.

American, ca. 1829, transition shelf clock, 30-hour time and strike wooden works, 31", signed George Marsh, $420. Credit: Prices4Antiques.com.

ciled splat and half columns, 28.5", 30-hour wooden time and alarm movement, very good as-found condition, $560

American, ca. 1830, Marsh, George, transition shelf clock with carved splat and half columns, 32", 30-hour wooden time and strike movement, good condition with some veneer damage (illustrated), $420

American, ca. 1830, Mitchell, A. G., transition shelf clock with carved splat

American, ca. 1835, transition shelf clock, 30-hour time, alarm, and strike wooden works, 26", signed Silas Hoadley, $1,008. Credit: Prices4Antiques.com.

and half columns, 29.5", 30-hour wooden time and strike movement, very good as-found condition, $1,904

American, ca. 1830, Smith, A., transition shelf clock with carved splat, 28", 30-hour wooden time and strike movement, very good condition, $1,008

American, ca. 1828, Sperry, Henry, transition shelf clock with stenciled splat and half columns, 26.75", 30-hour wooden time and alarm movement, fair condition with restoration, $308

American, ca. 1830, Terry, Eli and Sons, transition shelf clock with stenciled splat and half columns, 28.25", 30-hour wooden time and strike movement, very good as-found condition, $560

American, ca. 1835, Terry, Eli and Sons, transition shelf clock with stenciled splat and half columns, 28.5", 30-hour wooden time and strike movement, very good as-found condition with repainted tablet, $476

American, ca. 1840, Terry, Eli and Sons, transition shelf clock with stenciled splat and half columns, 28.5", 30-hour wooden time and strike movement, very good as-found condition, $1,568

American, ca. 1830, Terry, Eli and Sons, transition shelf clock with stenciled splat and half columns, 28.5", 30-hour wooden time and strike movement, fair condition with tablet replaced by a print, $392

American, ca. 1830, Seth Thomas, transition shelf clock, 29", 30-hour wooden time and strike movement, very good condition, missing hands, $560

American, ca. 1830, Seth Thomas, transition shelf clock with carved splat and stenciled half columns, 29.25", 30-hour wooden time and alarm movement, good condition, $896

	LOW	MID	HIGH
Transition Shelf Clocks (ca. 1830–40)	$300–$450	$500–$750	$800–$1,000+

WALNUT AND OAK GINGERBREAD CLOCKS are 8-day time and strike shelf clocks produced in the latter part of the nineteenth century and named for the fanciful gingerbread confections popular at the time. As they most often were found in the kitchen, they are just as commonly called kitchen clocks.

In construction and design, these clocks are a rectangular box mounted on a base surrounded by large flat areas of incised and applied walnut decoration in the walnuts and flat steam-impressed oak designs in the oaks. They have a full one-piece glazed door whose glass was decorated by silk screening.

American, walnut and oak gingerbread shelf clocks, 8-day time and strike, 20"–30". The photo on the left is offering six for $850 or $142 each. The photo on the right is offering two pressed oaks for $195. Credit (left): NAWCC TIMEXPO 2002. Credit (right): NAWCC Eastern States Regional 2002.

Abundant supply and reasonable prices make these attractive first purchases.

American, ca. 1900, Ansonia Clock Co., pressed-oak gingerbread shelf clock, 22.25", 8-day time and strike spring-driven movement, good condition, $120

American, ca. 1895, Attleboro Clock Co., pressed-oak gingerbread shelf clock, "AMERICUS" model, 22.25", 8-day time and strike spring-driven movement, good original condition, $407

American, ca. 1900, Attleboro Clock Co., pressed-oak gingerbread shelf clock, "PEERLESS ASSORTMENT F" model, 22", 8-day time and strike spring-driven movement, refinished case and repapered dial, $247

American, ca. 1885, Gilbert, William L., pressed-oak gingerbread shelf clock, "EGYPTIAN No. 60" model, 25", 8-day time and strike spring-driven movement, poor condition, top half-inch of the case missing, $121

American, ca. 1890, Gilbert, William L., walnut gingerbread shelf clock, 22", 8-day time and strike spring-driven movement, good condition, $192

American, ca. 1900, Gilbert, William L., pressed-oak gingerbread shelf clock, "EGYPTIAN No. 58" model, 23.5", 8-day time and strike spring-driven movement, excellent original condition, $220

American, ca. 1910, pressed-oak gingerbread shelf clock, 8-day time, alarm, and strike, 22", signed Waterbury Clock Co., $93. Credit: Prices4Antiques.com.

American, ca. 1895, incised-walnut gingerbread shelf clock, 8-day time and strike, 23", unknown maker, asking $175. Credit: NAWCC Eastern States Regional 2002.

American, ca. 1913, Gilbert, William L., pressed-oak gingerbread shelf clock, "IDEAL- MIRROR SIDE" model, 25", 8-day time and strike spring-driven movement, good condition, $275

American, ca. 1884, Ingraham and Co., walnut gingerbread shelf clock, 21.5", 8-day time and strike spring-driven movement, good original condition, $143

American, ca. 1890, Ingraham and Co., walnut gingerbread shelf clock, 21.5", 8-day time and strike spring-driven movement, good condition, $65

American, ca. 1890, Ingraham and Co., pressed-oak gingerbread shelf clock, 22.5", 8-day time and strike spring-driven movement, fair condition with loss of finish, $84

American, ca. 1896, Ingraham and Co., pressed-oak gingerbread shelf clock, "JEWEL" model, 21", 8-day time and strike spring-driven movement, good condition, $247

American, ca. 1900, Ingraham and Co., pressed-oak gingerbread shelf clock, "CABINET C" model, 15.5", 8-day time and strike spring-driven movement, good condition, $363

American, ca. 1900, Ingraham and Co., pressed-oak gingerbread shelf clock, "MAINE" model, 23", 8-day time and strike spring-driven movement, good condition, $616

American, ca. 1890, incised-walnut gingerbread shelf clock, 8-day time and strike, 22", signed Ansonia Clock Co., $110.

American, ca. 1895, incised-walnut gingerbread shelf clock, 8-day time, alarm, and strike, 23", signed Ansonia Clock Co., $120.

American, ca. 1900, Ingraham and Co., pressed-oak gingerbread shelf clock, 22", 8-day time and strike spring-driven movement, good condition, $156

American, ca. 1910, Ingraham and Co., pressed-oak gingerbread shelf clock, "GILA" model, 23", 8-day time and strike spring-driven movement, good refinished condition, $247

American, ca. 1915, Ingraham and Co., pressed-oak gingerbread shelf clock, "MT. VERNON" model, 22", 8-day time and strike spring-driven movement, poor condition, overpainted, $275

American, ca. 1905, New Haven Clock Co., pressed-oak gingerbread shelf clock, "NORWICH LINE-C" model, 25", 8-day time and strike spring-driven movement, excellent original condition, $302

American, ca. 1905, New Haven Clock Co., pressed-oak gingerbread shelf clock, "NORWICH LINE-A" model, 25", 8-day time and strike spring-driven movement, fair condition, stripped, $203

American, ca. 1900, maker unknown, pressed-oak gingerbread shelf clock, 23", 8-day time and strike spring-driven movement, original as-found condition, $137

American, ca. 1900, Waterbury Clock Co., pressed-oak gingerbread shelf clock, 22", 8-day time, alarm, and strike spring-driven movement, very good condition (illustrated), $93

American, ca. 1910, Waterbury Clock Co., pressed-oak gingerbread shelf clock, "FESTUS" model, 23", 8-day time and strike spring-driven movement, good condition, $121

American, ca. 1910, Waterbury Clock Co., pressed-oak gingerbread shelf clock, "HILLSDALE" model, 22", 8-day time and strike spring-driven movement, good restored condition, $151

American, ca. 1910, Waterbury Clock Co., pressed-oak gingerbread shelf clock, "HILLSDALE" model, 22", 8-day time and strike spring-driven movement, good restored condition, $151

American, ca. 1890, Welch, E. N., walnut gingerbread shelf clock, 23.5", 8-day time and strike spring-driven movement, good condition, $145

American, ca. 1890, Welch, E. N., walnut gingerbread shelf clock, "SMUG-GLER" model, 22", 8-day time and strike spring-driven movement, good condition, $176

American, ca. 1890, Welch, E. N., walnut gingerbread shelf clock, 25", 8-day time and strike spring-driven movement, good condition, $330

American, ca. 1890, Welch, E. N., walnut gingerbread shelf clock, 23", 8-day time and strike spring-driven movement, good refinished condition, $137

American, ca. 1900, Welch, E. N., walnut gingerbread shelf clock, 22", 8-day time and strike spring-driven movement, good condition, $440

American, ca. 1900, Welch, E. N., pressed-oak gingerbread shelf clock, "CABINET K No. 64" model, 17", 8-day time and strike spring-driven movement, good condition, $275

	LOW	MID	HIGH
Walnut and Oak Gingerbread Shelf Clocks (ca. 1885–1915)	$75–$150	$200–$300	$400+

WALNUT AND OAK PARLOR MANTEL CLOCKS were produced from the 1860s to the 1890s as "fancy" parlor clocks.

They can be described as rectangular cases mounted on an architectural base. They are crested by architectural features and flanked by carved, turned, or fluted columns. These ornate, very Victorian clocks often have carved figures or heads and mirrors. Their fully glazed doors were decorated with screened designs of foliage, birds, and geometric forms.

They are abundant and still fairly reasonable.

American, ca. 1885, walnut mantel clock, "Occidental," 8-day time and strike, 23", signed William L. Gilbert, $450. Credit: NAWCC TIMEXPO 2002.

American, walnut mantel clock, damaged (missing pieces of case), signed Ansonia Clock Co., asking $185. Credit: NAWCC Eastern States Regional 2002.

American, ca. 1875, American Clock Co., walnut shelf clock, "TURRET No. 11" model, 20.5", 8-day time, alarm, and strike spring-driven movement, as-found condition, $357

American, ca. 1880, Ansonia Clock Co., walnut shelf clock, "PARISIAN" model, 23", 8-day time and strike spring-driven movement, good restored condition with incorrect pendulum, $275

American, ca. 1885, Ansonia Clock Co., walnut and maple shelf clock, "EPSOM" model, 18", 8-day time, alarm, and strike spring-driven movement, good condition, $291

American, ca. 1900, Ansonia Clock Co., walnut shelf clock, "VALMA" model, 16.5", 8-day time and strike spring-driven movement, fair condition, $137

American, ca. 1901, Ansonia Clock Co., walnut shelf clock, "TRIUMPH" model, 25", 8-day time, alarm, and strike spring-driven movement, fair condition, $330

American, ca. 1875, Gilbert, William L., walnut shelf clock, "ALDINE" model, 19.5", 30-hour time and strike weight-driven movement, fair original condition, $99

American, ca. 1875, Gilbert, William L., walnut shelf clock, "DACCA" model, 18", 8-day time, alarm, and strike spring-driven movement, poor condition, missing carved top and missing finials, $330

American, ca. 1880, walnut mantel clock, "OCCIDENTAL" model, 8-day time and strike, 24", signed F. Kroeber, $500. Credit: NAWCC Eastern States Regional 2002.

American, ca. 1875, walnut mantel clock, "PATTI" model, 8-day time and strike, 19", signed E. N. Welch, $2,000. Credit: NAWCC Eastern States Regional 2002.

American, ca. 1885, Gilbert, William L., walnut shelf clock, "ALTAI" model, 20.25", 8-day time and strike spring-driven movement, excellent condition, $417

American, ca. 1885, Gilbert, William L., walnut shelf clock, "LATONA" model, 30.5", 8-day time and strike spring-driven movement, excellent original condition, $1,155

American, ca. 1885, Gilbert, William L., walnut shelf clock, "LUNA" model, 21.25", 8-day time, alarm, and strike spring-driven movement, excellent original condition, $1,320

American, ca. 1885, Gilbert, William L., walnut shelf clock, "OCCIDENTAL" model, 23", 8-day time and strike spring-driven movement, good restored condition, $577

American, ca. 1885, Gilbert, William L., walnut shelf clock, "OCCIDENTAL" model, 24", 8-day time and strike spring-driven movement, very good condition, $506

American, ca. 1885, Gilbert, William L., walnut shelf clock, "PAROLE" model, 20", 8-day time and strike spring-driven movement, fair condition, $154

American, ca. 1865, Ingraham and Co., walnut and maple shelf clock, "GRECIAN" model, 13.5", 8-day time, alarm, and strike spring-driven movement, good restored condition, $522

American, ca. 1875, Ingraham and Co., walnut and maple shelf clock, "GRECIAN" model, 14.5", 8-day time, alarm, and strike spring-driven movement, very good condition, $616

American, ca. 1875, Ingraham and Co., walnut and maple shelf clock, "GRECIAN" model, 14.5", 8-day time, alarm, and strike spring-driven movement, excellent restored condition, $660

American, ca. 1875, Ingraham and Co., walnut and maple shelf clock, "GRECIAN" model, 14.5", 8-day time, alarm, and strike spring-driven movement, good condition, $308

American, ca. 1875, Ingraham and Co., walnut and maple shelf clock, "GRECIAN" model, 14.5", 8-day time, alarm, and strike spring-driven movement, good condition with replaced dial, $257

American, ca. 1880, Ingraham and Co., walnut and maple shelf clock, "GRECIAN" model, 14.5", 8-day time, alarm, and strike spring-driven movement, excellent condition (illustrated), $220

American, ca. 1885, Ingraham and Co., walnut shelf clock, 21", 8-day time and strike spring-driven movement, good condition, $335

American, ca. 1890, Ingraham and Co., walnut shelf clock, "LIBERTY" model, 21", 8-day time, alarm, and strike spring-driven movement, good restored condition, $220

American, ca. 1865, walnut mantel clock, 8-day time and strike, 18", signed Noam Pomeroy, asking $295. Credit: NAWCC Eastern States Regional 2002.

American, ca. 1893, walnut mantel clock, "HUDSON" model, 8-day time, alarm, and strike, 24", signed Waterbury Clock Co., museum exhibit. Credit: Timex Museum.

American, ca. 1874, walnut mantel clock, 8-day time, alarm, and strike, 18", signed Waterbury Clock Co., museum exhibit. Credit: Timex Museum.

American, ca. 1884, oak mantel clock, 8-day time and strike, 26", signed Waterbury Clock Co., museum exhibit. Credit: Timex Museum.

American, ca. 1855, Jerome, Chauncey, walnut shelf clock, 8.25", 30-hour time-only spring-driven movement, fair condition with missing hands, $95

American, ca. 1860, Jerome, Chauncey, walnut shelf clock, 9.5", 30-hour time-only spring-driven movement, fair condition with missing glass, $112

American, ca. 1868, Kroeber, F., Clock Co., walnut shelf clock, 14.5", 8-day time, alarm, and strike spring-driven movement, very good condition, $632

American, ca. 1880, Kroeber, F., Clock Co., walnut shelf clock, 23", 8-day time, alarm, and strike spring-driven movement, good condition, $448

American, ca. 1880, Kroeber, F., Clock Co., walnut shelf clock, "ARTIC" model, 25", 8-day time, alarm, and strike spring-driven movement, fair condition, $1,760

American, ca. 1880, Kroeber, F., Clock Co., walnut shelf clock, "BATAVIA" model, 19.75", 8-day time, alarm, and strike spring-driven movement, very good condition, $770

American, ca. 1880, Kroeber, F., Clock Co., walnut shelf clock, "JAMESTOWN" model, 19", 8-day time and strike spring-driven movement, fair condition, $385

American, ca. 1880, Kroeber, F., Clock Co., walnut shelf clock, "JAVA" model, 18.5", 8-day time and strike spring-driven movement, good original condition, $330

American, ca. 1880, Kroeber, F., Clock Co., walnut shelf clock, "WINONA" model, 20", 8-day time, alarm, and strike spring-driven movement, good condition, $220

American, ca. 1882, Kroeber, F., Clock Co. , walnut shelf clock, "OCCI-DENTAL" model, 23.5", 8-day time and strike spring-driven movement, good condition, mirror side case, $840

American, ca. 1882, Kroeber, F., Clock Co., walnut shelf clock, "OCCI-DENTAL" model, 23.5", 8-day time, alarm, and strike spring-driven movement, fair condition, $840

American, ca. 1890, Kroeber, F., Clock Co., walnut shelf clock, 17", 8-day time and strike spring-driven movement, good restored condition, $412

American, ca. 1890, Kroeber, F., Clock Co., walnut shelf clock, "FLO-RETTA" model, 20", 8-day time, alarm, and strike spring-driven movement, fair condition, $330

American, ca. 1875, New Haven Clock Co., walnut shelf clock, "INDUS" model, 23.75", 30-hour time and strike weight-driven movement, fair condition, $420

American, ca. 1880, New Haven Clock Co., walnut shelf clock, "DANUBE" model, 24", 8-day time, alarm, and strike spring-driven movement, good restored condition, $264

American, ca. 1885, walnut mantel clock, 8-day time, alarm, and strike, 26", signed Ingraham Clock Co., asking $195. Credit: NAWCC Eastern States Regional 2002.

American, ca. 1880, walnut and maple mantel clock, "GRECIAN" model, 8-day time and strike, signed Ingraham Clock Co., $220. Credit: Prices4Antiques.com.

American, ca. 1880, walnut mantel clock, 8-day time, alarm, and strike, maker unknown, $175. Credit: NAWCC Eastern States Regional 2002.

American, ca. 1880, New Haven Clock Co., walnut shelf clock, "ELBE" model, 24", 8-day time, alarm, and strike spring-driven movement, good refinished condition, $280

American, ca. 1880, New Haven Clock Co., walnut shelf clock, "ESTELLE" model, 21", 8-day time, alarm, and strike spring-driven movement, fair restored condition, $165

American, ca. 1880, New Haven Clock Co., walnut shelf clock, "EUPHRATES" model, 21", 8-day time and strike spring-driven movement, very good condition, $145

American, ca. 1895, New Haven Clock Co., walnut shelf clock, "OCCIDENTAL" model, 24", 8-day time and strike spring-driven movement, fair condition, $495

American, ca. 1890, Russell and Jones, walnut shelf clock, 20", 8-day time, alarm, and strike spring-driven movement, fair condition, $264

American, ca. 1884, Terry Clock Co., walnut shelf clock, "HIGHLAND" model, 22.5", 8-day time, alarm, and strike spring-driven movement, good refinished condition, $330

American, ca. 1888, Terry Clock Co., walnut shelf clock, "HIGHLAND" model, 22.5", 8-day time, alarm, and strike spring-driven movement, good refinished condition, $220

American, ca. 1875, Seth Thomas, walnut and maple shelf clock, "GARFIELD" model, 24", 8-day time, alarm, and strike spring-driven movement, good condition, $1,870

American, ca. 1880, Seth Thomas, walnut shelf clock, 17", 8-day time, alarm, and strike spring-driven movement, very good condition, $112

American, ca. 1885, Seth Thomas, walnut and maple shelf clock, "GARFIELD" model, 29.5", 8-day time, alarm, and strike spring-driven movement, very good condition, $1,650

American, ca. 1885, Seth Thomas, walnut and maple shelf clock, "GREEK" model, 24", 8-day time, alarm, and strike spring-driven movement, good condition, $357

American, ca. 1885, Seth Thomas, walnut shelf clock, "LINCOLN V.P." model, 27.5", 8-day time and strike weight-driven movement, good condition, $1,568

American, ca. 1885, Seth Thomas, walnut shelf clock, "LINCOLN V.P." model, 27", 8-day time, alarm, and strike spring-driven movement, fair condition, $771

American, ca. 1885, Seth Thomas, walnut shelf clock, "LINCOLN V.P." model, 27", 8-day time, alarm, and strike spring-driven movement, very good refinished condition, $1,314

American, ca. 1886, Seth Thomas, walnut shelf clock, "ATLAS" model, 22.5", 8-day time and quarter strike spring-driven movement, good condition, $1,792

American, ca. 1886, Seth Thomas, walnut shelf clock, "LINCOLN V.P." model, 28.75", 8-day time and strike weight-driven movement, good restored condition, $2,035

American, ca. 1886, Seth Thomas, walnut shelf clock, "MOBILE" model, 22", 8-day time, alarm, and strike spring-driven movement, good condition, $462

American, ca. 1886, Seth Thomas, walnut shelf clock, "NORFOLK" model, 19.5", 8-day time, alarm, and strike spring-driven movement, good restored condition, $467

American, ca. 1886, Seth Thomas, walnut shelf clock, "RENO" model, 20", 8-day time, alarm, and strike spring-driven movement, good condition, $247

American, ca. 1885, maker unknown, walnut shelf clock, "RUBINA" model, 16.75", 8-day time and strike spring-driven movement, good condition, $154

American, ca. 1895, Waterbury Clock Co., walnut shelf clock, "NOR-WALK" model, 22.25", 8-day time and strike spring-driven movement, good condition, $275

American, ca. 1870, Welch, E. N., walnut shelf clock, "LUCCA" model, 23", 8-day time and strike spring-driven movement, very good condition, $672

American, ca. 1870, Welch, Spring, and Co., walnut shelf clock, "GER-STER" model, 18.5", 8-day time and strike spring-driven movement, fair condition, missing side gallery, $2,072

American, ca. 1870, Welch, Spring, and Co., walnut shelf clock, "PATTI" model, 19", 8-day time and strike spring-driven movement, fair condition, missing pendulum, $1,288

American, ca. 1875, Welch, Spring, and Co., walnut shelf clock, "PAREPA" model, 23", 8-day time, alarm, and strike spring-driven movement, poor condition, missing columns, $165

American, ca. 1875, Welch, Spring, and Co., walnut shelf clock, "SCALCHI" model, 20", 8-day time, alarm, and strike spring-driven movement, good restored condition, $1,045

American, ca. 1885, Welch, Spring, and Co., walnut and maple shelf clock, "DOLARO" model, 22", 8-day time, alarm, and strike spring-driven movement, very good original condition , $412

American, ca. 1890, Welch, Spring, and Co., walnut shelf clock, "NANON" model, 21.5", 8-day time and strike spring-driven movement, poor condition, $297

	LOW	MID	HIGH
Walnut and Oak Mantel Clocks (ca. 1860–95)	$150–$250	$350–$500	$600–$1,000+

English/British Shelf Clocks

English shelf clocks became a distinctive clock family in the seventeenth century with the appearance of the tall-case clock. The adoption of the pendulum from the Dutch, the invention of the anchor escapement in England, the development of reliable spring steel, and English craftsmanship accelerated the growth of the shelf clock industry. This British tradition would cross the Atlantic and form the foundation of clockmaking in America.

Ironically, this same British tradition of craftsmanship would stifle the English clock industry in the nineteenth century. Unable to compete with the importation of cheaper mass-produced American clocks, the British industry stagnated. Consequently there are fewer numbers and types of shelf clocks to introduce to the collector.

The great majority of these clocks are of high quality and house the renowned English fusee movement. Many of these clocks are still running, providing opportunities for collectors. I have tried to include those examples most often offered for sale.

Bracket clocks, ca. 1720–present
China-cased clocks, ca. 1880–1930
Lantern clocks, ca. 1620–1740, and reproductions, ca. 1850–1900
Skeleton clocks, ca. 1840–1900

ENGLISH BRACKET CLOCKS were made possible by eighteenth-century developments in the iron industry that produced reliable steel for clock and watch springs. The clocks appear in numbers by the early eighteenth century, and peak production occurred during the mid-nineteenth century. Historically they are associated with the wealthy and urban centers. These clocks, at their best, are wonderful examples of the skills and traditions of the British clockmaker. Cases reflect the same skills and traditions of the British cabinetmaker.

English, ca. 1860, Barwise, J., bracket clock, ebonized wood, molded-arch top, 15.5", 8-day fusee time and strike, good condition, $3,220

English, ca. 1880, Bright and Sons, bracket clock, oak, architectural-style case, 22.5", 8-day fusee time and strike, nest of three bells plus gong, excellent condition (illustrated), $990

English, ca. 1885, bracket clock, 8-day fusee time and strike (Westminster chimes), 24", signed W. H. and Son, $1,955. Credit: Prices4Antiques.com.

English, ca. 1880, bracket clock, 8-day fusee time and strike (Westminster chimes), 22.5", signed Bright and Sons, $990. Credit: Prices4Antiques.com.

English, ca. 1910, bracket clock, 8-day fusee time and strike (Westminster chimes), 18.5", maker unknown, $3,584. Credit: R. O. Schmitt Fine Arts.

English, ca. 1860, bracket clock, 8-day fusee time and strike, 19", signed Gamment, $1,586. Credit: Prices4Antiques.com.

English, ca. 1780, Child, Samuel, miniature bracket clock, mahogany molded-arch top, 8.5", 8-day fusee time-only, good condition, $4,600

English, ca. 1860, Gamment, bracket clock, mahogany Gothic case, 19", 8-day fusee time and strike, fair condition (illustrated), $1,568

English, ca. 1780, Graham, George, bracket clock, mahogany molded-arch top, 20", 8-day fusee time and strike, very good condition, $10,350

English, ca. 1770, Harrison, bracket clock, chinoiserie, bell-top case, 17", 8-day fusee time, strike, and calendar, good condition, $7,920

English, ca. 1870, Hurt and Wray, bracket clock, oak Victorian peaked roof, 22.5", 8-day fusee time and strike, nest of eight bells, fair condition, $1,650

English, ca. 1851, Kaiser, Joseph, bracket clock, ebonized wood, architectural-style case, 23", 8-day fusee time and strike, fair condition, some case damage, $2,640

English, ca. 1890, Leicester, Henry, bracket clock, mahogany balloon case, 19", 8-day fusee time-only, poor condition, $392

English, ca. 1870, Paris, T. J., bracket clock, walnut Victorian peaked roof, 37.25", 8-day fusee time and strike, nest of eight bells, good condition, $4,312

English, ca. 1830, Reeves, Richard, bracket clock, kingwood veneer, round-top case, 16.25", 8-day fusee time and strike, good original condition (illustrated), $1,680

English, ca. 1830, bracket clock, 8-day fusee time and strike, 16.25", signed Richard Reeves, $1,680. Credit: R. O. Schmitt Fine Arts.

English, ca. 1850, bracket clock, 8-day fusee time and strike, 17.5", maker unknown, $1,870. Credit: R. O. Schmitt Fine Arts.

English, ca. 1910, made for Starr, Theodore, and Co., bracket clock, mahogany architectural-style case, 18.5", 8-day fusee time and strike, nest of eight bells plus gong, very good condition (illustrated), $3,584

English., ca. 1880, Sutherland, bracket clock, mahogany bell-top case, 19.5", 8-day fusee time and strike, good condition, $1,210

English, ca. 1850, unattributed, bracket clock, mahogany with carving,

English, ca. 1880, bracket clock, 8-day fusee time and strike, nest of eight bells and gong, 29.5", maker unknown, $3,360. Credit: Prices4Antiques.com.

17.5", 8-day fusee time and strike, very good condition (illustrated), $1,870

English, ca. 1860, unattributed, bracket clock, rosewood, 13.25", 8-day fusee time and strike, very good condition, $977

English, ca. 1880, unattributed, bracket clock, oak Victorian peaked roof, 29.5", 8-day fusee time and strike, nest of eight bells plus gong, fair condition, some case damage (illustrated), $3,360

English, ca.1890, unattributed, bracket clock, mahogany, 26.5", 8-day fusee time and strike, Westminster chimes, very good condition, $3,450

English, ca. 1890, unattributed, bracket clock, mahogany, 27.5", 8-day fusee time and strike, nest of eight bells plus gong, very good original condition, $5,320

English, ca. 1900, unattributed, bracket clock, mahogany, 18", 8-day time and strike, good condition, $660

English, ca. 1950, unattributed, bracket clock, walnut, reproduction, 10.75", 8-day time and strike, good condition, $56

English, ca. 1820, Viner, Charles, bracket clock, mahogany molded-arch top, 29", 8-day fusee time and strike, nest of eight bells, good condition, $4,256

English, ca. 1890, W. H. and Son, bracket clock, rosewood, molded-arch top, 24", 8-day fusee time and strike, Westminster chimes, good condition (illustrated) $1,955

Scottish, ca. 1920, unattributed, bracket clock, mahogany, lancet-style case (Gothic), 12", 8-day time and strike, very good condition, $258

	LOW	MID	HIGH
English Bracket Clock (ca. 1720–1960)	$500–$1,500	$2,000–$3,000	$4,000–$6,000+

ENGLISH CHINA-CASED CLOCKS appear in Britain at the same time that they do in America (1880–1920). In fact, large numbers of American china-cased clocks made their way to England's shores. The clocks listed here are the English response, which used the established potteries of England for cases. Today they are pricey and sought after not only by clock collectors but also by china fanciers.

English, ca. 1915, Chesterfield, mantel clock, Royal Bonn china case, 6.75", 30-hour time-only, fair condition, $50

English, ca. 1900, Wedgwood case, 8-day time and strike, 13.5", maker unknown, $690. Credit: Prices4Antiques.com.

English, ca. 1910, Wedgwood case, 8-day time and strike, French movement, 11.25", maker unknown, $935. Credit: R. O. Schmitt Fine Arts.

English, ca. 1880, maker unknown, mantel clock, Wedgwood china, D-shaped case, 8.75", 8-day time only, excellent condition, $1,035

English, ca. 1890, maker unknown, mantel clock, Wedgwood china case, 12.5", 8-day time and strike, good condition, $500

English, ca. 1900, maker unknown, mantel clock, Copeland Spode china case, 11.5", 8-day time-only, very good condition, $467

English, ca. 1910, Wedgwood case, 8-day time and strike, 9.75", maker unknown, $1,955. Credit: Prices4Antiques.com.

English, ca. 1900, maker unknown, mantel clock, Wedgwood china case, 13.5", 8-day time and strike, good condition, some case restoration (illustrated), $690

English, ca. 1910, maker unknown, mantel clock, Wedgwood china case, 11.25", 8-day time and strike, French movement, very good condition (illustrated), $935

English, ca. 1910, maker unknown, mantel clock, Wedgwood china case, 9.75", 8-day time and strike, poor condition (illustrated), $1,955

English, ca. 1920, maker unknown, mantel clock, Royal Doulton china case, 10", 8-day time-only, good condition, $500

English, ca. 1930, maker unknown, mantel clock, Royal Doulton china case, 19", 8-day time-only, very good condition, $700

	LOW	MID	HIGH
English China-Cased Clocks (ca. 1880–1930)	$500–$699	$700–$999	$1,000+

ENGLISH LANTERN CLOCKS appeared about 1620. The earliest version was fitted with a balance escapement, which was replaced by the pendulum after 1700. These early versions were weight-driven, ran for 30 hours, and were meant to hang on the wall. Spring-driven versions appeared by the mid-seventeenth century and continued in production until the mid-eighteenth century. With the Jacobean Revival in the nineteenth century, they reappeared as mantel clocks outfitted with fusee movements.

Lantern clocks with original balance escapements command the highest prices, followed by those with anchor escapements. The nineteenth-century fusee reproductions are moving up in price. There are some twentieth-century "novelty" versions that are not particularly valuable.

English, ca. 1640, Bowyer, William, lantern clock, 15.5", 30-hour time and strike, balance wheel escapement, good restored condition, $7,840

English, ca. 1920, Coventry Astral, lantern clock, reproduction, 15", 30-hour time and strike, good condition, $156

English, ca. 1740, maker unknown, lantern clock, 16", 30-hour time and strike, poor condition, not running, $1,210

English, ca. 1890, maker unknown, lantern clock, reproduction, 15.25", 8-day fusee time and strike, good condition, $1,232

English, ca. 1890, maker unknown, lantern clock, reproduction, 15.25", 8-day fusee time and strike, good condition, $1,288

English, ca. 1920, lantern clock, reproduction, 30-hour time-only, 15", signed Coventry Astral, $156. Credit: Prices4Antiques.com.

English, ca. 1890, lantern clock, reproduction, 8-day fusee time and strike, 15.25", maker unknown, $1,232. Credit: R. O. Schmitt Fine Arts.

	LOW	MID	HIGH
English Lantern Clocks (ca. 1620–1950)	$200–$999	$1,000–$2,000	$5,000–$10,000+

ENGLISH SKELETON CLOCKS appeared around 1850 and went out of fashion about 1900. Although most skeleton clocks one finds are English, the style is probably French in origin. This clock style has no case and sits on a stand under a glass dome. The name comes from the fact that the plates have been cut away in a decorative pattern so the gear trains are visible. The original English versions struck once on each hour, but they evolved in time into full-striking clocks.

These clocks have always been popular, and their value continues to rise.

English, ca. 1850, Mayo and Son, skeleton clock, Gothic style, 12", 8-day fusee time-only, very good condition, new base and dome, $1,265

English, ca. 1850, unattributed, skeleton clock, 12.25", 8-day fusee time-only, good condition, replacement dome, $1,375

English, ca. 1855, Blackhurst, C., skeleton clock, 18.5", 8-day fusee time and strike, very good condition (illustrated), $3,740

English, ca. 1855, skeleton clock, 8-day double fusee time and strike, 18.5", signed C. Blackhurst, $3,740. Credit: Prices4Antiques.com.

English, ca. 1900, skeleton clock, 8-day single fusee time and strike, 18", maker unknown, $1,400. Credit: A. Zilberberg Collection.

English, ca. 1855, maker unknown, skeleton clock, 12", 8-day fusee time-only, poor condition, dome missing, $990

English, ca. 1860, Bennett, T., skeleton clock, 13", 8-day fusee time and strike, very good condition, dome and base (illustrated), $3,248

English, ca. 1860, Haycock, skeleton clock, 13", 8-day fusee time-only, very good condition, cracked dome, $1,650

English, ca. 1860, maker unknown, skeleton clock, 16", 8-day fusee time and strike, good condition, $460

English, ca. 1860, maker unknown, skeleton clock, 13", 30-day fusee time-only, fair condition, cracks in dial, $2,750

English, ca. 1870, Smith, J. and Sons, skeleton clock, 21.5", 8-day fusee time and strike, very good condition, $2,035

English, ca. 1870, Smith, J. and Sons, skeleton clock, 19", 8-day fusee time-only, good condition with replacement dome, $2,310

English, ca. 1870, maker unknown, skeleton clock, 16.5", 8-day fusee time-only, fair condition, dome wrong size, $1,925

English, ca. 1875, Evans, W. F., skeleton clock in the form of Westminster Abbey, 32", 8-day three fusee time and eight nested bells, strikes every fifteen minutes, good condition, $15,400

English, ca. 1890, Smith, John and Sons, skeleton clock, 19", 8-day fusee time and strike, very good condition, dome and base, $1,045

English, ca. 1860, skeleton clock,
8-day double fusee time and strike,
16", signed T. Bennett, $3,248.
Credit: R. O. Schmitt Fine Arts.

English, ca. 1890, maker unknown, skeleton clock, 15.25", 8-day fusee time-only, good condition, $977

English, ca. 1890, maker unknown, skeleton clock, 15", 8-day fusee time-only, good condition with replacement dome, $1,350

English, ca. 1900, maker unknown, skeleton clock, 16", 8-day fusee time-only, poor condition, dome missing, $660

English, ca. 1900, maker unknown, skeleton clock, 16", 8-day fusee time and strike, fair condition, dome wrong size, $896

English, ca. 1900, maker unknown, skeleton clock, 19", 8-day fusee time and strike, very good condition, $1,760

English, ca. 1900, maker unknown, skeleton clock, 19", 8-day fusee time and strike, good condition, $1,760

English, ca. 1900, maker unknown, skeleton clock, 15.25", 8-day fusee time and strike, fair condition, $935

English, ca. 1900, maker unknown, skeleton clock, 15.5", 8-day fusee time and strike, fair condition, dome missing, $880

	LOW	MID	HIGH
English Skeleton Clocks (ca. 1850–1900)	$800–$1,000	$2,000–$3,000	$4,000+

French Shelf Clocks

Shelf or mantel clocks have been the dominant French clock style from the start (France began to produce pendulum clocks in the 1600s). In

France the clock's case was of greater importance than the movement and caused the development of smaller movements. The fusee movement therefore never gained a foothold in France as it did in England. Style was more important than accurate time, and French clocks followed the fashions that emanated from Paris.

By the eighteenth century, French movement design had become standardized. French movements reflect the high standards of the French craftsman, and until the 1930s they remained durable and dependable.

French clocks have been collected since the Renaissance and into the twenty-first century.

Again I have tried to include those examples most often offered for sale.

Annular dial clocks, ca. 1770–1900
Architectural clocks, ca. 1840–1900
Baroque or Rococo clocks, ca. 1830–1910
Bracket clocks, ca. 1750–1900
Carriage clocks, ca. 1840–1920
China-cased clocks, ca. 1760–1910
Crystal regulator clocks, ca. 1880–1920
Figural clocks, ca. 1780–1900
Garniture clocks, ca. 1860–1920
Industry series clocks, ca. 1880–1900
Louis XVI clocks, ca. 1830–90
Lyre clocks, ca. 1760–1890
Marble/slate-cased clocks, ca. 1820–1920
Novelty clocks, ca. 1840–1900
Portico clocks, ca. 1820–90
Wood-cased clocks, ca. 1750–1920

FRENCH ANNULAR DIAL CLOCKS appeared in the mid-eighteenth century. They most often take the form of an urn with the dials (one for the hours and another for the minutes) as parallel bands at the top. On these clocks the dials move and a stationary pointer indicates the time. In the beginning these were the clocks of the wealthy. During the latter part of the nineteenth century, they were produced and reproduced in fair numbers. They are lovely to look at but expensive to own.

French, ca. 1790, maker unknown, annular dial mantel clock, ormolu and marble, Temple of Love, 17", 8-day time and strike, excellent condition, $14,000

Closeup of a French annular dial, ca. 1880, showing the stationary pointer in the form of a snake's tongue. Credit: R. O. Schmitt Fine Arts, $6,600.

French, ca. 1890, annular dial clock, 8-day time-only, 12", maker unknown, $4,125. Credit: R. O. Schmitt Fine Arts.

French, ca. 1875, maker unknown, annular dial mantel clock in the style of Louis XVI, 17", 8-day time and strike, good condition, $8,800

French, ca. 1880, maker unknown, annular dial mantel clock, 19", 8-day time and strike, fair condition with loss of gilding (illustrated), $6,600

French, ca. 1890, maker unknown, annular dial mantel clock, 12", 8-day time and strike, good restored condition (illustrated), $4,125

French, ca. 1890, maker unknown, annular dial mantel clock, supported by the Three Graces, 30", 8-day time and strike, very good condition, $14,300

French, ca. 1890, maker unknown, annular dial mantel clock, white marble, 11.75", 8-day time and strike, good condition, $3,640

	LOW	MID	HIGH
French Annular Dial Clocks (ca. 1760–1900)	$4,000–$5,000	$6,000–$8,000	$10,000+

FRENCH ARCHITECTURAL CLOCKS are decorative mantel clocks whose cases (usually brass) take various building or architectural forms. The movements they house are the standard French movements, 8-day time-only or time and strike. Striking in appearance, many are still affordable.

French, ca. 1890, architectural clock, 8-day time and strike, 16", maker unknown, $330. Credit: R. O. Schmitt Fine Arts.

French, ca. 1890, architectural clock, 8-day time and strike, 14", signed Japy Frères, $247. Credit: R. O. Schmitt Fine Arts.

French, ca. 1840, maker unknown, architectural mantel clock, cathedral form, 23.5", 8-day time and strike, excellent original condition, $6,105

French, ca. 1875, maker unknown, architectural mantel clock, 13.5", 8-day time and strike, good condition, $715

French, ca. 1890, Japy Freres, architectural mantel clock, fountain motif, 14", 8-day time and strike, good condition (illustrated), $247

French, ca. 1890, maker unknown, architectural mantel clock, 16", 8-day time and strike, fair condition, $330

French, ca. 1890, maker unknown, architectural mantel clock, temple motif, 13.5", 8-day time and strike, good condition (illustrated), $825

French, ca. 1890, maker unknown, architectural mantel clock, temple motif, 10.75", 8-day time and strike, good condition, $560

French, ca. 1890, maker unknown, architectural mantel clock, 20", 8-day time and strike, good condition, $880

French, ca. 1890, maker unknown, architectural mantel clock, 17", 8-day time and strike, very good condition, $990

French, ca. 1890, maker unknown, architectural mantel clock, 13.5", 8-day time and strike, fair condition, $385

French, ca. 1890, maker unknown, architectural mantel clock, 12.5", 8-day time and strike, fair condition, $412

French, ca. 1890, architectural clock, 8-day time and strike, 14", maker unknown, $825. Credit: R. O. Schmitt Fine Arts.

French, ca. 1890, maker unknown, architectural mantel clock, 16", 8-day time and strike, fair condition (illustrated), $330

French, ca. 1890, maker unknown, architectural mantel clock, Persian motif, 28", 8-day time and strike, very good condition, $3,025

French, ca. 1895, maker unknown, architectural mantel clock, bell tower motif, 19.5", 8-day time and strike, excellent condition, $4,785

	LOW	MID	HIGH
French Architectural Clocks (ca. 1840–1900)	$250–$500	$700–$900	$1,000–$3,000+

FRENCH BAROQUE AND ROCOCO CLOCKS are decorative mantel clocks whose cases (often brass) take various Baroque or Rococo forms. They house the standard French movements, 8-day time-only or time and strike. Many of these attractive clocks are still affordable.

French, ca. 1880, Susse Frères, Baroque/Rococo-style mantel clock, 23", 8-day time and strike, very good condition, $2,530

French, ca. 1830, maker unknown, Baroque/Rococo-style mantel clock, brass case, 11.5", 8-day time and strike, good condition (illustrated), $660

French, ca. 1870, maker unknown, Baroque/Rococo-style mantel clock, 17", 8-day time and strike, good condition, $220

French, ca. 1880, maker unknown, Baroque/Rococo-style mantel clock, 23", 8-day time and strike, fair condition, $440

French, ca. 1830, Rococo clock, 8-day time and strike, 11.5", maker unknown, $660. Credit: R. O. Schmitt Fine Arts.

French, ca. 1900, Baroque clock, 8-day time and strike, 19", maker unknown, $616. Credit: R. O. Schmitt Fine Arts.

French, ca. 1885, maker unknown, Baroque/Rococo-style mantel clock, 20", 8-day time and strike, fair condition, $715

French, ca. 1885, maker unknown, Baroque/Rococo-style mantel clock, 20", 8-day time and strike, fair condition, $440

French, ca. 1900, maker unknown, Baroque/Rococo-style mantel clock, brass case, 19", 8-day time and strike, very good condition (illustrated), $616

French, ca. 1900, maker unknown, Baroque/Rococo-style mantel clock, 19.5", 8-day time and strike, excellent condition, $1,210

French, ca. 1910, maker unknown, Baroque/Rococo-style, mantel clock, ormolu and marble, 15.5", 8-day time-only, good condition, $275

	LOW	MID	HIGH
French Baroque and Rococo Clocks (ca. 1830–1910)	$250–$450	$500–$900	$1,000–$2,000+

FRENCH BRACKET OR MANTEL CLOCKS appear in the seventeenth century, evolving from the Dutch Coster (Solomon Coster) clocks and independent of developments across the English Channel. Following the French tradition of the case being more important than the movement, these clocks became reflections of French style and taste—especially those done in the design of Boulle (tortoiseshell veneer inlaid with brass).

These are formal clocks meant to grace the best room in the house. The earliest versions are in museums and are thus beyond our means, but there are still nineteenth-century revival reproductions.

The term "bracket clock" originated in England after the seventeenth century, when people used the term because they believed that "old clocks" had been made to stand on brackets. There is no evidence to prove this and it is more logical to assume that these clocks were made to stand on tables so they could be moved from room to room. However, the term has stuck and today it is virtually synonymous with mantel and shelf clocks. In America the term usually means a fancier, more upscale clock.

French, ca. 1880, Japy Freres, bracket clock, Boulle case, 14", 8-day time and strike, very good condition (illustrated), $550

French, ca. 1880, Japy Freres, bracket clock, green Boulle case, 16.5", 8-day time and strike, good condition, $1,568

French, ca. 1890, Japy Freres, bracket clock, ebonized case with ormolu mounts, 15.25", 8-day time and strike, very good condition, $431

French, ca. 1880, Mage, bracket clock, Boulle case, 25", 8-day time and strike, good original condition, $5,880

French, ca. 1875, maker unknown, bracket clock, Boulle case, 59.5", 8-day time and strike, very good condition, $4,950

French, ca. 1890, bracket clock, Boulle case, 8-day time and strike, 14", signed Japy Frères, $550. Credit: Prices4Antiques.com.

French, ca. 1890, mantel clock, 8-day time and strike, 17.5", maker unknown, $2,128. Credit: R. O. Schmitt Fine Arts.

French, ca. 1880, maker unknown, bracket clock, walnut case with ormolu, 28", 8-day time and strike, good condition, $2,800

French, ca. 1880, maker unknown, bracket clock, Louis XIV–style case, 33.5", 8-day time and strike, very good condition, $4,200

French, ca. 1890, maker unknown, bracket clock, German-style case, 17.5", 8-day time and strike, excellent original condition (illustrated), $2,128

French, ca. 1890, maker unknown, bracket clock, Boulle case, 20.5", 8-day time and strike, good original condition, $672

French, ca. 1905, maker unknown, bracket clock, oak case, 21", 8-day time and strike (chimes), excellent original condition, $2,310

French, ca. 1910, maker unknown, bracket clock, cloisonné case, 12", 8-day time and strike, very good condition, $1,155

	LOW	MID	HIGH
French Bracket and Mantel Clocks (ca. 1750-1900)	$500–$1,000	$2,000–$3,000	$4,000–$5,000+

FRENCH CARRIAGE CLOCKS first appeared around the middle of the nineteenth century and achieved immediate popularity. They were produced in great numbers into the twentieth century. The carriage clock was the traveling clock (often with alarm) of its day. Quite often they were sold with leather traveling cases, most of which are gone today.

There was a carriage clock for everyone: simple time-only, time and alarm, repeaters, quarter strikers, and grand sonnerie (see Glossary). They were housed in a variety of cases ranging from classically simple to Baroque ornate. Carriage clocks are valued not only by their condition, but by the number of functions the movement can perform.

French, ca. 1900, Baveux Frères, carriage clock, Anglaise Riche style with Limoges panels, 7.25", 8-day time, strike, and repeat, good condition (illustrated), $5,500

French, ca. 1870, Bechot carriage clock, foliate case, 6.75", 8-day time, strike, and repeat, good condition, $1,595

French, ca. 1875, Brocot, A., carriage clock, silver over brass case, 8", 8-day time and strike, grande sonnerie, very good condition (illustrated), $2,464

French, ca. 1900, H and H, carriage clock, corniche-style case, 5.75", 8-day time and strike, fair condition, $420

Three of the many carriage clocks found at every show
and mart. Credit: NAWCC TIMEXPO 2002.

French, ca. 1860, Japy Freres, carriage clock, one-piece brass case, 7", 8-day
time-only, good condition, $550

French, ca. 1860, Japy Freres, carriage clock, one-piece brass case, 6.75",
8-day time, strike, and alarm, fair condition, $2,200

French, ca. 1885, Margaine, carriage clock, bamboo-style case, 7.5", 8-day
time, strike, repeat, and alarm, very good condition (illustrated), $3,472

French, ca. 1900, Maurice, E. and Co., carriage clock in the shape of a
lantern clock case, 10", 8-day time and strike, excellent condition, $693

French, ca. 1880, Rodanet, A. H., carriage clock, bamboo-style case, 7.5",
8-day time and strike, grand sonnerie, good original condition, $5,225

French, ca. 1900, carriage clock with leather carrying
case, 8-day time-only, 5.5", maker unknown, $198.
Credit: R. O. Schmitt Fine Arts.

French, ca. 1900, carriage clock with square sides, 8-day time-only, 4", maker unknown, $165. Credit: R. O. Schmitt Fine Arts.

French, ca. 1900, carriage clocks with serpentine corners, 8-day time-only, 5.75", maker unknown, $280. Credit: R. O. Schmitt Fine Arts.

French, ca. 1880, maker unknown, carriage clock, oval case, 5.5", 8-day time, strike, repeat, and alarm, good condition, $1,100

French, ca. 1900, maker unknown, carriage clock, traveling case, 5.5", 8-day time-only, very good condition (illustrated), $198

French, ca. 1900, maker unknown, carriage clock with serpentine corners, 5.75", 8-day time-only, very good condition (illustrated), $280

French, ca. 1900, maker unknown, carriage clock, corniche-style case, 4", 8-day time-only, very good condition (illustrated), $165

French, ca. 1900, maker unknown, carriage clock, enameled case, 6", 8-day time and alarm, good condition (illustrated), $797

French, ca. 1900, maker unknown, mini carriage clock, caryatid-style case, 3.25", 8-day time-only, very good condition (illustrated), $2,475

French, ca. 1900, maker unknown, carriage clock, 5.75", 8-day time and alarm, good condition, $336

French, ca. 1900, maker unknown, mini carriage clock, 4.25", 8-day time-only, fair condition, $168

French, ca. 1900, maker unknown, carriage clock with carrying case, 7", 8-day time-only, good condition, $209

French, ca. 1900, maker unknown, mini carriage clock with carrying case, 3", 8-day time-only, fair condition, $345

French, ca. 1900, carriage clock, Anglaise Riche–style case with signed Limoges-type panels, 8-day time, repeat, alarm, and quarter strike, 7.25", signed Baveau Freres, $5,500. Credit: R. O. Schmitt Fine Arts.

French, ca. 1875, carriage clock, 8-day Grand Sonnerie, 8", signed A. Brocot, $2,464. Credit: R. O. Schmitt Fine Arts.

French, ca. 1885, carriage clock with bamboo-style case, 8-day time, repeat, alarm, and quarter strike, 7.5", signed Margaine, $3,472. Credit: R. O. Schmitt Fine Arts.

French, ca. 1900, carriage clock with caryatid-style case, 8-day time-only, 3.25", maker unknown, $2,475. Credit: R. O. Schmitt Fine Arts.

French, ca. 1900, carriage clock with a champlève case, 8-day time and alarm, 6", maker unknown, $797. Credit: R. O. Schmitt Fine Arts.

French, ca. 1905, maker unknown, carriage clock with Aviary porcelain panels, 7.5", 8-day time and strike, excellent condition, $2,576

French, ca. 1910, maker unknown, mini carriage clock, 4.25", 8-day time-only, fair condition, $95

French, ca. 1910, maker unknown, carriage clock with enamel panels, 7.5", 8-day time-only, excellent condition, $1,725

French, ca. 1920, maker unknown, carriage clock, 5.25", 8-day time-only, good original condition, $218

French, ca.1920, maker unknown, carriage clock with carrying case, 5.75", 8-day time-only, good condition, $224

French, ca. 1900, maker unknown, made for J. E. Caldwell of Philadelphia, carriage clock with jewel and cloisonné decoration, 5.75", 8-day time and alarm, good condition, $1,540

	LOW	MID	HIGH
French Carriage Clocks (ca. 1850–1920)	$150–$350	$400–$850	$1,000–$3,000+

FRENCH CHINA-CASED CLOCKS appeared in the eighteenth century when Meissen porcelain cases were imported from Saxony (Germany) and fitted with French movements and ormolu mounts. These early clocks are generally in museums and beyond the scope of this guide. The establishment of major French potteries, such as Limoges, and their flourishing in the nineteenth century made it natural to continue the tradition of china-cased clocks.

Although the earliest examples are beyond the means of most collectors, their nineteenth-century counterparts are not, and they form a collectible area.

French, ca. 1890, C-J, china-cased mantel clock, 12", 8-day time and strike, good condition (illustrated), $192

French, ca. 1845, maker unknown, china-cased mantel clock, two-piece case, 19.5", 8-day time and strike, fair condition with repaired case, $1,210

French, ca. 1850, maker unknown, china-cased mantel clock, 13.5", 8-day time and strike, fair condition (illustrated), $825

French, ca. 1860, maker unknown, china-cased mantel clock, porcelain case with a seated sultan figure, 18", 8-day time and strike, good condition (illustrated), $1,150

French, ca. 1880, maker unknown, china-cased mantel clock, gilded bronze trim, 15", 8-day time and strike, poor condition, $715

French, ca. 1890, maker unknown, china-cased mantel clock, porcelain case of high quality, 17.75", 8-day time and strike, very good condition (illustrated), $1,100

French, ca. 1890, maker unknown, china-cased mantel clock, Limoges case, 12.5", 8-day time and strike, very good condition, $1,210

French, ca. 1890, maker unknown, china-cased mantel clock, figural, 11.5", 8-day time and strike, good condition, $1,210

French, ca. 1850, china-cased clock, 8-day time and strike, 18", maker unknown, $1,150. Credit: Prices4Antiques.com.

French, ca. 1890, china-cased clock, 8-day time and strike, 17.75", maker unknown, $1,100. Credit: R. O. Schmitt Fine Arts.

French, ca. 1850, china-cased clock, 8-day time and strike, 13.5", maker unknown, $825. Credit: R. O. Schmitt Fine Arts.

French, ca. 1890, china-cased clock, 8-day time and strike, 12", maker unknown, $192. Credit: R. O. Schmitt Fine Arts.

French, ca. 1890, maker unknown, china-cased mantel clock, bisque figure of girl with bird's nest, 10.25", 8-day time and strike, good condition, $1,035

French, ca. 1890, maker unknown, china-cased mantel clock, 12.5", 8-day time and strike, good condition, $308

French, ca. 1900, maker unknown, china-cased mantel clock, 13", 8-day time and strike, fair condition, $687

French, ca. 1900, maker unknown, china-cased mantel clock, 14", 8-day time and strike, good condition, $330

French, ca. 1900, maker unknown, china-cased mantel clock, Meissen-style porcelain case, 13", 8-day time-only, good condition $920

French, ca. 1900, maker unknown, china-cased mantel clock, blue Delft case, 13.75", 8-day time and strike, good condition, $935

French, ca. 1905, maker unknown, china-cased mantel clock, 8", 8-day time only, good condition, $224

	LOW	MID	HIGH
French China-Cased Clocks (ca. 1760–1910)	$200–$400	$600–$800	$1,000–$2,000

FRENCH CRYSTAL REGULATOR CLOCKS appeared at the end of the nineteenth century and their production continued into the twentieth. The case form with its glass panels indicates a close relationship to the carriage clock. Building upon the popularity of the carriage clock, the crystal regulator was large enough to contain a pendulum movement and be marketed as a mantel clock.

These handsome clocks are still available to the collector.

French, ca. 1895, H and H, crystal Regulator mantel clock, 10.75", 8-day time and strike, good condition, $840

French, ca. 1890, Japy Frères, crystal Regulator mantel clock, cloisonné decoration of the columns, 13", 8-day time and strike, excellent condition (illustrated), $1,980

French, ca. 1900, Japy Freres, crystal Regulator mantel clock, onyx columns and cloisonné base, 12.5", 8-day time and strike, excellent original condition, $2,200

French, ca. 1910, Japy Freres, crystal Regulator mantel clock, 10", 8-day time and strike, good condition, $920

French, ca. 1915, Japy Freres, crystal Regulator mantel clock, 8.5", 8-day time and strike, fair condition, $112

French, ca. 1900, Lardot and Boyon, crystal Regulator mantel clock with ormolu lion and green onyx, 18.5", 8-day time and strike, fair condition, $687

French, ca. 1900, crystal regulator, 8-day time and strike, 9", maker unknown, $550. Credit: Prices4Antiques.com.

French, ca. 1890, crystal regulator, 8-day time and strike, 13", Japy Frères, $1,980. Credit: R. O. Schmitt Fine Arts.

French, ca. 1900, crystal regulator, 8-day time and strike, 12", maker unknown, $825. Credit: Prices4Antiques.com.

French, ca. 1900, Marti, crystal Regulator mantel clock, oval case, 11", 8-day time and strike, good condition, $825

French, ca. 1900, Mougin, crystal Regulator mantel clock, 12.25", 8-day time and strike, good original condition, $952

French, ca. 1890, maker unknown, crystal Regulator mantel clock, 10", 8-day time and strike, good condition, $220

French, ca. 1890, maker unknown, crystal Regulator mantel clock, 16", 8-day time and strike, excellent condition, $2,035

French, ca. 1900, maker unknown, mini crystal Regulator mantel clock, 9", 8-day time and strike, excellent condition (illustrated), $550

French, ca. 1900, maker unknown, crystal Regulator mantel clock, 12", 8-day time and strike, excellent condition (illustrated), $825

French, ca. 1900, maker unknown, crystal Regulator mantel clock, oval case, 10.25", 8-day time and strike, excellent condition, $1,155

French, ca. 1900, maker unknown, crystal Regulator mantel clock with Limoges-style panels, 15", 8-day time and strike, good condition, replaced movement, $2,200

French, ca. 1900, maker unknown, crystal Regulator mantel clock, bow-front case with brilliants and cameo, 13", 8-day time and strike, excellent original condition, $1,320

	LOW	MID	HIGH
French Crystal Regulator Clocks (ca. 1880–1920)	$300–$500	$600–$900	$1,000–$2,500

FRENCH FIGURAL CLOCKS were some of the most magnificent clocks ever made, growing out of and reflecting the classical revival in France. In the last decades of the eighteenth century the French wedded the clock with the arts, producing the clocks we call figural today. The timepiece was cased in ormolu (see Glossary) or bronze, which was cast with figures depicting classical tableaus. The craftsmanship of the early clocks (1780–1820) was superb. As the nineteenth century progressed and figural clocks evolved into mass-produced replicas, the craftsmanship and materials declined in quality. Bronze and ormolu gave way to brass and spelter.

It is possible to divide these clocks by period, style, and subject. (These are rough divisions and you will find exceptions and additions to the descriptions.)

First Period, ca. 1780–1820: Classical and allegorical subjects; ormolu and bronze with fine detail; silk suspension movements

Second Period, ca. 1830–50: Allegorical, historical, and romantic subjects often depicted in contemporary dress; mainly ormolu cases resembling steps; mostly silk suspension movements

Third Period, ca. 1860–70: Allegorical and romantic subjects depicting "Commerce," "Industry," etc.; mainly gilded brass cases, sometimes with alabaster or marble parts; spring suspension movements

Fourth Period, ca. 1880–1900: Mostly Romantic subjects; mainly mass-produced plated spelter or white metal cases of poor design; spring suspension movements

These are wonderful clocks, and I hope you can find room for one in your collection.

French, ca. 1815, Dubuc, Jean-Baptiste, figural mantel clock, ormolu George Washington, 19", 8-day time and strike, excellent original condition (illustrated), $48,300

French, ca. 1820, maker unknown, figural mantel clock, ormolu seated classical maiden, 19.75", 8-day time and strike, very good condition (illustrated), $3,737

French, ca. 1820, maker unknown, figural mantel clock, ormolu nymph with urn, 14", 8-day time and strike, good condition, $1,456

French, ca. 1825, figural mantel clock, woman in classical garb and cupid with ormolu case, 8-day time and strike, 18", maker unknown, $1,456. Credit: R. O. Schmitt Fine Arts.

French, ca. 1815, figural mantel clock, George Washington with the seal of the United States, 8-day time and strike, 19", attributed to Jean-Baptiste Dubuc, $48,300. Credit: Prices4Antiques.com.

French, ca. 1825, maker unknown, figural mantel clock, ormolu lady with cupid, 18", 8-day time and strike, excellent original condition (illustrated), $1,456

French, ca. 1825, maker unknown, figural mantel clock, ormolu Eros and nymph, 23", 8-day time and strike, very good condition, $2,240

French, ca. 1825, maker unknown, figural mantel clock, ormolu, two allegorical figures with globe, 13", 8-day time and strike, very good condition, $805

French, ca. 1830, maker unknown, figural mantel clock, ormolu sailor's wife and child, 17", 8-day time and strike, good condition, $805

French, ca. 1830, maker unknown, figural mantel clock, ormolu seated figure representing Harvest, 11", 8-day time and strike, good original condition, $275

French, ca. 1830, maker unknown, figural mantel clock, ormolu seated woman and bird, 12.75", 8-day time and strike, fair condition, $448

French, ca. 1835, maker unknown, figural mantel clock, ormolu hunter and his dog, 16", 8-day time and strike, good condition, $467

French, ca. 1835, maker unknown, figural mantel clock, ormolu merman and lion with base and dome, 14", 8-day time and strike, very good condition, $1,008

French, ca. 1830, figural mantel clock, classical maiden with dove, ormolu case, 8-day time and strike, 19.75", maker unknown, $3,737. Credit: Prices4Antiques.com.

French, ca. 1890, figural mantel clock in the style of 1830, seated philosopher, ormolu case and bronze, 28", maker unknown, asking price unknown. Credit: NAWCC Eastern States Regional 2002.

French, ca. 1835, figural mantel clock, seated lady in contemporary dress, ormolu case, 8-day time and strike, 18", maker unknown, $850.

French, ca. 1840, figural mantel clock, seated young man with book, ormolu case, 17", maker unknown, $1,000. Credit: NAWCC Eastern States Regional 2002.

French, ca. 1840, figural mantel clock, showing how these clocks were usually displayed on base under glass dome. Credit: NAWCC Eastern States Regional 2002.

French, ca. 1870, figural mantel clock, allegorical figure of Commerce, gilded brass with alabaster inserts, 8-day time and strike, 19", maker unknown, $950.

French, ca. 1835, maker unknown, figural mantel clock, ormolu seated figure of man, 15", 8-day time and strike, good condition, $460

French, ca. 1840, maker unknown, figural mantel clock, marble and bronze figure of Christ and John the Baptist, 20", 8-day time and strike, good condition, $1,430

French, ca. 1840, maker unknown, figural mantel clock, ormolu allegorical figure of music, 22", 8-day time and strike, very good condition, $1,540

French, ca. 1840, Tourbier, figural mantel clock, ormolu figure of Darius, 17", 8-day time and strike, very good condition, $1,150

French, ca. 1840, maker unknown, figural mantel clock, ormolu with a seated figure of Napoleon's son, 18", 8-day time and strike, good condition, $1,375

French, ca. 1840, maker unknown, figural mantel clock, bronze seated figure of man in court dress, 17", 8-day time and strike, good condition, $660

French, ca. 1860, maker unknown, figural mantel clock, gilded brass, allegorical figure of Commerce, 16.5", 8-day time and strike, fair condition, $190

French, ca. 1860, Japy Frères, figural mantel clock, ormolu girl holding spaniel, 11", 8-day time and strike, good original condition, $2,310

French, ca. 1860, maker unknown, figural mantel clock, bronze figures of

French, ca. 1875, figural mantel clock, knight and Saracen locked in battle, gilded brass with alabaster inserts, 8-day time and strike, 16.25", maker unknown, $1,725. Credit: Prices4Antiques.com.

French, ca. 1880, figural mantel clock, two cupids, ormolu and bronze, 8-day time and strike, 9", maker unknown, $2,000. Credit: A. Zilberberg Collection.

two soldiers and a dog, 18.5", 8-day time and strike, very good condition, $1,980

French, ca. 1865, maker unknown, figural mantel clock, woman holding sheaf of wheat, 16", 8-day time and strike, fair condition, $467

French, ca. 1870, Bergys, T., figural mantel clock, seated muse and Sèvres plaques, 18", 8-day time and strike, very good condition, $3,450

French, ca. 1880, maker unknown, figural mantel clock, ormolu figures of a knight and a Saracen, 16.25", 8-day time and strike, excellent condition (illustrated), $1,725

French, ca. 1880, Charpentier, figural mantel clock, bronze with seated figure of classical maiden, 22.5", 8-day time and strike, excellent condition, $1,960

French, ca. 1880, maker unknown, figural mantel clock, bronzed spelter with figure of girl, 13", 8-day time and strike, excellent condition, $616

French, ca. 1890, Japy Fils, figural mantel clock, gilded spelter and onyx with figure of boy with hammer, 12.5", 8-day time and strike, good condition (illustrated), $575

French, ca. 1890, maker unknown, figural mantel clock, bronze with two putti, 16", 8-day time and strike, good condition (illustrated), $812

French, ca. 1890, figural mantel clock, standing child, gilded spelter and onyx, 8-day time and strike, 12.5", Japy Fils, $575. Credit: Prices4Antiques.com.

French, ca. 1890, maker unknown, figural mantel clock, bronzed spelter with a girl fishing, 24.5", 8-day time and strike, good condition, $550

French, ca.1890, maker unknown, figural mantel clock, gilded spelter with figure of a hunter, 13", 8-day time and strike, fair condition, $280

French, ca. 1900, Brevete, figural mantel clock, spelter with figure playing a violin, 12", 8-day time and strike, fair condition, $173

French, ca. 1890, figural mantel clock, winged putti, bronze spelter on marble base, 8-day time and strike, 16", maker unknown, $812. Credit: Prices4Antiques.com.

French, ca. 1900, maker unknown, figural mantel clock, gilded spelter with figure of a woman, 10.5", 8-day time and strike, fair condition, $190

French, ca. 1900, maker unknown, figural mantel clock, gilded spelter with figure of a woman and child on alabaster, 10", 8-day time and strike, fair condition, $275

	LOW	MID	HIGH
French Figural Mantel Clock (ca. 1780–1900)	$200–$500	$700–$1,000	$2,000–$4,000+

FRENCH GARNITURE CLOCKS are clocks of various styles that are accompanied by a pair of matching candelabra. These sets were designed to sit on a mantelpiece. Clocks with matching candelabra appeared during the eighteenth century in the homes of the wealthy, disappeared for a time, and regained popularity in the latter part of the nineteenth. Many clocks survive that were once parts of garnitures but have been separated from their candelabras.

Sought by decorators, garnitures have become quite pricey.

French, ca. 1875, Cerard garnitures, figural clock, 20", 8-day time and strike, good condition, $4,200

French, ca. 1880, maker unknown, garnitures, crystal regulator form with a

French, ca. 1890, mantel garniture, 8-day time and strike, 26", maker unknown, asking price unknown. Credit: NAWCC Eastern States Regional 2002.

French, ca. 1890, mantel garniture, 8-day time and strike, 24", maker unknown, asking price unknown. Credit: NAWCC Eastern States Regional 2002

cloisonné case, 15.5", 8-day time and strike, excellent original condition, $1,870

French, ca. 1890, Japy Frères, garnitures, steam hammer forge, 17.5", 8-day time and strike, very good condition, $3,737

French, ca. 1900, maker unknown, garnitures, crystal regulator, 19", 8-day time and strike, good condition (illustrated), $1,232

French, ca. 1890, mantel garniture, 8-day time and strike, 26", maker unknown, asking price unknown. Credit: NAWCC Eastern States Regional 2002.

French, ca. 1900, mantel garniture, 8-day time and strike, 19", maker unknown, $1,232. Credit: R. O. Schmitt Fine Arts.

	LOW	MID	HIGH
French Garnitures (ca. 1860–1920)	$1,000–$2,499	$2,500–$3,999	$4,000+

FRENCH INDUSTRY SERIES MANTEL CLOCKS, produced in the 1880s, encompassed models of engines, lighthouses, steam hammers, and the like in gleaming copper, brass, and steel. Earlier clocks (see French Figural Clocks) had represented French pride in allegorical terms. The industry series reflected French industry, commerce, and prosperity. From the outset these clocks were a commercial success, and they have become very collectible as well.

French, ca. 1880, maker unknown, industrial street clock, 23.5", 8-day time-only, with manual calendar, good condition, $5,880

French, ca. 1880, maker unknown, industrial clock, marine theme, 9", 8-day time-only, with barometer and thermometer, restored condition, $1,008

French, ca. 1880, maker unknown, industrial clock, windmill, 17.5", 8-day time- only, good original condition, $3,024

French, ca. 1885, maker unknown, industrial clock, horizontal steam boiler, 11", 8-day time and barometer, very good condition (illustrated), $5,500

French, ca. 1885, maker unknown, industrial clock, steam plant and regulator, 18.5", 8-day time-only, with barometer and thermometer, excellent condition, $14,575

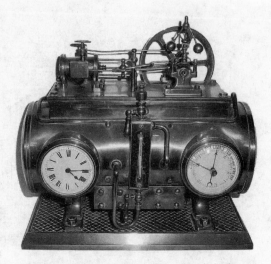

French, ca. 1880, industry series mantel clock, nautical theme, a binnacle containing two time dials, a compass, thermometer, and barometer, 20", maker unknown, asking $6,500. Credit: NAWCC TIMEXPO 2002.

French, ca. 1885, industry series mantel clock, horizontal steam engine, 8-day time, thermometer, and barometer, 11", maker unknown, $5,500. Credit: R. O. Schmitt Fine Arts.

French, ca. 1885, maker unknown, industrial clock, railway wagon with barrels, 8.5", 8-day time-only, with barometer and thermometer, good condition, $1,760

French, ca. 1890, maker unknown, industrial clock, steam hammer, 17.5", 8-day time-only, good condition, $1,650

French, ca. 1890, maker unknown, industrial clock, ship's quarter deck, 13", 8-day time and strike, good condition, $7,952

French, ca. 1890, maker unknown, industrial clock, marine themes, 15", 8-day time-only, with barometer and thermometer, good condition, $1,232

	LOW	MID	HIGH
French Industry Series Clocks (ca. 1880–95)	$1,000–$1,999	$2,000–$3,000	$4,000–$7,000+

FRENCH LOUIS XVI-STYLE CLOCKS consisted of a horizontal marble or alabaster base surmounted by two vertical marble or alabaster pillars crossed by a marble or alabaster lintel in classical forms with ormolu mounts. The round movement and dial were mounted in the center of the lintel. The clock and pillars were topped by finials, urns, or similar ornamentation. This nineteenth-century reproduction of clocks of the Ancien Regime has become known as Louis XVI–style. In some aspects, these clocks resemble the more famous portico clocks.

When faithful to their original proportions and details, these are handsome clocks. They appear as early as the 1820s and disappear by the end of the nineteenth century.

French, ca. 1860, Baudoin, Louis XVI–style mantel clock, 20.5", 8-day time and strike, good condition, $2,587

French, ca. 1855, Bourret, Louis XVI–style mantel clock, 26", 8-day time and strike, excellent condition (illustrated), $8,625

French, ca. 1860, Chapus, A., Louis XVI–style mantel clock, 16", 8-day time and strike, fair condition, $440

French, ca. 1860, Germain, Louis XVI–style mantel clock, 22", 8-day time and strike, very good condition, $8,625

French, ca. 1860, maker unknown, Louis XVI–style mantel clock, 16", 8-day time and strike, very good condition, $747

French, ca. 1880, maker unknown, Louis XVI–style mantel clock, 17.5", 8-day time and strike, very good original condition, $1,650

French, ca. 1855, Louis XVI–style mantel clock, 8-day time and strike, 26", Bourret, $8,625. Credit: Prices4Antiques.com.

French, ca. 1880, Louis XVI–style mantel clock, 8-day time and strike, 17", Bourret, $1,650. Credit: R. O. Schmitt Fine Arts.

French, ca. 1840, Louis XVI–style mantel clock, 8-day time and strike, 21", maker unknown, $1,000. Credit: Alessi Collection

French, ca. 1880, maker unknown, Louis XVI–style mantel clock, 20", 8-day time and strike, good condition, $690

French, ca. 1880, maker unknown, Louis XVI–style mantel clock, 15", 8-day time and strike, very good condition, $550

French, ca. 1885, Vincenti, Louis XVI–style mantel clock, 16.5", 8-day time and strike, good condition, $440

	LOW	MID	HIGH
French Louis XVI–Style Clocks (ca. 1830–90)	$700–$1,000	$1,500–$2,500	$3,000–$4,500+

FRENCH LYRE CLOCKS first appeared in France ca. 1785. The clock, its case shaped like the lyre of the ancients, is also interesting in that its pendulum was suspended at the top of the case. The bob was a circle set with paste gems which surrounded the dial and swung from side to side. Eighteenth-century examples command extremely high prices and rarely come up for sale. During the nineteenth century, the style was revived. Variations of the original form appeared, including models in which the pendulum swung behind the clock. No matter which variant, these revival clocks command high prices today.

French, ca. 1880, Cousard, lyre-form mantel clock, 14", 8-day time and strike, excellent condition, $4,070

French, ca. 1820, maker unknown, lyre-form mantel clock, 23", 8-day time and strike, very good condition, $1,344

French, ca. 1825, lyre-form mantel clock, 8-day time and strike, 21", maker unknown, $1,288. Credit: R. O. Schmitt Fine Arts.

French, ca. 1825, maker unknown, lyre-form mantel clock, 21", 8-day time and strike, good condition (illustrated), $1,288

French, ca. 1840, maker unknown, lyre-form mantel clock, 25.75", 8-day time and strike, very good condition, $4,400

French, ca. 1850, maker unknown, lyre-form mantel clock, 23", 8-day time and strike, excellent condition, $15,400

French, ca. 1880, maker unknown, lyre-form mantel clock, 19", 8-day time and strike, excellent condition, $6,325

French, ca. 1890, maker unknown, lyre-form mantel clock, 19", 8-day time and strike, good condition, $1,840

	LOW	MID	HIGH
French Lyre-Form Clocks (ca. 1760–1890)	$1,500	$3,000	$5,000+

FRENCH MARBLE MANTEL CLOCKS are generally the black slate clocks so popular in the last quarter of the nineteenth century. While genuine black marble does exist, the slate quarries of Belgium produced a slate that was preferable because it could be finished to a uniform high sheen and was ideal for clock cases.

These heavy, rich-looking cases appeared as early as the 1830s, but most of the clocks that reach the market today date from the 1880s and 1890s. For convenience, I have included true marble and alabaster period clocks with the "slates." Often underpriced and confused with American "blacks," they offer an opportunity to the beginning collector.

French, ca. 1825, alabaster mantel clock, column form, 8-day time and strike, 14", Mylius, $700.

French, ca. 1880, slate and strike, 10", Japy Frères, $300.

French, ca. 1820, maker unknown, marble/slate and alabaster mantel clock, alabaster case with urn finial, 15.5", 8-day time and strike, good condition, $336

French, ca. 1825, Detour, marble/slate and alabaster mantel clock, bronze-mounted red marble, 15.5", 8-day time and strike, excellent condition, $2,070

French, ca. 1870, Mene, P. J., marble/slate and alabaster mantel clock, bronze dog on top, 16", 8-day time and strike, good condition, $747

French, ca. 1880, maker unknown, marble/slate and alabaster mantel clock, temple form, 12.75", 8-day time and strike, fair condition, $115

French, ca. 1885, maker unknown, marble/slate and alabaster mantel clock, malachite insets, 13.25", 8-day time and strike, very good condition, $1,725

French, ca. 1885, Japy, marble/slate and alabaster mantel clock, seated Roman soldier, 18", 8-day time and strike, good condition, $385

French, ca. 1890, maker unknown, marble/slate and alabaster mantel clock, domed top, 11", 8-day time only, good condition, $115

French, ca. 1890, Julien, Henri, marble/slate and alabaster mantel clock, tambour form, 13", 8-day time and strike, very good condition (illustrated), $550

French, ca. 1890, maker unknown, marble/slate and alabaster mantel clock, domed top, 11.5", 8-day time and strike, very good condition, $392

French, ca. 1880, slate and marble mantel clock, temple form, 8-day time and strike, 12.75", maker unknown, $115. Credit: Prices4Antiques.com.

French, ca. 1890, slate and onyx mantel clock, arch-top form, 8-day time and strike, 11.5", maker unknown, $115. Credit: R. O. Schmitt Fine Arts.

French, ca. 1890, maker unknown, marble/slate and alabaster mantel clock, gable top, 11", 8-day time and strike, excellent condition, $112

French, ca. 1895, maker unknown, marble/slate and alabaster mantel clock, bronze trim, 6", 8-day time and strike, excellent restored condition, $715

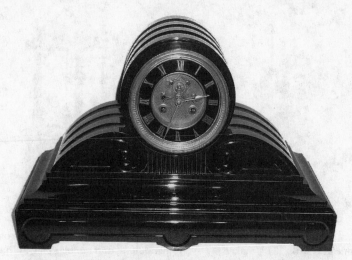

French, ca. 1890, slate mantel clock, tambour form, 8-day time and strike, 13", Henri Jullen, $550. Credit: R. O. Schmitt Fine Arts.

French, ca. 1895, Marti, marble/slate and alabaster mantel clock, temple form, 13.25", 8-day time and strike, good condition, $247

French, ca. 1900, maker unknown, marble/slate and alabaster, mantel clock, green onyx and ormolu, 9.5", 8-day time and strike, fair condition, $420

French, ca. 1900, Marti, marble/slate and alabaster mantel clock, American statue on top, 14", 8-day time and strike, fair condition, $201

	LOW	MID	HIGH
French Marble/Slate and Alabaster Mantel Clock (ca. 1830–1900)	$150–$250	$350–$550	$1,000–$3,000

FRENCH NOVELTY CLOCKS are clocks that no one knows how to classify. They are clocks that fall outside the mainstream or those that were made to amuse or bewilder. France, like many other countries, produced its share of these clocks. Better known and often better crafted clocks command hefty prices in the marketplace.

French, ca. 1900, Bontems, novelty clock, singing birds and waterfall under dome, 26", 8-day time only, fair condition, missing dome, $4,600

French, ca. 1890, Farcot, novelty clock, conical pendulum, 20.5", 8-day time and strike, fair condition, $3,850

French, ca. 1890, novelty conical clock, 8-day time and strike, 21", maker unknown, $3,960. Credit: R. O. Schmitt Fine Arts.

French, ca. 1900, novelty clock, rotary pendulum, and annular dial, 30-hour time-only, 7", maker unknown, $825. Credit: R. O. Schmitt Fine Arts.

French, ca. 1890, novelty mystery clock, 8-day time and strike, 24.5", Gullmet, $3,850. Credit: R. O. Schmitt Fine Arts.

French, ca. 1900, novelty gravity clock, 30-hour time only, 10", maker unknown, $145. Credit: Prices4Antiques.com.

French, ca. 1895, Farcot, novelty clock, conical pendulum with annular dial, 6.75", 8-day time and alarm, excellent original condition, $560

French, ca. 1880, maker unknown, novelty clock, singing birds, waterfall, and music box under dome, 23.5", 8-day time and strike, good condition, $5,225

French, ca. 1880, maker unknown, novelty clock, singing birds and waterfall under dome, 18", 8-day time-only, good condition, $2,475

French, ca. 1890, maker unknown, novelty clock, conical pendulum, 21", 8-day time and strike, good condition (illustrated), $3,960

French, ca. 1900, maker unknown, novelty clock, conical pendulum with annular dial, 7", 8-day time and alarm, very good condition (illustrated), $825

French, ca. 1900, maker unknown, novelty clock, conical pendulum with annular dial, 7", 8-day time and alarm, good condition, $577

French, ca. 1895, maker unknown, novelty clock, conical pendulum with annular dial, 6.75", 8-day time and alarm, excellent original condition, $1,100

French, ca. 1900, maker unknown, novelty clock, conical pendulum with annular dial, 7", 8-day time and alarm, excellent original condition, $550

French, ca. 1890, maker unknown, novelty clock, Eiffel Tower, 19.25", 8-day time-only, excellent original condition, $1,540

French, ca. 1890, novelty picture clock, 8-day time and music box, 25" × 35", maker unknown, $1,955. Credit: Prices4Antiques.com.

French, ca. 1910, maker unknown, novelty clock, gravity clock, 10", 8-day time-only, excellent condition (illustrated), $145

French, ca. 1910, maker unknown, novelty clock, gravity clock, 10", 8-day time-only, excellent condition, $179

French, ca. 1880, maker unknown, novelty clock, musical picture clock, 25" × 35", 8-day time with music box, good condition (illustrated), $1,955

French, ca. 1840, novelty clock, waterfall, fountain, 8-day time-only, 14", maker unknown, $2,310. Credit: R. O. Schmitt Fine Arts.

French, ca. 1890, novelty night clock, 30-hour time-only,
5", A. F. Frères, $532. Credit: R. O. Schmitt Fine Arts.

French, ca. 1900, maker unknown, novelty clock, mystery clock, 14.5",
8-day time-only, excellent condition (illustrated), $9,900

French, ca. 1890, maker unknown, novelty clock, mystery clock "Swinger,"
statue of a worker, 37", 8-day time-only, good condition, $3,360

French, ca. 1890, maker unknown, novelty clock, mystery clock, "Swinger,"

French, ca. 1900, novelty mystery clock,
8-day time-only, 14.5", maker unknown,
$9,900. Credit: R. O. Schmitt Fine Arts.

French, ca. 1890, not a clock but an
automaton, whistling bird in a cage,
clockwork mechanism, 22", maker
unknown, $1,430. Credit: R. O. Schmitt
Fine Arts.

statue of Diana, 25.5", 8-day time and strike, very good condition (illustrated), $3,850

French, ca. 1880, maker unknown, novelty clock, mystery clock, "Swinger," statue of Diana, 25", 8-day time and strike, good condition, $4,500

French, ca. 1890, maker unknown, novelty clock, night light clock, 5", 30-hour time only, excellent condition (illustrated), $532

French, ca. 1890, maker unknown, novelty clock, singing bird in cage, 22", whistling bird only, fair condition (illustrated), $1,430

French, ca. 1890, maker unknown, novelty clock, singing bird in cage, 22", whistling birds only, good condition, $1,650

French, ca. 1840, maker unknown, novelty clock, waterfall clock, 14", 8-day time only, good condition (illustrated), $2,310

	LOW	MID	HIGH
French Novelty Clocks (ca. 1840–1920)	There are so many varieties of novelty clocks that it is impossible to create a meaningful range.		

FRENCH PORTICO MANTEL CLOCKS grew from the classical architectural designs and proportions of eighteenth-century France. In their earliest form, they are often cased in stone and ormolu. Produced throughout the nineteenth century, they peaked in the 1880s and 1890s. The later clocks are most often in wood cases veneered in rosewood or mahogany and inlaid with brass or a contrasting veneer. The columns can be plain, fluted, or twisted. The movements are almost always 8-day time and strike. The early clocks have silk-thread suspensions and machine-turned or enameled dials.

There are few clocks that make a more handsome appearance on a mantel. Portico clocks are still available and collectible.

French, ca. 1880, Barbot, portico mantel clock with inlay and barley twist columns, 20", 8-day time and strike, good restored condition, $467

French, ca. 1880, Grange and Betout, portico mantel clock in rosewood-inlaid case, 20", 8-day time and strike, very good condition (illustrated), $1,008

French, ca. 1875, Japy Frères, portico mantel clock with barley twist columns, base, and dome, 24", 8-day time and strike, very good condition, $1,320

French, ca. 1880, portico clock, black marble with ormolu mounts, 8-day time and strike, 17.25", maker unknown, $392. Credit: Prices4Antiques.com.

French, ca. 1880, portico clock, white marble with ormolu mounts, 8-day time and strike, 20.5", maker unknown, $747. Credit: Prices4Antiques.com.

French, ca. 1880, Japy Freres, portico mantel clock with barley twist columns and brass decoration, 20", 8-day time and strike, good condition, $770

French, ca. 1880, Japy Freres, portico mantel clock in inlaid rosewood case with barley twist columns, 19", 8-day time and strike, good original condition (illustrated), $840

French, ca. 1890, Marti, portico mantel clock, ormolu case, 13.5", 8-day time and strike, very good condition, $1,485

French, ca. 1890, Roy, L. E., portico mantel clock inlaid with barley twist columns, 19.75", 8-day time and strike, poor condition, $402

French, ca. 1830, maker unknown, portico mantel clock with walnut-veneered case, 20", 8-day time and strike, good restored condition, $880

French, ca. 1840, maker unknown, portico mantel clock, rosewood case with satinwood inlay, 20", 8-day time and strike, excellent condition, $2,090

French, ca. 1850, maker unknown, portico mantel clock in marble and granite, 16.5", 8-day time and strike, good condition, $690

French, ca. 1860, maker unknown, portico mantel clock with the movement as the pendulum, 19.5", 8-day time and strike, very good condition, $5,610

French, ca. 1880, portico clock, inlaid rosewood case, 8-day time and strike, 20", Grange and Betout, $1,008. Credit: R. O. Schmitt Fine Arts.

French, ca. 1880, portico clock, inlaid rosewood case with twisted columns, 8-day time and strike, 19", Japy Frères, $840. Credit: R. O. Schmitt Fine Arts.

French, ca. 1865, maker unknown, portico mantel clock, 20", 8-day time and strike, good restored condition, $560

French, ca. 1870, maker unknown, portico mantel clock with ebonized case and barley twist columns, 20.5", 8-day time and strike, good restored condition, $1,372

French, ca. 1870, maker unknown, portico mantel clock inlaid with barley twist columns, 19", 8-day time and strike, good condition, $412

French, ca. 1875, maker unknown, portico mantel clock with floral inlay, 25", 8-day time and strike, excellent condition, $2,035

French, ca. 1880, maker unknown, portico mantel clock, 17.25", 8-day time and strike, very good condition (illustrated), $392

French, ca. 1880, maker unknown, portico mantel clock with white marble case, 20.5", 8-day time and strike, very good condition (illustrated), $747

French, ca. 1880, maker unknown, portico mantel clock, 19", 8-day time and strike, good condition, $990

French, ca. 1890, maker unknown, portico mantel clock, Baccarat crystal case, 12", 8-day time and strike, excellent condition, $9,900

French, ca. 1855, Vincenti et Cie, portico mantel clock, 16", 8-day time and strike, fair condition, $924

French, ca. 1880, Vincenti et Cie, portico mantel clock with white onyx case, 20", 8-day time and strike, good condition, $1,760

	LOW	MID	HIGH
French Portico Clocks (ca. 1820–1900)	$600–$800	$900–$1,500	$2,000–$3,000+

FRENCH WOOD-CASED MANTEL CLOCKS were produced in fair numbers throughout the nineteenth century and into the first quarter of the twentieth century. Too often the more spectacular cases of metal and stone overshadow these wood-cased clocks, and fewer of them have been imported to America. These clocks are quite reasonable in price and remain an opportunity for the collector.

French, ca. 1850, Planchon, wood-cased mantel clock, architectural form, 14", 8-day time and strike, good original condition, $1,120

French, ca. 1850, Pilfort, E., wood-cased mantel clock, architectural form, 12.75", 8-day time and strike, good condition, $616

French, ca. 1830, maker unknown, wood-cased mantel clock, architectural form, 12.5", 8-day time and strike, good condition, $230

French, ca. 1900, wood-cased mantel clock, lancet case, 8-day time and strike, 16.5", Vincenti Cie, $411. Credit: Prices4Antiques.com.

French, ca. 1900, wood-cased mantel clock, arched-top case, 8-day time and strike, 15", Vincenti Cie, $308. Credit: R. O. Schmitt Fine Arts.

French, ca. 1920, wood-cased mantel clock, mini balloon case, 8-day time-only, 9", maker unknown, $330. Credit: R. O. Schmitt Fine Arts.

French, ca. 1880, maker unknown, wood-cased mantel clock, scrolled bracket or tambour case, 14.5", 8-day time and strike, very good condition, $345

French, ca. 1900, maker unknown, wood-cased mantel clock, lancet case, 14", 8-day time and strike, good condition, $316

French, ca. 1900, Vincenti Cie, wood-cased mantel clock, arched top, 15", 8-day time and strike, very good condition (illustrated), $308

French, ca. 1910, Vincenti Cie, wood-cased mantel clock, lancet case, 16.5", 8-day time and strike, excellent condition (illustrated), $411

French, ca. 1910, maker unknown, wood-cased mantel clock, tambour case, 5", 8-day time only, very good condition (illustrated), $192

French, ca. 1880, wood-cased mantel clock, tambour case, 8-day time and strike, 14.5", maker unknown, $345. Credit: Prices4Antiques.com.

French, ca. 1920, wood-cased mantel clock, tambour case, 8-day time-only, 5", maker unknown, $192. Credit: Prices4Antiques.com

French, ca. 1920, maker unknown, wood-cased mantel clock, mini balloon case, 9", 8-day time-only, very good condition (illustrated), $330

French, ca. 1920, maker unknown, wood-cased mantel clock, mini lyre case, 11.25", 8-day time-only, very good condition, $275

	LOW	MID	HIGH
French Wood-Cased Clocks (ca. 1750–1920)	$150–$250	$350–$450	$550–$650+

Austrian Shelf Clocks

When Americans think of Austrian clocks it is most often of the famous wall clocks called Vienna Regulators. Austrian makers produced shelf/mantel clocks as well but they were overwhelmed in the market by the imported French and German clocks. However, Austrian clocks deserve mention as the collector will occasionally encounter them and they are often underpriced. The two major groups are

Annular-dial mantel clocks, ca. 1870
Mantel and shelf clocks, ca. 1800–20

AUSTRIAN ANNULAR-DIAL MANTEL CLOCKS are similar to the French clocks in that they are in the form of an urn, but they differ in that they are decorated in enamel over metal (often silver) and they are consider-

Austrian, ca. 1870, mini annular dial mantel clock, hand painted enamel, 8-day time only, 4.75", maker unknown, $2,420. Credit: R. O. Schmitt Fine Arts

ably smaller. They appeared for a short period in the 1870s and then disappeared. Quite beautiful, they command high prices when they appear at auction or in the showroom.

Austria, ca. 1870, maker unknown, mini annular-dial mantel clock, 4.75", 8-day time-only, very good condition (illustrated), $2,420

Austria, ca. 1870, maker unknown, mini annular-dial mantel clock, 4.75", 8-day time-only, excellent condition, $2,520

Austria, ca. 1870, maker unknown, mini annular-dial mantel clock, 5", 8-day time-only, good condition, $3,740

Austria, ca. 1870, maker unknown, annular-dial mantel clock, 7.25", 8-day time-only, excellent condition, $3,136

Austria, ca. 1870, maker unknown, annular-dial mantel clock, 7.25", 8-day time-only, good condition, $4,235

	LOW	MID	HIGH
Austrian Annular-Dial Clocks (ca. 1870)	$2,000–$3,499	$3,500–$4,999	$5,000

AUSTRIAN MANTEL CLOCKS followed French style in their case design, but used Austrian-designed movements. Among these designs was the 2-day time and strike brass spring-driven movement that was common to the region. Unable to compete with the French, Austrian clockmakers produced very few mantel clocks after the 1830s. If Empire- or Biedermeier-style clocks appeal to you, then there are some excellent and reasonably priced opportunities awaiting you in Austrian mantel clocks.

Austria, ca. 1790, maker unknown, mantel clock, portico-style case, gesso over wood, 29.5", 8-day time and strike, grand sonnerie and calendar, poor condition, $728

Austria, ca. 1810, Schlatter, Ignatz, mantel clock, portico-style case, marble columns, 18", 2-day time and strike, good condition (illustrated), $224

Austria, ca. 1810, maker unknown, mantel clock, portico-style case, silver over brass, 11.5", 30-hour time-only, good condition, $196

Austria, ca. 1820, maker unknown, mantel clock, portico-style case with ebonized columns and inlaid mahogany, excellent condition (illustrated), $500

Austria, ca. 1820, maker unknown, mantel clock, portico-style case, marble columns, 25", 2-day time and strike, fair condition, $165

Austria, ca. 1820, maker unknown, mantel clock, portico-style case, silver over brass, 18.5", 8-day time and strike, grand sonnerie, poor condition, $742

Austria, ca. 1870, maker unknown, mantel clock, portico-style case, marble columns, 22", 2-day time and strike, good condition, $880

Austrian, ca. 1810, mantel clock, portico-style case, 2-day time and strike, 18", Ignatz Schlatter, $224. Credit: R. O. Schmitt Fine Arts.

Austrian, ca. 1820, mantel clock, portico-style case, 2-day time and strike, 16", maker unknown, $500.

	LOW	MID	HIGH
Austrian Mantel Clocks (ca. 1780–1870)	$200–$300	$500–$700	$800–$1,000

German Shelf Clocks

The German clocks that the collector encounters today are the products of the second half of the nineteenth century after the German States had unified and the manufacturing revolution had transformed Germany into a major industrial power. Before unification in 1870, clockmaking was a small industry and primarily produced local clocks such as the Black Forest clocks of southwestern Germany (as well as Austria and Switzerland). After unification and the lowering of trade barriers, the small factories began a process of consolidation that would result in the large factories of Gustav Becker, Lenzkirch, Junghans, Winterhalder and Hofmeier, and others. These factories quickly competed with those in Austria, France, Britain, and the United States. Large numbers of German clocks were exported to America. The German industry would remain a major producer until World War II. After the war, the industry shrank and evolved, producing more and more movements for export. Most better mechanical clocks sold in America today contain German movements.

Major groups of German clocks are

Black Forest shelf clocks, ca. 1860–1920
China-case shelf clocks, ca. 1880–1930
Cuckoo shelf clocks, ca. 1860–present
400-day shelf clocks, ca. 1880–present
Mantel and bracket clocks, ca. 1880–1930
Novelty shelf clocks, ca. 1890–1930

GERMAN BLACK FOREST SHELF CLOCKS were brought home by early- to mid-nineteenth-century English and American travelers as souvenirs of the grand tour through the Rhine River and the Alps. As the century progressed, these handcarved cases and their clockworks became more sophisticated. Today the survivors of these nineteenth-century clocks command impressive prices based upon the carving and condition of the cases, not their movements.

German, Black Forest shelf clock,
hen on nest, 8-day time and strike,
14.5", maker unknown, $660.
Credit: R. O. Schmitt Fine Arts.

German, ca. 1875, Ed. Schirrmenn, Black Forest carved mantel clock, bird,
19", 8-day time and strike, very good condition, $1,680

German, ca. 1880, maker unknown, Black Forest carved mantel clock,
14.5", 8-day time and strike, very good condition (illustrated), $660

German, ca. 1880, maker unknown, Black Forest carved mantel clock, 14",
8-day time and strike, very good condition, $560

German, ca. 1880, maker unknown, Black Forest carved mantel clock, deer,
39", 8-day time and strike, very good condition, $5,040

German, ca. 1880, maker unknown, Black Forest carved mantel clock,
stags, 31", 8-day time and strike, very good condition, $3,080

German, ca. 1880, maker unknown, Black Forest carved mantel clock, eagle
and eaglets, 35", 8-day time and strike, very good condition, $4,760

German, ca. 1885, maker unknown, Black Forest carved mantel clock, deer,
36", 8-day time and strike, very good condition, $4,760

German, ca. 1885, maker unknown, Black Forest carved mantel clock,
birds and nest, 27.5", 8-day time and strike, very good condition, $3,080

German, ca. 1885, maker unknown, Black Forest carved mantel cuckoo
clock, 21.5", 8-day time and strike, very good condition, $952

	LOW	MID	HIGH
German Black Forest Shelf Clocks (ca. 1860–1920)	$500–$800	$1,500–$3,000	$4,500–$6,000

GERMAN CHINA-CASE MANTEL CLOCKS became fashionable in the last decades of the nineteenth century. In Germany as in France and England, there were two levels of cases. The most expensive were those of porcelain, produced by major potteries such as Meissen or R. S. Prussia. In America, there are more German china cases than in Germany, as they were imported by the thousands by companies such as the Ansonia Clock Company of New York.

German, ca. 1880, maker unknown, china mantel clock, Meissen porcelain case, 23.5", 8-day time and strike, fair condition with repairs to the case, $3,850

German, ca. 1890, maker unknown, china mantel clock, with floral design, marked R. S. Prussia, 14", 30-hour time-only, excellent condition, $600

German, ca. 1895, maker unknown, china mantel clock, 11.5", 30-hour time-only, excellent condition, $2,860

German, ca. 1900, maker unknown, china mantel clock with figures, 17", 8-day time and strike, fair condition with old repairs (illustrated), $517

German, ca. 1910, maker unknown, china mantel clock, 15.5", 30-hour time-only, very good condition (illustrated), $280

German, ca. 1910, china-case mantel clock, country scene, 30-hour time-only, 15.5", maker unknown, $280. Credit: R. O. Schmitt Fine Arts.

German, ca. 1890, china-case mantel clock, egg shaped, flanked by girls with baskets and a cherub finial, 17", maker unknown, $517. Credit: Prices4Antiques.com.

German, ca. 1910, maker unknown, china mantel clock, "Death of King Lear," 11", 30-hour time-only, excellent condition, $220

German, ca. 1920, Haller, T. E., china mantel clock, majolica case, 11.75", 30-hour time-only, fair condition, $825

	LOW	MID	HIGH
China-Case Mantel Clocks (ca. 1875–1930)	$300–$500	$600–$800	$1,000–$3,000+

GERMAN CUCKOO SHELF CLOCKS sit on the mantel or shelf and are spring-driven. Hardly known and rarely produced today, they are genuine cuckoo clocks. The general public believes that there is only one type of cuckoo clock: it hangs on the wall, has pinecone weights, and looks like a chalet with a little door at the top, out of which pops something that goes "cuckoo, cuckoo." This is the souvenir clock that you either love or hate. The genuine German cuckoo shelf clock is a lesser-known variant which was produced from the 1870s until World War II. They are getting hard to find today and prices are rising.

German, ca. 1880, maker unknown, shelf-style cuckoo clock, chalet with leaves and bird, 21", 2-day time and strike, good condition, $672

German, ca.1890, maker unknown, shelf-style cuckoo clock with fox and game birds, 34", 2-day time and strike, fair condition, $2,464

German, ca. 1900, maker unknown, shelf-style cuckoo clock with leaves and recumbent deer, 24.5", 2-day time and strike, poor condition, $868

German, ca. 1900, maker unknown, shelf-style trumpeter clock, chalet, 22", 30-hour time and strike, poor condition, $1,760

German, ca. 1910, maker unknown, shelf-style cuckoo clock, chalet, 19", 2-day time and strike, fair condition (illustrated), $207

German, ca. 1910, maker unknown, shelf-style cuckoo clock, chalet, 14", 30-hour time and strike, fair condition, $247

German, ca. 1910, maker unknown, shelf-style cuckoo clock with leaves, roebuck, and eagle, 32", 2-day time and strike, good condition, $2,200

German, ca. 1920, maker unknown, shelf-style cuckoo clock, chalet, 20", 30-hour time and strike, fair condition, $330

German, ca. 1925, maker unknown, shelf-style cuckoo clock, chalet with leaves and bird, 15", 2-day time and strike, very good condition (illustrated), $980

German, ca. 1910, cuckoo shelf clock, chalet form, 2-day time and strike, 19", maker unknown, $207. Credit: Prices4Antiques.com.

German, ca. 1920, cuckoo shelf clock, chalet form with birds and leaves, 2-day time and strike, 15", maker unknown, $980. Credit: R. O. Schmitt Fine Arts.

German, ca. 1925, maker unknown, shelf-style cuckoo clock, chalet with leaves, bird, and chamois, 24", 2-day time and strike, good condition, $1,680

	LOW	MID	HIGH
German Cuckoo Shelf Clocks (ca.1860–1940)	$300–$500	$700–$1,000	$2,000–$3,000

GERMAN 400-DAY CLOCKS are also known as anniversary clocks or torsion clocks. Outfitted with a spring-driven movement, an anchor escapement, and a rotary torsion pendulum, they run for one year on a single winding. This clock was invented by Anton Harder in Germany around 1880, and early forms were developed by Aaron Crane in the early nineteenth century in New Jersey.

These clocks are still being produced, although increasing numbers are outfitted with quartz movements. Early examples of this clock are steadily rising in price.

German, ca. 1883, Jahresuhrenfabrik, 400-day shelf clock under dome, 10", 400-day time-only movement, good condition (illustrated), $1,680

German, ca. 1885, maker unknown, 400-day shelf clock, crystal regulator case, 11.25", 400-day time-only movement, excellent condition (illustrated), $728

German, ca. 1900, maker unknown, 400-day shelf clock under dome, 15.5", 400-day time-only movement, poor condition with a cracked dome, AU$84

German, ca. 1905, maker unknown, 400-day shelf clock, crystal regulator case, 11", 400-day time-only movement, fair condition, $250

German, ca. 1906, Kienzle, 400-day shelf clock under dome, 16", 400-day time-only movement, very good condition, $467

German, ca. 1907, Becker, Gustav, 400-day shelf clock under dome, 11", 400-day time-only movement, very good condition, $212

German, ca. 1910, Jahresuhrenfabrik, 400-day shelf clock, crystal regulator case, 11", 400-day time-only movement, good condition, $440

German, ca. 1920, maker unknown, 400-day shelf clock under dome, 12.5", 400-day time-only movement, very good condition, $201

German, ca. 1920, Wurthner, 400-day shelf clock under dome, 12", 400-day time-only movement, very good condition, $112

German, ca. 1925, Montag, Sokol, and Co., 400-day shelf clock, under dome, 14.5", 400-day time-only movement, very good condition, $56

German, ca. 1883, 400-day mantel clock, circular case with glass dome, 400-day time-only movement, 10", Jahresuhrenfabrik, $1,680. Credit: R. O. Schmitt Fine Arts.

German, ca. 1885, 400-day mantel clock, crystal regulator–type case, 400-day time-only movement, 11.25", maker unknown, $728. Credit: Prices4Antiques.com.

German, ca. 1930, maker unknown, 400-day shelf clock under dome, 14", 400-day time-only movement, good condition, $134

German, ca. 1932, Keininger and Obergfell, 400-day shelf clock under dome, 11", 400-day time-only movement, fair condition, $247

German, ca. 1952, Keininger and Obergfell, 400-day shelf clock under dome, 16", 400-day time-only movement, good condition, $392

	LOW	MID	HIGH
German 400-day Shelf Clocks (ca. 1880-present)	$100-$200	$300-$500	$600-$1,000+

GERMAN MANTEL AND BRACKET CLOCKS copied American, British, and French styles in design and form during the later decades of the nineteenth century. The fast-growing German clockmaking industry produced a full spectrum of clocks, including mantel or bracket models, and developed its own unique styles by the 1880s and 1890s.

Many of these clocks crossed the Atlantic and can still be found at reasonable prices.

German, ca. 1900, Becker, Gustav, mantel or bracket clock, 12.5", 8-day time and strike, Westminster chimes, very good condition, $522

German, ca. 1909, Becker, Gustav, mantel clock or bracket clock, 14", 8-day time and strike, Westminster chimes, very good condition (illustrated), $504

German, ca. 1910, Becker, Gustav, mantel or bracket clock, 14", 8-day time and strike, Westminster chimes, good condition, $336

German, ca. 1910, Hamburg American Clock Co., mantel or bracket clock, 14", 8-day time and strike, Westminster chimes, good original condition, $246

German, ca. 1880, Junghans, mantel clock, steeple clock, 15.5", 30-hour time only, excellent condition (illustrated), $179

German, ca. 1890, Junghans, mantel or bracket clock, 17", 8-day time and strike, Westminster chimes, excellent condition (illustrated), $252

German, ca. 1904, Junghans, mantel clock, tambour-style case, 13.5", 8-day time and strike, Westminster chimes, fair condition, $347

German, ca. 1910, Junghans, mantel or bracket clock, 19", 8-day time and strike, Westminster chimes, good condition (illustrated), $275

German, ca. 1900, mantel clock, Vienna style, 8-day time only, 25", maker unknown, $190. Credit: Prices4Antiques.com.

German, ca. 1880, mantel clock, American, steeple style, 8-day time-only, 15.5", Junghans, $179. Credit: Prices4Antiques.com.

German, ca. 1915, Junghans, mantel or bracket clock, 15.5", 8-day time and strike, Westminster chimes, fair condition, $532

German, ca. 1920, Junghans, mantel or bracket clock, 21.5", 8-day time and strike, Thorens music box with disks, very good original condition, $3,360

German, ca. 1920, Junghans, mantel or bracket clock, 18", 8-day time and strike, good condition, $247

German, ca. 1920, Junghans, mantel or bracket clock, 12.75", 8-day time and strike, good condition (illustrated), $532

German, ca. 1795, Kandler, Paul, mantel or bracket clock, 20", 2-day time and strike, grand sonnerie, good condition, $1,100

German, ca. 1915, Kienzle, mantel or bracket clock, 17.5", 8-day time and strike, Westminster chimes, excellent condition, $550

German, ca. 1887, Lenzkirch, mantel or bracket clock, 11.5", 8-day time and strike, very good condition, $835

German, ca. 1900, Lenzkirch, mantel or bracket clock, 13.5", 8-day time and strike, fair condition, $137

German, ca. 1910, Lenzkirch, mantel or bracket clock, 14", 8-day time and strike, very good condition, $550

German, ca. 1890, bracket clock, French-style case, 8-day time, strike, and chime, 17", Junghans, $252. Credit: Prices4Antiques.com.

German, ca. 1920, bracket clock, English-style case, 8-day time, strike, and chime, 12.75", Junghans, $532. Credit: R. O. Schmitt Fine Arts.

German, ca. 1909, bracket clock, lancet-style case, 8-day time, strike, and chime, 14", Gustav Becker, $504. Credit: R. O. Schmitt Fine Arts.

German, ca. 1910, bracket clock, English-style case, 8-day time, strike, and chime, 19", Junghans, $275. Credit: Prices4Antiques.com.

German, ca. 1890, Müller and Co., mantel or bracket clock, Neuchâtel style, 19", 8-day time and strike, Westminster chimes, excellent original condition, $1,980

German, ca. 1900, Müller and Co., mantel or bracket clock, 21", 8-day time and strike, excellent condition, $2,475

German, ca. 1890, maker unknown, mantel or bracket clock, 16", 8-day time and strike, good original condition, $336

German, ca. 1900, maker unknown, mantel clock, Vienna Regulator style, 25", 8-day time-only, excellent condition (illustrated), $190

German, ca. 1910, maker unknown, mantel or bracket clock, 16", 8-day time and strike, good original condition, $264

German, ca. 1885, Winterhalder and Hofmeier, mantel or bracket clock, 25", 8-day time and strike, Westminster chimes, excellent original condition, $5,225

German, ca. 1890, Winterhalder and Hofmeier, mantel or bracket clock, 18", 8-day time and strike, good condition, $3,850

German, ca. 1900, Winterhalder and Hofmeier, mantel or bracket clock, 15", 8-day time and strike, very good original condition, $616

	LOW	MID	HIGH
German Mantel and Bracket Clocks (ca. 1880–1930)	$150–$400	$600–$950	$1,500–$2,500

GERMAN NOVELTY CLOCKS were produced by the German clock industry well into the twentieth century. Once quite common and poorly regarded, they have now become very collectible and prices are going up.

German, ca. 1925, Griesbaum, Karl Co., novelty shelf clock, whistler, carved peddler, 13.5", no time, whistles when wound, good condition, $1,210

German, ca. 1930, Griesbaum, Karl Co., novelty shelf clock, whistler, carved hobo, 7.5", no time, whistles when wound, good condition, $990

German, ca. 1935, Griesbaum, Karl Co., novelty shelf clock, whistler, carved hobo, 8.25", no time, whistles when wound, good condition, $990

German, ca. 1935, Griesbaum, Karl Co., novelty shelf clock, whistler, carved man, 13", no time, whistles when wound, good condition, $1,344

German, ca. 1910, novelty clock with moving eyes, 30-hour time-only, 9", maker unknown, $1,210. Credit: R. O. Schmitt Fine Arts.

German, ca. 1900, novelty clock, the monk rings the bell at the top at the alarm, 30-hour time and alarm, "MONK" model, 14", maker unknown, $644. Credit: R. O. Schmitt Fine Arts.

German, ca. 1935, Griesbaum, Karl Co., novelty shelf clock, whistler, carved drunk, 18.5", no time, whistles when wound, good condition, $728

German, ca. 1910, Junghans, novelty shelf clock, minstrel with moving eyes, 9.5", 30-hour time-only, good condition, $728

German, ca.1895, maker unknown, novelty shelf clock, monk alarm clock, 14", 30-hour time and alarm, poor condition, $825

German, ca. 1900, maker unknown, novelty shelf clock, monk alarm clock, 14", 30-hour time and alarm, good restored condition (illustrated), $644

German, ca. 1900, maker unknown, novelty shelf clock, monk alarm clock, 14", 30-hour time and alarm, very good original condition, $1,265

German, ca. 1910, maker unknown, novelty shelf clock, moving eyes, 9", 30-hour time-only, good condition (illustrated), $1,210

German, ca. 1920, maker unknown, novelty shelf clock, owl with moving eyes, 6", 30-hour time-only, fair condition, $71

	LOW	MID	HIGH
German Novelty Clocks (ca. 1890–1940)	$150–$450	$600–$900	$1,500–$2,500

Swiss Mantel and Shelf Clocks

Like Swiss wall clocks, Swiss mantel and shelf models were produced in small numbers and designed after clocks of neighboring nations. However, there is one clock which is unique to Switzerland, known around the world, and still being produced: LeCoultre's Atmos mantel clock.

This clock is wound by changes of temperature. The principle was first devised by a Frenchman named Reutter. In the original models, a change in atmospheric pressure was used to wind the mainspring, and they called the clock "Atmos" for this reason. This method proved to be unreliable, and the company switched to a system based on temperature changes.

Retail prices for new clocks far exceed the prices that they bring when they are resold. If you would like one of these quality clocks, consider buying a pre-owned model.

Switzerland, ca. 1949, LeCoultre, Atmos mantel clock, serial number 96515, 9", indefinite and time-only, good condition, $280

Switzerland, ca. 1950, LeCoultre, Atmos mantel clock, 9", time-only, good condition (illustrated), $632

Switzerland, ca. 1951, LeCoultre, Atmos mantel clock, serial number 51392, 9.25", time-only, fair condition , $385

Swiss, ca. 1950, Atmos mantel clock, time-only movement, 9", LeCoultre, $632. Credit: Prices4Antiques.com.

Swiss, ca. 1955, Atmos mantel clock, time-only movement, 9", LeCoultre, $420. Credit: Prices4Antiques.com.

Switzerland, ca. 1954, LeCoultre, Atmos mantel clock, serial number 47883, 9.5", indefinite and time-only, poor condition, $302

Switzerland, ca. 1955, LeCoultre, Atmos mantel clock, serial number 69254, 9", indefinite and time-only, very good condition (illustrated), $420

Switzerland, ca. 1955, LeCoultre, Atmos mantel clock, 9.25", indefinite and time-only, fair condition, $431

Switzerland, ca. 1955, LeCoultre, Atmos mantel clock, 9.25", indefinite and time-only, good condition, $302

Switzerland, ca. 1956, LeCoultre, Atmos mantel clock, 9", indefinite and time-only, very good condition with original box, $392

Switzerland, ca. 1957, LeCoultre, Atmos mantel clock, serial number 95518, 8.75", indefinite and time-only, fair condition, $577

Switzerland, ca. 1959, LeCoultre, Atmos mantel clock, serial number 102710, 9.25", indefinite and time-only, good condition, $417

Switzerland, ca. 1959, LeCoultre, Atmos mantel clock, serial number 118413, 9", indefinite and time-only, good condition, $440

Switzerland, ca. 1960, LeCoultre, Atmos mantel clock, 9.25", indefinite and time-only, very good condition (illustrated), $316

Switzerland, ca. 1960, LeCoultre, Atmos mantel clock, serial number 116480, 9", indefinite and time-only, excellent condition with original display box, $1,568

Switzerland, ca. 1962, LeCoultre, Atmos mantel clock, serial number 151136, 9", indefinite and time-only, fair condition, $1,606

Swiss, ca. 1960, Atmos mantel clock, time-only movement, 9.25", LeCoultre, $316. Credit: Prices4Antiques.com.

Switzerland, ca. 1965, LeCoultre, Atmos mantel clock, serial number 223713, 9", indefinite and time-only, good condition, $336

Switzerland, ca. 1965, LeCoultre, Atmos mantel clock, 9.25", indefinite and time-only, good condition, $495

	LOW	MID	HIGH
Swiss Atmos Mantel Clocks (ca. 1930–present)	$300–$500	$600–$800	$1,000–$2,000

CHAPTER 6

Where Do You Find Clocks?
or
Would You Buy a Purple Clock?

Clocks can be found almost anywhere, often in places where you would never expect to find them. I found my first antique clock in an antiques shop that specialized in trunks. My wife was looking at the trunks, and I was just standing there when I spotted a mantel clock and got to wondering how the thing worked. We left the shop with a trunk for my wife and a clock for me. It turned out to be a small spring-driven Ogee made by the Welch Clock Company in 1890.

Another time, I repaired a neighbor's chair and was given a Japanese schoolhouse clock that had belonged to her late husband; she had never liked the sound of that clock.

Garage Sales

If you frequent garage and yard sales, you surely run across clocks. They will range from battery and electric clocks, to windup alarm clocks, to Mom and Dad's old mantel clock, to an occasional real find. I once walked into a garage sale and came away with a Seth Thomas pillar and splat wooden-works clock from the 1820s and a Forrestville triple-decker with a beautiful lyre-shaped movement from the 1830s.

Flea Markets

Flea markets will also have some clocks, but be aware that very often this is where many married (a clock built from the parts of one or more other clocks), reproduction, and new clocks are sold to the unwary and innocent. If it looks too good to be in a flea market, you are right to be ultra cautious and suspicious.

Antiques Shops

Most antiques shops have a clock or two but the clocks are seldom rare and are usually overpriced. Antique clocks in these shops are specimens of the most common and thus most available. In shop after shop, you will find the black mantel clocks of the turn of the twentieth century, the ubiquitous tambour mantel clock of the 1920s and 1930s as well as assorted Ogees and Connecticut shelf clocks of the last quarter of the nineteenth century.

However, sometimes you do find something worth acquiring. Walking through a series of antiques shops in upstate New York, I found a lovely French figural mantel clock, ca. 1860–70, whose case had been spray-painted purple. The movement, dial, hands, and pendulum were original to the clock and all in working order. Minus the paint job, the $125 price was a quarter of its retail value. In another shop, I discovered an English gallery clock, ca. 1900–20, with an incredibly dirty movement. The price, $150, was also a bargain.

In high-end antiques shops, you should expect to find a better grade of clocks. Eighteenth- and nineteenth-century tall-case clocks, more English or Scottish than American, are common, as are European wall and mantel clocks and better American clocks, such as pillar and scrolls and actual Regulators. Here, too, you will often encounter many of the fine French clocks that were exported to the United States and Canada during the nineteenth century.

Clock Shops

Clock shops are disappearing from our world. As the general public has shifted more and more to the battery-driven clock and away from the mechanical clock, traditional clock shops have become an endangered species. They survived in past years on both the sale of clocks and their repair. Now there is too little to repair and too few customers to buy. Most contemporary clock shops offer lines of new clocks, virtually all imported.

Here and there a shop still exists that offers antique clocks for sale and provides comprehensive clock service. When you find one of these shops, frequent it and help keep it in business. This dealer will become an important asset to you and a major source of clock expertise. My experience has shown them to be invaluable to the collector and a major source of collectible clocks at fair market value. They love the field and are usually eager to talk with anyone who shows an interest.

The Internet

The world of the computer and the Internet will introduce you to many dealers and shops that would normally be out of your physical reach. Browse dealers' Web sites regardless of their area of origin. Often a clock or clock part that seems to be completely elusive in New York is obtainable on the West Coast or in the United Kingdom via the Web.

Buying clocks via the Internet from other than an established dealer or known source can be riskier. Hundreds of clocks are sold at online sites such as eBay. Here you must rely on the description, pictures, and your own expertise. Very often, clocks being offered for sale are poorly described, often lacking important details. Your own expertise must supply the important questions to be asked of the seller. However, this task is becoming a bit easier with the appearance of online clock appraisers to aid you.

Internet buying is a new and growing field of clock acquisition, but it still has not replaced the advantages of being able to actually see and examine the clocks that you are interested in. My first experience in buying a clock online netted me a clock with two major mechanical problems not mentioned in the description. After renegotiating the price via e-mail and doing some repair work, I finally wound up with a lovely German mantel clock. However, much time and hassle could have been avoided had I seen the clock in person.

House and Estate Sales

House and estate sales can be excellent clock sources. Virtually every house has a few clocks. The trick is to choose the right sale. The house sale that lists extensive baby clothes or baby and juvenile furniture is usually not a great source for collectible clocks. What you will find are clocks from the last twenty years or so, very few of which are collectible. Instead, look for house sales in older, established neighborhoods where the owners are retiring or moving. You have a much better chance of finding vintage clocks at this type of house sale.

Estate sales don't always imply the sale of a millionaire's property. Ordinary people die and their families dispose of their estates. Wonderful clocks can sometimes be found at these sales. Often the family found them in the attic or the basement or even the garage where the owner had stored them, dismissing them as "too old-fashioned."

In any estate sale, you must try to get there early before the "vultures and pickers" (so-called antiques dealers) arrive. If it looks like it might be a good house sale, the vultures and pickers will have staked out the place the night before and are waiting for the door to open so they can rush in to "cherry pick." Often, you find that the family has let these dealers in a day or so early, and the best has already disappeared. Fortunately for you, however, these dealers are not often clock oriented, unless they think they can buy the clock for a pittance.

Estate sales of the wealthy are excellent sources for very good clocks. Virtually every wealthy family had one or more fine clocks, often clocks that were passed down from an earlier generation. Here is often your best source for finding the tall-case clock that you have been looking for or a wonderful French fire-gilded figural mantel clock. A friend recently showed me a superb English eighteenth-century tall-case clock found at an estate sale and purchased for a fraction of its market value.

Auctions

Auctions are another major source of clocks. We are often attracted to them because of the lure of discovery and the possible bargain. For our purposes, there are two different types of auctions: the general auction, which has a bit of everything, and the specialized or clock auction, which concentrates just on horological items. Each has advantages and disadvantages.

The general auction usually offers a few clocks. Since most of the bidders are not clock experts, prices can range from very low to insanely high. It is possible to get a bargain at these auctions, but it will depend upon a number of things, such as: Did you get to the auction in time to preview and closely examine the clock? Did you treat with profound suspicion anything that you where told by the auctioneer? Auctioneers are not clock experts. Beware of pat expressions such as "It needs a little work," "It just needs a little cleaning and oiling," "We just got it in," or "It's been running for days." Trust only your own eyes and expertise, and remember, you never polish the case of a bronze clock

LOOK CLOSELY

For house and estate sales and auctions, carry a small kit including a couple of bench keys consisting of five or so different sizes in order to check the springs, a small flashlight so you can peer inside the case, a small loupe or magnifying glass that will enable you to closely see the condition of the movement and anything that might be printed on it and a small magnet to check for ferrous and nonferrous metals.

If a bench key test reveals a broken spring, you can estimate what spring replacement will cost in your bid.

Try the strike. If it doesn't work, it could be something minor or something requiring a repair shop. Estimate the higher expense when you are establishing what you will bid.

Check the beat. If the clock is out of beat, again estimate the cost of correction and subtract the amount from your bid.

How does the case look? Are any parts such as finials or hardware missing? Has the case been refinished to hide defects? Adjust your bid accordingly.

Now check the dial. Has it been replaced by either a different dial or one of the antiqued paper replacements? How do the hands look? Are they in place, and if so, are they original or replacements? If the latter, are they correct to the clock?

Look at the movement. Do you think the movement is original to the case? One indication that it is not are extra screw holes or closed-up holes where the original movement was removed. If the original movement is gone, skip the clock unless you need it for parts and then adjust your bid way down.

Is the clock label in place or is the label a reproduction? Is the pendulum still with the clock? How is the glass? Has the original glass been replaced with modern windowpane glass? All these things must affect your bid.

BIDDING

Now to the bid itself. First and foremost, it's important to set a limit on the amount that you are willing to spend for the clock. As the bidding starts and goes higher, you will discover how much willpower you have. Stick to your limit and never be drawn into a bidding duel. Too often, these duels are rigged to get you to increase what you will pay for that clock. When the bidding starts it is easy to get sucked in. You begin to think that if these other bidders want the clock, you must somehow have missed something and underestimated its value. Stick to your limit!

If you do make the winning bid, make sure all the parts that you examined at the preview are still with the clock. The items that most frequently get lost between preview and sale are the key, the pendulum, and the weights. If they are missing, refuse the clock until the items are found. If they can't be found, return the clock. The auctioneer will usually put it up again, and you will have another chance to bid, taking into account the missing parts.

CLOCK AUCTIONS

Clock auctions are quite different from the general auction. If the auction house specializes in clocks, you can expect management to know their clocks and accurately describe them in their catalog or on the floor. Clock auctions and their catalogs can be major sources of clock information. Some catalogs are works of art and classrooms in print. Clock auctions can bring you into contact with the entire spectrum of clocks plus a good number of collectors, dealers, and curators. Among the auction houses that are known for their clock auctions and catalogs are:

R. O. SCHMITT FINE ARTS
P.O. Box 1941
Salem, NH 03079
Tel: 603-893-5915
Fax: 603-893-9777
Web site: www.antiqueclockauction.com
E-mail: bob@roschmittfinearts.com
(Bob Schmitt does only clock auctions. His catalogs are wonderful.)

COTTONE AUCTIONS
Sam Cottone
15 Genessee Street
Mt. Morris, NY 14510
Tel: 585-658-3119
Web site: www.cottoneauctions.com

GENE HARRIS AUCTIONS
203 S. 18th Avenue
Marshalltown, IA 50158
Tel: 641-752-0600
Web site: www.geneharrisauctions.com

HORTON'S ANTIQUE CLOCKS
3864 Wyse Square
Lexington, KY 40510
Tel: 859-381-8633
Fax: 859-381-8733
Web site: www.hortonsantiqueclocks.com
E-mail: hortonsclocks@insightbb.com

WILLIAM J. JENACK
62 Kings Highway Bypass
Chester, NY 10918
Tel: 845-469-9095
Fax: 845-469-8445
Web site: www.jenack.com
E-mail: info@jenack.com

These auction houses also offer online catalogs.

Don't expect to find many bargains at these auctions because your fellow bidders will all be clock collectors or dealers. You will, however, have a much better chance of finding what you are looking for. Just know your limit and stick to it!

Go early, having done your homework before you get there. Know what you are looking for, know what you are looking at, and know what a fair price would be for the clock you see. Take what you are told at estate sales and general auctions with an enormous grain of salt! If there are any doubts that you cannot satisfy, don't buy the clock. Remind yourself, there are many other clocks out there, and the world will not end if you don't buy this particular clock.

Examining Your Clock: A Checklist

Over the years, numerous clock experts have devised checklists to aid the collector in examining a clock to obtain the best possible identification and help to establish its value.

The checklist included here is the one that I use and is an amalgam of ideas and categories borrowed from numerous experts in the field. I have found it useful as it forces me to look at a clock in a very objective way, making it far easier to do further research or draw a conclusion. I am sure you will find things to add or delete from this list to suit your own special circumstances.

CLOCK EVALUATION CHECKLIST

Place

Date

Kind of Clock

Asking Price

I. The Clock Case
  A. Type
    1. Type of clock
      a. tall case
      b. wall clock
      c. mantel or table clock
      d. portable
      e. marine
      f. other
    2. Style of clock
      a.
  B. Outside
    1. First impression: how does it look?
    2. Second impression: general condition?
      a. poor
      b. fair
      c. good
      d. excellent
    3. Material
      a. wood
      b. metal
      c. ceramic
      d. other
    4. Ornamentation
      a. veneer
      b. molding
      c. carving
      d. gilding
      e. paint
      f. stenciling
      g. mirror
      h. glass tablet with reverse painting decoration
    5. Replacement parts
      a. are the feet original?
      b. are the feet missing?

      c. are the feet replacements?

      d. does any part of the case look odd? out of proportion?

      e. does any part of the case appear to be altered?

      f. does the wood all match as to color and grain?

      g. do you see any plywood used in the case?

      h. is the backboard original and does it run the length of the case? (This is important in tall-case clocks.)

      i. does the hardware match?

  6. Finish

      a. does the case appear to have its original finish?

      b. paint

      c. stain

      d. varnish

      e. shellac/French polish

      f. other

      g. has the case been stripped and reveneered?

      h. has it been heavily stained or painted to mask repairs?

C. Inside

  1. First impression: does it look and smell like an old clock?

  2. Second impression: general condition.

      a. poor

      b. fair

      c. good

      d. excellent

  3. Interior layout

      a. movement is screwed to backboard

      b. movement is seated on board

      c. movement is pinned between wooden dividers

      d. movement is screwed to rear of the clock front

      e. movement is screwed to case sides with brackets

      f. movement is held by metal straps running to a backmounting plate

      g. other

  4. Written details

      a. clock label

      b. instructions for setting up

      c. dates

      d. repair (names or dates) or cleaning data

      e. owner's name, etc.

      f. other

  5. Construction
   a. do the wood glue blocks match or do they look new?
   b. have nails been used in the construction?
   c. have wood screws been used in the construction?

II. The Dial
 A. What is written on the dial?
  1. Name _____
  2. Date _____
  3. Location _____
  4. Maker _____
  5. Logo (sketch)
  6. Do you think anything has been added to the dial to enhance its value?
  7. Other
 B. Dial characteristics
  1. Shape
   a. round
   b. square
   c. arched
   d. oval
   e. other
  2. Type
   a. brass
   b. silvered
   c. enamel
   d. glass or plastic
   e. paper
   f. paper on metal
   g. paper on wood
   h. metal and/or cloth on wood
   i. painted metal
   j. painted wood
   k. other
 C. Hands
  1. Shape and size
   a. describe or sketch shape with length of minute and hour hands
  2. Material
   a. brass
   b. iron
   c. wood

       d. bone

       e. ivory

       f. plastic

       g. other

    3. Manufactured

       a. machine stamped

       b. cast

       c. hand cut

       d. do the hands appear to have been trimmed?

  D. Dial features

    1. Other indicators

       a. second hand

       b. calendar

       c. other

    2. Decoration

       a. painted

       b. printed

       c. applied

    3. Describe decoration/ornamentation

       a. _____

          _____

          _____

  E. Method of attaching dial to movement

    1. Description: _____

      _____

III. The Clock Movement

  A. First impression

    1. General condition

       a. poor

       b. fair

       c. good

       d. excellent

    2. Is the movement original to the case or a replacement?

  B. Second impression

    1. Function

       a. time only

       b. time and strike

       c. time and strike plus other

2. Duration
   a. 30-hour
   b. 8-day
   c. 2-week
   d. 31-day
   e. other
3. Construction
   a. wood
   b. iron
   c. brass
   d. other
4. Mounting
   a. rear mounted
   b. front mounted
   c. seated on board
   d. side mounted with brackets
   e. other
C. Power
1. motive power
   a. weight
   b. coiled spring
   c. electricity
   d. other
2. Control
   a. balance wheel
   b. crown verge/pendulum
   c. anchor/deadbeat escapement/pendulum
   d. spring balance
   e. other
3. Strike type
   a. rack and snail
   b. count wheel
   c. other
4. Pendulum
   a. located in rear of movement
   b. located in front of the movement
   c. off center
   d. compensated
   e. length of pendulum _____"/cm

Completely original clocks have greater value than those that are not. But remember, the older the clock, the more likely it is that parts have been replaced. This is usually found in the case, which often suffers more damage over time than the movement.

Judging the originality of a clock is a study in its own right, and volumes have been written on the subject. The checklist above merely touches on the subject, but it will get you started and help alert you to some of the marriages, forgeries, reproductions, and fakes out there.

Well, You Bought the Clock— Now What Do You Do with It?

MOVING YOUR CLOCK

You need to get your purchase home. There are some definite dos and don'ts about transporting clocks.

Never move a pendulum clock without first removing the pendulum or locking it in place!

Most clocks can be moved with the movement in the case. An exception: most tall-case clocks, where weight is a factor. Older tall-case clocks were constructed so the movement was readily removed when it was necessary to relocate the clock.

Weight-driven clocks must have their weights removed and their ropes, cords, chains, or gut fastened to prevent them tangling.

Stop your spring-driven movements by placing some folded paper or cardboard between the crutch and the backplate.

Make sure that your clock's door or bezel is closed and fastened. Remove keys if necessary and remember to protect the glass and dial.

As you are about to move the clock to its carton, remember to lift it from the bottom. This is especially important with antique clocks whose cases may have weakened with age. (You would not be the first person to try and lift the clock by its top and have the top come off in your hands.)

You are now ready to move your clock. Clocks should be moved in the vertical position whenever possible. Obviously, with large wall clocks this is not practical, so they are transported on their backs. This is also true of all tall-case clocks.

Pack and/or wrap your clock well. If shipping with a mover or a parcel service such as UPS, I have found it wise to wrap my clocks well with bubble wrap, place them inside a sturdy carton, pack the space between the clock and the sides of the carton with foam pellets, and seal the carton. Now repeat the process by placing your first carton inside of a larger carton and packing the space between the two with more foam pellets. Before sealing the outer carton, make sure that you have inserted your address, just in case the outer label is obliterated. Mark the carton FRAGILE. Insurance is also a sound precaution. Do the above and you have a fighting chance that your clock will come to you unscathed.

INSTALLING CLOCKS

So your clock made its voyage in good condition; it is time to install it in its new home.

Choose a location that ideally is out of traffic and protected from dust, moisture, too much heat or cold, and direct sunlight. Treat clocks much the same as you would a good wine.

Having found the perfect spot, start your clock by giving the pendulum a slight push. You should hear an even-sounding tick-tock that tells you that the clock is in beat and should run as intended.

"I installed the clock, but I don't hear the tick-tock and it does not run. What do I do?"

Why do clocks stop running? The most common reasons include:

The clock is not level or plumb.
Check surface from side to side and from front to back with a level (floor and mantel clocks); check wall and clock for plumb (wall clocks); adjust surface or clock accordingly.

The clock's pivot holes are dry or surrounded by congealed oil.
(Read section below on cleaning clock movements.)

The tick-tock, or beat, is very uneven.
(Read section below on adjusting clock beat.)

The clock weights are "hanging up" on the inside of the case.
Plumb the case so the weights descend without touching the case.

The pendulum rubs on something and the clock stops.
Plumb the case so the pendulum hangs straight down and does not touch the movement or the case.

Hands catch on each other and the clock stops.
Carefully rebend the hands so they do not make contact with each other.

The escapement is damaged (usually when the clock was moved).
Take the clock to the repair shop.

The clock weight has fallen to the bottom of the clock.
Replace cordage or repair chain and reattach weight to hook or pulley.

The key turns without winding the spring, indicating that the spring has broken.
Take the clock to the repair shop.

Clock gear train jams because of wear.
Take the clock to the repair shop.

Tall-case and mantel clocks must be placed on firm and level surfaces to permit their pendulums to function properly.

Tall-case clocks tend to be top-heavy, especially when fully wound. It is good practice to fasten them to the wall. It is common to find holes in the backboards of old clocks indicating just how common this practical suggestion was.

Remember, any clock fastened to the wall must be plumb so there will be no contact between the pendulum and the backboard. Also, make sure the weights don't rub along the backboard or catch on the front of the case as they descend.

Wall clocks should have at least two wall attachments to prevent them from moving sideways when winding.

ADJUSTING THE BEAT

If your clock does not have an even tick-tock when you start the pendulum or has no tick-tock at all, the most likely explanation is that the clock is out of beat. Before you rush your clock into the repair shop, here are a few things to try.

Start by rechecking your surface for level. If you find that the surface cannot be leveled and you are sure that this is the place for the clock, there are a number of things to do to adjust the beat to the surface.

The crudest and most common method is to raise one side or the other of the clock until the tick-tock sounds even. The disadvantage of this method is obvious: it looks terrible. However, it does give you an idea of how much the clock must be adjusted to bring it back into beat.

Better clocks, especially many tall-case clocks, have a device called a beat setter. A beat setter is a fine screw that adjusts the distance between the crutch and pendulum, thereby bringing the clock into beat. See if a small adjustment to the beat setter doesn't solve the problem.

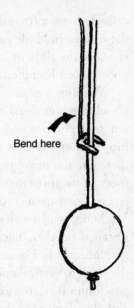

Bend here

How do you adjust the beat? In most older tall-case, wall and mantel clocks, adjust the beat by carefully bending the crutch (it is intended to be bent). The crutch is bent ONLY from side to side and NEVER in and out. The crutches of older clocks will show clear evidence of earlier adjustments. In the past, floors and mantels were not always as level as they are today.

Slowly bend the crutch a slight amount to the right or left, replace the pendulum, and try the results. If the tick-tock has gotten worse, bend the crutch rod in the opposite direction. In a few tries you will get the knack of this technique, and your clock will be running in beat on a less-than-perfect surface.

Mantel clocks are much more difficult to bring into beat, as you must turn the clock around to reach the movement. A trick that you can try here is to place the clock on another surface that is similarly off level but that allows you to walk behind the clock so you can adjust the beat without turning the clock around each time. When adjusted, return the clock to its spot and it should run in beat.

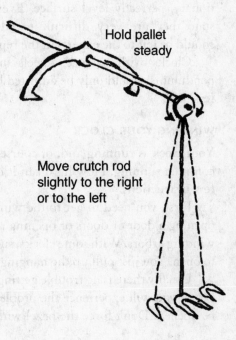

Hold pallet steady

Move crutch rod slightly to the right or to the left

Some mantel clocks, most often European, are constructed with crutch rods that can be adjusted by changing the rod's angle to the pallet. This can be done because there is a friction fit where the crutch rod joins the pallet arbor. In these cases, hold the pallet steady and push the crutch rod a slight amount either to the right or left. You are achieving the same results as above but without bending the crutch rod.

Winding a clock with a circular movement (many French clocks have circular movements) can sometimes cause the movement to shift if it is not securely fastened and thus to lose its beat. Always check that the movement is securely fastened to the case. However, often you can adjust these circular movements by loosening their case screws and very slightly rotating the movement until the clock is back in beat. Then retighten the screws holding the movement to the case.

Many wall clocks have graduated scales installed on their backboards just below the pendulum bob. These scales are to help you set the clock to vertical and set the beat. When the pendulum is started and everything is vertical and the clock is in beat, the pendulum will swing an equal distance on both sides of the center mark on the scale. If this does not happen, adjust the crutch until the pendulum swings equally to either side.

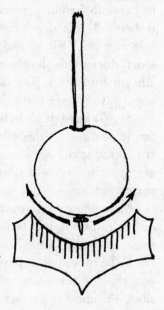

The 400-day clocks require a solid, stationary, perfectly level surface. Even in this state they are very difficult to adjust and should be left to the experts in the repair shop.

Clocks with balance wheels instead of pendulums should only be adjusted by a professional.

WINDING YOUR CLOCK

Your clock is running and, of course, needs to be periodically wound to continue running. How hard can it be to wind your clock? Easy, with a few instructions.

First, you need to get to the winding mechanism. This will require opening a door or doors or opening a bezel that protects the dial and the winding arbors. With some clocks, such as cuckoo clocks, there is nothing to open. You just pull up the hanging weights by their chains.

Usually there is no trouble getting to the winding mechanism. On occasion you will experience the problem of a very tight bezel which must be opened. Don't force the bezel with your hand, as doing so is liable to damage the bezel and/or break the glass. Instead, insert a thin metal blade in the bezel on the side opposite the hinge; with a slight pry outward, the bezel should pop open. Locked doors with missing keys are another story and are often best left to a locksmith so you do not damage the clock case by trying to force the lock.

Be careful how you wield your key, as damage to the dial is common when winding. French clocks, with their wonderful enameled dials, very often show damage around the winding holes caused by careless winding.

Use only the correct size key, one that fits snugly and does not slip when turned. Keys too large in diameter or too loose on the winding shaft will cause damage to the winding holes by binding. Many clocks are outfitted with ferrules in the winding holes to protect the dial. If these are missing, they should be replaced, because they serve an important function.

Most clock movements are wound in one direction. Trying to wind a clock in the wrong direction can cause serious damage to the movement. Front-winding clocks, such as English wall clocks, generally are wound clockwise (although there are many, many exceptions) while rear-winding movements, such as French carriage clocks, are generally wound counterclockwise. In some striking clocks, the time and strike springs are wound in opposite directions. Always carefully test the direction before you wind your clock for the first time. (I once stripped teeth off an American wooden-works clock by not heeding my own advice.)

Try to establish a consistent winding schedule, winding your 30-hour clocks at the same time each day and your 8-day clocks on the same day each week.

But what to do when you won't be there to wind your clocks at their scheduled times? I stop my weight-driven pendulum clocks as well as my spring-driven pendulum clocks. Spring-driven clocks without pendulums I let run down.

Determine the number of turns each clock needs to run for its full period and don't wind past that. Overwinding a clock, be it weight-driven or spring-driven, can cause serious problems, ranging from broken springs to broken cases.

Too much pressure on a fully wound spring can damage the end of the spring, causing premature spring failure. As you wind your clock, you will feel the growing tension on the spring and be able to determine easily when the spring is wound enough to keep the clock running for its required time.

Do not overwind weight-driven movements by pulling the weight all the way to the top, as this can cause dislodging of the pulley or the weight.

Dislodged pulleys will stop the clock and falling weights can severely damage the case and/or the floor, as well as scaring you out of a year's growth when they crash down.

In weight-driven movements, especially tall-case clocks, watch the weights as you wind the clock. They often swing slightly and can interfere with the pendulum.

If you have occasion to rehang your weights (especially in tall-case clocks), consider limiting the rope, cord, chain, or gut so the weights do not reach all the way to the case bottom. If you have too much cord and you forget to wind the clock, the weight can reach the bottom and detach, causing problems when rewinding.

Another old trick is to allow the time side of the movement to have a bit more cord than the strike side. Then, if you forget to wind the clock, the strike will remain correct in relation to the hands instead of being able to run on after the time side has stopped and being out of sequence.

Periodically examine your rope, cord, chain, or gut weight supports for any signs of failure such as fraying, loose strands, and so on. If you notice a problem, repair it as soon as possible as a free-falling weight can cause great damage. When you heft your first cast-iron weight from a tall-case clock, you will quickly realize what "great damage" can mean.

SETTING THE TIME

You have returned from vacation and you need to start up and reset the time on your clocks. Simple to do, but just remember the following things.

The minute hands are designed to be moved forward without causing any damage to the movement. Don't do this with the hour hand as it is meant to move forward only in company with the minute hand. When you move the minute hand forward, the hour hand will follow in a normal fashion.

Hands are delicate even if they don't look particularly delicate. When moving the minute hand, hold it close to its center. This will minimize the chances of breaking or bending the hand (particularly true of the minute hands of smaller clocks, such as carriage clocks).

On striking clocks, ALWAYS allow the clock to strike fully at each hour and half-hour (if it strikes on the half-hour) before moving the minute hand forward.

The hands of a striking clock should never be turned backwards—

with one exception. If the clock is running a few minutes fast, it is safe to turn the hand back within the following limit: from five minutes after the hour up to the next strike, but not past it. If your clock is really gaining a lot of time, stop it and adjust the pendulum. Restart the pendulum when the correct time is reached.

It is very easy to bend the minute hand when moving it, so it is wise to make sure that the minute hand does not "hang up" on the hour hand as they pass each other. This will cause your clock to stop and is one of the most common causes of clock stoppage.

Finally, how do you handle the seasonal changes in time from standard to daylight savings and back? When changing from standard time to daylight savings time, slowly move the minute hand forward to the correct time. Remember to allow the clock to chime as necessary. When moving back to standard time, the easiest way is to stop the clock for an hour.

REGULATING THE SPEED OF YOUR CLOCK

All clocks have a method to adjust their speed or going rate. On pendulum clocks, the going rate is controlled by changing the operating length of the pendulum. You can do this by moving the nut located at the top or bottom of the pendulum bob. Lower the bob and the clock will lose time; raise the bob and the clock will gain time.

Many mantel clocks manufactured after the middle of the nineteenth century make this job easier by providing an adjustment on the clock front. At the top of the dial, you will see a small, square shaft linked to a mechanism that raises or lowers the pendulum's suspension spring. Turning the shaft clockwise usually causes the clock to gain time, while turning it counterclockwise causes the clock to lose time.

Clocks with balance wheels are adjusted by a lever that alters the length of the hairspring in the escapement. Often this lever is accompanied by a graduated scale indicating fast and slow. These clocks need only very small adjustments.

In warm weather, the pendulum will expand and the clock lose time, while in winter's colder weather, the pendulum will contract and the clock will gain time. Rarely do seasonal differences in temperature (winter to summer) necessitate pendulum adjustment. If your clock is equipped with a compensating pendulum (see Glossary), this problem should not exist. Given the climate controls found in most homes today, this problem has become virtually extinct.

ADJUSTING THE STRIKE

Striking clocks are designed to strike or chime unless they have been provided with a mechanism to turn the strike off and on. Essentially, these clocks use two methods to produce a strike or chime at the correct time and number. These two methods are the count wheel and the rack and snail (see Glossary). Both are forms of programming that, working in conjunction with the hands, cause the clock to strike the correct number at the correct time. At times, the strike may be out of sequence because the clock either didn't strike or struck before it should have. To fix this problem, the clock must restrike the hours until the correct sequence is again reached.

Most striking movements have a lever installed on the movement, which, when lifted or depressed, causes the strike train to be released and the clock to strike. An inspection of your movement will usually indicate this lever. To correct your clock's strike pattern, lift or depress this lever and let the clock strike. Do this for as many times as it is necessary to correct the problem.

If your clock continues to have this problem, it usually indicates the necessity for cleaning and lubricating the movement.

If you are unhappy with the sound of your clock's strike, the sound can often be altered by adjusting the way the hammer hits the bell, gong, tube, or coil. However, before you start adjusting the hammer, check to see if the bell, gong, etc., is securely attached as this can have a major effect upon the sound. It is also wise to listen to the strike before you buy the clock, because it may be a sound that you can't live with.

CONSERVE, REPAIR, AND RESTORE

Clocks were built to run and should be put in condition to run. The only exception that I can think of would be if you owned a totally unique clock with great historical value that was not in working order. Since any changes that you make to a clock will be permanent, I would suggest that you do nothing but enjoy the clock as is.

However, the vast majority of us will never own a clock that falls into that category. The clocks that we will acquire will range from mass-produced clocks existing in the hundreds of thousands to handcrafted clocks produced in very small numbers. I believe that these clocks should be put in working order.

Repairs should only be undertaken by a trained repairperson, and the repairs should be guaranteed. My hope is that as your hobby grows, you will take advantage of some of the fine repair courses offered by instructors from the National Association of Watch and Clock Collectors and the time will arrive when you will be able to do most of your own repair work.

Now on to conservation and restoration. Before we proceed, ask yourself why you wish to conserve or restore your clock. Remember, anything that you do will permanently affect the clock.

If you have a clock of considerable age, my suggestion is to take your questions to a professional clock restorer. Major questions that must be answered are: How much and what kind of restoration work must be done? What will this work do to the value of the clock and your investment? With newer clocks, particularly those produced since the middle of the nineteenth century, these questions are much easier to answer. Proper restoration will most likely increase their value.

However, I must stress *proper* restoration. This does not include replacing the movement with something "better" or redoing the case in a different color and changing the hardware.

My own rule is: the older and more valuable the clock, the less I do in the way of restoration. Here I think in terms of conservation, doing just enough work to stabilize the piece and prevent further deterioration.

With newer and less valuable clocks, I might think in terms of restoration, returning the clock, as far as possible, to its condition when it was new. Another caution: I recommend restoration only when I believe that it would enhance the value of the clock or when the owner has a particular attachment to the piece.

If you have decided to go ahead, remember that work of poor quality will only lower the value of the clock. Again, my hope is that you will enroll in some of the fine restoration courses that are offered and learn to do much of this work yourself. There is a tremendous satisfaction derived from bringing a clock back to life.

CLEANING THE CLOCK MOVEMENT

When you see the pivot holes of your clock movement are dry, they have a buildup of gunk around them, or the oil is dirty, these are sure signs that the movement needs cleaning.

Clock movements, like any kind of machinery, require lubrication as part of their maintenance. Oil, needed to lubricate the moving parts of the clock, dries out or oxidizes into a gummy substance. Oil attracts dust and the minute particles of metal produced by a running clock. All of this produces a situation in which wear increases. If you ignore these conditions, you are guaranteeing expensive repairs in the future.

Unless you have learned how to clean a movement and have had some practice, I do not recommend trying it yourself. Find a professional to do the job.

After being cleaned and relubricated, the movement should not need cleaning again for years, depending upon the environment in which the clock runs. A rule that you might follow would be to oil your clock every five years and clean it every ten.

CHAPTER 7

How Do I Learn More About Clocks?

You cannot become a serious collector of clocks without becoming a student. To aid you in this process, various resources are available. Leading the list is the National Association of Watch and Clock Collectors (NAWCC), founded in 1943. I strongly recommend that you fill out the application in this book and take advantage of membership in this organization.

Advantages include its renowned bulletin, published six times a year and including articles on both clocks and watches. The association also publishes *The Mart* on the same schedule. This companion publication contains member advertisements for both buying and selling. The trade section of *The Mart* represents booksellers, dealers offering parts, movements, clocks, and services such as restoration of dials and the like. Specialized bulletins are also published occasionally.

Of particular value to the collector is the association's library of papers, books, publications, and videotapes, which members can borrow. NAWCC headquarters in Columbia, Pennsylvania, houses the library, the finest clock museum in the country, and a school of horology. Courses are offered in watch- and clockmaking and repair.

Beyond its national headquarters, the NAWCC sponsors local chapters that hold regular meetings with lectures and marts allowing members to exchange horological information and items.

Regional conventions, organized by local chapters, are held around the country, and a national convention is held annually in July. At $60 a year, membership is a major bargain. You will receive value far exceeding the cost of your dues.

The American Clock and Watch Museum in Bristol, Connecticut, accepts public membership, publishes a journal, offers research facilities, and has a first-rate American clock collection.

Credit: NAWCC TIMEXPO 2002.

Overseas, the United Kingdom offers membership in the British Horological Institute, a very worthwhile organization. Germany, France, and Switzerland have active collector societies as well.

Museums and Collections

To study clocks you must see as many as possible. This includes collections in museums, antique shops, and auction houses.

Major collections of clocks can be seen at:

THE AMERICAN CLOCK AND WATCH MUSEUM
100 Maple St.
Bristol, CT 06010

THE HENRY FORD MUSEUM
Greenfield Village
Dearborn, MI 48120

THE HENRY FRANCIS DUPONT MUSEUM
Winterthur Museum
Winterthur, DE 19735

THE NATIONAL MUSEUM OF CLOCKS AND WATCHES (NAWCC)
514 Poplar St.
Columbia, PA 17512

MEMBERSHIP APPLICATION

National Association of Watch and Clock Collectors

New Member Name: _____

Street: _____

City: _____

State/Country: _____   Zip: _____

Ph. Work: (_____)_____

Home: (_____)_____

Fax: (_____)_____

E-mail: _____

Are you a former member of NAWCC? _____

If yes, your membership #: _____

Date of Birth: _____ / _____ / _____

Occupation: _____

Specify horological interest or related hobbies:

_____

_____

Sponsor Name: *Frederick W. Korz*

Member #: *60650*

Enclose with remittance and send to: **NAWCC, Inc., 514 Poplar Street, Columbia, PA 17512–2130**

Ph: (717) 684-8261 • Fax: (717) 684-0878 • www.nawcc.org

Annual dues: U.S. New Members $60 (1st year), International $55.

Payment must be in U.S. funds drawn on a U.S. bank, by international money order, or with VISA, MasterCard, Discover, or American Express.

Cardholder's Name: _____

Credit Card #: _____

Exp. Date: _____ / _____

Amt. to be Charged to Credit Card: _____

Signature: _____

OLD STURBRIDGE VILLAGE
Sturbridge, MA 01566

THE SMITHSONIAN INSTITUTION
Washington, DC 20001

THE TIME MUSEUM
7801 East State St.
Rockford, IL 61101

Clock Supplies

The three major suppliers of clock material in America are

S. LAROSE, INC.
3223 Yanceyville St.
P.O. Box 21208
Greensboro, NC 27420
888-752-7673
orders@slarose.com
www.slarose.com

MERRITT'S ANTIQUES, INC.
1860 Weavertown Road
P.O. Box 277
Douglasville, PA 19518–0277
800-345-4101
www.merritts.com

TIMESAVERS
P.O. Box 12700
Scottsdale, AZ 85260
800-552-1520
info@timesavers.com
www.timesavers.com

All three firms publish extensive catalogs, offer excellent service, and are members of NAWCC.

There are numerous smaller suppliers whose services are best located through the pages of *The Mart*.

GLOSSARY

acanthus   A large, leafed plant of Mediterranean origin. Representations of this leaf have been used as architectural decoration since classical times. Used especially on the capitals of Corinthian columns.

acid etching   A method of decorating glass tablets. This method was developed to reduce clock manufacturing costs and is found in some American shelf clocks after 1840.

acorn clock   An American nineteenth-century shelf clock design. The cases were made from laminated wood which was steam-bent and formed into an inverted acorn shape. These cases and clocks were made by the Forrestville Manufacturing Company in ca. 1850 and are rather rare.

Act of Parliament clock   This name, derived from a 1797 Act of Parliament (repealed in 1798), is a misnomer which has been applied to an English "time-only," usually weight-driven clock having a large dial (unglazed) and a small trunk. Fable says that these clocks were put into inns and taverns for public use after people sold their clocks and watches to avoid the annual tax imposed by the 1797 law.

advertising clock   Mostly American clocks of the latter part of the nineteenth century whose dials and/or door panels bore the names and logos of various businesses. Beware of reproductions.

alarm   At a predetermined time, a mechanical attachment rings a bell or activates some other sound-making device. The device is found on many Connecticut shelf clocks of the nineteenth century. The existence of a brass disk numbered 1–12 surrounding the hand shafts in the center of the dial indicates an alarm.

alarm clock   Although alarm mechanisms as part of a clock have been known since the seventeenth century, a clock produced primarily as an alarm clock is the creation of the second half of the nineteenth century. The French produced one of the first commercially successful portable alarm clocks in about 1865. By the last quarter of the nineteenth century, first America and then Germany produced huge quantities of these small, inexpensive portable clocks.

amplitude   The distance that a pendulum bob moves as it swings.

anchor escapement   Invented about the middle of the seventeenth century in England and generally attributed to Dr. Robert Hooke, although some authorities claim William Clement as the inventor. Another name for a recoil escapement, it was utilized from the beginning in long-case clocks.

anniversary clock   See **400-day clock**

apparent time   Also known as solar time. Often referred to as the time shown on a sundial. Time based upon the rotation of the earth in relation to the sun.

apron   The decoration below the base of a clock. It can include the feet or be found between them.

Arabic numerals   The numerals found on a chapter ring or dial are shown either in Arabic (1, 2, 3, and so on) or Roman (I, II, III, and so on) form. When Roman numerals are used on clock dials, it is traditional to use IIII for the number 4 rather than IV. The presence of Arabic or Roman numerals has little bearing on dating a clock.

arbor   This is the shaft (axle) to which a pinion and a wheel are attached. A typical arbor would consist of a shaft with a pivot at each end, attached to which are a pinion at one end and toothed wheel at the other.

arch-top clock   Refers to any type of clock case where the arch rises directly from the sides. First appears in English and some Continental clocks around the end of the eighteenth century.

architectural-top clock   A clock case in which the top (a hood in a long-case clock and the top in a mantel clock) assumes the form of a classical pediment. These tops may or may not be supported by corresponding classical columns.

astronomical clock   A very precise clock that was used by astronomers. The clock mechanism shows not only the time but also sidereal time (time measured by successive transits of a star). Very complicated versions often showed the positions of planets, the day and month, the phases of the moon, the tides, time in other parts of the world; and so on. These clocks are far more likely to be English or Continental than American. They date from ca. seventeenth to late nineteenth century.

Atmos clock   Manufactured in Switzerland by the LeCoultre Company, this clock's movement is wound mostly by changes of temperature. The principle was invented by the Frenchman Jean-Léon Reutter in the first quarter of the twentieth century. As originally envisioned, the winding system was to use changes in atmospheric pressure, thus the name "Atmos." Today's versions use a change in temperature to wind the mainspring.

auto clock   Clocks designed to be mounted in the instrument panel of an automobile.

automaton   This type of clock covers a very wide range. These clocks, besides telling time, encompass and interact with other mechanisms that produce music, animate figures, open and close portals on the clock, and so on at a predetermined time and in a specific order. Automata first appear around the middle of the eighteenth century.

back plate   The rear plate of a clock movement. Most clock movements consist of two plates separated by pillars. Between these plates reside the barrels, gears, pinions, arbors, and so on which comprise the motion and striking trains of the clock.

balance spring   Often called a balance wheel, it consists of a circular spring which oscillates around its center and controls the speed at which a clock or watch runs.

balance staff   The arbor (shaft) on which the balance spring is fixed.

balloon clocks   "Balloon" refers to the shape of a waisted clock case resembling a hot air balloon that evolved in England around the middle of the eighteenth century. It was a mantle clock about 12 inches or so high. The case was often constructed of exotic woods such as mahogany, satinwood, or ebony. The French manufactured clocks in this shape during the last quarter of the nineteenth century. The English clocks are more valuable.

banding   A contrasting strip of veneer placed for decorative purposes around the perimeter of a door or panel on a clock case.

banjo clock   The popular name given to a clock type first invented and produced by Simon Willard of Massachusetts in the late eighteenth century. Willard patented this clock in 1802 as the "Improved Timepiece." The movement was a brass 8-day time-only with a 20–26" pendulum. Popular from the outset, the banjo clock was copied and modified by many makers in New England. Collectors should be aware of many copies, reproductions, and rebuilt banjo clocks that have had the Willard name added to increase their salability. By the 1840s, Edward Howard's plain style banjo clock came to dominate the market. Twentieth-century banjo clocks by major manufacturers such as Sessions are quite common.

barrel   The cylindrical container that holds the mainspring in a clock. This arrangement to contain the mainspring is more often found in European clocks. Most American clocks made before the twentieth century had unenclosed springs. "Barrel" may also refer to the drum upon which the weight line is wound; this usage is generally British.

barrel arbor   The shaft within the barrel around which the spring is wound.

barrel hook   The projection on the inside wall of the barrel to which one end of the spring is attached.

base   The bottom of a column. "Base" is sometimes used to identify the bottom portion of a long-case (grandfather) clock. See **plinth**.

basket-top clock   Most often a bracket clock that has a pierced ormolu top. This shape/style first appeared in England in the middle of the seventeenth century.

battery clock   Any electrically-powered clock whose power comes from a battery. Electric-battery-powered clocks appeared as early as the 1840s. They were not commercially important until the twentieth century. They are found everywhere today in the form of quartz movements.

bearing   Support for the pivot or arbor where it passes through the plate. At various times, the bearing has been made from brass, wood, ivory, and jewels.

beat   The sound made by the teeth of the escape wheel as they strike the pallets of the escapement with each swing of the pendulum. More commonly known as the "tick-tock." When a clock is said to be "in beat," the intervals between the "tick" and the "tock" are even.

beehive clock   A nineteenth-century Connecticut shelf clock that was thought to resemble the shape of the traditional straw coil beehive. These were the first mass-produced American clocks with coil springs. Sometimes also called a flatiron clock because of its shape. The actual shape of the clock is closer to a Gothic arch.

bell-top clock   The top of a clock (either a bracket/mantel or tall-case clock) that resembles a handbell. Appears in both England and Holland toward the end of the seventeenth century.

bench key   A circular arrangement of various sized clock keys used by the clockmaker or repairman as a "master set" to eliminate many separate keys.

bezel   A ring, usually metal (brass), which surrounds the dial and holds the glass.

bim-bam clock   A clock whose striking mechanism hits two bells or gongs or rods successively for each hour. Very often this same movement will differentiate the half-hour from the hour by striking only one bell, gong, or rod.

birdcage clock   A clock base upon which is fixed a birdcage containing a mechanical bird. On the hour these mechanical birds flutter their wings, turn their heads, revolve, all accompanied by a whistled melody. First appeared on the Continent during the last quarter of the eighteenth century.

Black Forest clock   Generic term used for clocks and movements produced in the Black Forest region of southwestern Germany. Their history extends from the seventeenth century. Traditionally, the movements, dials, cases, hands, and so on were produced as piecework by the region's farmers during the winter. The early weight-driven movements are an interesting mix of wooden plates and arbors combined with metal wheels and pinions. Often the strike mechanism is coupled with bellows and reeds which produce the sounds of birds (cuckoo), musical instruments, and drums and cymbals. The most famous of these clocks is the cuckoo clock. More recently the term has been used to include the many far more sophisticated clocks produced by major German manufacturers, such as Junghans, Lenzkirch, Hamburg American, and others whose businesses were located in the region.

black mantel clock   American mantel clocks produced ca. 1880 to 1910; so called because their cases were designed to resemble the black marble or slate cases that had become such an important import from Europe. American companies competed by producing their own wooden, iron, and marble black-cased clocks. Large numbers of these clocks can still be found in yard sales, antiques shops, and auctions. Most often they are 8-day spring-driven clocks that strike a wire gong on the hour and half hour.

blinking-eye clock   A clock whose case is in the form of an animal or human. The eyes of the figure are attached to the escapement so they move in conjunction with the pendulum. First appeared in Germany in the seventeenth or eighteenth century. Produced as novelty clocks in nineteenth-century America and Germany. Numerous reproductions exist, and the collector should take care to establish the authenticity of any such clock before purchasing.

bluing   The process of coloring clock parts, almost always the hands, by heat and/or chemical means to obtain a blue-black color.

bob   The weight at the bottom of the pendulum rod. The raising or lowering of this weight causes the clock to run faster or slower.

boss   A round or oval metal disk on a dial that generally contains the name of the clock's maker.

boudoir clock   A European term referring to a type of small clock, often with a folding case, that appeared around the middle of the nineteenth century. The cases were usually highly decorated and frequently designed and used as traveling clocks.

Boulle clock   A mantel, wall, or table clock whose case was veneered in tortoiseshell with brass inlay and date from ca. 1650 to 1730. These clocks were produced in the style of the great seventeenth-century French cabinetmaker Charles Andre Boulle. "Buhl" is a variation of Boulle.

box case   Term used to describe Eli Terry's earliest mass-produced woodenworks shelf clock case. This clock became the prototype of his far more famous pillar and scroll clock.

box chronometer   A very precise clock which was essential to a ship's navigation. With the use of clocks such as these the navigator could establish Greenwich Mean Time and with the aid of a sextant the ship's position. The earliest of these marine clocks appear in the second half of the eighteenth century. By the last quarter of the eighteenth century it became common to box these chronometers with the clock mounted on gimbals. Collectors should approach buying marine chronometers with caution and only with an expert's advice as many clocks called chronometers are not true chronometers.

box-on-box   Antiquated name for a Massachusetts shelf clock.

bracket clock   The name is supposedly derived from the fact that the earliest versions were made to sit on brackets. However, the literature and the clocks themselves show little evidence that they ever sat on brackets. Instead, these are more correctly called table clocks. They first appeared in England and Holland around the middle of the seventeenth century and became quite popular as they could be moved from room to room. This type of clock is still made. At the peak of their popularity in the first half of the eighteenth century, their movements and casework reflected the finest workmanship of the period. Victorian reproductions of these clocks exist and can be excellent buys. Twentieth-century reproductions do not approach the workmanship of the originals or their Victorian counterparts.

break-arch clock   Similar to the arch-top clock, but the arch is broken on each side by a horizontal step. This architectural feature appears on clocks in the last quarter of the eighteenth century. Also known as a broken-arch clock.

Brocot clock   Named after Achille Brocot (1817–78), a Parisian clockmaker who invented the pin pallet escapement for pendulum clocks and a form of pendulum suspension that can be adjusted or regulated from the clock's face.

(This is most frequently found on French clocks of the second half of the nineteenth century.) Brocot also developed a visible escapement that was found on many movements imported into the United States.

Brocot escapement   This is a form of the **deadbeat escapement** invented by Achille Brocot in about 1850 (see **Brocot clock**). It was very popular with French clockmakers from the 1860s until the end of the century.

bronze looking-glass clock   American shelf clock created and produced by Chauncey Jerome of Connecticut, ca. 1830. Jerome produced this case design in competition with Eli Terry's extremely popular pillar and scroll case. It consisted of a rectangular box topped by a bronze powder–stenciled splat, bronze powder–stenciled half columns flanking the door, and a mirror in place of the painted glass tablet in the lower section of the door. This clock case almost always housed either a 30-hour or 8-day wooden movement driven by cast iron weights. This clock made a fortune for Chauncey Jerome because it could be produced and sold for less than the pillar and scroll, plus it coincided with the fashion for stenciling furniture (especially chairs).

bushing   When a pivot hole has worn to the point of affecting a movement's operation, it is drilled out and the hole filled with a predrilled bushing, a metal lining for decreasing the diameter of a hole. The predrilled hole in the bushing is then enlarged to receive the pivot. As this procedure is labor intensive and costly, clocks and their movements should be inspected carefully before being purchased.

calendar movement   Any clock movement that not only tells the time but also indicates the day, month, or year. They have been made almost from the beginning of clockmaking. In mass-produced mechanical movements, they reached their heyday in America in the second half of the nineteenth century. There has been a further resurgence of popularity with the arrival of the quartz or electronic movement.

cam   An irregularly shaped rotating part of a clock mechanism that gives a special motion to anything resting on the cam (interconnected wheels and pinions that control the clock's strike). Most commonly found in certain strike trains.

cam follower   The arm that follows the shape of the cam (see **cam**). Found in strike trains using a rack-and-snail escapement.

camelback clock   A common name for the mantel clock that is also known as a tambour or Napoleon's hat clock. Possibly the most commonly encountered clock. The basic form appeared in the second half of the nineteenth century, and it achieved its present form during the first half of the twentieth century.

candle clock A medieval method of timekeeping. A candle was divided by notching into a fixed number of divisions of equal size. As the candle burned down, a crude record was kept of the passage of time. This was a device to use during the night hours when the sundial was unusable.

cannon pinion The hollow pinion that fits over the center wheel shaft and to which the minute hand is fitted.

capital The topmost part of an architectural column. Usually carved or molded with decoration. Very often used on clocks of classical design. The hoods of many tall-case clocks utilize architectural columns with ornate capitals.

carriage clock This small portable table/desk clock is forever associated with France, although it was also made in England and America as well as in France. Appearing in the mid-nineteenth century, it seems to have evolved from the French Pendule d'Officier desk clock. It was made in very large numbers well into the 1920s. Quartz-driven versions are still being made. The original clock consisted of a spring-driven drive train regulated by a platform escapement. This brass plate movement with its porcelain dial was housed in a five-sided glass and brass case with a carrying handle on top. Carriage clocks were made as simple timepieces at first, but evolved to include alarms, strike trains (once on the half hour and the number of hours on the hour), repeaters (repeated the previous hour), quarter strike (petite sonnerie), full strike (grande sonnerie where the clock struck the quarters plus the full hour on each quarter), etc. Most of these clocks demonstrate the fine craftsmanship of the French clockmaking industry.

cartel clock An elongated wall clock appearing in France around the second quarter of the eighteenth century. The case is most often a Baroque design made of fire-gilded bronze (ormolu). The value of these clocks is most often determined by the quality of the case. Although they appeared throughout most of the eighteenth century, they were abundantly reproduced in the last quarter of the nineteenth century.

cartouche The term used to denote a decorative panel, usually containing an inscription, found on a clock face or dial.

carved column and splat clock In an attempt to compete with the popular Jerome bronze-stenciled half column and splat mantel clocks, George Mitchell of Connecticut produced a similarly shaped mantel clock with carved splat and half columns in about 1830. These carved column clocks usually command a higher price than do the stenciled clocks, even though they generally have similar wooden movements and dials.

case-on-case clock Another name for the Massachusetts shelf clock of the late eighteenth to early nineteenth century.

center seconds A clock that has its second hand on the same arbor as the hour and minute hands.

center wheel The second wheel or gear of the time train that rotates once per hour.

chaise clock This is a clock that looks like a very large watch. It could be carried in a large pocket or in a chaise (coach), hence their name. Also known as a coach or goliath clock in Europe. First produced in the eighteenth century and made until the nineteenth century, their value depends upon the quality of the movement and casework. Rare.

chamber or **domestic clock** Along with the Gothic clock, these iron-framed, uncased, weight-driven clocks were the first house clocks, appearing in the fifteenth century. Having only an hour hand and regulated by a foliot escapement, these clocks were notoriously inaccurate. However, they hold the distinction of being the common ancestors of all Western clocks. Original clocks command very high prices when they come up for sale. Many later copies of these clocks can be found.

chamfer-top clock An architectural term referring to a clock case whose top is constructed in beveled or chamfered steps. A style that was introduced in England in about 1815. Most often seen on smaller mantel clocks. Variations of this design would be revived in American clocks in the latter part of the nineteenth century.

chapter ring The ring on the dial upon which the numerals or "chapters" are painted or engraved.

chapters The hour numerals on the dial.

Chelsea clock Clocks made by the Chelsea Clock Company of Massachusetts. Although the company made a wide range of clocks, the ship's bell clock is best known. These high-grade clocks were supplied to the United States Navy and Weather Service for many years. The movements are time and strike with platform escapements, and each clock is numbered in series.

chiming clock Traditionally a clock that chimes on the quarters and the half hour as well as striking the hour. Originally, chiming meant only striking the melody on bells. Today chiming clocks strike bells, tubes, wires, and gongs. Among the most familiar of this category of clock are those that produce the Westminster melody.

china clock Clock type that married the mass-produced American clock movement with mass-produced china or porcelain clock cases primarily made in Germany. Extremely popular at the turn of the twentieth century. Do not buy if the case shows any damage.

chinoiserie "In the style of the Chinese" is the literal meaning of this term. It is used to describe the case and some dial decoration that first appeared in the seventeenth century. Case makers attempted to imitate the Oriental lacquered furniture that was imported primarily from China. Unable to duplicate the multilayered lacquer surfaces of the Orient, European craftsmen produced a facsimile using plaster, glue, varnishes, and shellac. The ground was most often red although other color grounds are known (black, blue, and green being the most frequently used alternatives). Upon the ground, imitation Chinese motifs were drawn (most often in gold or black). Longcase and bracket clocks were the usual recipients of this style of decoration. Chinoiserie decoration did not hold up well and was subject to much cracking and flaking. Another form of chinoiserie may sometimes be found in the china and porcelain cased clocks of Europe.

circa Latin term meaning "about." Used to indicate an approximate date. Can be abbreviated as c., ca., cir., circ., or C.

clepsydra clock From the Greek meaning "water stealer or thief." Name given to the famous water clocks of ancient Greece and Rome. A mechanical device to measure time by the steady flow of water through a small hole. Tradition holds that they were developed in ancient Athens for use in the Agora to limit the time allotted to public speakers. They were never accurate.

click A pawl that keeps the ratchet wheel from moving backwards. The name comes from the sound made when the clock is wound. Also known in the United Kingdom as "clickwork."

clickwork See click

clock A timepiece. A device for measuring time usually utilizing pointers that move around a dial. Different from a watch in that it is not meant to be carried on one's person.

cock The bridge or bracket that supports the pendulum of a clock.

collet The brass collar used to fit a wheel to its arbor. More commonly it is used to identify the dome-shaped washer (also called a hands collet) that secures the hands of a clock.

column A vertical circular shaft usually with a capital at the top and a base at the bottom. An architectural feature on many clock cases. Some are incorporated into the case itself and some are freestanding. Most often found at the corners of cases.

column clock   A style of clock that was most common in France starting in the eighteenth century and continuing into the nineteenth century. They appear to have started as bracket clocks with short pendulums and become pedestals as clocks became more a part of a room's decoration. Eventually the pedestal and clock became one and the long pendulum was hidden within the column. Some column clocks were constructed with a glass door showing the working pendulum. These last column clocks are sometimes mistakenly referred to as French grandfather clocks.

compensated balance   A balance spring or wheel that corrects for the effects of heat and cold upon its operation. This is most commonly achieved by constructing the balance from two different metals.

compensating pendulum   Heat and cold affect the length of a pendulum. When it is hot, the pendulum rod expands (lengthens) and the clock runs slower. The reverse occurs when it is cold. To keep the clock accurate required a pendulum of constant length. This was achieved by constructing a pendulum that compensated for changes in temperature. Most often this was done by constructing the pendulum from a combination of metals, often iron, brass, and mercury, that expanded and contracted at different rates.

Congreve clock   A form of novelty clock invented in the early nineteenth century by William Congreve of the Woolrich Arsenal in England. A steel ball rolls down a zigzag-shaped grooved inclined plate until the ball strikes a lever that causes the inclined plate to tilt in the opposite direction. This continues until the spring that provides the motive power to tilt the plane runs down (usually eight days). Each time the plane tilts a rod connected to the plane and the timepiece mounted above advances the clock hands a fixed amount of time (usually a minute). For a variety of reasons, these clocks are not accurate, but they are great fun to watch in operation.

contrate wheel   A wheel or gear in the teeth is at right angles to the plane of the wheel. This type of gear is used to transmit motion at a right angle.

cornice   The top horizontal molding of a clock case.

cornucopia   The classical "horn of plenty"—a cone out of which tumbles all manner of riches. This motif was frequently used in clock case and dial decoration from the seventeenth to the nineteenth century.

cottage clock   Small, inexpensive mantel clocks of 30-hour or 8-day duration first made in Connecticut in the second half of the nineteenth century.

The movements were spring-powered and very often time-only. By the last decades of the nineteenth century, their manufacture had spread to the German clock factories of the Black Forest region that penetrated the American and world markets with their cheaper versions of the cottage clock.

count wheel   A wheel with a series of notches spaced at increasing intervals, also known as a locking plate or locking wheel. When the strike train is released on the hour, a detent is raised and the clock strikes. The detent rides the wheel until a notch is reached; then it drops into the notch and the strike train stops. This was a feature of virtually all 30-hour long-case clocks built in the United States and in the British Isles and a common feature of most of Connecticut clocks with a striking mechanism produced during the nineteenth century.

Crane clock   Aaron Dodd Crane, a nineteenth-century New Jersey inventor and clockmaker, experimented with pendulum design. He developed a rotary pendulum (also known as a torsion pendulum). Its weight consists of a group of balls that rotated, twisting the thin steel of the rod. When the twist reached its maximum, the weights stopped and they begin to rotate in the opposite direction. The motive power of these movements allowed them to run for a year at a winding. These clocks never became very popular and consequently are rare. They are not to be confused with the ubiquitous German 400-day or "anniversary clocks" whose pendulums look like the Crane pendulum but operate on a different principle.

cresting   The carved decoration above the cornice of a clock case. A common feature of long-case clocks.

cross banding   Cross cut or cross-grained veneer used as decoration on a clock case.

cross cut   Wood that has been cut across the grain. Cross-cut wood was glued to a wood backing whose grain ran at right angles to the cross-grain; often used for and moldings. Vertical grain moldings were a common feature of many English seventeenth-century tall-case clocks.

crown wheel   The escape wheel of a verge escapement. So called because the teeth of the wheel are at right angles to its spokes.

crown wheel escapement   See **verge escapement**

crutch   The part of the clock movement that is attached to the pallet arbor. It encompasses, via a fork or loop, the pendulum and imparts the clock's power to it.

crystal regulator   A French clock housed in a case with glass on all sides. Appeared during the 1880s. Usually contained a good movement with a compensated pendulum and visible escapement. Many were imported to America by jewelry firms such as Tiffany & Co. Some were manufactured by American makers such as Waterbury, but their quality was generally not so fine as the French imports. See **French four glass regulator.**

cuckoo clock   The most famous of the many Black Forest–style clocks. Attributed to Anton Ketterer of Schonwald, Germany, during the first half of the eighteenth century. Produced in huge numbers from the second half of the nineteenth century until the present. The weight-driven movement strikes the hour and half hour on a wire gong. At the hour a door at the top of the case opens and a model of a cuckoo appears accompanied by the sound of the cuckoo produced by bellows and reeds.

cylinder escapement   Sometimes called a horizontal escapement. This movement was an English invention of the seventeenth century. It was adopted for use in watches during the eighteenth century. In the nineteenth century, it was adopted for use in cheap clocks. The lever escapement replaced it in the latter part of the nineteenth century.

deadbeat escapement   This is an improved version of the anchor escapement and was invented by George Graham of England in about 1715. It has greater accuracy than the anchor escapement because there is virtually no recoil imparted to the escape wheel. Usually found on true regulator and high-precision clocks.

depth   The technical term used to describe the amount of penetration between two meshing gears.

detent   A locking device. Very often an arm that acts as a stop or a click (pawl) on a ratchet wheel that allows motion in only one direction. See also **count wheel.**

dial   The face of a clock containing a circle (chapter ring) that is divided into hours, minutes, and, rarely, seconds. The style, construction, materials, and decoration of the dial often reflect the age that produced it and allows one to date the clock.

dial clock   These are almost always English clocks that were made for offices or public spaces. They are timepieces (time-only) generally with well-made fusee movements. English dial clocks have a reputation for durability and are most often housed in oak cases. By the end of the nineteenth century, the Germans began to manufacture a spring-driven version that is inferior in construction to the English clocks. The collector should be careful to inspect the movement as some German manufacturers put English names on their dials.

dial pillar   The pillars (columns) that allow the dial to be attached to the front plate of a movement.

double-basket-top clock   Very similar to the basket-top clock (see above), but having a smaller inverted basket on top. First appeared in England and Holland around the mid-eighteenth century.

double-decker   A Connecticut shelf clock design that gives the impression of a two-section clock. Often used in the 1830s on carved and stenciled column and splat clocks.

drop   The distance traveled by the escape wheel between escape and lock or from pallet to pallet.

drop dial   A dial clock with an extended lower part of the case to allow a longer pendulum. Another extremely popular clock that was made in large numbers from the last quarter of the nineteenth century through the first quarter of the twentieth. Made in England, Germany, and America. In America, this clock is often referred to as a "schoolhouse clock," as thousands of them decorated the walls of classrooms. With the expansion of rural electrification in the 1930s and 1940s, these clocks were replaced and production waned.

drum   The cylinder or barrel upon which the gut, cord, or cable of a weight-driven movement is wound.

drum clock   This term refers to a clock whose movement is fitted into a brass cylinder. The cylinder is then inserted into an outer case of some other material, often china.

dummy winders   These are imitation winding squares that were painted on 30-hour weight-driven long-case clock dials to mimic the appearance of 8-day longcase clocks. They first appeared in the third quarter of the eighteenth century on the "white dials" of English and American long-case clocks and on painted wooden dials in both America and Germany.

Dutch clocks   Common term used to refer generically to all Dutch clocks made in Friesland and Zaandam.

8-day movement   It has been common practice during the last three centuries for clockmakers to produce two main movements: a movement with sufficient motive power to run for 8 days and a movement with sufficient motive power for 30 hours. In America, these became our two standard types of movement from the eighteenth century through the first quarter of the twentieth century. This was a logical development of the U.S. clockmaking industry, which had grown from British roots. English clockmakers had been making these movements for generations. French makers tended to concentrate on 8-day movements although many of these "8-day movements" ran for 14 days or more. German makers made movements of many different durations. The 8-day movements required a slightly different gearing arrangement and therefore cost more to manufacture. The customer paid more for an 8-day clock than for one running 30 hours.

electric clocks   Simply, a clock driven and/or controlled by electricity. The electric power may be supplied either by cord and plug or by battery.

Empire clocks   In America, "Empire clocks" refer to the case designs produced ca. 1830 to 1850. These cases reflect the furniture styles of the period. As such, they often have stenciled decorations on their columns, splats, and lower door panels. Others have carved columns and splats abounding with acanthus leaves and other motifs that were common on the furniture. Many of these clocks were the 30-hour wooden-works shelf clocks produced so prolifically in Connecticut at the time. In Europe, this term referred to French clocks produced ca. 1790 to 1820. These were high-quality clocks housed for the most part in wonderful figural ormolu cases depicting all manner of motifs from the classical to the patriotica. French Empire clocks would become the roots of the figural clocks that follow throughout the nineteenth century.

endless cord   The term used to describe Huygens's invention of maintaining power in a clock by suspending the weight from an continuous cord or chain. Most commonly encountered on British 30-hour tall-case clock movements.

engine clock   Term used to describe a clock that incorporates some miniaturized form of industrial equipment or machinery; also known as an industrial clock. Often this included steam engines, locomotives, lighthouses, drop forges, and the like. Some of these clocks were produced as early as the 1850s in America and England. However, they reached the pinnacle of their development in France during the 1880s in the wonderful "French industry series" produced by Guilmet. These clocks usually included an 8-day movement, barometer, and thermometer. A second spring provided power for the miniature machinery. These clocks are scarce and bring high prices.

English Regulator clock   These were weight-driven tall-case clocks with a deadbeat escapement and a compensated pendulum. These clocks were exceedingly accurate and their dials often indicated far more than just the time. Similar clocks were made on both sides of the Atlantic and were the most accurate timekeepers known until the twentieth century. The term "Regulator" indicated accuracy in the public's mind. However, the name was increasingly attached to mass-produced clocks in the last half of the nineteenth century, and "Regulator" quickly lost its significance.

equation of time   This is the difference between time shown on the sundial (solar time) and time shown by a clock (mean time). This difference can be as much as 16 minutes. Solar and mean time coincide four times a year—December 25, April 15, June 14, and August 31.

escape wheel   The final wheel or gear of the time train of a clock. This wheel imparts the impulse to the pendulum. In the British Isles, it is referred to as the scape wheel.

escapement   The mechanism that momentarily stops the motion of a clock and sends the motive power of that movement to the pendulum or balance. The major types of escapements are: (1) anchor escapement, (2) cylinder escapement, (3) deadbeat escapement, (4) verge escapement, (5) lever escapement, and (6) pin-pallet escapement. (See individual entries.)

escutcheon   The decorative hardware surrounding a keyhole, usually brass, but can be found made from wood, bone, or ivory.

false plate   The iron bracket required to attach a "white" or painted iron dial to the movement. It first appeared in the mid-eighteenth century. British and American tall-case clocks appearing around the same time used the same type of movements, and by the 1780s, American makers were often buying English painted dials, their false plates, and rough-cast clock components.

finial   Decorative ornaments found at the top of various styles of clock cases, especially tall-case clocks. They can be of metal or wood, and can be cast, carved, or turned. They are found in a multitude of shapes—balls, cones, flames, acorns, pineapples, and so on.

first wheel   Also called the "great wheel," it is the first gear of a clock train. This is the gear that provides power to the rest of the train as it is attached to the barrel or drum that contains the wound spring or weight.

flambeau finial   A finial in the form of a flame.

flat ogee   An American clock case of the first half of the nineteenth century that resembles an ogee case. The difference: the front molding is flat.

fleur-de-lis   A stylized form of the flower of the lily. Much used in heraldry and on the royal arms of France. Used on some dials to indicate the half hour. Often seen on eighteenth-century dials.

floating balance clock   An inexpensive alternative to the platform lever escapement. A mid-twentieth-century German invention with a suspended balance designed to be a pendulum replacement for short pendulum movements. These clocks can be moved without affecting their accuracy and they do not have to be completely level to run. Frequently used by manufacturers such as Hermele.

fluting   Vertical grooves separated by sharp ridges found on columns and pilasters. Part of the architectural decoration found on many clock cases.

fly   A rotating vane on the final arbor of the strike train that regulates the speed of the strike.

foliot   One of the earliest controllers in a mechanical clock. A bar balance used with verge escapements on very early clocks. Seen on fifteenth-century clocks. Regulation of this escapement was by moving weights attached to ends of the foliot and was very inaccurate. It is occasionally seen today in some replica clocks.

fountain clock   Also called a waterfall clock. Most often French clocks dating from the mid-nineteenth century. The case contains two movements—the spring-driven clock movement and another spring-driven movement to rotate a twisted glass rod. The case depicts a fountain, spring, or waterfall and the twisted glass rod represents water. The rotation of this glass rod furnishes the illusion of moving water. See **automaton**.

400-day clock   Also known as an "anniversary" or "torsion" clock. The invention of this clock is attributed to Anton Harder in about 1880 in Germany. The movement is meant to run for a year on a single winding. The movement has an anchor escapement with a torsion pendulum. The pendulum "rod" is a strip of wire with a circular disk or a group of decorative globes as a "bob." The pendulum twists, and the bob rotates first in one direction and then in the opposite direction. See **Atmos clock** and **Crane clock**. Countless numbers of these clocks have been manufactured and they are still being manufactured today with battery-powered quartz movements. They have little collectible value except for the earliest models.

fourth wheel   The fourth wheel or gear in a train of gears. It rotates once a minute.

French four glass regulator   Usually called a "crystal regulator." These French clocks are, in one sense, large versions of the carriage clock (see above) with a pendulum rather than a platform escapement. Often outfitted with outside Brocot escapements and compensated pendulums, these clocks are well made and accurate timekeepers. Appearing in about 1860, they reached the peak of their popularity in the 1890s. There are American versions of this clock. See **crystal regulator**.

Friesland clocks   Dutch wall clocks made in the Friesland region of Holland. First appearing in the early part of the eighteenth century, they are characterized by very elaborate ornamentation. The movement is weight-driven. Many contemporary reproductions exist. See **Zaanse clocks.**

front plate   The movement plate just behind the dial of a plate framed clock movement.

front wind   Any clock that is wound from the front instead of the rear.

fusee   A conical pulley with a spiral groove for a chain (the fusee chain) that was attached to a mainspring. The purpose of this arrangement is to compensate for the reduction of power produced by the mainspring as it unwinds. The fusee guarantees a constant torque to the wheel (gear) train. The principle and the fusee pulley have been known since the fifteenth century. More commonly found on English clocks than on American.

gallery clock   A large round wall clock that began life on the walls of public institutions such as banks, railway stations, libraries, and the like. See **railway clocks.**

gathering pallet   Part of a rack-and-snail striking mechanism. The gathering pallet advances the "rack" one tooth for each strike of the clock. At the end of the rack, the strike mechanism locks.

gesso   A form of plaster of Paris that is used on some wood clock surfaces to prepare a ground for painting.

gilding   Refers to either the process of electrically or chemically plating metal with a thin film of gold or the mechanical process of applying thin gold sheets to a prepared wood or glass surface. Considered to be an indication of a "better" clock. Much used on Continental clocks, especially French. American clockmakers often used "bronze stenciling" or "gold" paint (really brass) to imitate the more expensive gold.

gingerbread   Common name given to the very ornate kitchen clocks produced in America between 1890 and 1910.

girandole clock   American wall clock designed by Lemuel Curtis in about 1815. The construction of the case and movement are similar to the banjo clock. The major difference between the Curtis and Willard clocks is the shape of the bottom of the case. The Willard banjo clocks terminate in a box shape while the Curtis clocks terminate in a round shape. As the round shape of the Curtis clocks resembled the framed round mirrors known as Girandoles, that were fashionable during this Federal period, the name stuck. This is a rare clock, and collectors should be aware that many fine reproductions can be encountered.

going barrel   Mainspring barrel (cylinder that contains the mainspring) that incorporates the first (great) wheel.

going train   The set of wheels (gears) that drives the hands of the clock. In a striking clock and America this is called the time train.

gold leaf   See **gilding**

gong   Hardened and tempered wire wound in the shape of a flattened spiral that replaced the traditional bell for striking the hours on many clocks. Appeared in the latter part of the eighteenth century. Very common on American clocks from the 1830s on.

Gothic clock   (1) A specific style of early domestic clock made in Europe from about 1450 to 1600. This early type of clock was built of iron and was meant to hang on a wall or sit on a bracket. They were weight-driven and the earliest examples have foliot escapements. They are called Gothic clocks after the age in which they were produced. (2) Other Gothic clocks whose cases reflected in various ways the pointed top shape of the Gothic arch. Most of these clocks were shelf clocks and American in manufacture. The American clocks took advantage of the inexpensive brass spring-driven movements first introduced by Chauncey Jerome in the 1850s. Among the most popular of these clocks was the **steeple clock**.

Graham pendulum   A compensated pendulum invented by George Graham during the first quarter of the eighteenth century and also called the mercury pendulum. The bob consists of a glass or metal cylinder filled with measured quantity of mercury. As the rod lengthens in the heat, the mercury expands upwards compensating for changes in rod length. See **compensating pendulum**.

grande sonnerie   In French, the big or full strike. The French term today refers to a pattern of striking bells or gongs. The clock strikes the quarter followed immediately by striking the previous hour. Multiple bells or gongs are used so the listener can distinguish the quarter from the hour. Many nineteenth-century French carriage clocks incorporated this feature.

grandfather clock   More properly known as a long-case or tall-case clock, these came into existence shortly after the invention of the anchor escapement (1670s) allowed the enclosing of pendulum and weights within a case.

The term "grandfather clock" is American and derives from a popular song of the 1870s—"My Grandfather's Clock."

grandmother clock A shorter version of a tall-case or "grandfather" clock.

gravity clock A clock that relies upon its own weight to drive the going train as it has no mainspring. Very often these clocks were made in Germany and are considered to be novelty clocks. Also known as rack clocks, they were made in America by companies such as Ansonia. They appeared around the beginning of the twentieth century and were never considered accurate or well-made.

great wheel The first wheel (gear) in a train.

Greenwich time The local mean time at Greenwich, England, used as a basis for the calculation of longitude.

gridiron pendulum Invented by John Harrison of Yorkshire, England, in about 1725, it is another form of the compensated pendulum. The gridiron pendulum is constructed of alternating rods of steel and brass. The two different coefficients of expansion tend to cancel each other out, maintaining the accuracy of the pendulum.

groaner movement A 30-hour wooden-works movement invented by Chauncey Boardman of Connecticut (ca. 1827) to circumvent the Terry wooden-works movement patent. Boardman's movement struck a bell mounted on the top of the movement. The sound of the wooden gears meshing gained this clock the nickname of "groaner."

gut line Weight-driven clocks have their weights suspended by lines that are wound around barrels or drums. In earlier days, weights were suspended by woven wire cable or gut cable, fashioned from animal intestines. Later, lines were fashioned from woven cotton or linen. By the mid-twentieth century, braided synthetics, such as nylon, replaced earlier materials, such as gut.

hairspring The fine spring that regulates the balance wheel.

hammer That part of the strike train that hits the bell, gong, rod, and so on.

hands The pointers of a clock.

hollow column clock Rare Connecticut weight-driven shelf clocks introduced in about 1830. Their cases had full columns made of wood or tin which were hollow. The weights, driving the movement, descended within these columns.

hood   The top portion of a long-case clock that is removable to allow access to the dial and movement.

hood, rising   The earliest form of a tall-case hood, dating from the seventeenth century. The hoods had no door, just fixed glass, and to gain access to the dial and movement, the hoods had to be lifted off. Later hoods had both a glazed door and slid forward.

hoop wheel   That wheel (gear) of the strike train that has detents affixed at right angles. Regularly spaced, the detents regulate the striking hammer.

horology   The study and measurement of time and those instruments we commonly call clocks and watches.

hourglass clock   A rare Connecticut shelf clock form introduced by Joseph Ives circa 1840. Like the acorn case, the hourglass case was constructed from steam-bent laminated wood and shaped like an hourglass. It was powered by Ives wagon springs. This is a rare clock.

impulse face   That part of the escapement which receives an impulse from the escape wheel.

inclined plane clock   Invented at the end of the seventeenth century, this is essentially a weight-driven drum clock whose weight, seeking the low point, drives the clock slowly down an inclined plane. When the mechanism reaches the bottom, it is lifted and moved back to the top. Examples from the seventeenth and eighteenth centuries are rare. Modern versions are worth far less. Essentially, these clocks fall into the category of novelty clocks.

inside-outside escapement   This is a purely American term that describes an escapement used by Eli Terry in some of his pillar and scroll clocks. The escapement is directly behind the dial (inside) and directly outside the front plate.

inverted bell-top clock   The shape of the top of a clock that appears in the first quarter of the eighteenth century. Found on both tall-case and bracket clocks England and on some French clocks.

iron-front clocks   Connecticut shelf clocks of the mid-nineteenth century. The face (front) of these clocks were cast from iron. The movement was housed in a wooden box fastened to the reverse of the iron front. One of the most prolific of manufacturers of these cast iron fronts was Müller (Mueller) and Sons of New York City.

Japanese lantern clock   Before the Meiji period began in 1868, the Japanese had developed their own unique clockmaking industry. By the 1870s, traditional Japanese clocks and methods of telling time were being replaced by Western clocks and calendars. The traditional Japanese clock came in two forms—the lantern clock and the pillar clock. The original Japanese lantern clock resembles its European counterpart and undoubtedly owes much to early European clocks that entered Japan with those few European merchants who were allowed to trade in Japan prior to Perry's visit in the 1850s. These clocks were of 6-hour duration and had no hands; instead, the dial (which had the hour zones engraved on it) rotated and a fixed pointer indicated the hour zone. The clocks were weight-driven with foliot balance wheel escapements. These clocks are rare.

Japanese pillar clock   The Japanese pillar clock resembles a vertically oriented rectangular box with a vertical dial making up the front of the clock. The dial resembles a thermometer with the hour marks replacing the degree marks. Time is indicated by a pointer mounted on a slide which in turn is connected to the time train (gears). As the length of the Japanese hour varied during the year, the hour marks' positions can be altered. Very often these clocks are spring-driven. These clocks are scarce and went out of production with the adoption of Western timekeeping and clock technology after 1860.

japanning   The European term for the Oriental, and specifically Japanese, art of applying multiple layers of lacquer to wood in order to provide a ground for decoration. This form of decoration was highly prized in the West. During the seventeenth and eighteenth centuries, Western craftsmen attempted to imitate this work. On a few documented rare occasions, British clock cases were actually shipped to the Orient to be japanned. See **chinoiserie.**

jewels   Bearings originally made from precious stones such as rubies. Today these jewels are made synthetically. More commonly found in watch movements, they can be found in platform escapements and some very small clocks.

kidney dial   The dials of Massachusetts shelf clocks, ca. 1790–1800, often had a very distinctive opening that resembled the shape of a kidney or kidney bean.

labels   A paper label identifying the manufacturer of a clock and often including useful information, such as how to maintain and regulate the movement. They seem to be a curiously American invention, appearing on some of the tall-case clocks produced around 1800 to 1810. They were virtually universal in the cases of American shelf clocks from the beginning, but were never a feature of European clocks until the latter part of the nineteenth century, when they began to appear in the cases of German clocks. This is understandable, as the German firms entered mass production and the world market by imitating American clock styles. It is possible that the idea evolved from the English watchmaker's tradition of placing an engraved or lithographed disk of paper inside the back of a watch when it was repaired. Labels are of major importance in identifying clocks.

ladder movement   American brass spring-driven 1-day shelf clock movements invented by Silas B. Terry. They were so called because the gear train was positioned between the plates so each wheel was almost directly over the one below it.

lamp clock   A nonmechanical form of timekeeping whose origin is lost in the late Middle Ages; essentially, a glass or horn reservoir that has the hours painted or engraved vertically on the side. The reservoir is filled with oil and a wick is added. As the wick burns, the oil level lowers. One reads the time by comparing the oil level with the hour scale on the side. This type of clock was obviously used most often during the night.

lancet-top clock   Clock case design first appearing at the end of the eighteenth century in England. It is a case whose shape resembles a Gothic arch. The name derives originally from the shape of the head of a lance, but by the time of these case designs, the shape more clearly resembles the familiar medical scalpel.

lantern clock   In England the Gothic clock of the sixteenth century evolved into the seventeenth-century lantern clock, which in various forms existed well into the eighteenth century. The English sometimes call this a "birdcage clock." The earliest version was a 30-hour weight-driven clock with a large bell on top, a large brass dial, and one hand indicating the hour. They were meant to hang on a wall or sit on a bracket fastened to the wall. Early clocks were fitted with a balance (foliot) escapement. By the mid-seventeenth century the balance escapement was replaced by the newly invented pendulum. Many reproductions of this clock have been made since the eighteenth century. Victorian reproductions were fitted with fusee movements. Twentieth-century reproductions almost invariably show poorer workmanship than their nineteenth-century counterparts.

lantern pinion   A pinion consisting of two circular disks (usually brass) separated by regularly spaced rods (usually steel). A very common feature of American shelf clock movements. Not much used in European movements, except in Germany. In mass production this is the cheapest form of pinion to produce.

leaf pinion   A pinion in which the leaves (teeth) are machined to be an integral part of the gear.

leaves   The "teeth" of the leaf pinion are called leaves. The term "teeth" has traditionally been reserved for use with wheels, but leaves function in exactly the same way as teeth.

lenticle   The glass window set into the door of a long-case clock so the motion of the pendulum may be observed. They are almost always circular in shape.

lever escapement   A form of balance escapement invented in England by Thomas Mudge in 1770. The name comes from the fact that two levers engage the pallets of the escape wheel.

lever movement   See **marine movement**

lifting piece   Levers that release and lock the strike train of a movement.

lighthouse clock   An American shelf clock invented by Simon Willard of Massachusetts in about 1820. The dial and movement are housed under a glass dome that is supported by a column and base. The arrangement re-sembles the shape of a lighthouse, hence the name. The term also applies to nineteenth-century French clocks whose case is a model of a lighthouse. The American clock is rare.

lines   Weight-driven clocks suspend their weights by lines that are wound on drums or barrels. These lines can be made from stranded wire (used with the heaviest weights), gut, or cord. Today, gut and cord have been replaced by synthetic cordage such as nylon. See **gut**.

locking plate   A disk (wheel) with notches cut into the edge at increasing intervals to control the number of times the clock strikes. In America, this is called the count wheel.

long-case clock   The long-case clock evolved in Britain and Holland from early attempts to encase the weights and pendulum of seventeenth-century bracket clocks such as the lantern clock. This became feasible with the inven-tion of the anchor escapement and its short arca. In a sense, the encased bracket clock moved from the wall to the floor by about 1670. It is also known as a tall or tall-case clock.

looking-glass clock   An American wall clock invented ca. 1815–20 by Joseph Ives, it had a tall, rather flat case containing a full-length mirror in the door. The term has also been used to mean the Chauncey Jerome shelf clock invented in about 1825 to compete with Eli Terry's pillar and scroll clock. In Jerome's clock the looking glass fills the bottom panel of the door.

lunar dial   A dial that shows the phases of the moon on a separate disk that is connected by gears to the going (time) side of the movement.

lunette   The area of the hood of a tall-case clock that holds the top (arch) of a breakarch dial.

lyre clock   An interesting clock design that first appeared in France during the last quarter of the eighteenth century. The entire clock takes the shape of a lyre. Particularly impressive specimens have the pendulum attached at the top and the bob consists of a circle that surrounds the dial and swings on a short arc from side to side. The bob is usually decorated with faux jewels. This clock was reproduced in France during the second half of the nineteenth century. In America the term applies to a Federal-style wall clock made in about 1810 whose case is designed to resemble a lyre. Both types are scarce.

mainspring   The coiled steel strip that supplies power to the time and strike sides of a clock movement. Although known since the fifteenth century, spring steel was costly to produce and hard to work until the Industrial Revolution. Steel mainsprings did not commonly appear in American clocks until around 1840 when inexpensive spring steel became available.

maintaining power gear   This was a device that maintained power to the movement while it was being wound. Normally while being wound, motive power to the pallets of the escapement would momentarily cease affecting the time.

mantel clock   Technically, a clock designed to stand on a mantelpiece. However, the term is often used to indicate shelf clocks as well, and in Britain, bracket clocks.

marble clocks   Generally refers to the black marble clock cases that appeared in Europe toward the middle of the nineteenth century. Except in very rare instances, these cases are made from slate. Much of the slate came from quarries in Belgium and most of the works were French pendule movements. The finished clock was produced in France. Marble clocks were extremely popular in the second half of the nineteenth century and they remained in production until about 1920. They were exported to Britain and America in large numbers, often with porcelain dials bearing the names of the retailers who sold them. American clock manufacturers competed by producing three kinds of these clocks: (1) marble-cased (cases often supplied from France), (2) black enameled cast-iron-cased clocks, and (3) black-painted wooden-cased clocks. These American clocks are still found in abundance. German manufacturers did the same as their American counterparts, but not on as large a scale.

marine movement clocks   Wall clocks with lever escapements that were suitable for use on ships. Most of the American-made clocks produced with this name never went to sea. Well-made marine movement clocks were produced for nautical use (usually with strike) and many more, of far cheaper construction, were made for domestic use (usually without a strike).

marquetry   Decorative wood inlay used in some clock cases, marquetry was very popular in tall-case clocks of the seventeenth century and was used in many French cases of the later seventeenth century and the eighteenth century. The inlay was in the form of natural subjects such as flowers and fruit.

Massachusetts shelf clock   Clock and case first produced in Massachusetts in about 1765. Most of these clocks were produced by the famous Willard family of clockmakers although there were other makers. The movement was an 8-day timekeeper, although occasional movements with strike were produced. Often considered to be America's first shelf clock. Also referred to as "half clock," case-on-case, and box-on-box. These clocks show attributes usually seen on tall-case clocks, perhaps not unusual considering that Willards' primary production in the eighteenth century was tall-case clocks.

master clock   A term that appears with the widespread use of electric clocks in public buildings in about 1900. A "master clock" controls a series of "slave clocks" via electrical impulses which cause the geared hands of the "slaves" to advance in concert with the master.

matching hands   Hands on which the minute hand reflects an elongated version of the design found on the hour hand.

mean time   The time indicated by most clocks in general use. It is calculated by averaging all of the "solar days" throughout the year.

minute-repeating clocks   Clocks, usually small, having a mechanism fitted that allows the hours, quarters, or minutes to be repeated when a button or pull is activated. Often found on eighteenth- and nineteenth-century watches, it is less often found on clocks. One form of clock that utilizes this feature is the French carriage clock. It is almost always a mark of a higher-grade clock.

mirror clock   Any clock whose case incorporates a mirror, usually in the door, in its design. In America, Chauncey Jerome invented the looking-glass shelf clock in about 1825 to compete with Terry's pillar and scroll clock. In Jerome's clock the looking glass fills the bottom panel of the door.

mock pendulum   A pendulum that performs no function in the escapement and is used only for decoration. Battery-driven quartz movements sometimes use mock or false pendulums to simulate the appearance of a mechanical movement.

month clock   Any clock that runs for about a month on one winding. Usually these movements run for 32 days. Most of the inexpensive reproduction antique clocks imported from India and Korea have 31-day movements.

moon dial   A secondary dial on a clock that indicates the age and phases of the moon. Common to tall-case clocks since the eighteenth century, these dials can also be found on some smaller clocks (such as bracket clocks) as well.

Morbier clock   French clock produced as early as the mid-eighteenth century around the village of Morbier in the Jura Department. By the nineteenth century they were found throughout much of the Alpine region of eastern France and western Switzerland. These are 8-day weight-driven time and strike clocks that are singular in having a vertical strike rack and automatically restrike approximately five minutes after the hour. They are found as tall-case clocks, recognized by their pear-shaped cases, and as wall clocks with very ornate brass sheet work around the dial and very long ornate brass pendulums. The names found on the dials are almost always those of the retailer. They are also known as Comtoise clocks. The earliest examples have verge escapements and later examples have anchor escapements.

motion train   Also known as the "going train," these are gears that drive the dial hands.

motion work   A British term that indicates the total gear train that drives the hands. It also refers to the gearing that allows the hour hand to revolve once every 12 hours and the minute hand to revolve once every hour. See **motion train.**

movement   The mechanism or works that provide the regulated motive power of a clock. A "timekeeper" movement contains only the time train and escapement. A "time and strike" movement contains a time train plus a strike train and escapement. Motive power may derive from weight, spring, or electricity.

musical clock   Simply, a clock whose movement plays a tune when it strikes.

mystery clocks   The name given to a variety of clocks whose movements have been designed to make it difficult for the observer to understand how they function. Primarily a novelty of the nineteenth century, they frequently were products of very imaginative and talented French clockmakers. They were also produced by American and German clock companies at the turn of the twentieth century. Among the most common clocks of this variety are the "mystery swinger" clocks, in which the pendulum is suspended from the upraised arm of the figure.

New Hampshire mirror clock A rectangular wall clock only about 4–5" deep by 36" high and about 16" wide. The dial and 8-day weight-driven movement is mounted in the top section. The remainder of the clock front consists of a mirror. It is a rare clock and was not widely produced outside New Hampshire. It appeared in about 1820 and was no longer made by 1850.

night clock A clock that indicates the hour at night by means of a light shining through a pierced dial.

off-center pendulum An American term indicating a pendulum that is not hung in the center. Used in reference to early shelf clocks with wooden movements made by Eli Terry or Seth Thomas.

OG Case The "OG" stands for ogee, a molding having an S shape in profile. By the 1840s the ogee shape had been fashionably incorporated into much furniture. Capitalizing on the public's familiarity with this shape, Chauncey Jerome began to construct shelf clock cases using OG molding as the face. These cases were fitted with his one-day brass movement. Jerome's famous first shipment of clocks to England in 1842 consisted of OG clocks. The OG case became one of the most prolifically produced clock cases in American clockmaking.

ogee A molding having an S shape in profile. Used on the face of the famous OG case.

oil sink The shallow concentric depression surrounding pivot holes, designed to hold lubricating oil.

one-second pendulum A pendulum whose arc takes one second to travel from side to side.

organ clock A clock whose case houses a pipe organ. The organ is operated by a pin barrel like that found in music boxes. Wind is supplied by bellows and pumped by levers tripped by the pin barrel. They appeared in the middle of the eighteenth century as novelty clocks for the upper classes. The same sort of clock also appeared among Black Forest clockmakers a bit later and often added cymbals, whistles, bells, and drums to the organ.

ormolu clock Generic term for any clock housed in a gilded metal case, in particular, "fire-gilded." The term means 'ground or powdered gold.' Brass or bronze cases were coated with a compound of ground gold and mercury. The mercury was driven off as a vapor by heating the case. After cooling, the cases had a uniform coating of gold that was then burnished. This procedure was particularly dangerous to the gilders as mercury vapors are toxic. Today the term refers to brass cases and fittings that have been electroplated.

It has sometimes been incorrectly used to identify electroplated base metals (spelter, pot metal, and so on.). Many late-nineteenth-century figural clocks produced in France and in America were of base metals that had been electroplated. The original ormolu clocks first appeared in the seventeenth century.

Orrery clock   A specialized clock consisting of spheres (representing heavenly bodies) mounted on rods and connected to clockwork that causes them to revolve and rotate. They are also called mechanical planetariums. They appeared in the first quarter of the eighteenth century as a by-product of the astronomical advances of the Scientific Revolution.

outside escapement   A term first used in America to describe the placement of the escape wheel, anchor, crutch, and pendulum rod in front of the dial on some experimental pillar and scroll clocks produced by Eli Terry. The term also describes the Brocot escapement, which was often placed on the face of the dial on "better made" French clocks of the nineteenth century. Many American mantel clocks, particularly those made to compete with French black marble and figural clocks, featured outside escapements.

pallet   Those parts of the escapement that alternately halt and release the escape wheel.

papers   See **labels**

paperweight clocks   Late-nineteenth-century clocks (ca. 1880–1900) with cases of glass; small, 4–6 inches.

papier-mâché clocks   Small, usually American, shelf clocks whose cases are made from molded papier-mâché. Often found with mother-of-pearl inlays. The clocks date from ca. 1860s.

parcel-gilt   An antiquated term that means 'partially gilded.'

parquetry   A decorative inlay utilizing veneer to form geometric designs. They are often found on many clock cases of the seventeenth and eighteenth centuries.

patent timepiece   Simon Willard's name for his banjo clock.

pediment-top clock   A clock case whose top is a sloping roof. Also known as an architectural clock, it is derived from the form of the pediment of Greek temples such as the Parthenon.

pendulum   A weight hung from a fixed point and allowed to swing freely. Christiaan Huygens of Holland is given credit for first using (1657) the principle of the pendulum to regulate the speed of the movement. He combined the pendulum with the verge escapement. The result was a far more accurate clock.

pendulum bob See **bob**

petite sonnerie clock Generally, a French carriage clock that strikes the quarters with a "ting-tang" sound. See **carriage clocks**.

picture clock A painting, on canvas or board, that has a steeple or tower as part of the scene. A small clock is mounted on the back so its dial becomes a clock in the steeple or tower. First appearing in Europe in the middle of the eighteenth century, these clocks were made throughout the nineteenth century and into the twentieth century, particularly in Switzerland.

pilaster An architectural term indicating a rectangular column attached to a flat surface with a capital and base. Frequently used as decoration on clock cases.

pillar and scroll The name given to the case design created by Eli Terry in the second decade of the nineteenth century. Its form, a box having delicate feet, slender tapered columns, and a broken arch top, made this clock one of the most handsome ever produced. Invented by Terry, the movement was weight-driven—30-hour wooden-works time and strike with a painted wooden dial. This was the first American mass-produced clock. Terry was unable to protect his patent, so the clock was copied by many makers in the 1820s and 1830s.

pillars The posts that hold the plates of a clock movement together.

pin pallet escapement A French escapement, invented around the middle of the eighteenth century, in which the pins stand out from the side of the escape wheel. It is mainly found on lower-priced European clocks.

pin wheel escapement A French escapement invented in the early eighteenth century by the French clockmaker Amant. It is a form of the deadbeat escapement and was often used in larger turret clocks.

pinion Small toothed gears that intermesh with wheels in clock movements. The teeth are called leaves. These gears are usually cut from the same metal as the arbor. See **lantern pinion**.

pivot The turned and reduced end of an arbor that rotates within the pivot hole of a clock plate.

plates Pieces of metal or wood, between which the pivoted gear trains of clocks run. The plate behind the dial is called the front plate and the one behind it the back plate.

platform   The small metal plate affixed to the movement of a carriage clock that carries a watch escapement and balance.

plinth   A term usually associated with tall-case clocks. It can mean two things: the part of the clock case below the trunk, or the bottom-most molding of the clock case. In the British Isles it is sometimes called the "kicking strip."

pull repeater   Usually a cord or wire attached to the strike train that allows one to release the striking mechanism between hours.

R-A regulator   Not really a regulator, but a regulator look-alike that had a pendulum bob containing the letters "R" (for retard) and "A" (for advance). See **regulator**.

rack   The toothed lever in a rack-and-snail strike movement. The distance that the rack moves determines how many times the clock strikes.

rack-and-snail strike   A striking system invented in England by Edward Barlow in the last quarter of the seventeenth century. It is a system that is directly connected to the hour hand, ensuring that the strike will not be out of sequence with the hour. Commonly found on 8-day tall-case movements and most European clocks, it has come to replace the count wheel.

railway clock   A term often used in the British Isles to identify the gallery-style wall clocks that began to appear in railway stations by the 1850s. See **gallery clock**.

ratchet   A spring-loaded click that engages a set of teeth when a movement is wound so power is transmitted to a set of gears.

ratchet wheel   A wheel with saw-shaped teeth that can rotate in only one direction.

rate   The amount of time a clock gains, loses, or remains steady.

rating nut   The nut found below the pendulum bob that is used to regulate clock speed by raising and lowering the bob.

recoil   The momentary backward movement of the escape wheel in recoil escapements such as the anchor or verge.

recoil escapement   See **anchor escapement** and **verge escapement**

regulator   Usually refers to a clock with a long compensated pendulum and a deadbeat escapement. A regulator, with precise and often complicated movements, was frequently found in workshops and institutions where exact time was required. Clock manufacturers of the later nineteenth century often used the designation "Regulator" on mass-produced clocks to increase sales. Beware—not all "regulators" are Regulators.

religieuse clock   A shelf/table clock of the late seventeenth century. "Religieuse" is French for 'nun,' and the round chapter ring set against a dark case was thought to look something like a nun in habit. These clocks are quite rare and usually only seen in museums.

repeater   A clock that can be made to strike the previous hour. Many French carriage clocks were repeaters.

reverse painting   Many American clockmakers of the nineteenth century used the technique of reverse glass painting to decorate the lower panel of a shelf clock's doors. Also known as eglomis, it is the technique of painting the last details first and the first details last.

ripple molding   Applied clock case molding made by steam-pressing wood strips. Very fashionable on certain American shelf clocks during the 1840s. The form parallels the furniture style known as "spool" and "Jenny Lind."

roller pinion   A rare form of the pinion invented by Joseph Ives in the 1830s. It is a lantern pinion using rollers instead of wires to reduce friction.

rotary pendulum   A torsion pendulum invented by the New Jersey clockmaker Aaron Dodd Crane. The pendulum consists of a steel ribbon with a ball or group of balls at the end that rotate until the ribbon reaches its twist limit and then reverses direction.

round top   Any clock case whose top is in the shape of a half arc.

scapewheel   See **escape wheel**

seat board   The wooden platform on which the clock movement sits.

second wheel   The second gear of a gear train.

set-up   The amount of wound spring remaining after the clock movement has run down.

shelf clock   Simply, a clock designed to sit on a shelf. A mantel clock is essentially the same thing. Most mass-produced American clocks of the nineteenth century were shelf or mantel clocks. The English bracket clock is a shelf clock.

ship's bell clock   A wall clock with a lever or balance escapement that was designed to function aboard a ship. The strike sounds one to six bells every half hour to indicate "watches."

ship's clock   A lever escapement movement usually housed in a round brass case with a flange so the clock can be fastened to a bulkhead. Also known as a marine clock.

silvering   The silver plating of all or certain parts, often the chapter ring, of a brass dial. Most often used on tall-case clock dials.

skeleton clock   A clock whose movement is housed between plates that have been pierced to show the mechanism. Usually found fixed to a wooden base and covered with a glass dome. They first appeared around the middle nineteenth century generally in England. Fine French examples are known.

slave clock   Not a clock at all, but merely a dial and hands remotely controlled by a "master clock."

snail   The eccentric cam in a rack-and-snail striking mechanism that determines the number of hours to be struck.

solar time   Time indicated by the sun and measured on a device such as a sundial. Also known as "apparent" or "true" time.

Sonora chime clock   A mantel-style clock manufactured by the Seth Thomas Clock Company that struck a series of tuned and cupped bells.

spade hand   Clock hands whose ends resemble the shape of the spade found in a deck of playing cards.

spandrel   The corner spaces between the chapter ring and corners of a clock dial are called spandrels, and they are often filled with decoration. This decoration can appear as a metal casting, engraving, or paint.

splat   A decorative wood panel found at the top of a clock case. Most commonly associated with American shelf clocks of the first half of the nineteenth century. They were often carved or stenciled.

Staartklok   See **Friesland clock**

steeple clock   An American shelf clock invented by Elias Ingraham in the 1840s; one of the most popular clock case designs made in the nineteenth century. The shape, as its name suggests, resembles a steeple or steeply pitched roof flanked by pointed spires. This case remained in production until the twentieth century.

stenciled clock   Common term used to identify many American shelf clocks, ca. 1820–40, usually with wooden movements, which have painted and stenciled columns and splats.

stenciled column clock   The name refers to the large number of American shelf clocks, usually with 30-hour wooden movements, produced between 1825 and 1840. Credit is given to Chauncey Jerome for introducing this style of clock. Sometimes called column and splat clocks, the splat and columns were first painted with a black ground and then stenciled with bronze powders. See **bronze looking glass clock.**

stenciling   Painting over a perforated plate or template.

Stoel clock   See **Friesland clock**

Stoeltjesklok   See **Friesland clock** and **Zaandam clock**

store clock   Common name given to the rectangular box clocks commonly found in stores in the first part of the twentieth century. They often had dials and glass doors that contained advertising.

strap plate or frame   The use of wood or brass strips (straps) fastened together to form an open plate.

strawberry corners   An English term used to indicate the painted spandrel designs on early white dials of tall-case clocks. The term is used generically to indicate these early painted motifs whether or not they included strawberries.

sundial   One of the earliest devices to show the time of day by the shadow of a standard (gnomon) on a base.

sunray clock   A clock whose circular motif is decorated with a sun whose rays emanate from the center. First introduced in France during the reign of Louis XIV, the Sun King, it has been reproduced throughout the years.

suspension   The method of supporting the pendulum of a clock. Can be by spring, silk thread, or knife-edge.

suspension spring   Simply the spring from which the pendulum is suspended.

swinging clock   Essentially a novelty clock produced in the last decades of the nineteenth century in France. The traditional pendulum is replaced by a figure on a swing. A modified anchor escapement allowed the figure/pendulum to swing fore and aft. The popularity of this clock caused it to be copied and produced in cheaper form both in Germany and America.

table clock   The original meaning of this term referred to the very early (ca. 1520) spring-driven clocks made in Europe. The spring-driven movement allowed clocks to be moved from room to room and displayed on tables. A far newer meaning designates small clocks that sat on side tables in bedrooms and living rooms. French carriage clocks, cottage clocks, and even alarm clocks would fit this designation.

tablet   Decorated, usually painted, glass panels found in many American, and some German, shelf and wall clocks. From about 1800 to 1835 the designs were reverse glass paintings. After about 1840, the designs were usually decals, stencils, or etched glass.

tall-case clock   See **grandfather clock** and **long-case clock**

tall clock   See **grandfather clock** and **long-case clock**

tavern clock   Usually another name for the so-called Act of Parliament clocks. It can also be used to describe the electric advertising wall clocks (beer and soft drink companies) of the twentieth and twenty-first centuries.

teardrop clock   American Victorian walnut parlor/mantel clocks with rounded tops and hanging finials.

telluhr clock   Telluhr translated from German means 'plate clock.' A circular wall clock that appeared in Germany in the second quarter of the eighteenth century. On early examples, the pendulum was placed on the front of the clock. The cases were made of metal often silvered or gilded.

term clock   The name "term" here is used in the architectural sense, indicating a trunk, pillar, or pedestal. Simply put, it refers to a clock mounted upon a trunk, pillar, or pedestal. This form of clock is almost always of French origin and is rarely seen outside of palaces or museums.

third wheel   The third gear in a clock train.

30-hour movement   A clock movement designed to run for approximately 30 hours on one winding. In the English clockmaking tradition, which was transplanted to America in the seventeenth century, the two most common movements produced were the 8-day and 30-hour. The 30-hour movement was cheaper to produce, and most mass-produced American clocks were therefore concentrated on it.

time clock   A clock connected to a printing mechanism. In one use, an employer can check the comings and goings of employees. The employee inserts a timecard in a slot and the synchronous mechanism imprints the time on the card.

timekeeper   Strictly speaking, it means a clock that tells time only, without striking, chiming, or calendar function. In more common usage, this term merely means any clock.

time-only   See **timekeeper**

tin-plate movement   American-made (especially Connecticut) clock movements whose plates were made of tinned iron as a way to save brass and reduce costs, ca. 1860s.

ting-tang   The sounding of the quarter hours on two different bells. Common on French carriage clocks.

Torrington movement   The Torrington, Connecticut, clockmakers of the 1820s attempted to avoid infringing on Eli Terry's wooden movement patent by producing their own 30-hour movement, oriented horizontally rather than vertically. Torrington movements can be identified by their winding holes at 3 and 9 P.M.

torsion pendulum   See **Crane clock**

tower clock   See **turret clock**

train   A set of interconnected wheels and pinions terminating in the escape wheel.

transition clock   Another attempt to avoid infringing upon the Terry patent. Various Connecticut clockmakers produced case designs that were about the size of the pillar and scroll clock but employed carved or stenciled features that later carried over into clocks such as the "carved column" clocks.

travel clocks   Small, portable clocks with nonpendulum escapements.

triple-decker clock   Large weight-driven Connecticut shelf clocks (ca. 1830–50), whose fronts consist of upper and lower doors with a fixed panel between.

true time   See **solar time**

trumpeter clock   Another form of the Black Forest clock commonly called the cuckoo clock. In this variety a trumpeter replaces the cuckoo and on the hour appears and plays a tune.

trunk   That part of a tall-case clock found between the hood and base (plinth).

tubular chime clock   Tall-case clocks that employ graduated brass tubes in place of rods, bells, or gongs. They appear in the tall-case clocks of the late nineteenth century.

turret clock   Also called a tower clock. A large clock constructed for use in the towers of churches and public buildings.

urn clock   A clock in the form of an urn. Time is indicated by two rotating bands, one for the hour and one for the minute, at the top of the urn. A fixed hand indicates the time. These clocks appear around the middle of the eighteenth century in France and are another indication of the brilliance of French clockmakers.

verge   Term used to indicate that part of the escapement that includes the pallets.

verge escapement   The earliest form of clock escapement, used from the fifteenth century until the nineteenth century. In its earliest versions, it employed the foliot followed by the balance wheel, bar balance, and finally the Huygens's pendulum.

vernis Martin clock   An English term indicating a clock whose case was decorated with a finish similar in appearance to Japanese lacquer. An early eighteenth-century cabinetmaker, Robert Martin of Paris, introduced a varnish (vernis) finish that resembled Oriental lacquer.

Vienna Regulator   A weight-driven wall clock that originated among the clockmakers of Vienna, Austria, in the first half of the nineteenth century. The early movements are precise and very well made. In the latter part of the nineteenth century the German clockmakers of the Black Forest such as Junghans would adapt this form and produce an inferior version, which captured the market and virtually destroyed the Viennese clockmaking industry. American manufacturers were equally quick to adapt this popular clock form to mass production. See **regulator**.

visible escapement clock   Simply, a clock in which the escapement is visible from the front. Commonly found on many French clocks employing the Brocot escapement. The American manufacturer Ansonia frequently used an outside escapement on many of its mantel clocks of the last quarter of the nineteenth century.

wag-on-the-wall clock   An American term that may have its roots in Dutch horological history. Essentially, it is nothing more than a tall-case movement, dial, hands, weights, and pendulum, mounted as a working unit on the wall, eliminating the need for a case. The same arrangement was also produced in the Black Forest region of Germany and sold throughout Europe in the eighteenth and early nineteenth centuries.

wagon-springs   Flat-leaved springs invented by Joseph Ives and used to power some Connecticut shelf and wall clocks, ca. 1825–55. Clocks using these springs are rare and command high prices.

wall clocks   The term refers to any clock that was manufactured to hang upon a wall.

warning   The sound indicating the partial unlocking of the strike train just before the moment of striking.

weights   Masses of stone, lead, cast iron, or cylinder-enclosed scrap used to provide motive power in clocks. Early clocks usually had weights of lead and later ones had cast iron. Many early American tall-case clocks with wooden movements used "tin-can" weights (cylinders made of thin sheet iron and filled with scrap iron).

wheel   A clock gear, usually brass, that engages a pinion as part of a gear train.

winding square   The square end of an arbor used for winding a clock.

Zaandam clock   Probably the earliest form of Dutch wall clock. In form it is a lantern clock seated on a wall bracket with exposed weights. They appeared around the beginning of the seventeenth century. The early examples had verge escapements with foliot. After 1660 the foliot was replaced by the Huygens pendulum. By the end of the seventeenth century the anchor escapement and long pendulum appeared. The clock was made into the nineteenth century. Reproductions are still being produced.

Zappler clock   An eighteenth-century German clock resembling the Telluhr clock, but made to stand on a table.

BIBLIOGRAPHY

This short bibliography should help you get started exploring the world of clocks. I have tried to list the most current works whenever possible. A few of these books are out of print, but they are important enough to list. There are so many others that you will discover that collecting clock books is a field in itself. The vast majority of these works can be obtained from booksellers specializing in horological works. See the end of the bibliography for a listing of some of these booksellers. Lastly, I have included some personal notes about the entries after the citation in brackets.

ESSENTIAL

NAWCC. *Master Index to the Bulletin of the National Association of Watch and Clock Collectors, Inc.* Columbia, PA: NAWCC, 1994. [All NAWCC publications through 1993.]

NAWCC. *NAWCC Bulletin Index.* Columbia, PA: NAWCC, 2002. [All NAWCC publications from 1994 through 2002.]

CLOCK IDENTIFICATION

Baillie, G. H. *Watchmakers and Clockmakers of the World.* Vol. 1. Colchester, U.K.: N.A.G. Press, 1988. (See Loomes for Vol. 2.) [This is the place to start identifying a maker's name; best for British makers.]

Carle, Donald de. *Watch and Clock Encyclopedia.* Suffolk, U.K.: St. Edmundsbury Press, 1995. [Uselful reprint, with additions and excellent illustrations, of the original 1950 edition.]

Kochmann, Karl. *Clock and Watch Trademark Index of European Origin.* Sacramento, CA: Clockworks Press, 2001. [Essential when trying to track down a trademark on movement or dial.]

Loomes, Brian. *Watchmakers and Clockmakers of the World.* Vol. 2. Colchester, U.K.: N.A.G. Press, 1992. (See Baille for Volume 1.) [Continues what Baille started.]

Smith, Alan, editor. *The International Dictionary of Clocks*. London, U.K.: Chancellor Press, 1996. [Useful, with excellent illustrations.]

Spittler, Sonya, Thomas Spittler, and Chris Bailey. *American Clockmakers and Watchmakers*. Fairfax, VA: Arlington Book Co., 2000. [Start here to identify American makers.]

CLOCK REPAIR AND RESTORATION

Balcomb, Philip E. *The Clock Repair Primer*. Tell City, IN: Tempus Press, 1986. [Clear, with excellent illustrations.]

Conover, Steven G. *Clock Repair Basics*. Reading, PA: Clockmakers Newsletter, 1996. [Clear, concise, with excellent illustrations.]

————. *Clock Repair Skills*. Reading, PA: Clockmakers Newsletter, 2002. [Clear, concise, with excellent illustrations.]

Fried, Henry B. *Bench Practices for Watch and Clockmakers*. Fairfax, VA: Arlington Book Company, 1997. [First-rate instruction and advice.]

Penman, Laurie. *The Clock Repairer's Handbook*. Devon, U.K.: David and Charles, 1992. [Good, clear, useful work from across the Atlantic.]

Vernon, John. *The Grandfather Clock Maintenance Manual*. New York, NY: Van Nostrand Reinhold, 1983. [Concentrates on tall-case clocks and their care.]

AMERICAN CLOCKS

Bailey, Chris. *Two Hundred Years of American Clocks and Watches*. Englewood Cliffs, NJ: Prentice-Hall, 1975. [Start here for an overview of American clocks.]

Balcomb, Philip E. *The Clock Book: An Overview of Heirloom and Contemporary Clocks in American Homes*. Tell City, IN: Tempus Press, 1996. [Useful work with first-class line drawings.]

Ball, Robert W. D. *American Shelf and Wall Clocks: A Pictorial History For Collectors*. Atglen, PA: Schiffer Publishing Ltd., 1992. [Excellent photographs of most American clocks.]

Distin, William H., and Robert Bishop. *The American Clock*. New York, NY: E. P. Dutton, 1976. [Good survey with excellent photographs.]

Linz, Jim. *Electrifying Time: Telechron and GE Clocks, 1925–55*. Atglen, PA: Shiffer Publishing Ltd., 2001. [Good information that has been hard to locate before now.]

Ly, Tran Duy. *American Clocks*. Vols. 1–3.
Ansonia Clocks and Watches.
Calendar Clocks.

Gilbert Clocks.

Ingraham Clocks and Watches.

Longcase Clocks and Standing Regulators. Pt. 1

New Haven Clocks and Watches.

Sessions Clocks.

Seth Thomas Clocks and Movements.

Waterbury Clocks and Watches.

Welch Clocks.

All are published by the author who is the Arlington Book Co. Inc.—Fairfax, VA. [These titles are wonderful advanced studies on America's best known clocks produced by a gentleman who pays attention to detail.]

Palmer, Brooks. *A Treasury of American Clocks.* New York, NY: Macmillan, 1967. [An out-of-print pioneering pictorial study that is still useful.]

———. *The Book of American Clocks.* New York, NY: Macmillan, 1966. [Another out-of-print useful pioneering pictorial study.]

Roberts, Kenneth D. *The Contributions of Joseph Ives to Connecticut Clock Technology.* Bristol, CT: American Clock and Watch Museum, 1970. [If you are studying early Connecticut clocks, you will need this work.]

Roberts, Kenneth D., and Snowden Taylor. *Eli Terry and the Connecticut Shelf Clock.* Rev. 2d ed. Chelsea, MI: Bookcrafters, 1994. [If you are studying early Connecticut clocks, you will need this work.]

———. *Forestville Clockmakers.* Fitzwilliam, NH: Ken Roberts Publishing Co., 1992. [If you are studying early Connecticut clocks, you will need this work.]

———. *Jonathan Clark Brown and the Forestville Manufacturing Co.* Fitzwilliam, NH: Ken Roberts Publishing Co., 1988. [If you are studying early Connecticut clocks, you will need this work.]

Stein, Mark V. *Twentieth Century Modern Clocks.* Baltimore, MD: Radiomania Books, 2002. [Fills a long existing gap in published information about contemporary clocks.]

FOREIGN CLOCKS

Bassermann-Jordan, Ernst von. *The Book of Old Clocks and Watches.* New York, NY: Crown Publishers, 1964. [Out of print, but worth the hunt.]

Heuer, Peter, and Klaus Maurice. *European Pendulum Clocks.* West Chester, PA: Schiffer Publishing Ltd., 1988. [Another fine European work brought to America.]

BRITISH CLOCKS

Cescinsky, Herbert and Malcolm R. Webster. *English Domestic Clocks*. New York, NY: Bonanza Books, 1948. [Excellent introduction to English clocks.]

Loomes, Brian. *Brass Dial Clocks*. Suffolk, U.K.: Antique Collectors' Club, 1998. [British longcase clocks.]

———. *Painted Dial Clocks*. Woodbridge, U.K.: Antique Collector's Club, 1997. [More about British longcase clocks.]

Roberts, Derek. *British Longcase Clocks*. West Chester, PA: Schiffer Publishing, Ltd., 1990. [Good standard reference.]

Robey, John. *The Longcase Clock Reference Book*. Vols. 1 and 2. Derbyshire, U.K.: Mayfield Books, 2001. [If you are interested in longcase clocks, this is the work for you.]

Shenton, Alan, and Rita Shenton. *Collectable Clocks 1840–1940*. Woodbridge, U.K.: Antique Collectors' Club, 1994. [Much needed information about British clocks other than longcase and bracket clocks.]

CANADIAN CLOCKS

Connell, James E. *The Charlton Price Guide to Canadian Clocks*. Toronto, Ontario: Charlton Press, 1995. [There is little available in the United States about Canadian clocks.]

FRENCH CLOCKS

Ly, Tran Duy. *French Clocks and Bronzes*. Fairfax, VA: Arlington Book Co., 2001. [One of the advanced studies on well-known clocks produced by a gentleman who pays attention to detail.]

Maitzner, Francis, and Jean Moreau. *Comtoise Clocks: The Morbier and The Morez*. Paris, France: Stampa, 1990. [Excellent work.]

Niehüser, Elke. *French Bronze Clocks, 1700–1830*. Atglen, PA: Schiffer Publishing Ltd., 1999. [Another fine European work brought to America.]

Roberts, Derek. *Carriage and Other Traveling Clocks*. Atglen, PA: Schiffer Publishing, 1993. [Looks like a coffee table book, but far more useful.]

Terwilliger, Charles, editor. *A Century of Fine Carriage Clocks*. Bronxville, NY: Clock Trade Enterprises, 1987. [Wonderful treatment of carriage clocks.]

Thorpe, Nicolas M. *The French Marble Clock*. Colchester, U.K.: N.A.G. Press, 1993. [Wonderful book that includes all aspects of French marble clocks; this book was a labor of love.]

GERMAN CLOCKS

Kochmann, Karl. *Black Forest Clockmaker and the Cuckoo Clock*. Concord, CA: Antique Clock Publishing, 1996. [Pioneering work in English in this area.]

————. *The Gustav Becker Story.* Concord, CA: Antique Clock Publishing, 1993. [Pioneering work in English in this area.]

————. *Lenzkirch Clock Factory and Winterhalder and Hofmeier Clocks.* Concord, CA: Kochmann, 1995. [Pioneering work in English in this area.]

Ly, Tran Duy. *Gustav Becker Clocks.* Fairfax, VA: Arlington Book Co., 2000. [One of the advanced studies on well-known clocks produced by a gentleman who pays attention to detail.]

Ortenburger, Rick. *Black Forest Clocks.* West Chester, PA: Schiffer Publishing Ltd., 1991. [Wonderful work dealing with much of the German clockmaking industry after 1870. Absolutely first-rate photos.]

BOOKSELLERS

ARLINGTON BOOK CO.
2706 Elsmore Street
Fairfax, VA 22031-1409
Tel: 703-280-2005
Fax: 703-280-5300
Web site: www.arlingtonbooks.com
E-mail: tranduyly@aol.com

RITA SHENTON HOROLOGICAL BOOKSELLERS
142, Percy Road
Twickenham TW2 6JG
United Kingdom
Tel: 4420 8894 6888
Fax: 4420 8893 8766
Web site: www.shentonbooks.com
E-mail: rita@shentonbooks.com
[Includes many books that are not available in the United States.]

TRANTIQUES BOOK AND CLOCK CO.
929 Woodland Avenue
East Norriton, PA 19403
Tel: 610-584-6231
Fax: 610-584-0346
Web site: www.trantiques.com
E-mail: trantiques_info@yahoo.com

USBOOKS.COM
312 Autumn Circle
Bluff City, TN 37618
Tel: 423-391-0222
Fax: 423-391-0211
Web site: www.usbooks.com
E-mail: info@usbooks.com

Index